Stress, Well-Being, and Performance in Sport

Stress, Well-Being, and Performance in Sport provides the first comprehensive and contemporary overview of stress in sport and its implications for performance and well-being. It explores how athletes', coaches', and support staffs' performances can be enhanced while simultaneously optimizing their well-being in competitive sport.

Divided into four sections following the stress process, *Stress, Well-Being, and Performance in Sport* covers key topics including:

- Appraising and Coping With Stress in Sport
- Responses to and Outcomes of Stress in Sport
- Moderators of the Stress Process in Sport
- Stress Management to Promote Thriving in Sport

Bringing together theory and practice, each chapter discusses conceptual and theoretical issues, current research, and innovative practical implications. Written by scholars around the globe, *Stress, Well-Being, and Performance* offers an international perspective. It is important reading for students, professionals working in the field of sport psychology, as well as coaches, athletes, and support staff.

Rachel Arnold, PhD, is a Senior Lecturer in Sport and Performance Psychology at the Department for Health, University of Bath, UK. She is a Chartered Psychologist and Associate Fellow of the British Psychological Society, registered Practitioner Psychologist with the Health and Care Professions Council, accredited Sport and Exercise Scientist with the British Association of Sport and Exercise Sciences, Chartered Scientist with the Science Council, and Senior Fellow of the Higher Education Academy. Alongside her consultancy experience, Dr Arnold has published widely in the area of stress, performance, and well-being, and received awards for her research from the Association for Applied Sport Psychology, and the British Psychological Society.

David Fletcher, PhD, is Director of Performance Psychology and Management at Loughborough University, UK. His experience of consulting with high-level performers spans the past 20 years and includes working closely with Olympic and world champions from a variety of sports, special forces and emergency services, and senior leaders and their teams in FTSE 100 and Fortune 500 companies. Dr Fletcher has published widely in performance psychology and consulting, including ground-breaking research studies in scientific journals and practical articles that demystify complex human phenomena.

Routledge Psychology of Sport, Exercise and Physical Activity

Series Editor: Andrew M. Lane

University of Wolverhampton, UK

This series offers a forum for original and cutting edge research exploring the latest ideas and issues in the psychology of sport, exercise and physical activity. Books within the series showcase the work of well-established and emerging scholars from around the world, offering an international perspective on topical and emerging areas of interest in the field. This series aims to drive forward academic debate and bridge the gap between theory and practice, encouraging critical thinking and reflection among students, academics and practitioners. The series is aimed at upper-level undergraduates, research students and academics, and contains both authored and edited collections.

Available in this series:

For more information about this series, please visit: www.routledge.com/sport/series/RRSP

Stress, Well-Being, and Performance in Sport

Edited by Rachel Arnold
and David Fletcher

Routledge
Taylor & Francis Group

NEW YORK AND LONDON

First published 2021
by Routledge
52 Vanderbilt Avenue, New York, NY 10017

and by Routledge
2 Park Square, Milton Park, Abingdon, Oxon, OX14 4RN

Routledge is an imprint of the Taylor & Francis Group, an informa business

Library of Congress Cataloging-in-Publication Data
A catalog record for this book has been requested

ISBN: 978-0-367-27267-8 (hbk)
ISBN: 978-0-367-70089-8 (pbk)
ISBN: 978-0-429-29587-4 (ebk)

Typeset in Baskerville
by Apex CoVantage, LLC

Contents

Figures

Tables

Acknowledgments

We sincerely thank the authors who contributed chapters to this book. Our appreciation is extended to Professor Daniel Gould and Professor Sir Cary L. Cooper for their foreword and epilogue contributions respectively. Thanks also to the staff at Taylor & Francis Group who have guided us throughout the publication process. Finally, we acknowledge and thank our families and friends for their love, support, encouragement, and inspiration.

Contributors

Rachel Arnold, Department for Health, University of Bath, United Kingdom.

Daniel J. Brown, School of Sport, Health, and Exercise Science, University of Portsmouth, United Kingdom.

Sir Cary L. Cooper, Alliance Manchester Business School, University of Manchester, United Kingdom.

J. D. DeFreese, Department of Exercise and Sport Science, University of North Carolina at Chapel Hill, United States.

Faye F. Didymus, Carnegie School of Sport, Leeds Beckett University, United Kingdom.

Robert C. Eklund, College of Education, Florida State University, United States.

David Fletcher, School of Sport, Exercise, and Health Sciences, Loughborough University, United Kingdom.

Paul Freeman, School of Sport, Rehabilitation, and Exercise Sciences, University of Essex, United Kingdom.

Genevieve Gordon-Thomson, Leicester De Montfort Law School, De Montford University, United Kingdom.

Daniel Gould, Institute for the Study of Youth Sports, Michigan State University, United States.

Kate Gwyther, Orygen, Centre for Youth Mental Health, University of Melbourne, Australia.

Kate Hays, English Institute of Sport, United Kingdom.

Sinikka Heisler, Department of Performance Psychology, German Sport University, Germany.

Marc V. Jones, Department of Psychology, Manchester Metropolitan University, United Kingdom.

Emma Kavanagh, Department of Sport and Event Management, Bournemouth University, United Kingdom.

Sylvain Laborde, Department of Performance Psychology, German Sport University, Germany; Normandie Université Caen, France.

Carolina Lundqvist, Department of Behavioural Sciences and Learning, Linköping University, Sweden.

Lee J. Moore, Department for Health, University of Bath, United Kingdom.

Emma Mosley, School of Sport, Health, and Social Sciences, Solent University, United Kingdom.

Michael Passaportis, School of Sport, Health, and Exercise Science, University of Portsmouth, UK.

Rosemary Purcell, Orygen, Centre for Youth Mental Health, University of Melbourne, Australia.

Daniel J. A. Rhind, School of Sport, Exercise, and Health Sciences, Loughborough University, United Kingdom.

Simon Rice, Orygen, Centre for Youth Mental Health, University of Melbourne, Australia.

Katherine A. Tamminen, Faculty of Kinesiology and Physical Education, University of Toronto, Canada.

Samuel J. Vine, College of Life and Environmental Sciences, University of Exeter, United Kingdom.

Christopher R. D. Wagstaff, School of Sport, Health, and Exercise Science, University of Portsmouth, United Kingdom.

Courtney C. Walton, Orygen, Centre for Youth Mental Health, University of Melbourne, Australia; School of Psychology, The University of Queensland, Australia.

Mark R. Wilson, College of Life and Environmental Sciences, University of Exeter, United Kingdom.

Foreword

Many years ago as a 20-year-old collegiate athlete and second-year undergraduate student majoring in physical education, I was lucky enough to enroll in my first sport psychology course. I loved the course and was drawn to it because what was being discussed helped me better understand my own experiences as an athlete and the content seemed highly applicable to my future goal of becoming a coach. An area of particular interest to me was stress and anxiety. I think this was the case because I was a somewhat high trait anxious individual and became nervous before I competed. The anxiety would usually dissipate after the first hit in American football or after the first points scored in my wrestling matches (usually by my opponent because I was tight). Not thinking I could do anything about my nervousness, especially in wrestling, I worked extremely hard to get in tremendous physical condition, so I had the stamina to comeback from losing the first few points or having a slow start because I was nervous. The good news was that my anxiety was not so severe that I choked. However, it did affect my performance at the start of contests and, more importantly, limited the enjoyment I had competing. It was for this reason that I was so excited to hear Rainer Martens (who would later become my doctoral adviser) speak at my college during my undergraduate days and talk about the inverted-U hypothesis. The idea of having an optimal level of arousal that would lead to best performance and finding that fine line between psyching up and psyching out resonated with me. From that moment on, I was hooked on sport psychology. These experiences as an athlete also spurred my interest as a researcher whether it was studying sources of stress in young athletes, how stress, anxiety, and emotions influenced athletic performance and/or stress induced burnout in tennis players.

Ironically, about eight years after my undergraduate days, I was a young assistant professor teaching sport psychology at Michigan State University when I received a referral from a clinical psychologist who asked if I would be willing to see if I could help a young figure skater that had tremendous difficulties handling stress. This 12-year-old girl would become so nervous during competitions that she would actually vomit on the ice! Feeling I was the young skater's last option and despite not having any applied training (few physically educated trained professionals did in the late 1970s), I said I would try. I tried progressive muscle relaxation, but the young skater indicated that she did not like "feeling like rubber". This was a problem as while sport psychology research at the time discussed how anxiety influenced performance, little information existed to guide one helping athletes cope with heightened stress, so I had little knowledge of anxiety management techniques beyond physical relaxation. Later, after searching the general psychology literature, I was able to use cognitive-behavioral thought control strategies with her which helped this young skater manage her anxiety, stay in the sport, and later go on to be a coach.

I bring up these personal examples here because my desire to understand stress, anxiety, coping, and their relationship to athletic performance had a great deal to do with my pursuing a career as a researcher and practitioner in sport psychology. It is also evident that when I compare what we knew in sport psychology about stress and anxiety and their effects on performance 40 years ago to today, we knew very little. Over my career, I have witnessed an unbelievable trajectory of research and corresponding knowledge in the area. In fact, it is very difficult to keep up with all the stress-related sport psychology research being published today, so there is a need for a book that integrates and presents the diverse array of research being conducted around the world.

It was for this reason I was so excited to learn about Rachel Arnold and David Fletcher's book *Stress, Well-Being, and Performance in Sport*. Designed to provide an overview and synthesis of stress in sports research and outline implications for performance and well-being, the book brings together the most active researchers in the area today. I especially like the theory to practice orientation of the book. The authors do an excellent job of not only summarizing the research and theory on the various stress-related topics but also critiquing it and providing direction for future research and theory. In addition to covering more traditional topics such as sources of stress and coping in sport, a vast array of newer and more contemporary topics such as group emotions, unconscious coping strategies, the influence of stress on quality of life and well-being, thriving, and pressure training are discussed. The publishing of this book will certainly help advance research and theory in the area.

At the same time, those interested in assisting athletes and other performers better handle stress will find the same rigor and attention to detail characterizing the presentation of research focused on implications for practice. Students will also find the book useful because of its comprehensive nature. It is organized around four key areas: appraising and coping with stress in sport; responses to and outcomes of stress in sport; moderators of the stress process in sport; and stress management to promote thriving in sport. Not only did I really like the emphasis in the book placed on stress and performance, but I also appreciated learning about the latest research examining the relationship between stress and well-being for those involved in sport.

The bottom line is that if you are a researcher interested in the effects of stress on performance and the overall well-being of the athlete, or a practitioner trying to help performers better deal with stress and enjoy the sport experience more, *Stress, Well-Being, and Performance in Sport* is a must read. It is a major contribution to the field, and I commend both the editors and the authors for their excellent contributions.

Daniel Gould, PhD

Gwen Norrell Professor of Youth Sports and Student-Athlete Well-Being; Director, Institute for the Study of Youth Sports; Michigan State University, United States.

Introduction

Rachel Arnold and David Fletcher

The context of elite sport can be highly stressful for those performing within it and, as a result, offers a natural laboratory for examining
humans' responses to demanding situations. Indeed, stress in sport has
been and continues to be a popular and widely researched area, particularly given the significant implications it can hold for individuals'
well-being and performance. Although it has long been recognized that
stress can have powerful effects on performance in the sport domain, it
is only more recently that its effects on well-being and its implications
for sport welfare policy have been considered. How athletes', coaches',
and support staffs' performances can be enhanced while simultaneously
optimizing their well-being within a highly demanding environment is
arguably one of the most pressing and important issues in contemporary sport. Indeed, in an independent report to the British government
on Duty of Care in Sport, Baroness Tanni Grey-Thompson (2017) suggested that:

> The most important element in sport is the people involved, whether
> they are taking part, volunteering, coaching or paid employees. The
> success of sport, in terms of helping people achieve their potential,
> making the most of existing talent, and attracting new people to
> sport relies on putting people—their safety, wellbeing and welfare—
> at the centre of what sport does. However, recent media reports and
> anecdotal evidence from across a range of sports has led to questions
> about whether welfare and safety really are being given the priority
> they deserve. At a time of success for British sport in terms of medals,
> championships and profile, this raises challenging questions about
> whether the current balance between welfare and winning is right
> and what we are prepared to accept as a nation. . . . Winning medals
> is, of course, really important, but should not be at the expense of
> the Duty of Care towards athletes, coaches and others involved in
> the system. . . . It is clear that the drive for success and desire to win
> should not be at the cost of the individuals involved.
>
> (p. 4)

For the critic who may argue that sport is not a "life or death" performance domain and thus, not as worthy of scholarly study or funding as
other pressurized contexts, it is perhaps worth exemplifying the importance of examining and optimizing performance and well-being in sport.
Taking performance first, success in elite sport can generate a positive
impact on the economy and employment (Ashton, Gerrard, & Hudson, 2003; Critchlow, 2015); enhance national identity, pride, and the
"feel-good factor" (Hilvoorde, Elling, & Stokvis, 2010; Wicker, Prinz, &
von Hanau, 2012); and positively impact sport participation frequency
and re-engagement (Weed et al., 2015). Turning to well-being, as Grey-
Thompson's (2017) quote highlights, the success of sport relies on prioritizing the well-being of those operating within it. At an individual
level, it is also noteworthy that high levels of psychological functioning
and adaptive responses to emotions are crucial for optimal performance
(see, e.g., Lundqvist, 2011; Rathschlag & Memmert, 2009). Additionally,
focusing on optimal well-being and motivation in sport can reap further
benefits for retention within the sporting context, and thus the resultant health benefits of continued engagement (cf. Green, 2005). Furthermore, Lundqvist (2011) illuminates the importance of well-being for
athletes in the context of competition, and the transfer of this outside
the milieu of sport (see also Chapter 6; cf. Downward & Rasciute, 2011).
Given these findings, it is essential for scholars to continue to examine
stress in the sport setting, so that optimal performance and well-being
can be achieved and, ultimately, a positive and sustainable impact can
be witnessed at the individual, team, organization, community, national,
and international levels. However, in order to make progress in a field of
inquiry and achieve the aforementioned aims and desired impact, it is
necessary to first review and learn from the scholarly work that has been
done to date.

Historical Developments in the Field

Pre-1990: The Early Years

When reviewing the academic study of stress in 1990, Jones and Hardy
observed that stress had been a popular area within sport psychology,
with research conducted classified into three main areas: stress responses,
stress and performance, and stress management. Beginning with stress
responses, most of the research in the early years focused on the competitive stress response, and in particular, competitive anxiety. To elaborate (see also Jones & Hardy, 1990), this anxiety research focused on
its: multidimensional conceptualization (e.g., state/trait and cognitive/
somatic; see, e.g., Jones & Hardy, 1989); cognitive, physiological, and
behavioral measurement (see, for a review, Martens, Vealey, & Burton,
1990; see also Landers, Christina, Hatfield, Daniels, & Doyle, 1980);

antecedents (see, e.g., Gould, Petlichkoff, & Weinberg, 1984; Scanlan & Passer, 1978; Scanlan & Lewthwaite, 1984); temporal patterning (see, e.g., Mahoney & Avener, 1977; Parfitt & Hardy, 1987); and individual differences (see, e.g., Martens & Gill, 1976).

Turning from stress responses to stress and performance, in the early years, a precise relationship between stress and performance appeared elusive (Jones & Hardy, 1990; see also Kleine, 1990; McAuley, 1985). Specifically, Jones and Hardy (1990) observed how prior research had been hampered by a lack of precision in defining and conceptualizing key constructs (e.g., anxiety and arousal). Furthermore, despite researchers in the early years debating the merits of various theories, such as drive theory (Spence & Spence, 1966) and the inverted-U hypothesis (Martens & Landers, 1970), a main motive for Jones and Hardy writing their 1990 book was concerns over slow theoretical advancement relating to the stress-performance relationship in sport (see also Jones & Hardy, 1989). In response, they reviewed literature on and forwarded ideas for the future study of multidimensional anxiety (Parfitt, Jones, & Hardy, 1990), cognitive processes underlying the stress-performance relationship (Jones, 1990), and catastrophe (Hardy, 1990) and drive theories (Kerr, 1990). With regard to empirical studies on the stress and performance link in the early years, research measuring the subcomponents of performance across a diversity of sports began to indicate that stress may impair or, under some circumstances, enhance performance (Burton, 1988; Jones & Hardy, 1988, 1990). Interestingly, an early study on the sources of stress identified by sport performers forwarded various performance-related stressors (e.g., not performing up to one's ability, losing; Gould, Horn, & Spreeman, 1983). As well as a focus on the outcome of performance, an additional line of inquiry in the early years was the relationship between stress and injury (Andersen & Williams, 1988; Hardy & Riehl, 1988; Passer & Seese, 1983).

With regard to stress management, one of the earliest references to stress in sport comes from the late 1920s and 1930s when the United States Olympic physicians realized that one of their main tasks was to help athletes reduce tension, often using relaxation, during the Olympic Games (Kornspan, 2007; Kornspan & MacCracken, 2001, 2003). Other stress and anxiety management work in the early years focused on self-regulation (see, e.g., Hardy & Nelson, 1988), cognitive and biofeedback (De Witt, 1980), COPE (Anshel, 1990), and stress inoculation training (see, e.g., Mace & Carroll, 1986); as well as developing goal setting (see, e.g., Hardy, Maiden, & Sherry, 1986), imagery (see, e.g., Suinn, 1983), hypnosis (see, e.g., Naruse, 1965), coping (see, e.g., Crocker, Alderman, Murray, & Smith, 1988), anxiety and activation control skills (see, e.g., Davidson, 1978; Hardy & Nelson, 1988), and performance routines (see, for a review, Boutcher, 1990). An interesting further line of inquiry in the early years was the exploration of stress-seeking behaviors in the sporting context (see, e.g., Robinson, 1985).

1991–2001: Establishment of the Field

Following the seminal publication of Jones and Hardy's (1990) and Martens et al.'s (1990) books, the period from 1991 to 2001 witnessed the field of stress and anxiety in sport becoming more established, with scholars from across the globe beginning to study the topic with more frequency and depth. A key feature of this period was the critique and further refinement of theoretical models formerly proposed for application to explaining performance in sports settings, including those which are arousal-based such as the inverted-U hypothesis, drive theory, and reversal theory (see, for a review, Jones, 1995b; see also Kerr, 1993), and those which are anxiety-based such as the catastrophe model (Hardy & Parfitt, 1991; Hardy, Parfitt, & Pates, 1994), and multidimensional anxiety-based approaches (Jones, 1995b). Expanding on the latter approach, research during this period was plentiful (see, for a review, Jones, 1995b) and examined the nature of the competitive anxiety response (e.g., state/trait, cognitive/somatic, and role of self-confidence) and specific antecedents of cognitive and somatic anxiety (e.g., expectations of success, changing room preparation, gender, sport, and skill level). Furthermore, research found that performers experienced a steady increase in anxiety in the buildup to a performance, which then continued during performance for those less experienced, but reduced for those with more experience and who were competing at higher levels (cf. Jones, 1995b). Extending this, it was also shown that while cognitive anxiety remained relatively stable in the buildup to a competition, somatic anxiety increased rapidly near an event starting (cf. Jones, 1995b). To enable more advanced research in this period, some scholars focused on advancing the measurement of anxiety (Jones, 1995b), for example, via shorter measures, using those of a psychophysiological nature, and by examining dimensions other than solely the intensity of symptoms (e.g., frequency of cognitive intrusions; Swain & Jones, 1993).

An additional dimension which was a popular area of study in the context of sport during this period was the direction of the anxiety response, and in particular, the extent to which the intensity of anxiety symptoms was labeled as either positive or negative on a facilitative-debilitative continuum (see, e.g., Jones, 1991, 1995a, 1995b; Jones, Hanton, & Swain, 1994; Jones & Swain, 1992; Jones, Swain, & Hardy, 1993; Woodman & Hardy, 2001), the role of individual differences in this model (see, for a review, Mellalieu, Hanton, & Fletcher, 2006), and the subsequent links between the direction dimensions and performance (Jones et al., 1993; Swain & Jones, 1996). Utilizing the research conducted on the direction dimensions of anxiety, Hardy (1997) aimed to debunk three common recommendations made in applied sport psychology literature; one of which was that cognitive anxiety is always detrimental to performance and should therefore be reduced where possible. Invited to respond to this article, Burton and Naylor (1997) disagreed with how Hardy (1997) had both defined competitive anxiety (i.e., not distinguishing between anxiety and other positive outcomes with similar symptoms) and advocated the measurement of its symptoms (e.g., not separately measuring anxiety and other positive emotions, not having standard intensity prompts for rating direction, and not accounting for symptom quality vs. quantity). Responding to the article, Hardy (1998) made a plea that anxiety researchers seriously reconsider the definition and measurement of basic constructs underpinning anxiety-performance research.

In line with a stimulus-based conceptualization of stress, a body of research during this period identified various "sources of stress" that sport performers encountered (see, e.g., Gould, Jackson, & Finch, 1993; James & Collins, 1997; Scanlan, Stein, & Ravizza, 1991). Examples included refereeing decisions, coach and teammate influences, and social support. Moving from a stimulus- to a response-based conceptualization, there were early endeavors in this period which focused on how an athlete responded and coped with such sources of stress (see, e.g., Blascovich & Tomaka, 1996; Crocker, 1992; Gould, Eklund, & Jackson, 1993). Furthermore, research also investigated antecedents of coping, including those which were social and environmental, person-related, and developmental (see, e.g., Anshel & Wells, 2000; Madden, Kirkby, & McDonald, 1989; Ntoumanis & Biddle, 1998), as well as how coping linked to other theoretically important variables such as appraisal, emotions, social support, and performance (Campen & Roberts, 2001; Crocker & Graham, 1995; Gaudreau, Lapierre, & Blondin, 2001; Gould, Bridges, Udry, & Beck, 1997; Ntoumanis & Biddle, 1998, 2000; Prapavessis & Grove, 1995). Linked to theory, debate initiated during this period around the conceptualization of coping in sport and whether it represented trait-like behavioral tendencies or state-like responses to specific life encounters (Bouffard & Crocker, 1992; Crocker & Isaak, 1997; Haney & Long, 1995; Pensgaard & Ursin, 1998; Udry, 1997). To provide more definitive conclusions for this debate, it was necessary to strengthen measures of coping; therefore, this was also a focus of activity during the period (see, for a review, Crocker, Kowalski, & Graham, 1998).

While the attention of this period was predominantly on anxiety and arousal, there was also a collection of work beginning to emerge which examined broader emotions in sport (see also Chapter 4). Summarizing this research, Hanin (2000) published a pivotal text which reviewed emotion definitions, theoretical frameworks, and linkages between emotions and athletic performance, emotional exhaustion, and mental health. A focal theoretical framework of Hanin's work during this period was the Individual Zones of Optimal Functioning (IZOF) model, which describes, explains, and predicts how performance related psychobiosocial states, of which subjective emotional experiences (e.g., emotions, mood, affect, and feelings) are a critical component, affect individual and team activity (see, for a review, Hanin, 1997, 2000). An alternative theoretical framework applied to competitive sport during this period to explain the relationship between emotions and performance was the Cognitive-Motivational-Relational Theory of Emotion (see, for a review, Lazarus, 2000a, 2000b). Turning from theories to empirical literature, Cerin, Szabo, Hunt, and Williams (2000) forwarded a critical review of the temporal patterning of competitive emotions, which emphasized the need to expand research from a narrow focus on pre-competitive anxiety to more precisely considering competitive anxiety as a set of patterns of emotions as opposed to a unitary affect.

2002–2010: The Millennial Period

At the turn of the millennium, there was a proliferation of studies that emerged on the sources of stress that sport performers encounter. While it is beyond the scope of this chapter to review each of these, it is worth noting that in this period stressors began to be classified as predominantly personal, competitive, and organizational in nature (see, for a review, Arnold & Fletcher, 2012; Fletcher, Hanton, & Mellalieu, 2006; Mellalieu et al., 2006; see also Chapter 1) and were found as being prevalent across a variety of sports. Turning from stressors to responses, this period also witnessed two new theoretical approaches to understanding stress in performance contexts. Following an extensive review and synthesis of the stress literature, Fletcher and colleagues (Fletcher & Arnold, 2017; Fletcher & Fletcher, 2005; Fletcher et al., 2006; Fletcher & Scott, 2010) developed a meta-model of stress, emotions, and performance that outlines the theoretical relationships among key processes, moderators, and consequences of the stress process. The model offers a supraordinate perspective of the stress-emotion-performance relationship and provided the first serious consideration of the transactional nature of stress as a dynamic process in the sport literature. At its most fundamental level, the meta-model postulates that stressors arise from the environment an individual operates in, are mediated by the processes of appraisal and coping, and, as a consequence, individuals respond in different ways. This ongoing process is moderated by personal and situational characteristics, and results in well-being and performance-related outcomes.

Several years later, a second theory focused specifically on athletes' appraisals was proposed in the sport literature—The Theory of Challenge and Threat States in Athletes (TCTSA; Jones, Meijen, McCarthy, & Sheffield, 2009; see also Chapter 2)—which hypothesizes that certain factors (e.g., self-efficacy) determine a challenge or threat state in response to competition, which can be indicated by distinct patterns of neuroendocrine, cardiovascular (CV), and emotional responses, and these states then influence various outcomes (e.g., effort, attention, and performance; see also Chapters 2 and 5). Additional appraisal-related research during this period explored properties of stress appraisals (Thatcher & Day, 2008), the role of control in secondary appraisals (see, e.g., Campbell & Jones, 2002), factors which may influence appraisals (e.g., mental toughness; Kaiseler, Polman, & Nicholls, 2009), and the relationships between appraisals and other components (e.g., emotions and outcomes) of the stress process (Adie, Duda, & Ntoumanis, 2008; Uphill & Jones, 2007).

The work on emotions in sport during this period continued to investigate various antecedents of emotions (see, e.g., Uphill & Jones, 2007) and the effects of emotions on outcomes (see, e.g., Vast, Young, & Thomas, 2010). One interesting extension on the latter line of enquiry was the investigation of the spread of emotions within sports teams (see, e.g., Moll, Jordet, & Pepping, 2010). Theoretical frameworks of emotion continued to be refined and applied to new sporting situations (Hanin, 2002; Robazza, 2006), and recommendations were also forwarded for how to optimally control emotions in sport (Jones, 2003). There was still a tendency during this period to focus attention on the emotion of anxiety, with research tracking within-person anxiety experiences (see, e.g., Hanton, Thomas, & Maynard, 2004) and illustrating its performance-impairing effects across multiple sporting tasks (see, e.g., Wilson, Wood, & Vine, 2009; see also Chapters 4 and 5).

Turning from emotions to coping, a pivotal systematic review was published during this period by Nicholls and Polman (2007). Specifically, the results shed light on the variety of coping strategies used by athletes in the studies synthesized, differences in coping by age and gender, as well as forwarding evidence for both the trait and process coping perspectives, and support for three different models of coping effectiveness (Nicholls & Polman, 2007; see also Hoar, Kowalski, Gaudreau, & Crocker, 2006). A further formative resource for coping was published by Nicholls (2010), which brought together the work conducted during this period on conceptualizing coping, the identification of methodological issues (e.g., measurement and research design), coping and moderating variables (e.g., gender, age, and culture), coping and related constructs (e.g., personality, self-determination, achievement goals, and self-esteem), and future-oriented aspects of coping (see also Chapter 3). An additional seminal systematic review conducted within this period was on burnout in sport (Goodger, Gorely, Lavallee, & Harwood, 2007). The review illustrated that research had been conducted on both athlete and coach burnout, with psychological (e.g., coping with adversity), situational (e.g., training load), and demographic (e.g., gender) correlates of burnout identified (Goodger et al., 2007; see also Cresswell & Eklund, 2006). Given that burnout is a chronic disorder, it is also important to note that this period witnessed longitudinal investigations of burnout (Cresswell & Eklund, 2005; Lemyre, Treasure, & Roberts, 2006). While intervention work on burnout is sparse, Raedeke and colleagues (2002) did provide insight into how coaches can help by maintaining flexibility with physical training, fostering social support, and making engagement exciting (see also Chapter 7). With regard to broader stress management literature during this period, studies underscored the importance of athletes developing relaxation, imagery, self-talk, goal setting, and self-regulation skills, as well as their self-confidence (see, for a review, Thomas, Mellalieu, & Hanton, 2009; see also Chapter 12).

2011–Present Time: Contemporary Focus

A notable extension that occurred in this contemporary period was the examination of various components of the stress process simultaneously (see, e.g., Britton, Kavanagh, & Polman, 2019; Didymus & Fletcher, 2017b; Larner, Wagstaff, Thelwell, & Corbett, 2016; Nicholls, Polman, & Levy, 2012). That said, the in-depth inquiry into separate stress process components also continued. Taking stressors first, work during this period advanced understanding of particular types of stressors (e.g., organizational; Arnold & Fletcher, 2012), their measurement (see, e.g., Arnold, Fletcher, & Daniels, 2013; Ntwanano, Toriola, & Didymus, 2017), and individual differences across samples (Arnold, Fletcher, & Daniels, 2016; Arnold, Wagstaff, Steadman, & Pratt, 2017; Evans, Wadey, Hanton, & Mitchell, 2012; see also Chapter 1). This period also witnessed rapid escalation of the work on appraisals in sport. To exemplify the diversity of work on appraisals during this period (see also Chapter 2), scholars examined appraisals during competitions (Martinent & Ferrand, 2014), the consistency of challenge and threat evaluations (Moore, Freeman, Hase, Solomon-Moore, & Arnold, 2019), alternative conceptualizations of appraisal (Uphill, Rossato, Swain, & O' Driscoll, 2019), the relationship between challenge/threat appraisals and various outcomes (e.g., performance, attention, and CV indices; Hase, O'Brien, Moore, & Freeman, 2018; Trotman, Williams, Quinton, & Veldhuijzen van Zanten, 2018; Vine, Freeman, Moore, Chandra-Ramanan, & Wilson, 2013), appraisals of specific stressors (Didymus & Fletcher, 2012; Hanton, Wagstaff, & Fletcher, 2012), gender differences (Kaiseler, Polman, & Nicholls, 2012b), and the role of social identity in appraisal (Rees, Haslam, Coffee, & Lavallee, 2015). Advancements during this period were also evident in the measurement of stress responses, with scholars beginning to adopt psychophysiological assessments alongside more traditional methods (see, e.g., Hudson, Davison, & Robinson, 2013; MacDonald & Wetherell, 2019; Morales et al., 2013; Quested et al., 2012).

Crocker and colleagues (2015) provide an overview of coping research during the former years of this period (see also Chapter 3). To elaborate, as well as critically discussing work on its conceptualization, they discuss research examining coping as both an individual- and group-level construct, studies examining coping over time, and explore communal coping and interpersonal emotion regulation. Similar to appraisal, scholarly work on coping during this period has been wide-ranging, exploring avenues such as dyadic coping (Staff, Didymus, & Backhouse, 2017), coping within competitive situations (Martinent & Nicolas, 2016), the socialization of coping (Tamminen, McEwen, & Crocker, 2016), dispositional coping (Nicholls, Levy, & Perry, 2015; Nicholls, Perry, Jones, Morley, & Carson, 2013), and furthering knowledge on coping effectiveness (Nieuwenhuys, Vos, Pijpstra, & Bakker, 2011; see also Chapter 3). Turning to emotions, three main lines of inquiry are deemed noteworthy during this period. First, the examination of emotions as a social phenomenon has blossomed, with various studies examining group emotions and performance (see, e.g., Campo, Champely et al., 2019; Campo, Mellalieu, Ferrand, Martinent, & Rosnet, 2012; Tamminen, Palmateer et al., 2016) or the transfer of emotions (e.g., coach to group; van Kleef, Cheshin, Koning, & Wolf, 2019). Second, there has been an abundance of research during this period on the relationship between emotion regulation and performance (see, e.g., Lane et al., 2015; Rathschlag & Memmert, 2015; Tamminen & Crocker, 2013; Tamminen, Gaudreau, McEwen, & Crocker, 2016; Wagstaff, 2014). The third emerging line of emotional inquiry during this period has been on emotional abilities and regulation in sports organizations (see, e.g., Wagstaff, Fletcher, & Hanton, 2012; Wagstaff, Hanton, & Fletcher, 2013; see also Chapter 4).

A novel focus of research during this period has been around the outcomes of the stress process, including burnout, well-being, mental health, and thriving (see also Chapters 6–8 and 13). Gustafson, DeFreese, and Madigan (2017) provide an insightful review of the work conducted during this contemporary period on burnout, including the various models, measurement, antecedents, and suggestions for its prevention and treatment. For well-being, Lundqvist (2011) forwarded a review of conceptual considerations for well-being at the start of the period. Later in the period, a debate was published around if elite sport is bad for athletes (see, e.g., MacIntyre, Barr, & Butler, 2015; Martindale, Collins, & Richards, 2014, 2015), with a final piece on this topic concluding in 2017 that there is still much to be done regarding the measurement of mental health in elite sport before more definitive conclusions can be drawn (Lebrun & Collins, 2017). Additionally, scholars have identified (and compared to the general population) how elite athletes score with regard to their well-being and mental health (see, e.g., Gouttebarge et al., 2019; Gulliver, Griffiths, Mackinnon, Batterham, & Stanimirovic, 2015; Houltberg, Wang, Qi, & Nelson, 2018; MacDougall, O'Halloran,

Sherry, & Shields, 2016; Rice et al., 2016). With regard to improving well-being and mental health, Breslin and Leavey's (2019) study is particularly enlightening. Furthermore, various sporting organizations have created consensus statements on bolstering mental health in elite sport (Henriksen et al., 2019; Reardon et al., 2019; Schinke, Stambulova, Si, & Moore, 2018). Continuing the theme of management, scholarly work has also examined the treatment of specific disorders in elite sport (see, e.g., Doherty, Hannigan, & Campbell, 2016), help-seeking behaviors in athletes (Gulliver, Griffiths, & Christensen, 2012), and how mental health can be transformed toward mental wealth (Uphill, Sly, & Swain, 2016). Rather than exploring how athletes might succumb to demands and experience undesirable outcomes, research within this period has also illuminated the topic of thriving—that is, how an athlete may experience development and success in response to competitive encounters (see also Chapter 13). Within this topic, scholarly work has clearly defined and conceptualized thriving (Brown, Arnold, Fletcher, & Standage, 2017), as well as identifying the personal and contextual enablers and process variables underpinning it (Brown, Arnold, Reid, & Roberts, 2018; Brown, Arnold, Standage, & Fletcher, 2017), and making recommendations for how it can be facilitated (Brown & Arnold, 2019).

Although available space precludes a detailed review of all research developments, several influential moderators of the stress process have received substantial attention during this contemporary period. These include personality (Allen, Greenlees, & Jones, 2013; Kaiseler, Polman, & Nicholls, 2012a; Roberts & Woodman, 2015; see also Chapter 10), resilience and growth (Fletcher, 2019; Fletcher & Sarkar, 2013; see also Chapter 9), and social support (see, e.g., Arnold, Edwards, & Rees, 2018; Hartley & Coffee, 2019; see also Chapter 11). An additional innovative line of inquiry that has emerged during this period is that of safeguarding and duties of care in elite sport (see also Chapter 14). This has taken the form of international organization consensus statements (Mountjoy et al., 2016), duties of care reports to governments and on individual sports (Grey-Thompson, 2017; Phelps, Kelly, Lancaster, Mehrzad, & Panter, 2017), and academic papers on areas such as human rights, safeguarding, and abuse in sport (see, e.g., Adams & Kavanagh, 2018; Kavanagh, Brown, & Jones, 2017; Rhind, McDermott, Lambert, & Koleva, 2015). The final topic for review in this period is stress management (see also Chapter 12). Rumbold, Fletcher, and Daniels (2012) published a seminal systematic review early in this period on stress management interventions used with sport performers. The findings suggested that a variety of stress management interventions (e.g., cognitive, multimodal, and alternative) are associated with athletes' optimized stress experience and enhanced performance. Following this review, scholars have adopted multiple strategies to address athletic stress, such as cognitive-behavioral strategies (Didymus & Fletcher, 2017a; Olmedilla et al., 2019), imagery (Quinton, Veldhuijzen van Zanten, Trotman, Cumming, & Williams, 2019; Williams, Veldhuijzen van Zanten, Trotman, Quinton, & Ginty, 2017), and emotional intelligence training programs (Campo, Laborde, Martinent, Louvet, & Nicolas, 2019).

Aims and Structure of the Book

The aim of this book is to provide a comprehensive overview of stress in sport and the performance and well-being implications for those operating in this domain. In doing so, the book bridges the gap between theory and practice, by bringing together and exploring recent theoretical advances, original and cutting-edge research, a series of best practice recommendations, and novel suggestions for stimulating future research on this topic. Rather than focusing on isolated or narrow components of the stress process, the book provides a contemporary and complete perspective by showcasing the work of well-established and emerging scholars from across the globe who, collectively, offer an international perspective on established themes and emerging areas of interest associated with the topic of stress, well-being, and performance in sport. The book is directed at students (undergraduate and postgraduate), academics, professionals working in the field of sport psychology (neophyte and experienced practitioners), and psychologists and individuals outside of the sports domain with an interest in stress, performance, and well-being.

By logically progressing through the transactional stress process, the book covers four key areas: (i) appraising and coping with stress in sport, (ii) responses to and outcomes of stress in sport, (iii) moderators of the stress process in sport, and (iv) stress management to promote thriving in sport.

Appraising and Coping With Stress in Sport

Common to most contemporary theories of stress is the transaction between an individual and their surrounding environment, with their ability to respond appropriately to and manage the demands encountered critical in determining the strain subsequently experienced. Chapter 1, by Rachel Arnold and David Fletcher, provides a review of the original and contemporary research on the various stressors, hassles, and adversity encountered by sport performers, with a particular focus on their conceptualization. Indeed, the chapter offers a detailed and critical insight into the scholarly work conducted on the type, dimensions, properties and other characteristics of stressors, hassles, and adversity, before concluding with insightful suggestions for their optimal management via primary interventions. Given that appraisals lie at the heart of stress transactions, it is not surprising that a considerable amount of research has taken place on this topic in the sports domain over the past decade. In Chapter 2, Faye F. Didymus and Marc V. Jones take stock of this momentum, providing a timely update on relevant terminologies and conceptual distinctions, before reviewing the psychological and psychophysiological literature on primary and secondary appraising in sport. The authors finish the chapter by highlighting future research priorities and implications for applied practice. To conclude this section, Chapter 3, by Katherine A. Tamminen, critically considers the major theoretical perspectives and research on coping in sport, with a particular focus on how it relates to performance and well-being. Furthermore, the chapter provides discussion of recent research advances on proactive coping and communal coping in sport, before summarizing with practical implications forwarded to help athletes improve their coping.

Responses to and Outcomes of Stress in Sport

Continuing the theme of a transactional relationship, this section explores the various reactions and responses that a sport performer has to the stressors they encounter, and the implications of these for important health, well-being, and performance-related outcomes in sport. Chapter 4, by Christopher R. D. Wagstaff and Katherine A. Tamminen, considers both the historical research on emotion in sport, which has been largely from an intrapersonal perspective, alongside more recent advances in emotion research conducted via an interpersonal lens (i.e., the occurrence and experience of emotions within groups and teams). The chapter also discusses how research on emotions in sport can inform educational interventions delivered across multiple levels of an organizational hierarchy. Chapter 5, by Lee J. Moore, Samuel J. Vine, and Mark R. Wilson, provides a review of the literature and theoretical models that examine and explain how athletes' responses to stress impact attention and performance in sporting scenarios. With specific emphasis placed on Vine and colleagues' (2016) integrative framework of stress, attention, and visuomotor performance, the chapter summarizes supporting evidence, alongside forwarding applied suggestions for optimizing attention and performance under pressure. In Chapter 6, Carolina Lundqvist highlights the need for proactively stimulating well-being and quality of life in athletes, so that they can remain functional in both the sporting environment and their broader lives. Together with outlining underpinning definitions and frameworks, the chapter offers an overview of well-being and quality of life research conducted in sport, and provides a summarizing model of the life- and sport-related factors and resources which can impact on elite athletes' evaluations of well-being, quality of life, and functionality in both life and sport contexts. Chapter 7, by J. D. DeFreese and Robert C. Eklund, outlines research and theory on burnout in sport with specific emphasis on the psychological stress and coping model. The chapter highlights how the current evidence on burnout in sport can be used to guide both prevention and symptom mitigation efforts of this aversive experiential state for both athlete and other sport-related populations (e.g., coaches and officials). In the final chapter of this section (Chapter 8), Simon Rice, Courtney C. Walton, Kate Gwyther, and Rosemary Purcell provide a topical and timely update on the state of knowledge in relation to mental health in sport. After offering insight into underpinning frameworks and contemporary consensus and position statements, the chapter progresses through various strategies that can be employed for both athletes and their wider support systems to maintain optimal mental health.

Moderators of the Stress Process in Sport

This section of the book focuses on select personal and situational characteristics that can have a powerful influence on the stress process, by buffering or exacerbating the relationship between a performer and their environment (i.e., affecting performers' vulnerability or resilience to stressors), or between their responses and resultant outcomes (i.e., influencing whether responses are positive or negative in tone; cf. Fletcher et al., 2006). Chapter 9, by David Fletcher, reviews existing literature on the personal and situational influences that determine why some athletes benefit and grow from stress-related encounters and, subsequently, develop resilience, optimize their well-being, and enhance performance. Specific emphasis is placed on theoretical and empirical advancements in resilience and growth research in sport and how these can inform practitioners in more effectively supporting those operating in the sports domain to experience positive outcomes. Chapter 10, by Sylvain Laborde, Sinikka Heisler, and Emma Mosley, begins with a definition of personality, before providing a concise overview of personality research in sport as it relates to stress. Following this, the chapter turns its focus to examining how the activation of certain personality traits in pressured situations can lead to performance decrements, via an impact on executive function. In the final chapter of this section, Chapter 11, Paul Freeman discusses the theory and literature in sport which examines social support and, specifically in line with the title of this section, how it influences and interacts with stress, appraisals, coping, and outcomes (e.g., performance and well-being). Following this, the chapter provides recommendations for applied practice, with specific emphasis on helping performers to recognize the supportive resources available to them, facilitating the development of supportive environments, and considering the factors that can influence the effectiveness of social support.

Stress Management to Promote Thriving in Sport

As well as each of the aforementioned chapters including specific practical implications for the respective topics covered, the final section of this book comprises innovative and pioneering areas in sport that are, ultimately, designed to optimize the stress process for performers. Chapter 12, by David Fletcher and Rachel Arnold, reviews the main concepts, theory, and literature on the psychosocial preparation of athletes for performance in pressurized competition, with a particular focus on stress and pressure training. The chapter highlights evidence-based practical guidelines and recommendations for developing and implementing stress and pressure training, and makes the case for this becoming an increasingly important component of preparing performers for competition. Chapter 13, by Daniel J. Brown, Michael Passaportis, and Kate Hays, introduces the notion of human thriving; specifically, describing recent opportune advances in sport-based literature to conceptualize thriving as concurrently perceiving a high level of performance and experiencing a high level of well-being. The chapter proceeds to explain the role of enabler and process variables in both predicting and promoting thriving in sport, before illustrating how these empirical advances are being implemented into an applied framework used by sport psychologists working in British Olympic and Paralympic sport to deliver impactful psychology systematically, to ultimately enable athletes and the staff that support them to thrive. In the final chapter of this section, Chapter 14, Emma Kavanagh, Daniel Rhind, and Genevieve Gordon-Thomson, effectively highlight the pressing and newsworthy requirements for considering and prioritizing duty of care and welfare practices in sporting environments. After discussing risks to welfare in the performance environment (e.g., abuse and non-accidental violence), the chapter makes specific recommendations and a call to action for a more joined up approach to safeguarding in sport and implementation of the duty of care to protect the welfare and well-being of everyone involved.

References

Adams, A., & Kavanagh, E. J. (2018). The capabilities and human rights of high performance athletes. *International Review for the Sociology of Sport.* Advance online publication. Doi:10.1177/1012690218791139

Adie, J. W., Duda, J. L., & Ntoumanis, N. (2008). Achievement goals, competition appraisals, and the psychological and emotional welfare of sport participants. *Journal of Sport and Exercise Psychology, 30,* 302–322. Doi:10.1123/jsep.30.3.302

Allen, M. S., Greenlees, I., & Jones, M. (2013). Personality in sport: A comprehensive review. *International Review of Sport and Exercise Psychology, 6,* 184–208. Doi:10.1080/1750984x.2013.769614

Andersen, M. B., & Williams, J. M. (1988). A model of stress and athletic injury: Prediction and prevention. *Journal of Sport and Exercise Psychology, 10,* 294–306. Doi:10.1123/jsep.10.3.294

Anshel, M. H. (1990). Toward validation of a model for coping with acute stress in sport. *International Journal of Sport Psychology, 21,* 58–83.

Anshel, M. H., & Wells, B. (2000). Personal and situational variables that describe coping with acute stress in competitive sport. *Journal of Social Psychology, 140*, 434–450. Doi:10.1080/00224540009600483

Arnold, R., Edwards, T., & Rees, T. (2018). Organizational stressors, social support, and implications for subjective performance in high-level sport. *Psychology of Sport & Exercise, 39*, 204–212. Doi:10.1016/j.psychsport.2018.08.010

Arnold, R., & Fletcher, D. (2012). A research synthesis and taxonomic classification of the organizational stressors encountered by sport performers. *Journal of Sport and Exercise Psychology, 34*, 397–429. Doi:10.1123/jsep.34.3.397

Arnold, R., Fletcher, D., & Daniels, K. (2013). Development and validation of the Organizational Stressor Indicator for Sport Performers (OSI-SP). *Journal of Sport & Exercise Psychology, 35*, 180–196. Doi:10.1123/jsep.35.2.180

Arnold, R., Fletcher, D., & Daniels, K. (2016). Demographic differences in sport performers' experiences of organizational stressors. *Scandinavian Journal of Medicine & Science in Sports, 26*, 348–358. Doi:10.1111/sms.12439

Arnold, R., Wagstaff, C. R. D., Steadman, L., & Pratt, Y. (2017). The organizational stressors encountered by athletes with a disability. *Journal of Sports Sciences, 35*, 1187–1196. Doi:10.1080/02640414.2016.1214285

Ashton, J. K., Gerrard, B., & Hudson, R. (2003). Economic impact of national sporting success: Evidence from the London stock exchange. *Applied Economics Letters, 10*, 783–785. Doi:10.1080/1350485032000126712

Blascovich, J., & Tomaka, J. (1996). The biopsychosocial model of arousal regulation. In M. P. Zanna (Ed.), *Advances in experimental social psychology* (pp. 1–51). Cambridge, MA: Elsevier.

Bouffard, M., & Crocker, P. R. E. (1992). Coping by individuals with physical disabilities with perceived challenges in physical activity: Are people consistent? *Research Quarterly for Exercise and Sport, 63*, 410–417. Doi:10.1080/02701367.1992.10608763

Boutcher, S. H. (1990). The role of performance routines in sport. In J. G. Jones & L. Hardy (Eds.), *Stress and performance in sport* (pp. 231–246). New York: John Wiley & Sons.

Breslin, G., & Leavey, G. (Eds.). (2019). *Mental health and well-being interventions in sport: Research, theory and practice.* New York: Routledge.

Britton, D. M., Kavanagh, E. J., & Polman, R. C. J. (2019). A path analysis of adolescent athletes' perceived stress reactivity, competition appraisals, emotions, coping, and performance satisfaction. *Frontiers in Psychology*. Advance online publication. Doi:10.3389/fpsyg.2019.01151

Brown, D. J., & Arnold, R. (2019). Sports performers' perspectives on facilitating thriving in professional rugby contexts. *Psychology of Sport and Exercise, 40*, 71–81. Doi:10.1016/j.psychsport.2018.09.008

Brown, D. J., Arnold, R., Fletcher, D., & Standage, M. (2017). Human thriving: A conceptual debate and literature review. *European Psychologist, 22*, 167–179. Doi:10.1027/1016-9040/a000294

Brown, D. J., Arnold, R., Reid, T., & Roberts, G. (2018). A qualitative exploration of thriving in elite sport. *Journal of Applied Sport Psychology, 30*, 129–149. Doi:10.1080/10413200.2017.1354339

Brown, D. J., Arnold, R., Standage, M., & Fletcher, D. (2017). Thriving on pressure: A factor mixture analysis of sport performers' responses to competitive encounters. *Journal of Sport and Exercise Psychology, 39,* 423–437. Doi:10.1123/jsep.2016-0293

Burton, D. (1988). Do anxious swimmers swim slower? Reexamining the elusive anxiety-performance relationship. *Journal of Sport and Exercise Psychology, 10,* 45–61. Doi:10.1123/jsep.10.1.45

Burton, D., & Naylor, S. (1997). Is anxiety really facilitative? Reaction to the myth that cognitive anxiety always impairs sport performance. *Journal of Applied Sport Psychology, 9,* 295–302. Doi:10.1080/10413209708406488

Campbell, E., & Jones, G. (2002). Cognitive appraisal of sources of stress experienced by elite male wheelchair basketball players. *Adapted Physical Activity Quarterly, 19,* 100–108. Doi:10.1123/apaq.19.1.100

Campen, C., & Roberts, D. C. (2001). Coping strategies of runners: Perceived effectiveness and match to precompetitive anxiety. *Journal of Sport Behavior, 24,* 144–161.

Campo, M., Champely, S., Louvet, B., Rosnet, E., Ferrand, C., Pauketat, J. V. T., & Mackie, D. M. (2019). Group-based emotions: Evidence for emotion-performance relationships in team sports. *Research Quarterly for Exercise and Sport, 90,* 54–63. Doi:10.1080/02701367.2018.1563274

Campo, M., Laborde, S., Martinent, G., Louvet, B., & Nicolas, M. (2019). Emotional intelligence (EI) training adapted to the international preparation constraints in rugby: Influence of EI trainer status on EI training effectiveness. *Frontiers in Psychology.* Advance online publication. Doi:10.3389/fpsyg.2019.01939

Campo, M., Mellalieu, S., Ferrand, C., Martinent, G., & Rosnet, E. (2012). Emotions in team contact sports: A systematic review. *The Sport Psychologist, 26,* 62–97. Doi:10.1123/tsp.26.1.62

Cerin, E., Szabo, A., Hunt, N., & Williams, C. (2000). Temporal patterning of competitive emotions: A critical review. *Journal of Sports Sciences, 18,* 605–626. Doi:10.1080/02640410050082314

Cresswell, S. L., & Eklund, R. C. (2005). Changes in athlete burnout and motivation over a 12-week league tournament. *Medicine and Science in Sports and Exercise, 37,* 1957–1966. Doi:10.1249/01.mss.0000176304.14675.32

Cresswell, S. L., & Eklund, R. C. (2006). Athlete burnout: Conceptual confusion, current research and future research directions. In S. Hanton & S. D. Mellalieu (Eds.), *Literature reviews in sport psychology* (pp. 91–126). Hauppauge, NY: Nova Science Publishers.

Critchlow, A. (2015). Britain's sport industry hitting top form. *The Telegraph.* Retrieved from www.telegraph.co.uk/finance/11580773/Britains-sport-industry-hitting-top-form.html

Crocker, P. R. E. (1992). Managing stress by competitive athletes: Ways of coping. *International Journal of Sport Psychology, 23,* 161–175.

Crocker, P. R. E., Alderman, R. B., Murray, F., & Smith, R. (1988). Cognitive-affective stress management training with high performance youth volleyball players: Effects on affect, cognition, and performance. *Journal of Sport and Exercise Psychology, 10,* 448–460. Doi:10.1123/jsep.10.4.448

Crocker, P. R. E., & Graham, T. R. (1995). Coping by competitive athletes with performance stress: Gender differences and relationships with affect. *The Sport Psychologist, 9,* 325–338. Doi:10.1123/tsp.9.3.325

Crocker, P. R. E., & Isaak, K. (1997). Coping during competitions and training sessions: Are youth swimmers consistent? *International Journal of Sport Psychology, 28,* 355–369.

Crocker, P. R. E., Kowalski, K. C., & Graham, T. R. (1998). Measurement of coping strategies in sport. In J. L. Duda (Ed.), *Advances in sport and exercise psychology measurement* (pp. 149–161). Morgantown, WV: Fitness Information Technology.

Crocker, P. R. E., Tamminen, K. A., & Gaudreau, P. (2015). Coping in sport. In S. Hanton & S. Mellalieu (Eds.), *Contemporary advances in sport psychology: A review* (pp. 28–67). New York: Routledge.

Davidson, R. J. (1978). Specificity and patterning in biobehavioral systems: Implications for behaviour change. *American Psychologist, 33,* 430–436. Doi:10.1037/0003-066x.33.5.430

De Witt, D. J. (1980). Cognitive and biofeedback training for stress reduction with university athletes. *Journal of Sport and Exercise Psychology, 2,* 288–294. Doi:10.1123/jsp.2.4.288

Didymus, F. F., & Fletcher, D. (2012). Getting to the heart of the matter: A diary study of swimmers' appraisals of organisational stressors. *Journal of Sports Sciences, 30,* 1375–1385. Doi:10.1080/02640414.2012.709263

Didymus, F. F., & Fletcher, D. (2017a). Effects of a cognitive-behavioral intervention on field hockey players' appraisals of organizational stressors. *Psychology of Sport and Exercise, 30,* 173–185. Doi:10.1016/j.psychsport.2017.03.005

Didymus, F. F., & Fletcher, D. (2017b). Organizational stress in high-level field hockey: Examining transactional pathways between stressors, appraisals, coping and performance satisfaction. *International Journal of Sports Science & Coaching, 12,* 252–263. Doi:10.1177/1747954117694737

Doherty, S., Hannigan, B., & Campbell, M. J. (2016). The experience of depression during the careers of elite male athletes. *Frontiers in Psychology, 7,* 1069. Doi:10.3389/fpsyg.2016.01069

Downward, P., & Rasciute, S. (2011). Does sport make you happy? An analysis of the well-being derived from sports participation. *International Review of Applied Economics, 25,* 331–348. Doi:10.1080/02692171.2010.511168

Evans, L., Wadey, R., Hanton, S., & Mitchell, I. (2012). Stressors experienced by injured athletes. *Journal of Sports Sciences, 30,* 917–927. Doi:10.1080/02640414.2012.682078

Fletcher, D. (2019). Psychological resilience and adversarial growth in sport and performance. In E. O. Acevedo (Ed.), *The Oxford encyclopaedia of sport, exercise, and performance psychology* (pp. 731–756). New York: Oxford University Press.

Fletcher, D., & Arnold, R. (2017). Stress in sport: The role of the organizational environment. In C. R. D. Wagstaff (Ed.), *An organizational psychology of sport: Key issues and practical applications* (pp. 83–100). London, UK: Routledge.

Fletcher, D., & Fletcher, J. (2005). A meta-model of stress, emotions and performance: Conceptual foundations, theoretical framework, and research directions [Abstract]. *Journal of Sports Sciences, 23,* 157–158.

Fletcher, D., Hanton, S., & Mellalieu, S. D. (2006). An organizational stress review: Conceptual and theoretical issues in competitive sport. In S. Hanton & S. D. Mellalieu (Eds.), *Literature reviews in sport psychology* (pp. 321–374). Hauppauge, NY: Nova Science Publishers.

Fletcher, D., & Sarkar, M. (2013). Psychological resilience: A review and critique of definitions, concepts, and theory. *European Psychologist, 18,* 12–23. Doi:10.1027/1016-9040/a000124

Fletcher, D., & Scott, M. (2010). Psychological stress in sports coaches: A review of concepts, research and practice. *Journal of Sports Sciences, 28,* 127–137. Doi:10.1080/02640410903406208

Gaudreau, P., Lapierre, A. M., & Blondin, J. P. (2001). Coping at three phases of a competition: Comparison between pre-competitive, competitive, and post-competitive utilization of the same strategy. *International Journal of Sport Psychology, 32,* 369–385.

Goodger, K., Gorely, T., Lavallee, D., & Harwood, C. (2007). Burnout in sport: A systematic review. *The Sport Psychologist, 21,* 127–151. Doi:10.1123/tsp.21.2.127

Gould, D., Bridges, D., Udry, E., & Beck, L. (1997). Coping with season-ending injuries. *The Sport Psychologist, 11,* 379–399. Doi:10.1123/tsp.11.4.379

Gould, D., Eklund, R. C., & Jackson, S. A. (1993). Coping strategies used by U.S. Olympic wrestlers. *Research Quarterly for Exercise and Sport, 64,* 83–93. Doi:10.1080/02701367.1993.10608782

Gould, D., Horn, T., & Spreeman, J. (1983). Sources of stress in junior elite wrestlers. *Journal of Sport and Exercise Psychology, 5,* 159–171. Doi:10.1123/jsp.5.2.159

Gould, D., Jackson, S. A., & Finch, L. M. (1993). Sources of stress in national champion figure skaters. *Journal of Sport and Exercise Psychology, 15,* 134–159. Doi:10.1123/jsep.15.2.134

Gould, D., Petlichkoff, L., & Weinberg, R. S. (1984). Antecedents of, temporal changes in, and relationships between CSAI-2 subcomponents. *Journal of Sport Psychology, 6,* 289–304. Doi:10.1123/jsp.6.3.289

Gouttebarge, V., Castaldelli-Maia, J., Gorczynski, P., Hainline, B., Hitchcock, B., Kerkhoffs, G., . . . Reardon, C. (2019). Occurrence of mental health symptoms and disorders in current and former elite athletes: A systematic review and meta-analysis. *British Journal of Sports Medicine.* Advance online publication. Doi:10.1136/bjsports-2019-100671

Green, B. C. (2005). Building sport programs to optimize athlete recruitment, retention, and transition: Toward a normative theory of sport development. *Journal of Sport Management, 19,* 233–253. Doi:10.1123/jsm.19.3.233

Grey-Thompson, T. (2017). *Duty of care in sport: Independent report to government.* London, UK: HMSO.

Gulliver, A., Griffiths, K. M., & Christensen, H. (2012). Barriers and facilitators to mental health help-seeking for young elite athletes: A qualitative study. *BMC Psychiatry, 12,* 157. Doi:10.1186/1471-244x-12-157

Gulliver, A., Griffiths, K. M., Mackinnon, A., Batterham, P. J., & Stanimirovic, R. (2015). The mental health of Australian elite athletes. *Journal of Science and Medicine in Sport, 18,* 255–261.

Gustafson, H., DeFreese, J. D., & Madigan, D. J. (2017). Athlete burnout: Review and recommendations. *Current Opinion in Psychology, 16,* 109–113. Doi:10.1016/j.copsyc.2017.05.002

Haney, C. J., & Long, B. C. (1995). Coping effectiveness: A path analysis of self-efficacy, control, coping, and performance in sport competitions. *Journal of Applied Social Psychology, 25,* 1726–1746. Doi:10.1111/j.1559-1816.1995.tb01815.x

Hanin, Y. L. (1997). Emotions and athletic performance: Individual zones of optimal functioning model. *European Yearbook of Sport Psychology, 1,* 29–72.

Hanin, Y. L. (2000). *Emotions in sport.* Champaign, IL: Human Kinetics.

Hanin, Y. L. (2002). Individual optimal recovery in sports: An application of the IZOF model. In M. Kellman (Ed.), *Enhancing recovery: Preventing underperformance in athletes* (pp. 199–217). Champaign, IL: Human Kinetics.

Hanton, S., Thomas, O., & Maynard, I. (2004). Competitive anxiety responses in the week leading up to competition: The role of intensity, direction and frequency dimensions. *Psychology of Sport and Exercise, 5,* 169–181. Doi:10.1016/s1469-0292(02)00042-0

Hanton, S., Wagstaff, C. R. D., & Fletcher, D. (2012). Cognitive appraisals of stressors encountered in sport organizations. *International Journal of Sport and Exercise Psychology, 10,* 276–289. Doi:10.1080/1612197X.2012.682376

Hardy, C. J., & Riehl, R. E. (1988). An examination of the life stress-injury relationship among noncontact sport participants. *Behavioral Medicine, 14,* 113–118. Doi:10.1080/08964289.1988.9935132

Hardy, L. (1990). A catastrophe model of performance in sport. In J. G. Jones & L. Hardy (Eds.), *Stress and performance in sport* (pp. 81–106). New York: John Wiley & Sons.

Hardy, L. (1997). The Coleman Roberts Griffith address: Three myths about applied consultancy work. *Journal of Applied Sport Psychology, 9,* 277–294. Doi:10.1080/10413209708406487

Hardy, L. (1998). Responses to the reactants on three myths in applied consultancy work. *Journal of Applied Sport Psychology, 10,* 212–219. Doi:10.1080/10413209808406389

Hardy, L., Maiden, D. S., & Sherry, K. (1986). Goal setting and performance: The effects of performance anxiety. *Journal of Sports Sciences, 4,* 233–234.

Hardy, L., & Nelson, D. (1988). Self-regulation training in sport and work. *Ergonomics, 31,* 1573–1583. Doi:10.1080/00140138808966807

Hardy, L., & Parfitt, G. (1991). A catastrophe model of anxiety and performance. *British Journal of Psychology, 82,* 163–178. Doi:10.1111/j.2044-8295.1991.tb02391.x

Hardy, L., Parfitt, G., & Pates, J. (1994). Performance catastrophes in sport: A test of the hysteresis hypothesis. *Journal of Sports Sciences, 12,* 327–334. Doi:10.1080/02640419408732178

Hartley, C., & Coffee, P. (2019). Perceived and received dimensional support: Main and stress buffering effects on dimensions of burnout. *Frontiers in Psychology, 10,* 1724–1734. Doi:10.3389/fpsyg.2019.01724

Hase, A., O'Brien, J., Moore, L., & Freeman, P. (2018). The relationship between challenge and threat states and performance: A systematic review. *Sport, Exercise, and Performance Psychology, 8,* 123–144. Doi:10.1037/spy0000132

Henriksen, K., Schinke, R., Moesch, K., McCann, S., Parham, W. D., Larsen, C. H., & Terry, P. (2019). Consensus statement on improving the mental health of high performance athletes. *International Journal of Sport and Exercise Psychology.* Advance online publication. Doi:10.1080/1612197X.2019.1570473

Hilvoorde, I., Elling, A., & Stokvis, R. (2010). How to influence national pride? The Olympic Medal Index as a unifying narrative. *International Review for the Sociology of Sport, 45,* 87–102. Doi:10.1177/1012690209356989

Hoar, S. D., Kowalski, K. C., Gaudreau, P., & Crocker, P. R. E. (2006). A review of coping in sport. In S. Hanton & S. D. Mellalieu (Eds.), *Literature reviews in sport psychology* (pp. 47–90). Hauppauge, NY: Nova Science Publishers.

Houltberg, B. J., Wang, K. T., Qi, W., & Nelson, C. S. (2018). Self-narrative profiles of elite athletes and comparisons on psychological well-being. *Research Quarterly for Exercise and Sport, 89*, 354–360. Doi:10.1080/02701367.2018.148 1919

Hudson, J., Davison, G., & Robinson, P. (2013). Psychophysiological and stress responses to competition in team sport coaches: An exploratory study. *Scandinavian Journal of Medicine & Science in Sports, 3*, 279–285. Doi:10.1111/sms.12075

James, B., & Collins, D. (1997). Self-presentational sources of competitive stress during performance. *Journal of Sport and Exercise Psychology, 19*, 17–35. Doi:10.1123/jsep.19.1.17

Jones, J. G. (1990). A cognitive perspective on the processes underlying the relationship between stress and performance in sport. In J. G. Jones & L. Hardy (Eds.), *Stress and performance in sport* (pp. 17–42). New York: John Wiley & Sons.

Jones, J. G. (1991). Recent developments and current issues in competitive state anxiety research. *The Sport Psychologist, 4*, 152–155.

Jones, J. G. (1995a). Competitive anxiety in sport. In S. J. H. Biddle (Ed.), *European perspectives on exercise and sport psychology* (pp. 128–153). Champaign, IL: Human Kinetics.

Jones, J. G. (1995b). More than just a game: Research developments and issues in competitive anxiety in sport. *British Journal of Psychology, 86*, 449–478. Doi:10.1111/j.2044-8295.1995.tb02565.x

Jones, J. G., Hanton, S., & Swain, A. B. J. (1994). Intensity and interpretation of anxiety symptoms in elite and non-elite sport performers. *Personality and Individual Differences, 17*, 657–663. Doi:10.1016/0191-8869(94)90138-4

Jones, J. G., & Hardy, L. (1988). The effects of anxiety upon psychomotor performance. *Journal of Sport Sciences, 6*, 59–67. Doi:10.1080/02640418808729794

Jones, J. G., & Hardy, L. (1989). Stress and cognitive functioning in sport. *Journal of Sports Sciences, 7*, 41–63. Doi:10.1080/02640418908729821

Jones, J. G., & Hardy, L. (1990). *Stress and performance in sport.* New York: John Wiley & Sons.

Jones, J. G., & Swain, A. B. J. (1992). Intensity and direction dimensions of competitive state anxiety and relationships with competitiveness. *Perceptual and Motor Skills, 74*, 467–472. Doi:10.2466/pms.1992.74.2.467

Jones, J. G., Swain, A. B. J., & Hardy, L. (1993). Intensity and direction dimensions of competitive state anxiety and relationships with performance. *Journal of Sports Sciences, 11*, 525–532. Doi:10.1080/02640419308730023

Jones, M. V. (2003). Controlling emotions in sport. *The Sport Psychologist, 17*, 471–486. Doi:10.1123/tsp.17.4.471

Jones, M. V., Meijen, C., McCarthy, P. J., & Sheffield, D. (2009). A theory of challenge and threat states in athletes. *International Review of Sport and Exercise Psychology, 2*, 161–180. Doi:10.1080/17509840902829331

Kaiseler, M., Polman, R., & Nicholls, A. R. (2009). Mental toughness, stress, stress appraisal, coping, and coping effectiveness in sport. *Personality and Individual Differences, 47*, 728–733. Doi:10.1016/j.paid.2009.06.012

Kaiseler, M., Polman, R., & Nicholls, A. R. (2012a). Effects of the Big Five personality dimensions on appraisal, coping, and coping effectiveness in sport. *European Journal of Sport Science, 12,* 62–72. Doi:10.1080/17461391.2010.551410

Kaiseler, M., Polman, R., & Nicholls, A. R. (2012b). Gender differences in appraisal and coping: An examination of the situational and dispositional hypothesis. *International Journal of Sport Psychology, 43,* 1–14.

Kavanagh, E. J., Brown, L., & Jones, I. (2017). Elite athletes experience of coping with emotional abuse in the coach-athlete relationship. *Journal of Applied Sport Psychology, 29,* 402–417. Doi:10.1080/10413200.2017.1298165

Kerr, J. H. (1990). Stress and sport: Reversal theory. In J. G. Jones & L. Hardy (Eds.), *Stress and performance in sport* (pp. 107–131). New York: John Wiley & Sons.

Kerr, J. H. (1993). An eclectic approach to psychological interventions in sport: Reversal theory. *The Sport Psychologist, 7,* 400–418. Doi:10.1123/tsp.7.4.400

Kleine, D. (1990). Anxiety and sport performance: A meta-analysis. *Anxiety Research, 2,* 113–131. Doi:10.1080/ 08917779008249330

Kornspan, A. S. (2007). The early years of sport psychology: The work and influence of Pierre De Coubertin. *Journal of Sport Behavior, 30,* 77–93.

Kornspan, A. S., & MacCracken, M. J. (2001). Psychology applied to sports in the 1940s: The work of Dorothy Hazeltine Yates. *The Sport Psychologist, 15,* 342–345. Doi:10.1123/tsp.15.3.342

Kornspan, A. S., & MacCracken, M. J. (2003). The use of psychology in professional baseball: The pioneering work of David F. Tracy. *A Journal of Baseball History and Culture, 11,* 36–43. Doi:10.1353/nin.2003.0016

Landers, D. M., Christina, R., Hatfield, B. D., Daniels, F. S., & Doyle, L. A. (1980). Moving competitive shooting into the scientist's lab. *American Rifleman, 128,* 36–37.

Lane, A. M., Devonport, T. J., Friesen, A. P., Beedie, C. J., Fullerton, C. L., & Stanley, D. M. (2015). How should I regulate my emotions if I want to run faster? *European Journal of Sport Science, 11,* 1–8. Doi:10.1080/17461391.2015.1080305

Larner, R. J., Wagstaff, C. R. D., Thelwell, R. C., & Corbett, J. (2016). A multistudy examination of organizational stressors, emotional labor, burnout, and turnover in sport organizations. *Scandinavian Journal of Medicine and Science in Sports, 27,* 2103–2115. Doi:10.1111/sms.12833

Lazarus, R. S. (2000a). Cognitive-motivational-relational theory of emotion. In Y. L. Hanin (Ed.), *Emotions in sport* (pp. 39–64). Champaign, IL: Human Kinetics.

Lazarus, R. S. (2000b). How emotions influence performance in competitive sports. *The Sport Psychologist, 14,* 229–252. Doi:10.1123/tsp.14.3.229

Lebrun, F., & Collins, D. (2017). Is elite sport (really) bad for you? Can we answer the question? *Frontiers in Psychology, 8,* 1–6. Doi:10.3389/fpsyg.2017.00324

Lemyre, P. N., Treasure, D. C., & Roberts, G. C. (2006). Influence of variability in motivation and affect on elite athlete burnout susceptibility. *Journal of Sport and Exercise Psychology, 28,* 32–48. Doi:10.1123/jsep.28.1.32

Lundqvist, C. (2011). Well-being in competitive sports—The feel-good factor? A review of conceptual considerations of well-being. *International Review of Sport and Exercise Psychology, 4,* 109–127. Doi:10.1080/1750984X.2011.584067

MacDonald, D., & Wetherell, M. A. (2019). Competition stress leads to a blunting of the cortisol awakening response in elite rowers. *Frontiers in Psychology.* Advance online publication. Doi:10.3389/fpsyg.2019.01684

MacDougall, H., O'Halloran, P., Sherry, E., & Shields, N. (2016). Needs and strengths of Australian Para athletes: Identifying the subjective, psychological, social, and physical health and well-being. *The Sport Psychologist, 30*, 1–12. Doi:10.1123/tsp.2015-0006

Mace, R., & Carroll, D. (1986). Stress inoculation training to control anxiety in sport: Two case studies in squash. *British Journal of Sports Medicine, 20*, 115–117. Doi:10.1136/bjsm.20.3.115

MacIntyre, T., Barr, J., & Butler, C. (2015). The good, the bad and the ugly of elite sport: A reply to Martindale, A., Collins, D., & Richards, H. (2014). It's good to talk . . . Is elite sport good for you? Sport and Exercise Psychology Review, 10, 68–76. *Sport & Exercise Psychology Review, 11*, 88–90.

Madden, C. C., Kirkby, R. J., & McDonald, D. (1989). Coping styles of competitive middle distance runners. *International Journal of Sport Psychology, 20*, 287–296.

Mahoney, M. J., & Avener, M. (1977). Psychology of the elite athlete: An exploratory study. *Cognitive Therapy and Research, 1*, 135–141.

Martens, R., & Gill, D. L. (1976). State anxiety among successful competitors who differ in competitive trait anxiety. *Research Quarterly, 47*, 698–708.

Martens, R., & Landers, D. M. (1970). Motor performance under stress: A test of the inverted U hypothesis. *Journal of Personality and Social Psychology, 16*, 29–37. Doi:10.1037/h0029787

Martens, R., Vealey, R. S., & Burton, D. (1990). *Competitive anxiety in sport.* Champaign, IL: Human Kinetics.

Martindale, A., Collins, D., & Richards, H. (2014). It's good to talk . . . Is elite sport good for you? *Sport & Exercise Psychology Review, 10*, 68–76.

Martindale, A., Collins, D., & Richards, H. (2015). Is elite sport (still) good for you? A response to the reply. . . *Sport & Exercise Psychology Review, 11*, 91–94.

Martinent, G., & Ferrand, C. (2014). A field study of discrete emotions: Athletes' cognitive appraisals during competition. *Research Quarterly for Exercise and Sport, 86*, 51–62. Doi:10.1080/02701367.2014.975176

Martinent, G., & Nicolas, M. (2016). A latent profile transition analysis of coping within competitive situations. *Sport, Exercise, and Performance Psychology, 5*, 218–231. Doi:10.1037/spy0000062

McAuley, E. (1985). State anxiety: Antecedent or result of sport performance. *Journal of Sport Behavior, 8*, 71–77.

Mellalieu, S. D., Hanton, S., & Fletcher, D. (2006). A competitive anxiety review: Recent directions in sport psychology research. In S. Hanton & S. D. Mellalieu (Eds.), *Literature reviews in sport psychology* (pp. 1–45). Hauppauge, NY: Nova Science Publishers.

Moll, T., Jordet, G., & Pepping, G. J. (2010). Emotional contagion in soccer penalty shootouts: Celebration of individual success is associated with ultimate team success. *Journal of Sports Sciences, 28*, 983–992. Doi:10.1080/02640414.2010.484068

Moore, L. J., Freeman, P., Hase, A., Solomon-Moore, E., & Arnold, R. (2019). How consistent are challenge and threat evaluations? A generalizability analysis. *Frontiers in Psychology.* Advance online publication. Doi:10.3389/fpsyg.2019.01778

Morales, J., Garcia, V., García-Massó, X., Salvá, P., Escobar, R., & Buscá, B. (2013). The use of heart rate variability in assessing precompetitive stress in high-standard judo athletes. *International Journal of Sports Medicine, 34,* 144–151. Doi:10.1055/s-0032-1323719

Mountjoy, M., Brackenridge, C., Arrington, M., Blauwet, C., Carska-Sheppard, A., Fasting, K., . . . Budgett, R. (2016). The IOC consensus statement: Harassment and abuse (non-accidental violence) in sport. *British Journal of Sports Medicine, 50,* 1019–1029. Doi:10.1136/bjsports-2016-096121

Naruse, G. (1965). The hypnotic treatment of stage fright in champion athletes. *International Journal of Clinical and Experimental Hypnosis, 13,* 63–70. Doi:10.1080/00207146508412927

Nicholls, A. R. (2010). *Coping in sport: Theory, methods, and related constructs.* Hauppauge, NY: Nova Science Publishers.

Nicholls, A. R., Levy, A. R., & Perry, J. L. (2015). Emotional maturity, dispositional coping, and coping effectiveness among adolescent athletes. *Psychology of Sport and Exercise, 17,* 32–39. Doi:10.1016/j.psychsport.2014.11.004

Nicholls, A. R., Perry, J. L., Jones, L., Morley, D., & Carson, F. (2013). Dispositional coping, coping effectiveness, and cognitive social maturity among adolescent athletes. *Journal of Sport and Exercise Psychology, 35,* 229–238. Doi:10.1123/jsep.35.3.229

Nicholls, A. R., & Polman, R. C. J. (2007). Coping in sport: A systematic review. *Journal of Sports Sciences, 25,* 11–31. Doi:10.1080/02640410600630654

Nicholls, A. R., Polman, R. C. J., & Levy, A. R. (2012). A path analysis of stress appraisals, emotions, coping, and performance satisfaction among athletes. *Psychology of Sport and Exercise, 13,* 263–270. Doi:10.1016/j.psychsport.2011.12.003

Nieuwenhuys, A., Vos, L., Pijpstra, S., & Bakker, F. C. (2011). Meta experiences and coping effectiveness in sport. *Psychology of Sport and Exercise, 12,* 135–143. Doi:10.1016/j.psychsport.2010.07.008

Ntoumanis, N., & Biddle, S. J. H. (1998). The relationship of coping and its perceived effectiveness to positive and negative affect in sport. *Personality and Individual Differences, 24,* 773–788. Doi:10.1016/s0191-8869(97)00240-7

Ntoumanis, N., & Biddle, S. J. H. (2000). Relationship of intensity and direction of competitive anxiety with coping strategies. *The Sport Psychologist, 14,* 360–371. Doi:10.1123/tsp.14.4.360

Ntwanano, A., Toriola, A., & Didymus, F. (2017). Development and initial validation of an instrument to assess stressors among South African sports coaches. *Journal of Sports Sciences, 36,* 1378–1384. Doi:10.1080/02640414.2017.1385264

Olmedilla, A., Moreno-Fernández, I. M., Gómez-Espejo, V., Robles-Palazón, F. J., Verdú, I., & Ortega, E. (2019). Psychological intervention program to control stress in youth soccer players. *Frontiers in Psychology.* Advance online publication. Doi:10.3389/fpsyg.2019.02260

Parfitt, C. G., & Hardy, L. (1987). Further evidence for the differential effects of competitive anxiety upon a number of cognitive and motor sub-systems. *Journal of Sports Sciences, 5,* 62–63.

Parfitt, C. G., Jones, J. G., & Hardy, L. (1990). Multidimensional anxiety and performance. In J. G. Jones & L. Hardy (Eds.), *Stress and performance in sport* (pp. 43–80). New York: John Wiley & Sons.

Passer, M. W., & Seese, M. D. (1983). Life stress and athletic injury: Examination of positive versus negative events and three moderator variables. *Journal of Human Stress, 9,* 11–16. Doi:10.1080/0097840X.1983.9935025

Pensgaard, A. M., & Ursin, H. (1998). Stress, control, and coping in elite athletes. *Scandinavian Journal of Medicine and Science in Sports*, 8, 183–189. Doi:10.1111/j.1600-0838.1998.tb00190.x

Phelps, A., Kelly, J., Lancaster, S., Mehrzad, J., & Panter, A. (2017). *Report of the independent review panel into the climate and culture of the world class programme in British cycling*. London, UK: UK Sport.

Prapavessis, H., & Grove, J. R. (1995). Ending batting slumps in baseball: A qualitative investigation. *Australian Journal of Science and Medicine in Sport*, 27, 14–19.

Quested, E., Bosch, J. A., Burns, V. E., Cumming, J., Ntoumanis, N., & Duda, J. L. (2012). Basic psychological need satisfaction, stress-related appraisals, and dancers' cortisol and anxiety responses. *Journal of Sport and Exercise Psychology*, 33, 828–846. Doi:10.1123/jsep.33.6.828

Quinton, M. L., Veldhuijzen van Zanten, J., Trotman, G. P., Cumming, J., & Williams, S. E. (2019). Investigating the protective role of mastery imagery ability in buffering debilitative stress responses. *Frontiers in Psychology*. Advance online publication. Doi:10.3389/fpsyg.2019.01657

Raedeke, T. D., Lunney, K., & Venables, K. (2002). Understanding athlete burnout: Coach perspectives. *Journal of Sport Behavior*, 25, 181–206.

Rathschlag, M., & Memmert, D. (2009). The influence of self-generated emotions on physical performance: An investigation of happiness, anger, anxiety, and sadness. *Journal of Sport and Exercise Psychology*, 35, 197–210. Doi:10.1123/jsep.35.2.197

Rathschlag, M., & Memmert, D. (2015). Self-generated emotions and their influence on sprint performance: An investigation of happiness and anxiety. *Journal of Applied Sport Psychology*, 27, 186–199. Doi:10.1080/10413200.2014.974783

Reardon, C., Hainline, B., Miller Aron, C., Baron, D., Baum, A., Bindra, A., . . . Engebretsen, L. (2019). Mental health in elite athletes: International Olympic Committee consensus statement (2019). *British Journal of Sports Medicine*, 53, 667–699. Doi:10.1136/bjsports-2019-100715

Rees, T., Haslam, S. A., Coffee, P., & Lavallee, D. (2015). A social identity approach to sport psychology: Principles, practice, and prospects. *Sports Medicine*, 45, 1083–1096. Doi:10.1007/s40279-015-0345-4

Rhind, D. J. A., McDermott, J., Lambert, E., & Koleva, I. (2015). A review of safeguarding cases in sport. *Child Abuse Review*, 24, 418–426. Doi:10.1002/car.2306

Rice, S. M., Purcell, R., De Silva, S., Mawren, D., McGorry, P. D., & Parker, A. G. (2016). The mental health of elite athletes: A narrative systematic review. *Sports Medicine*, 46, 1333–1353. Doi:10.1007/s40279-016-0492-2

Robazza, C. (2006). Emotion in sport: An IZOF perspective. In S. Hanton & S. D. Mellalieu (Eds.), *Literature reviews in sport psychology* (pp. 127–158). Hauppauge, NY: Nova Science Publishers.

Roberts, R., & Woodman, T. (2015). Contemporary personality perspectives in sport psychology. In S. Hanton & S. D. Mellalieu (Eds.), *Contemporary advances in sport psychology: A review* (pp. 1–27). Abingdon, UK: Routledge.

Robinson, D. W. (1985). Stress seeking: Selected behavioural characteristics of elite rock climbers. *Journal of Sport and Exercise Psychology*, 7, 400–404. Doi:10.1123/jsp.7.4.400

Rumbold, J. L., Fletcher, D., & Daniels, K. (2012). A systematic review of stress management interventions with sport performers. *Sport, Exercise and Performance Psychology*, 1, 173–193.

Scanlan, T. K., & Lewthwaite, R. (1984). Social psychological aspects of competition for male youth sport participants: I. Predictors of competitive stress. *Journal of Sport and Exercise Psychology, 6,* 208–226. Doi:10.1123/jsp.6.2.208

Scanlan, T. K., & Passer, M. W. (1978). Factors related to competitive stress among male youth sport participants. *Medicine and Science in Sports, 10,* 103–108.

Scanlan, T. K., Stein, G. L., & Ravizza, K. (1991). An in-depth study of former elite figure skaters: III. Sources of stress. *Journal of Sport and Exercise Psychology, 13,* 102–120. Doi:10.1123/jsep.13.2.103

Schinke, R. J., Stambulova, N. B., Si, G., & Moore, Z. (2018). International Society of Sport Psychology position stand: Athletes' mental health, performance, and development. *International Journal of Sport and Exercise Psychology, 16,* 622–639. Doi:10.1080/1612197x.2017.1295557

Spence, J. T., & Spence, K. W. (1966). The motivational components of manifest anxiety: Drive and drive stimuli. In C. D. Spielberger (Ed.), *Anxiety and behaviour* (pp. 291–326). New York: Academic Press.

Staff, H. R., Didymus, F. F., & Backhouse, S. H. (2017). Coping rarely takes place in a social vacuum: Exploring antecedents and outcomes of dyadic coping in coach-athlete relationships. *Psychology of Sport and Exercise, 30,* 91–100. Doi:10.1016/j.psychsport.2017.02.009

Suinn, R. M. (1983). Imagery and sports. In A. A. Sheikh (Ed.), *Imagery: Current theory, research, and application.* New York: John Wiley & Sons.

Swain, A. B. J., & Jones, G. (1993). Intensity and frequency dimensions of competitive state anxiety. *Journal of Sports Sciences, 11,* 533–542. Doi:10.1080/02640419308730024

Swain, A. B. J., & Jones, G. (1996). Explaining performance variance: The relative contribution of intensity and direction dimensions of competitive state anxiety. *Anxiety, Stress, and Coping, 9,* 1–18. Doi:10.1080/10615809608249389

Tamminen, K. A., & Crocker, P. R. (2013). "I control my own emotions for the sake of the team": Emotional self-regulation and interpersonal emotion regulation among female high-performance curlers. *Psychology of Sport and Exercise, 14,* 737–747. Doi:10.1016/j.psychsport.2013.05.002

Tamminen, K. A., Gaudreau, P., McEwen, C. E., & Crocker, P. R. E. (2016). Interpersonal emotional regulation among adolescent athletes and their teammates: A Bayesian multilevel model of sport enjoyment and commitment. *Journal of Sport & Exercise Psychology, 38,* 541–555. Doi:10.1123/jsep.2015-0189

Tamminen, K. A., McEwen, C. E., & Crocker, P. R. E. (2016). Perceptions matter: Parental support, pressure, and the socialization of adolescent athletes' coping. *International Journal of Sport Psychology, 47,* 335–354. Doi:10.7352/IJSP2016.47.000

Tamminen, K. A., Palmateer, T. M., Denton, M., Sabiston, C., Crocker, P. R. E., Eys, M., & Smith, B. (2016). Exploring emotions as social phenomena among Canadian varsity athletes. *Psychology of Sport and Exercise, 27,* 28–38. Doi:10.1016/j.psychsport.2016.07.010

Thatcher, J., & Day, M. C. (2008). Re-appraising stress appraisals: The underlying properties of stress in sport. *Psychology of Sport & Exercise, 9,* 318–335. Doi:10.1016/j.psychsport.2007.04.005

Thomas, O., Mellalieu, S. D., & Hanton, S. (2009). Stress management in applied sport psychology. In S. D. Mellalieu & S. Hanton (Eds.), *Advances in applied sport psychology: A review* (pp. 124–161). New York: Routledge.

Trotman, G. P., Williams, S. E., Quinton, M. L., & Veldhuijzen van Zanten, J. J. C. S. (2018). Challenge and threat states: Examining cardiovascular, cognitive and affective responses to two distinct laboratory stress tasks. *International Journal of Psychophysiology, 126*, 42–51. Doi:10.1016/J.IJPSYCHO.2018.02.004

Udry, E. (1997). Coping and social support among injured athletes following surgery. *Journal of Sport and Exercise Psychology, 19*, 71–90. Doi:10.1123/jsep.19.1.71

Uphill, M. A., & Jones, M. V. (2007). The antecedents of emotions in elite athletes. *Research Quarterly for Sport and Exercise, 78*, 79–89. Doi:10.1080/02701367.2007.10599406

Uphill, M. A., Rossato, C. J. L., Swain, J., & O' Driscoll, J. (2019). Challenge and threat: A critical review of the literature and an alternative conceptualization. *Frontiers in Psychology*. Advance online publication. Doi:10.3389/fpsyg.2019.01255

Uphill, M., Sly, D., & Swain, J. (2016). From mental health to mental wealth in athletes: Looking back and moving forward. *Frontiers in Psychology, 7*, 93–98. Doi:10.3389/fpsyg.2016.00935

van Kleef, G. A., Cheshin, A., Koning, L. F., & Wolf, S. A. (2019). Emotional games: How coaches' emotional expressions shape players' emotions, inferences, and team performance. *Psychology of Sport and Exercise, 41*, 1–11. Doi:10.1016/j.psychsport.2018.11.004

Vast, R. L., Young, R. L., & Thomas, P. R. (2010). Emotions in sport: Perceived effects on attention, concentration, and performance. *American Psychologist, 45*, 132–140. Doi:10.1080/00050060903261538

Vine, S. J., Freeman, P., Moore, L. J., Chandra-Ramanan, R., & Wilson, M. R. (2013). Evaluating stress as a challenge is associated with superior attentional control and motor skill performance: Testing the predictions of the Biopsychosocial Model of Challenge and Threat. *Journal of Experimental Psychology, 19*, 185–194. Doi:10.1037/a0034106

Vine, S. J., Moore, L. J., & Wilson, M. R. (2016). An integrative framework of stress, attention, and visuomotor performance. *Frontiers in Psychology, 7*(1671), 1–10. Doi:10.3389/fpsyg.2016.01671.

Wagstaff, C. R. D. (2014). Emotion regulation and sport performance. *Journal of Sport and Exercise Psychology, 36*(4), 401–412. Doi:10.1123/jsep.2013-0257

Wagstaff, C. R. D., Fletcher, D., & Hanton, S. (2012). Exploring emotion abilities and regulation strategies in sport organizations. *Sport, Exercise, and Performance Psychology, 1*, 268–282. Doi:10.1037/a0028814

Wagstaff, C. R. D., Hanton, S., & Fletcher, D. (2013). Developing emotion abilities and regulation strategies in a sport organization: An action research intervention. *Psychology of Sport and Exercise, 14*, 476–487. Doi:10.1016/j.psychsport.2013.01.006

Weed, M., Coren, E., Fiore, J., Wellard, I., Chatziefstathiou, D., Mansfield, L., & Douse, S. (2015). The Olympic Games and raising sport participation: A systematic review of evidence and an interrogation of policy for a demonstration effect. *European Sport Management Quarterly, 15*, 195–226. Doi:10.1080/16184742.2014.998695

Wicker, P., Prinz, J., & von Hanau, T. (2012). Estimating the value of national sporting success. *Sport Management Review, 15*, 200–210. Doi:10.1016/j.smr.2011.08.007

Williams, S. E., Veldhuijzen van Zanten, J., Trotman, G. P., Quinton, M. J., & Ginty, A. T. (2017). Challenge and threat imagery manipulates heart rate and anxiety responses to stress. *International Journal of Psychophysiology, 117,* 111–118. Doi:10.1016/j.ijpsycho.2017.04.011

Wilson, M. R., Wood, G., & Vine, S. J. (2009). Anxiety, attentional control, and performance impairment in penalty kicks. *Journal of Sport and Exercise Psychology, 31,* 761–775. Doi:10.1123/jsep.31.6.761

Woodman, T., & Hardy, L. (2001). Stress and anxiety. In R. Singer, H. A. Hausenblas, & C. M. Janelle (Eds.), *Handbook of research on sport psychology* (pp. 290–318). New York: John Wiley & Sons.

Section I

Appraising and Coping With Stress in Sport

1 Stressors, Hassles, and Adversity

Rachel Arnold and David Fletcher

The sporting environment imposes numerous demands on sport performers and other individuals who function within it. Indeed, as first acknowledged by Hardy, Jones, and Gould (1996) performers do not operate in a vacuum in sport but instead in a highly complex social and organizational environment which can exert a major influence on them and their performances. Although it may be appealing to some scholars and practitioners to delve into examining and managing how a performer appraises and copes with stressors encountered in sport or the consequences of these responses, it is fundamental that they first understand comprehensively the demands that precede and are triggering such responses and outcomes. This plea is in accordance with early definitions of stress (i.e., stimulus based; see, for a review, Fletcher, Hanton, & Mellalieu, 2006), whereby the environmental conditions faced by individuals are emphasized. In addition, in more recent interaction- and transaction-based definitions and conceptualizations of stress, the environment in which an individual operates is a fundamental and primary feature (Fletcher et al., 2006; see also the Introduction chapter).

The majority of stressor-related research in the sports domain has tended to focus on the type of stressor that is encountered by performers, rather than the dimensions and properties of these. Notwithstanding the importance of stressor type, it should be recognized that this is only one way of conceptualizing stressors. Indeed, as an example of further conceptualization, although some demands may be encountered by sport performers more regularly (e.g., daily hassles), others may present as a more major, one-off adversity. The purpose of this current chapter, therefore, is to review the research to date on stressors, hassles, and adversity in sport. This chapter will begin with definitions of the key terms used in research on this topic, before outlining research conducted on the various ways in which stressors, hassles, and adversity can be conceptualized (e.g., type, dimensions, properties, and other characteristics). The chapter will then progress to summarizing future research directions for the area, before suggesting practical implications.

Definitions

Stressors have been defined as "the environmental demands (i.e., stimuli) encountered by an individual" (Fletcher et al., 2006, p. 359) and encompass various events, situations, and circumstances experienced throughout the lifespan. In competitive sport, stressors and other factors that "increase the importance of performing well on a particular occasion" (Baumeister, 1984, p. 610) are collectively referred to as pressure. Such pressure has the potential to impinge on performers' working memory and information processing capacity and can contribute or add to cognitive load (cf. Miller, 1956; Sweller, 1988; Wine, 1971; see also Chapter 5).

Depending on how often stressors are encountered and how demanding they are, stressors can be conceived as daily hassles or major life events (Harkness & Hayden, 2020a). Daily hassles are experienced frequently but are not that demanding in isolation (Kanner, Coyne, Schaefer, & Lazarus, 1981; Wright, Aslinger, Bellamy, Edershile, & Woods, 2020) and have been defined as the "irritating, frustrating, distressing demands and troubled relationships that plague us day in and day out" (Lazarus & Delongis, 1983, p. 247). Major life events, in contrast, are experienced infrequently but are highly demanding (Dohrenwend & Dohrenwend, 1974; Holmes & Rahe, 1967) and have been defined as "the 'obstacles, dangers, challenges, and threats' that are imposed by the dynamic physical and social environments people must overcome throughout their lives" (Monroe & Slavich, 2020, p. 7).

Regardless of whether a stressor or combination of stressors is conceived as a daily hassle(s) or major life event(s), if they are typically associated with maladaptive responses and adjustment difficulties, they can be referred to as adversity (Fletcher & Sarkar, 2013; Luthar & Cicchetti, 2000; see also Chapter 9). Adversity represents ostensibly negative life circumstances (Luthar & Cicchetti, 2000; McLaughlin, 2020). As such, adversity should not be conflated with intraindividual processes, such as cognitive evaluations and affective responses; rather, an individual's appraisal of and subjective meaning associated with adversity will determine the nature of his or her response to adversity (cf. Harkness & Hayden, 2020b; Lazarus & Folkman, 1984). If an individual responds maladaptively, has difficulty adjusting, and is in a distressed state, this is referred to as trauma (cf. Bovin & Marx, 2011; Brewin, Lanius, Novac, Schnyder, & Galea, 2009; Krupnik, 2019, 2020). As Tedeschi, Shakespeare-Finch, Taku, and Calhoun (2018) put it, "whether or not an [adverse] event is [perceived] traumatic[ally], is in the eye of the beholder" (p. 4). Hence, consistent with Fletcher (2019; see also Howells, Sarkar, & Fletcher, 2017), the terms "adversity" and "trauma" should not be used interchangeably or to both include the event and individuals' cognitive and affective responses, but rather to distinguish between an event (likely to be associated with negative responses) and actual negative responses (to an event).

Conceptualization

Type

Over the past few decades, a wide range of stressors have been identified that performers in sport encounter. Collectively, the stressors identified in this work have been associated with competitive performances, the sport organization within which a performer operates, and personal "non-sporting" life events (Fletcher et al., 2006). Although the primary focus has been identifying the stressors encountered by athletes, some studies have focused on the stress experiences of other "performers" in the sporting environment (e.g., coach, support staff, parents, officials). The remainder of this section will provide a summary of this work conducted with athletes and other performers in sport; however, given that comprehensive stressor reviews exist (see Arnold & Fletcher, 2012b; Fletcher & Arnold, 2017; Hanton, Neil, & Mellalieu, 2008; Sarkar & Fletcher, 2014), there will be a particular focus on significant research developments on each stressor type, studies that have been conducted since these reviews were published, and how each stressor type might be measured.

Competitive Stressors

These stressors are defined as the "environmental demands associated primarily and directly with competitive performance" (Mellalieu, Hanton, & Fletcher, 2006, p. 3). Research on competitive stressors has typically either (i) identified pre-performance stressors that athletes encounter or (ii) examined antecedents of the competitive anxiety response (Mellalieu et al., 2006). Although readers are directed to Mellalieu et al. (2006; see also Hanton et al., 2008) for a more comprehensive discussion of the latter line of enquiry, the former will be discussed herein. Specifically, early exploratory research involved scholars studying sport performers' general sources of stress and, in the process, identifying various competitive stressors (see, e.g., Anshel & Wells, 2000; Gould, Jackson, & Finch, 1993; Holt & Hogg, 2002; James & Collins, 1997; Noblet & Gifford, 2002; Scanlan & Passer, 1979; Scanlan, Ravizza, & Stein, 1989; Scanlan, Stein, & Ravizza, 1991). Examples of competitive stressors include, but are not limited to, inadequate preparation, injury, underperforming, self-presentation, superstitions, and opponent rivalry.

Recognizing that early work did not typically differentiate between the origins of stressors, Hanton and colleagues (2005) distinguished between and directly compared competitive stressors with those of an organizational nature. They found that although competitive stressors were experienced and recalled less than organizational stressors, the mean number of participants recalling competitive stressors was higher than those recalling organizational demands, therefore, reflecting the inherent and endemic nature of competitive stressors in sport. In comparison, some studies have found that performers encounter similar numbers of competitive and organizational demands (McKay, Niven, Lavallee, & White, 2008). In contrast to this, Mellalieu, Neil, Hanton, and Fletcher (2009) found that competitive demands were encountered more than those emanating from the organization; however, this was in reference to pre-competitive experiences. Additionally, it was found that the total number of stressors reported was similar for elite and non-elite athletes, with certain stressors being more specific to, or prevalent for, each of the two groups (Mellalieu et al., 2009).

Two further studies of note in this area, which have been published since the aforementioned reviews, examined competitive stressors and framed them as part of the larger transactional stress process (Curran & Hill, 2018; Neil, Hanton, Mellalieu, & Fletcher, 2011). First, Neil and colleagues (2011) examined performance and organizational stressors encountered in a competition environment and athletes' subsequent appraisals, emotions, further appraisals, and behaviors. Athletes' experiences of both single and multiple competitive stressors were presented, as well as their responses to concomitant competitive and organizational demands, with the authors concluding that athletes have differing appraisals in relation to the specific demands encountered and consequently experience certain emotions (Neil et al., 2011). Second, Curran and Hill (2018) conducted a novel examination of recurrent exposure to a specific competitive stressor: underperformance. Specifically, the study examined athletes' perfectionism and self-conscious emotions following repeated competitive failure, finding that those higher in perfectionism experience pronounced distress following repeated competitive failure.

Turning to measurement and the methodologies used to examine competitive stressors, the availability of self-report measures has reflected the focus of the literature in this area; that is, the majority of measures typically assess pre-competitive anxiety (i.e., an emotional response) rather than stressors (see, e.g., Cox, Martens, & Russell, 2003; see also Chapter 4). Self-report measures that do exist have typically assessed a single competitive stressor (e.g., self-presentation; Williams, Hudson, & Lawson, 1999) rather than the diversity of aforementioned demands. Thus, in the absence of a reliable and valid measurement tool to assess competitive stressors holistically, adopted methodologies for examining this type of stressor have typically involved either interviews with sport performers (see, e.g., Mellalieu et al., 2009), think aloud protocols (Nicholls & Polman, 2008), or the adoption of a stressor checklist (see, e.g., Nicholls, Holt, Polman, & Bloomfield, 2006). More recently, the literature has proposed psychophysiological measures of "pre-competition stress" such as cortisol and heart rate variability (see, e.g., Morales et al., 2013). It is important for scholars, however, to demonstrate critical methodological and theoretical awareness regarding the exact component of the stress process being assessed by these psychophysiological measurements (i.e., stressors or physical responses to them) and the shortcomings that need to be considered when employing such measurements in the sports domain (Gerber et al., 2012).

Organizational Stressors

These stressors are defined as the "environmental demands associated primarily and directly with the organization within which an individual is operating" (Fletcher et al., 2006, p. 359). Similar to competitive stressors, a number of organizational stressors were also identified in early studies exploring the sources of stress encountered in sport. Specifically, in a synthesis of the research on this type of stressor, Arnold and Fletcher (2012b) analyzed 34 studies (with a combined sample of 1,809 participants) to yield 640 distinct organizational stressors. These were then abstracted into 31 subcategories which formed four categories: leadership and personnel issues (e.g., the coach's behaviors and personality, sports officials, and the media), cultural and team issues (e.g., teammates behaviors and personality, goals, and cultural norms), logistical and environmental issues (e.g., facilities, selection, and the structure of training), and performance and personal issues (e.g., finances, career transitions, and diet). Several studies have provided support for this classification (see, for a review, Fletcher & Arnold, 2017). Since this seminal synthesis, there have typically been three main lines of inquiry regarding organizational stressors in sport. These are (i) examining the organizational stressors encountered by, and comparing between, specific groups of performers; (ii) investigating relationships between organizational stressors and other components of the transactional stress process; and (iii) developing the measurement of organizational stressors. Although it is beyond the scope of this chapter to provide a comprehensive review, a summary of each line of inquiry is offered.

It is evident in the organizational stressor literature since 2012 that there has been a shift in the scholarly focus from purely identifying organizational stressors encountered by a group of performers from a different sport and/or country to that studied previously (for an exception, see Sohal, Gervis, & Rhind, 2013). Instead, a new line of inquiry has focused on examining particular groups of performers and the differences between their stressor encounters. With regard to different groups, studies have been conducted on the organizational stressors encountered by disabled athletes (Arnold, Wagstaff, Steadman, & Pratt, 2017; Whittingham, Barker, Slater, & Arnold, 2020) and wounded, injured, and sick military veterans in the lead up to, during, and after international competition (Roberts, Arnold, Bilzon, Turner, & Colclough, 2019; Roberts, Arnold, Gillison, Colclough, & Bilzon, 2020). Additionally, studies have explored the types of stressors encountered by injured athletes' (Evans, Wadey, Hanton, & Mitchell, 2012) and captains' of sports teams (Smith, Arnold, & Thelwell, 2018). Furthermore, there is an emerging body of literature which examines the stressors (organizational and other types) encountered by performers other than the athletes themselves operating in sports environments, including coaches (see, e.g., Didymus, 2016; Fletcher & Scott, 2010; Ntwanano, Toriola, & Didymus, 2017), support staff (see, e.g., Arnold, Collington, et al., 2019; Fletcher, Rumbold, Tester, & Coombes, 2011), parents (see, e.g., Harwood & Knight, 2009), and officials (see, e.g., Voight, 2009).

Fletcher, Hanton, Mellalieu, and Neil (2012) provided the first comparison between different groups of performers' encounters of overall organizational stressors. The study found that organizational stressors were encountered proportionately more by elite performers than their non-elite counterparts, with some demands being common across groups (e.g., training and competition environment, exposure to injury, and officials' decisions) and some unique to each group (e.g., travel, accommodation, funding, and media mentioned more by elite performers). Extending this research, Arnold, Fletcher, and Daniels (2016) examined if the organizational stressors that sport performers encountered varied as a function of gender, sport type, and performance level. For gender, it was found that males encountered higher dimensions of logistics and operations stressors than females, and females encountered higher dimensions of selection stressors than males. Furthermore, performers in team-based sports encountered higher dimensions of logistics and operations, team and culture, and selection stressors than those competing in individual-based sports. Turning to performance level, those competing at higher performance levels (e.g., national/international) typically experienced organizational stressors more frequently, at a higher intensity, and for a longer duration than those competing at lower levels (e.g., regional/university or county/club).

A second line of inquiry has involved investigating relationships between organizational stressors and further components of the transactional stress process. Specifically, studies have been conducted which examine the relationship of organizational stressors with, either singularly or a combination of, appraisals (Bartholomew, Arnold, Hampson, & Fletcher, 2017; Didymus & Fletcher, 2012, 2014, 2017; Hanton, Wagstaff, & Fletcher, 2012; Neil et al., 2011; see also Chapter 2), emotions (Arnold, Fletcher, & Daniels, 2013; Fletcher, Hanton, & Wagstaff, 2012; Larner, Wagstaff, Thelwell, & Corbett, 2016; Neil et al., 2011; see also Chapter 4), motivation (Bartholomew et al., 2017; Kristiansen,

Halvari, & Roberts, 2012), coping (Arnold, Fletcher, & Daniels, 2017; Didymus & Fletcher, 2014, 2017; Kristiansen et al., 2012; see also Chapter 3), social support (Arnold, Edwards, & Rees, 2019; see also Chapter 11), and outcomes including burnout (Larner et al., 2016; Tabei, Fletcher, & Goodger, 2012; Wagstaff, Hings, Larner, & Fletcher, 2018; see also Chapter 7), growth/mastery (Sohal et al., 2013), turnover (Larner et al., 2016), performance (Arnold, Fletcher, et al., 2017; Arnold, Edwards, et al., 2019; Didymus & Fletcher, 2017; Roberts et al., 2019, 2020; Simms, Arnold, Turner, & Hays, 2020), well-being (Arnold, Fletcher, et al., 2017; Roberts et al., 2019, 2020; see also Chapter 6), verbal/physical behaviors (Fletcher, Hanton, & Wagstaff, 2012), and physical and mental health (Roberts et al., 2019, 2020; Simms, Arnold, Turner, et al., 2020; see also Chapter 8). In addition to conceptualization as a primary variable, organizational stressors have also been examined as variables influencing other relationships in sport (cf. Gump & Matthews, 1999). An example of this is evident in a study conducted by Tamminen, Sabiston, and Crocker (2019) which found that coaching-related and team and culture-related organizational stressors moderated the relationship between esteem support and secondary appraisal.

The final line of inquiry on the topic of organizational stressors has involved developments in measurement. Arnold and Fletcher (2012a) recognized that no measure existed to comprehensively assess, in a reliable and valid way, the organizational stressors that sport performers encountered. The authors, therefore, reviewed four main areas of existing psychometric issues in organizational stressor research (viz. conceptual and theoretical, item development, measurement and scoring, and analytical and statistical), with implications for sport psychologists wishing to measure the phenomenon in a sports context discussed (Arnold & Fletcher, 2012a). Informed by these issues and implications as well as extensive qualitative work in the area, the first comprehensive measure of organizational stressors was developed— labeled the Organizational Stressor Indicator for Sport Performers (OSI-SP; Arnold et al., 2013). Specifically, the OSI-SP is a 23-item indicator which assesses the frequency, intensity, and duration of organizational stressors encountered by sport performers, consisting of five subscales: goals and development, logistics and operations, team and culture, coaching, and selection. Analyses indicated that the OSI-SP displays adequate internal consistency and content, factorial, discriminant, concurrent, and cross-cultural validity (Arnold et al., 2013; Arnold, Ponnusamy, Zhang, & Gucciardi, 2017). Furthermore, invariance testing of the OSI-SP components makes it possible for researchers to assess the organizational stressors across different groups and make meaningful comparisons between them (Arnold et al., 2013; Fletcher & Arnold, 2017).

Personal Stressors

This final type of stressor is defined as the environmental demands associated primarily and directly with personal "non-sporting" life events (Fletcher et al., 2006). Early work identifying general sources of stress that sport performers encounter highlighted various personal stressors, including family issues, the death of a significant other, relocation, and the work-life interface (see, e.g., Giacobbi et al., 2004; Gould et al., 1993; McKay et al., 2008; Noblet & Gifford, 2002; Scanlan et al., 1991; Thelwell, Weston, & Greenlees, 2007). There is a growing body of literature which examines the stressors experienced by student-athletes who are required to balance their sporting involvement with their academic studies (see, e.g., Cosh & Tully, 2015; Kristiansen, 2017). Indeed, Kristiansen (2017) suggests that pursuing a dual career can present a challenging balancing act for student-athletes and to do so effectively they often require the support of coaches, clubs, lifestyle managers, family, and educational institutions.

Turning to the relationship between life stress and outcomes, research exists which examines the relationship between life stress and injury in sport (Ivarsson et al., 2017; Williams & Andersen, 1998). Notwithstanding the importance of this work, there is a limited understanding of how life stress might impact other outcomes such as performance and well-being in sport. An early insight into the life stress and performance relationship was demonstrated by Felsten and Wilcox (1993), who found that higher levels of daily life stress were related to poorer figure skating performances. Furthermore, Aquilina (2010) sampled athletes across three countries (France, Finland, and the United Kingdom) and found that, despite reporting various demands placed upon them (e.g., balance of dual career), pursuing educational experiences could facilitate sporting development and performances with both careers being mutually complementary. In terms of examining personal stressors, scholars have typically adopted measures of daily hassles, conducted interviews, or taken life histories. To further the measurement of this stressor type, Lu and colleagues (2012) developed and initially validated a measure of student-athletes' life stress. The measure is labeled the College Student-Athletes' Life Stress Scale (CSALSS), and it has demonstrated evidence of adequate factorial structure, criterion validity, and reliability.

Dimensions

When measuring stress, scholars have often implied demand by asking about the presence of a stressor in a surrounding environment (Dewe, 1991). Although this can be helpful in identifying which stressors an individual is encountering, it wrongly assumes that the presence of a stressor equates with it being demanding (Arnold & Fletcher, 2012a).

To overcome this, it is important that multiple dimensions are considered when investigating the stressors encountered by an individual. Indeed, Arnold, Fletcher, and Carr (2010) identified eight critical dimensions of organizational stressors (viz. duration, intensity, timing, prevalence, quantity, specificity, closeness, and weighting) which were proposed to help provide more insightful depictions of stressors. Although it is beyond the scope to discuss each of these in turn, the dimensions that have been given most attention in the sport psychology literature and measurement tools are discussed subsequently.

Frequency

The frequency of a stressor refers to its occurrence and specifically how often the performer has encountered or is encountering it per a specific unit of time (Arnold et al., 2013). To measure this dimension in the sports context, an indicator has been developed, which asks participants "How often did this stressor place a demand on you?" to which respondents indicate their answer on a Likert scale ranging from 0 (Never) to 5 (Always) (Arnold et al., 2013). When validating this indicator, Arnold et al. (2013) suggested that the frequency scale alone may sometimes be adequate for practitioners requiring a shorter version of the indicator. Following this recommendation, some scholars have just adopted the frequency subscale of the OSI-SP in their investigations (see, e.g., Arnold, Edwards, et al., 2019; Larner et al., 2016; Wagstaff et al., 2018). Within these studies, an examination of direct relationships has revealed significant positive relationships between the frequency of organizational stressors and burnout, surface acting (Larner et al., 2016; Wagstaff et al., 2018), and subjective performance (coaching stressors in particular; Arnold, Edwards, et al., 2019).

Outside of sport psychology, psychometricians have developed measures which focus on assessing the frequency of stressors. For example, the Perceived Stress Scale (PSS; Cohen, Karmarck, & Mermelstein, 1983) includes the stem "In the last month, how often have you [X]". This measure has been used in various sport psychology studies (see, e.g., Gustafsson, Sagar, & Stenling, 2016; Raedeke & Smith, 2004); however, it is important to acknowledge that the scale assesses the frequency of various components of the stress process (e.g., stressors, coping, control, emotions, and feelings) rather than stressor frequency in isolation. Although the frequency of a stressor is a significant dimension to consider given that it can relate to sport performers' health, well-being, and performance (Arnold, Edwards, et al., 2019; Larner et al., 2016; Simms, Arnold, Hays, et al., 2020), it is advised that, where possible, it is considered alongside other dimensions such as intensity and duration to provide a more complete representation of encountered stressors. This is important because it could be the case that although a particular stressor is encountered frequently it is not deemed to be very intense or long-lasting (e.g., more of a daily hassle); similarly a stressor occurring infrequently could be very intense or long-lasting (e.g., a more major life event).

Intensity

The intensity of a stressor refers to its level or, specifically, the felt strength of a stressor (Arnold & Fletcher, 2012a). To assess this dimension, there is an indicator which has been developed in the sports context which asks participants "How demanding was this pressure?" to which respondents indicate their answer on a Likert scale ranging from 0 (No demand) to 5 (Very high) (Arnold et al., 2013). Examples of intense life events might be the death of a family member or parental divorce. A core point of discussion in the literature, around which there is varied opinion and little resolution, relates to the intensity of events and, specifically, when a life event or an environmental exposure is considered to not be sufficiently impactful or severe enough to be qualified as a life event (Monroe & Slavich, 2020). While major life events are discussed here within the intensity section, some taxonomies classify major life events on the basis of their frequency or duration of event exposure (Pillow, Zautra, & Sandler, 1996). Major life events have been extensively studied outside of the sports domain, where they have been related to changes in physical activity (Engberg et al., 2012), subjective well-being (Luhmann, Hofmann, Eid, & Lucas, 2012), and mental and physical health (Tennant, 2001; Tosevski & Milovancevic, 2006).

Sport psychology researchers have found that major (non-sport) life events appear to be a consistent feature in the early lives of the world's best athletes (Fletcher, 2019; Sarkar & Fletcher, 2017; see also Chapter 9). Such events include the death or serious illness of a significant family member, parental divorce or serious relationship problems, unstable or unsettled home environment (e.g., witnessing, or undergoing personal experience of, physical or verbal abuse), frequently moving home (with a subsequent loss of friendship groups), the perception of being sent away from parents (e.g., boarding school), difficulty at school (e.g., low achievement, bullying, and loneliness), serious injury or illness, diagnosis of developmental-related disorders (e.g., attention-deficit/hyperactivity disorder [ADHD], speech impediment, and dyslexia), and symptoms of compromised mental health (e.g., obsessive-compulsive disorder, depression, suicidal thoughts, self-harm, substance abuse, and eating disorder) (Hardy et al., 2017; Howells & Fletcher, 2015; Sarkar, Fletcher, & Brown, 2015). Lower elite-level athletes who, while performing in international competition, do not attain or sustain the highest possible success at this level, appear to experience fewer major (non-sport) life events in their early lives (Collins, MacNamara, & McCarthy,

2016; Hardy et al., 2017; Savage, Collins, & Cruickshank, 2016). Turning back to the world's best athletes, as their careers commence and progress, major life events may be sport or non-sport in nature, with further sport specific examples including an athlete being told that he or she will never be a world-class performer, not being selected for an Olympic team, and perceived underperformance in Olympic competition (Hardy et al., 2017; Howells & Fletcher, 2015; Sarkar et al., 2015). These later life events, which are sometimes referred to turning points or critical moments, while appearing to be experienced by the majority of the world's best athletes, do not appear to be universally experienced in the same way that early life events are (Hardy et al., 2017; see also Fletcher, 2019; Sarkar & Fletcher, 2017; see also Chapter 9).

In contrast to major life events, daily hassles have typically been characterized as being of a relatively low intensity in isolation (cf. Hahn & Smith, 1999). A comparison of daily hassles and major life events can be made in their ability to predict outcomes; several studies have found that daily hassles provide a more powerful and substantially better assessment of stress than life events in predicting health and well-being (Chamberlain & Zika, 1990; Serido, Almeida, & Wethington, 2004). In addition to identifying the daily hassles encountered by sport performers (see section on type of stressors), scholars have also examined daily hassles alongside more major life changes as antecedents of sports injuries (Johnson, 2007).

Duration

Scholars examining the duration of stressors typically distinguish between those of an acute (i.e., generally of a short-term duration) and chronic (i.e., typically longer lasting) nature (Lepore, 1995; Pratt & Barling, 1988). To assess the duration of stressors in sport, an indicator has been developed which asks participants "How long did this pressure place a demand on you for" to which participants respond on a scale from 0 (No time) to 5 (A very long time) (Arnold et al., 2013). A source of ambiguity in the literature examining the duration of stress relates to where acute stress ends and chronic stress begins, or to put it more simply: when does a short-term stressor become longer-lasting? In an attempt to offer clarity on this debate, Smyth, Zawadzki, and Gerin (2013) suggested that rather than viewing the duration of stressors as a dichotomy, it would be better thought of as a continuum ranging from a single, brief acute stress episode to chronic stress comprising repeated activations, low or slow adaptation, and delayed or a failure to return to homeostasis.

Within the sports context, Anshel and colleagues have extensively studied acute stressors and their relationship with appraisal, coping, emotion, affect, and performance (Anshel & Andersen, 2002; Anshel & Delaney, 2001; Anshel, Williams, & Williams, 2000). Frequently cited acute stressors identified in the studies include receiving a bad call from the umpire or making a physical game error. Furthermore, Anshel and Delaney (2001) suggested that athletes typically make negative appraisals of the acute stressors followed by avoidance coping strategies; however, they also suggested that approach coping was evident if a positive appraisal was made. Turning to stressors of a more chronic nature, Schinke et al. (2012) have suggested that examples of these for National Hockey League (NHL) players relate to retaining a roster spot, and managing one's NHL lifestyle and media demands. Furthermore, Tenenbaum and colleagues (2003) identified that elite cyclists encountered chronic stressors such as an extended injury rehabilitation period and homesickness for immigrated athletes from out of the country. Moreover, those cyclists who appraised the chronic stressors as manageable displayed a constructive psychological response, using flexibility and constructive social support coping strategies, to subsequently spur successful adaptation (Tenenbaum et al., 2003; see also Schinke et al., 2012).

Severity

Monroe and Simons (1991) suggested that the severity of a stressor refers to the degree to which an individual perceives that a stressor(s) has the potential to negatively impact on his or her own life. Alternatively, Vagg and Spielberger (1999) suggested that the severity of the stressor refers to the amount of adjustment it requires for an individual to deal with it. Within the sport psychology literature, stressor severity has typically been examined by the sum of stressor frequency, intensity, and duration together (cf. Arnold, Fletcher, et al., 2017). More recently, McLoughlin and colleagues (2021) used the Adult STRAIN (Slavich & Shields, 2018) to assess the total count and severity of lifetime stressor exposure to find that it significantly predicted greater depression and anxiety symptoms and worse well-being. Regardless of the way in which stressor severity is defined and operationalized, it is an essential dimension to measure considering its contribution to the risk of developing a major illness (cf. Boscarino, 2004; Vagg & Spielberger, 1999). Notwithstanding this contribution, scholars have warned that popularly adopted subjective ratings of stressor severity can be influenced by systematic biases such as a respondent's neuroticism which must be taken into account in study designs (cf. Espejo et al., 2011). Similarly, Sarkar and Fletcher (2013) have noted that subjective ratings of stressor severity can confound the dimension with an individual's response, thus leading to spurious conclusions.

A concept related to stressor severity (and other stressor dimensions) is allostatic load. Specifically, allostatic load refers to "the failure or exhaustion of normal physiological processes that occurs in response to severe, frequent, or chronic stressors" (Katz, Sprang, & Cooke, 2012, p. 469; see also McEwen, 2006). There is an abundance of literature operational-izing allostatic load and examining both the antecedents and outcomes of the physiological dysregulation (see, for a review, Beckie, 2012; Juster, McEwen, & Lupien, 2010). Within the sports context, the allostatic stress paradigm has been used to aid understanding of effectively evaluating measures of training load and recovery. To indicate the extent of allo-static disruption in athletic recovery, physiological markers (e.g., heart rate variability) are often adopted (Kellman et al., 2018). Scholars have contended, however, that subjective markers (e.g., session rating of per-ceived exertion [RPE]) can reflect both the allostatic load and an ath-lete's appraisal of demands (Coyne, Haff, Coutts, Newton, & Nimphius, 2018); therefore, they suggest that training load measures are chosen on a case-by-case basis depending on the particular sport and training envi-ronment. Similarly, on the topic of injury prediction, Galambos, Terry, Moyle, and Locke (2005) have suggested that in addition to utilizing psychological measures for predicting injury, physiological indicators of allostatic load (e.g., stress hormones) should also be used.

Properties

For an event or situation to be appraised as stressful, both personal and situational factors are required to be present (Lazarus & Folkman, 1984). Indeed, when assessing an event encountered, a performer will consider how relevant it is to their personal welfare and by its situational characteristics (Lazarus, 2000). Examples of personal factors include goals at stake, personal resources, and individual beliefs (Lazarus, 1999). Turning to situational factors, Lazarus and Folkman (1984) suggest that underpinning all situations perceived as stressful are certain underlying properties. Specifically, they identified eight properties and highlighted that if just one of the identified properties is present, a situation that has personal significance and meaning will be appraised as stressful. The eight properties forwarded by Lazarus and Folkman (1984) are as follows: novelty (i.e., situations that a person has not previously expe-rienced or read/heard about), predictability (i.e., a situation becomes unpredictable when established expectancies are no longer met), event uncertainty (i.e., the subjective or objective probability of an event occur-ring), imminence (i.e., the amount of time and period of anticipation before an event), duration (i.e., the length of an event), temporal uncer-tainty (i.e., uncertainty around the precise timings of a definitely occur-ring event), ambiguity (i.e., a lack of situational clarity due to unclear or insufficient information needed for appraisal), and timing in relation to life cycle (i.e., appraising events in relation to other stressful events in a person's life cycle occurring at the same time).

Initial research examining the situational properties in the sports domain has tended to focus on the properties in isolation (see, e.g.,

Dugdale, Eklund, & Gordon, 2002; Marchant, Andersen, & Morris, 1997). Thatcher and Day (2008) provided the first examination of all eight properties in competitive sport and, with a sample of national standard trampolinists, found that participants experienced all of the underlying properties. Furthermore, given the unlikely occurrence of true novelty in sport, the authors suggested the need to modify the novelty definition to "a situation with a change or difference that has not been previously experienced" (Thatcher & Day, 2008, p. 333). In addition to verifying the original eight properties, Thatcher and Day (2008) identified two possible new properties specific to the sporting environment. These were self and other comparison (i.e., comparing performance with that of another individual) and inadequate preparation (i.e., where participants felt they were not prepared for competition). Notwithstanding the important contribution that this study offers by providing the first application of Lazarus and Folkman's (1984) situational properties to the sporting environment, future research needs to link these antecedents to further components of the stress process (e.g., appraisal, emotion). One example of this is the work conducted by Didymus and Fletcher (2012), which examined the transactional alternatives (e.g., harm/loss, threat, challenge) that athletes' experience in relation to each situational property. In contrast to Thatcher and Day (2008), the authors only found support for seven out of the eight properties, with temporal uncertainty identified as not being influential in swimmers' appraisals of organizational stressors. Furthermore, although Thatcher and Day (2008) discussed the unlikely occurrence of true novelty in sport, novelty was found to be the most frequently cited property in Didymus and Fletcher's (2012) study. In terms of the links between the properties and transactional alternatives, the findings illustrated that imminence was associated with the greatest number of threat appraisals, novelty was associated with the greatest number of challenge appraisals, and duration was associated with the greatest number of harm/loss appraisals (Didymus & Fletcher, 2012; see also Chapter 2). In 2017, Didymus and Fletcher provided further support for the notion that situational properties are influential in determining transactional alternatives; however, also identified that both temporal uncertainty and imminence did not appear in field hockey players' appraisals of organizational stressors.

Other Characteristics

Internal/External

A further characteristic of stressors relates to how much influence the sport performer has over the stressor. To elaborate, the literature (cf. Mellalieu et al., 2009; Alsentali & Anshel, 2015) has distinguished between stressors that the performer causes or places on him or herself (internal) and stressors that the performer has no influence over [their occurrence] and that have been caused by factors other than the athlete (external). Examples of internal stressors are low self-esteem, a fear of failure, and high personal expectations, while examples of external stressors are bereavement, injuries, unexpected weather conditions, and a bad referee call (Alsentali & Anshel, 2015; Newman, Howells, & Fletcher, 2016; Suinn, 2005). When considering the internal/external conceptualization of stressors, it is worth noting that some researchers have reported that athletes' internal responses to external stressors have subsequently become internal stressors in their own right (Evans et al., 2012; Howells & Fletcher, 2015).

The internal/external nomenclature has also been used to categorize specific stressors. For example, there has been a growing literature base on training load in sport and specifically how this can be separated into two measurable components of internal and external load (see, for a review, Impellizzeri, Marcora, & Coutts, 2019). Specifically, *external* load is the physical work that is prescribed in a sport performer's training plan (e.g., the quality and quantity of exercise and how it is organized) with examples including velocity generated, distance covered, or weight lifted. The purpose of prescribing a training program using external load indicators is to elicit a desired psychophysiological response, and *internal* training load indicators assess this bodily response during exercise (Impellizzeri et al., 2019). Examples of internal training load indicators include perceived exertion and heart rate. There has been a tendency in the literature to focus on the examination of external load, perhaps linked to the rise in the development of sophisticated assessment technologies; however, given the importance of internal load in determining outcomes, it is crucial that future scholarly work attempts to advance the measurement of internal load in sport, so that it can be used as a primary measure when monitoring sport performers (Impellizzeri et al., 2019).

Objective/Subjective

A frequently discussed characteristic of stressors is whether they are objectively or subjectively represented. To explain the distinction between the two, Fletcher et al. (2006) suggest that objective stressors are the demands as they exist independent of an individual's perceptions, whereas subjective stressors are the demands that an individual perceives. There is considerable debate in the literature around whether stressors should be studied subjectively, objectively, or by using a combination of both methods (cf. Arnold & Fletcher, 2012a). From a subjective standpoint, scholars argue that focusing on how individuals interpret environmental conditions enables a true understanding of the stress process, and is the critical factor in determining if a demand is significant (Arnold & Fletcher, 2012a; Fletcher et al., 2006). On the other hand, scholars have argued that certain stressors transcend individual cognitions; therefore, objective measures can establish consensus on significant stressors and avoid the measurement confounding criticism that is often directed toward subjective measures (Arnold & Fletcher, 2012a; Fletcher et al., 2006). However, given that objective measures are still ultimately underpinned by an individual's subjective perspective of their environment (Frese & Zapf, 1988), some researchers have begun to adopt a triangulation strategy whereby multiple methods are incorporated into a study design (Arnold & Fletcher, 2012a).

Within the sports literature, scholars interested in assessing the load placed upon athletes have often incorporated both subjective and objective measures into their study designs. As one example, Borresen and Lambert (2008) assessed the training load of athletes by asking them to rate their perceived exertion (RPE; subjective measure) and by measuring their heart rate (objective measure). The authors found that the subjective measures provided reasonably accurate assessments of training load compared to the objective measures, but they could deviate in accuracy when the intensity and duration of training changed (Borresen & Lambert, 2008). Furthermore, scholars have combined objective physiological measures (e.g., cortisol and secretory immunoglobulin-A) with subjective self-report questionnaires (e.g., the OSI-SP; Arnold et al., 2013) in studies conducted to examine organizational stress experiences of sport performers over time (Roberts et al., 2019). Interestingly, within Roberts and colleagues' (2019) study, organizational stressor intensity was positively related to cortisol exposure at competition. Outside of the sports domain, self-reported stress has also shown an association with objective physiological stress (Fohr et al., 2015). Specifically, Fohr and colleagues (2015) found that the higher the subjective self-reported stress, the higher the objective heart rate variability-based stress, even when adjusted for the effects of age and sex and accounting for physical activity and body fat percentage; however, the subjective and objective measures were affected by different factors such as physical activity.

Conscious/Unconscious

A stressor characteristic which has not received any attention to date in the sports-related literature is that relating to conscious and unconscious stress representations. Outside of the sports setting, scholars have examined conscious and unconscious representations of trauma experiences and suggested that conscious thought relates to trauma experiences that can be articulated, whereas the unconscious represents unformulated thought (Wrenn, 2003). Moreover on the topic of perseverance cognition (PC), which is when an individual makes cognitive representations of past stressful events (i.e., rumination) or events that are feared in the future (i.e., worry), research has found that unconscious PC is an even more important source of stress-related and prolonged physiological activity than conscious PC (Brosschot, 2010; Brosschot, Verkuil, & Thayer, 2010). Brosschot and colleagues (2010, 2014) suggest, therefore, that unconscious PC may yield new and important markers of chronic stress and disease. Despite unconscious stress being a common phenomenon, with many humans often feeling good or bad without necessarily understanding why (Brosschot, 2010), trying to measure processes which are outside of an individual's awareness has proved more complex (cf. Somerfield & McCrae, 2000). A variety of measures have been forwarded for unconscious measurement, including the manipulation of emotional versions of unconscious thought, indirectly measuring unconscious emotional cognition, and via implicit affect (IA) tests (Brosschot, 2010; Brosschot et al., 2014). Interestingly, when using IA tests, Brosschot and colleagues (2014) found that physiological stress recovery was associated with IA, thus concluding that unconscious stress is possibly responsible for a considerable part of prolonged unhealthy stress-related physiological activity.

The lack of attention to conscious and unconscious representations of stress in the sports literature seems surprising given the extensive relevance of this characteristic to the sporting context. However, given the renewed recognition by cognitive researchers of the sports context as a dynamic natural laboratory to investigate relationships between thoughts and action, and extensive work conducted on the links between thinking and action for the performance states of flow and choking (Moran, 2012), scholars are encouraged to conduct future work on conscious and unconscious representations of stressors in sport.

Challenge/Hindrance

A further stressor characteristic which has not received any attention to date in the sports-related literature is that relating to whether the stressor is a challenge or a hindrance. This distinction has arisen from recognition that job demands are not as homogenous as initially proposed in the widely adopted Job Demands-Resources model (JD-R model; Bakker & Demerouti, 2007). To explain, challenge stressors have been identified as demands which require some energy but are stimulating and that individuals tend to appraise as potentially promoting their growth and achievement, whereas hindrance stressors are health-impairing job demands that hinder optimal functioning (Podsakoff, LePine, & LePine, 2007; Van den Broeck, De Cuyper, De Witte, & Vansteenkiste, 2010). Research on this topic has emphasized the importance of distinguishing between challenge and hindrance stressors given that the two are differentially associated with, and can help to explain the differential effects of stressors on, various outcomes (Podsakoff et al., 2007). These outcomes include, but are not limited to, the following: psychological strains and turnover intentions (Abbas & Raja, 2019); safety compliance and participation (Clarke, 2012); exhaustion (Van den Broeck et al., 2010); well-being and life satisfaction (Flinch-baugh, Luth, & Li, 2015); sleep quality (French, Allen, & Henderson, 2019); perceived supervisory and organizational support (Haar, 2006); flourishing and self-esteem (Kim & Beehr, 2020); the learning component of thriving (Prem, Ohly, Kubicek, & Korunka, 2017); and individual and team job performance (Laethem, Beckers, de Bloom, Sianoja, & Kinnunen, 2019; LePine, Podsakoff, & LePine, 2005; Pearsall, Ellis, & Stein, 2009).

Given the importance of many of these outcomes in the sporting domain, it is pressing for research conducted with sport performers to identify and disentangle challenge and hindrance stressors and consider the differential effects that each might have. Within these investigations, it will also be essential for researchers to examine the mediators (e.g., appraisal, motivation, attitudes, and emotions) and moderators (e.g., conscientiousness, neuroticism, and psychological capital) of the challenge/hindrance stressor and outcomes relationship as has been done outside of sport to date (Abbas & Raja, 2019; González-Morales & Neves, 2015; Kim & Beehr, 2018; Min, Kim, & Lee, 2015; Podsakoff et al., 2007; Rodell & Judge, 2009; Webster, Beehr, & Christiansen, 2010). Furthermore, given the types of demands that sport performers encounter (e.g., competitive, organizational, and personal), it would also be insightful to examine how challenge and hindrance demands encountered in each domain (e.g., sport and life) impact the challenge and hindrance demands and outcomes experienced in the other. Nonetheless, despite this apparent promise, some caution is required because of the potential to conflate subjective stressors (i.e., perceived stimuli) with cognitive appraisals (e.g., challenge or threat reactions), thus creating tautological distillations of what are, in reality, complex person-environmental transactions (cf. Fletcher et al., 2006).

Practical Implications

The overriding implication of the stressor research in sport is that practitioners should seek to prevent, reduce, and/or eliminate environmental demands that are associated with distress and detrimental effects on well-being and/or performance (cf. Fletcher & Arnold, 2017; Fletcher et al., 2006; Fletcher & Scott, 2010; Hanton & Fletcher, 2005). This approach to stress management is known as a primary intervention (cf. Hargrove, Quick, Nelson, & Quick, 2011; Quick & Quick, 1979) because it attempts to manage stress at its origin by adapting the environment to optimize the demands that individuals encounter. Aside from the ethical obligation and duty of care to safeguard individuals' psychosocial health (see also Chapter 14), this approach is often the most direct and effective way to manage stress by targeting the cause through the proactive prevention and/or the reactive reduction or removal of stressors.

Primary stress management should be implemented systematically and underpinned by a diagnostic assessment of an athlete's (sport and non-sport) environment, including psychosocial demands, constraints, and risks. Such a "stress audit" (Fletcher et al., 2006; Hanton & Fletcher, 2005) should involve multidisciplinary biopsychosocial indicators, the design and delivery of a bespoke environmentally focused intervention, the ongoing monitoring of any changes over time, and the evaluation of any effects on athletes (see also Arnold, Fletcher, et al., 2017; Didymus & Fletcher, 2017; Rumbold, Fletcher, & Daniels, 2018). Consistent with this approach, it should be emphasized that experiencing stress should not be seen as a sign of weakness in a performer (Fletcher et al., 2006) or a lack of mental toughness on the part of the athlete; rather, that "any individual, no matter what his or her psychological make-up is, will succumb at some point (his or her "breaking point") to (extreme) adversity and hardship" (Fletcher & Sarkar, 2016, p. 139). To maximize the effectiveness of stress management, Fletcher and Arnold (2017) highlighted that practitioners will likely need to develop professional competence in leadership coaching and management consulting (Fletcher & Hanton, 2003; Fletcher et al., 2006; Fletcher & Wagstaff, 2009; Hanton et al., 2005; Hanton & Fletcher, 2005; Jones, 2002; Rumbold, Fletcher, & Daniels, 2012; Tabei et al., 2012; Woodman & Hardy, 2001a, 2001b), be sensitive to the political realities of sport organizations (cf. Fletcher et al., 2006; Fletcher & Wagstaff, 2009; Gardner, 1995; Hardy et al., 1996; Ravizza, 1988), and develop multilevel approaches to manage the stressors in athletes' lives (cf. Arnold, Fletcher, et al., 2017; Fletcher et al., 2006; Fletcher, Hanton, Mellalieu, et al. 2012; see also Chapter 12).

Conclusion

Numerous stressors, hassles, and adversities have been identified in sport psychology research to date that are encountered by sport performers. Moreover, environmental demands are a fundamental and primary feature of stress conceptualizations and theories. That said, the focus of the majority of stressor-related research in the sports domain to date has been on the types of stressors that are encountered by performers (e.g., competitive, organizational, and personal), rather than the dimensions or properties of these. It is hoped that this chapter provides a foundation for future work on stressors, hassles, and adversity by both synthesizing the research to date on the types, dimensions, and properties of demands and integrating this alongside innovative future research directions suggested to advance knowledge, understanding, and practice moving forward. Furthermore, the chapter has identified and discussed other characteristics of stressors, hassles, and adversity that have already received attention within the domain of sport (internal/external and objective/subjective) and novel characteristics examined outside which sports scholars and practitioners should further explore in the future (e.g., conscious/unconscious and challenge/hindrance). Finally, the chapter has forwarded several recommendations for designing, implementing, and evaluating primary stress management interventions that focus on the stressors, hassles, and adversity encountered, so that performers can ultimately experience optimal performance and well-being in competitive sport.

References

Abbas, M., & Raja, U. (2019). Challenge-hindrance stressors and job outcomes: The moderating role of conscientiousness. *Journal of Business and Psychology, 34*, 189–201.

Alsentali, A. M., & Anshel, M. H. (2015). Relationship between internal and external acute stressors and coping style. *Journal of Sport Behavior, 38*, 357–375.

Anshel, M. H., & Andersen, D. I. (2002). Coping with acute stress in sport: Linking athletes' coping style, coping strategies, affect and motor performance. *Anxiety, Stress and Coping: An International Journal, 15*, 193–209. Doi:10.1080/10615800290028486

Anshel, M. H., & Delaney, J. (2001). Sources of acute stress, cognitive appraisals, and coping strategies of male and female child athletes. *Journal of Sport Behavior, 24*, 329–354.

Anshel, M. H., & Wells, B. (2000). Personal and situational variables that describe coping with acute stress in competitive sport. *Journal of Social Psychology, 140*, 434–450. Doi:10.1080/00224540009600483

Anshel, M. H., Williams, L. R. T., & Williams, S. M. (2000). Coping style following acute stress in competitive sport. *The Journal of Social Psychology, 140*, 751–773. Doi:10.1080/00224540009600515

Aquilina, D. (2010). A study of the relationship between elite athletes' educational development and sporting performance. *The International Journal of the History of Sport, 30*, 374–392. Doi:10.1080/09523367.2013.765723

Arnold, R., Collington, S., Manley, H., Rees, S., Soanes, J., & Williams, M. (2019). "The team behind the team": Exploring the organizational stressor experiences of sport science and management staff in elite sport. *Journal of Applied Sport Psychology, 31*, 7–26. Doi:10/1080/10413200.2017.1407836

Arnold, R., Edwards, T., & Rees, T. (2019). Organizational stressors, social support, and implications for subjective performance in high-level sport. *Psychology of Sport and Exercise, 39*, 204–212. Doi:10.1016/j.psychsport.2018.08.010

Arnold, R., & Fletcher, D. (2012a). Psychometric issues in organizational stressor research: A review and implications for sport psychology. *Measurement in Physical Education and Exercise Science, 16*, 81–100. Doi:10.1080/1091367X.2012.639608

Arnold, R., & Fletcher, D. (2012b). A research synthesis and taxonomic classification of the organizational stressors encountered by sport performers. *Journal of Sport and Exercise Psychology, 34*, 397–429. Doi:10.1123/jsep.34.3.397

Arnold, R., Fletcher, D., & Carr, M. (2010). *Understanding performer-organization transactions in elite sport: A qualitative exploration of stressor dimensions.* Paper presented at the meeting of the British Association of Sport and Exercise Sciences, Glasgow, UK.

Arnold, R., Fletcher, D., & Daniels, K. (2013). Development and validation of the Organizational Stressor Indicator for Sport Performers (OSI-SP). *Journal of Sport & Exercise Psychology, 35,* 180–196. Doi:10.1123/jsep.35.2.180

Arnold, R., Fletcher, D., & Daniels, K. (2016). Demographic differences in sport performers' experiences of organizational stressors. *Scandinavian Journal of Medicine & Science in Sports, 26,* 348–358. Doi:10.1111/sms.12439

Arnold, R., Fletcher, D., & Daniels, K. (2017). Organizational stressors, coping, and outcomes in competitive sport. *Journal of Sports Sciences, 35,* 694–703. Doi: 10.1080/02640414.2016.1184299

Arnold, R., Ponnusamy, V., Zhang, C.-Q., & Gucciardi, D. F. (2017). Cross-cultural validity and measurement invariance of the Organizational Stressor Indicator for Sport Performers (OSI-SP) across three countries. *Scandinavian Journal of Medicine & Science in Sports, 27,* 895–903. Doi:10.1111/sms.12688

Arnold, R., Wagstaff, C. R. D., Steadman, L., & Pratt, Y. (2017). The organizational stressors encountered by athletes with a disability. *Journal of Sports Sciences, 35,* 1187–1196. Doi:10.1080/02640414.2016.1214285

Bakker, A. B., & Demerouti, E. (2007). The job demands-resources model: State of the art. *Journal of Managerial Psychology, 22,* 309–328. Doi:10.1108/02683940710733115

Bartholomew, K. J., Arnold, R., Hampson, R. J., & Fletcher, D. (2017). Organizational stressors and basic psychological needs: The mediating role of athletes' appraisal mechanisms. *Scandinavian Journal of Medicine & Science in Sports, 27,* 2127–2139. Doi:10.1111/sms.12851

Baumeister, R. F. (1984). Choking under pressure: Self-consciousness and paradoxical effects of incentives on skillful performance. *Journal of Personality and Social Psychology, 46,* 610–620. Doi:10.1037/0022-3514.46.3.610

Beckie, T. M. (2012). A systematic review of allostatic load, health, and health disparities. *Biological Research for Nursing, 14,* 311–346. Doi:10.1177/1099800412455688

Borresen, J., & Lambert, M. I. (2008). Quantifying training load: A comparison of subjective and objective measures. *International Journal of Sports Physiology and Performance, 3,* 16–30. Doi:10.1123/ijspp.3.1.16

Boscarino, J. A. (2004). Posttraumatic stress disorder and physical illness: Results from clinical and epidemiologic studies. *Annals of the New York Academy of Sciences, 1032,* 141–153. Doi:10.1196/annals.1314.011

Bovin, M. R., & Marx, B. P. (2011). The importance of the peritraumatic experience in defining traumatic stress. *Psychological Bulletin, 137,* 47–67. Doi:10.1037/a0021353

Brewin, C. R., Lanius, R. A., Novac, A., Schnyder, U., & Galea, S. (2009). Reformulating PTSD for *DSM-V:* Life after criterion. *Journal of Trauma Stress, 22,* 366–373. Doi:10.1002/jts.20443

Brosschot, J. F. (2010). Markers of chronic stress: Prolonged physiological activation and (un)conscious perseverance cognition. *Neuroscience and Biobehavioral Reviews, 35,* 46–50. Doi:10.1016/j.neubiorev.2010.01.004

Brosschot, J. F., Geurts, S. A. E., Kruizinga, I., Radstaak, M., Verkuil, B., Quirin, M., . . Kompier, M. A. J. (2014). Does unconscious stress play a role in prolonged cardiovascular stress recovery? *Stress and Health, 30,* 179–187. Doi:10.1002/smi.2590

Brosschot, J. F., Verkuil, B., & Thayer, J. F. (2010). Conscious and unconscious perseverative cognition: Is a large part of prolonged physiological activity due to unconscious stress? *Journal of Psychosomatic Research, 69,* 407–416. Doi:10.1016/jpsychores.2010.02.002

Chamberlain, K., & Zika, S. (1990). The minor events approach to stress: Support for the use of daily hassles. *British Journal of Psychology, 81,* 469–481. Doi:10.1111/j.2044-8295.1990.tb02373.x

Clarke, S. (2012). The effect of challenge and hindrance stressors on safety behavior and safety outcomes: A meta-analysis. *Journal of Occupational Health Psychology, 17,* 387–397. Doi:10.1037/a0029817

Cohen, S., Karmarck, T., & Mermelstein, R. (1983). A global measure of perceived stress. *Journal of Health and Social Behavior, 24,* 385–396.

Collins, D., MacNamara, Á., & McCarthy, N. (2016). Super champions, champions, and almost: Important differences and commonalities on the rocky road. *Frontiers in Psychology, 6,* 1–11. Doi:10.3389/fpsyg.2015.02009

Cosh, S., & Tully, P. J. (2015). Stressors, coping, and support mechanisms for student athletes combining elite sport and tertiary education: Implications for practice. *The Sport Psychologist, 29,* 120–133. Doi:10.1123/tsp.2014-0102

Cox, R. H., Martens, M. P., & Russell, W. D. (2003). Measuring anxiety in athletics: The revised Competitive State Anxiety Inventory-2. *Journal of Sport and Exercise Psychology, 25,* 519–533. Doi:10.1123/jsep.25.4.519

Coyne, J. O. C., Haff, G. G., Coutts, A. J., Newton, R. U., & Nimphius, S. (2018). The current state of subjective training load monitoring—A practical perspective and call to action. *Sports Medicine, 4,* 58–68. Doi:10.1186/s40798-018-0172-x

Curran, T., & Hill, A. P. (2018). A test of perfectionistic vulnerability following competitive failure among college athletes. *Journal of Sport and Exercise Psychology, 40,* 269–279. Doi:10.1123/jsep.2018-0059

Dewe, P. J. (1991). Measuring work stressors: The role of frequency, duration, and demand. *Work and Stress, 5,* 77–91.

Didymus, F. F. (2016). Olympic and international level sports coaches' experiences of stressors, appraisals, and coping. *Qualitative Research in Sport, Exercise and Health, 9,* 214–232. Doi:10.1080/2159676X.2016.1261364

Didymus, F. F., & Fletcher, D. (2012). Getting to the heart of the matter: A diary study of swimmers' appraisals of organizational stressors. *Journal of Sports Sciences, 30,* 1375–1385. Doi:10.1080/02640414.2012.709263

Didymus, F. F., & Fletcher, D. (2014). Swimmers' experiences of organizational stress: Exploring the role of cognitive appraisal and coping strategies. *Journal of Clinical Sport Psychology, 8,* 159–183. Doi:10.1123/jcsp.2014-0020

Didymus, F. F., & Fletcher, D. (2017). Organizational stress in high-level field hockey: Examining transactional pathways between stressors, appraisals, coping and performance satisfaction. *International Journal of Sports Science and Coaching, 12,* 252–263. Doi:10.1177/1747954117694737

Dohrenwend, B. S., & Dohrenwend, B. P. (Eds.). (1974). *Stressful life events: Their nature and effects.* Oxford, UK: John Wiley & Sons.

Dugdale, J. R., Eklund, R. C., & Gordon, S. (2002). Expected and unexpected stressors in major international competition: Appraisal, coping and performance. *The Sport Psychologist, 16,* 20–33. Doi:10.1123/tsp.16.1.20

Engberg, E., Allen, M., Kukkonen-Harjula, K., Peltonen, J. E., Tikkanen, H. O., & Pekkarinen, H. (2012). Life events and change in leisure time physical activity: A systematic review. *Sports Medicine, 42,* 433–447. Doi:10.2165/11597610-000000000-00000

Espejo, E. P., Ferriter, C. T., Hazel, N. A., Keenan-Miller, D., Hoffman, L. R., & Hammen, C. (2011). Predictors of subjective ratings of stressor severity: The effects of current mood and neuroticism. *Stress and Health, 27,* 23–33. Doi:10.1002/smi.1315

Evans, L., Wadey, R., Hanton, S., & Mitchell, I. (2012). Stressors experienced by injured athletes. *Journal of Sports Sciences, 30,* 917–927. Doi:10.1080/02640414.2012.682078

Felsten, G., & Wilcox, K. (1993). Relationships between life stress and performance in sports: Much theory, but very little data. *Journal of Sport Behavior, 16,* 99–110.

Fletcher, D. (2019). Psychological resilience and adversarial growth in sport and performance. In E. O. Acevedo (Ed.), *The Oxford encyclopedia of sport, exercise, and performance psychology* (pp. 731–756). New York: Oxford University Press.

Fletcher, D., & Arnold, R. (2017). Stress in sport: The role of the organizational environment. In C. R. D. Wagstaff (Ed.), *The organizational psychology of sport: Key issues and practical applications* (pp. 83–100). New York: Routledge.

Fletcher, D., & Hanton, S. (2003). Sources of organizational stress in elite sport performers. *The Sport Psychologist, 17,* 175–195. Doi:10.1123/tsp.17.2.175

Fletcher, D., Hanton, S., & Mellalieu, S. D. (2006). An organizational stress review: Conceptual and theoretical issues in competitive sport. In S. Hanton & S. D. Mellalieu (Eds.), *Literature reviews in sport psychology* (pp. 321–374). Hauppauge, NY: Nova Science Publishers.

Fletcher, D., Hanton, S., Mellalieu, S. D., & Neil, R. (2012). A conceptual framework of organizational stressors in sport performers. *Scandinavian Journal of Medicine and Science in Sports, 22,* 545–557. Doi:10.1111/j.1600-0838.2010.01242.x

Fletcher, D., Hanton, S., & Wagstaff, C. R. D. (2012). Performers' responses to stressors encountered in sport organisations. *Journal of Sports Sciences, 30,* 349–358. Doi:10.1080/02640414.2011.633545

Fletcher, D., Rumbold, J., Tester, R., & Coombes, M. (2011). Sport psychologists' experiences of organizational stressors. *The Sport Psychologist, 25,* 363–381. Doi:10.1123/tsp.25.3.363

Fletcher, D., & Sarkar, M. (2013). Psychological resilience: A review and critique of definitions, concepts and theory. *European Psychologist, 18,* 12–23. Doi:10.1027/1016-9040/a000124

Fletcher, D., & Sarkar, M. (2016). Mental fortitude training: An evidence-based approach to developing psychological resilience for sustained success. *Journal of Sport Psychology in Action, 7,* 135–157. Doi:10.1080/21520704.2016.1255496

Fletcher, D., & Scott, M. (2010). Psychological stress in sports coaches: A review of concepts, research, and practice. *Journal of Sports Sciences, 28,* 127–137. Doi:10.1080/02640410903406208

Fletcher, D., & Wagstaff, C. R. D. (2009). Organizational psychology in elite sport: Its emergence, application and future. *Psychology of Sport and Exercise, 10,* 427–434. Doi:10.1016/j.psychsport.2009.03.009

Flinchbaugh, C., Luth, M. T., & Li, P. (2015). A challenge or hindrance? Understanding the effects of stressors and thriving on life satisfaction. *International Journal of Stress Management, 22*, 323–345. Doi:10.1037/a0039136

Fohr, T., Tolvanen, A., Myllymäki, T., Järvelä-Reijonen, E., Rantala, S., Korpela, R., . . Kujala, U. M. (2015). Subjective stress, objective heart rate variability-based stress, and recovery on workdays among overweight and psychologically distressed individuals: A cross-sectional study. *Journal of Occupational Medicine and Toxicology, 10*, 39–47. Doi:10.1186/s12995-015-0081-6

French, K. A., Allen, T. D., & Henderson, T. G. (2019). Challenge and hindrance stressors and metabolic risk factors. *Journal of Occupational Health Psychology, 24*, 307–321. Doi:10.1037/ocp0000138

Frese, M., & Zapf, D. (1988). Methodological issues in the study of work stress: Objective versus subjective measurement of work stress and the question of longitudinal studies. In C. Cooper & R. Payne (Eds.), *Causes, coping and consequences of stress at work* (pp. 375–411). New York: John Wiley & Sons.

Galambos, S. A., Terry, P. C., Moyle, G. M., & Locke, S. A. (2005). Psychological predictors of injury among elite athletes. *British Journal of Sports Medicine, 39*, 351–354. Doi:10.1136/bjsm.2005.018440

Gardner, F. (1995). The coach and team psychologist: An integrated organizational model. In S. M. Murphy (Ed.), *Sport psychology interventions* (pp. 147–175). Champaign, IL: Human Kinetics.

Gerber, M., Brand, S., Lindwall, M., Elliot, C., Kalak, N., Hermann, C., . . Jonsdottir, I. H. (2012). Concerns regarding hair cortisol as a biomarker of chronic stress in exercise and sport science. *Journal of Sport Science and Medicine, 11*, 571–581.

Giacobbi Jr., P. R., Lynn, T. K., Wetherington, J. M., Jenkins, J., Bodendorf, M., & Langley, B. (2004). Stress and coping during the transition to university for first-year female athletes. *The Sport Psychologist, 18*, 1–20. Doi:10.1123/tsp.18.1.1

González-Morales, M., & Neves, P. (2015). When stressors make you work: Mechanisms linking challenge stressors to performance. *Work and Stress, 29*, 213–229. Doi:10.1080/02678373.2015.1074628

Gould, D., Jackson, S. A., & Finch, L. M. (1993). Sources of stress in national champion figure skaters. *Journal of Sport and Exercise Psychology, 15*, 134–159. Doi:10.1123/jsep.15.2.134

Gump, B. B., & Matthews, K. A. (1999). Do background stressors influence reactivity to and recovery from acute stressors? *Journal of Applied Social Psychology, 29*, 469–494. Doi:10.1111/j.15591816.1999.tb01397.x

Gustafsson, H., Sagar, S. S., & Stenling, A. (2016). Fear of failure, psychological stress, and burnout among adolescent athletes competing in high level sport. *Scandinavian Journal of Medicine and Science in Sports, 27*, 2091–2102. Doi:10.1111/sms.12797

Haar, J. M. (2006). Challenge and hindrance stressors in New Zealand: Exploring social exchange theory outcomes. *The International Journal of Human Resource Management, 17*, 1942–1950. Doi:10.1080/09585190601000147

Hahn, S. E., & Smith, C. S. (1999). Daily hassles and chronic stressors: Conceptual and measurement issues. *Stress Medicine, 15*, 89–101. Doi:10.1002/(sici)1099-1700(199904)

Hanton, S., & Fletcher, D. (2005). Organizational stress in competitive sport: More than we bargained for? *International Journal of Sport Psychology, 36,* 273–283.

Hanton, S., Fletcher, D., & Coughlan, G. (2005). Stress in elite sport performers: A comparative study of competitive and organizational stressors. *Journal of Sports Sciences, 23,* 1129–1141. Doi:10.1080/02640410500131480

Hanton, S., Neil, R., & Mellalieu, S. D. (2008). Recent developments in competitive anxiety direction and competition stress research. *International Review of Sport and Exercise Psychology, 1,* 45–47. Doi:10.1080/17509840701827445

Hanton, S., Wagstaff, C. R., & Fletcher, D. (2012). Cognitive appraisals of stressors encountered in sport organizations. *International Journal of Sport and Exercise Psychology, 10,* 276–289. Doi:10.1080/1612197X.2012.682376

Hardy, L., Barlow, M., Evans, L., Rees, T., Woodman, T., & Warr, C. (2017). Great British medalists: Psychosocial biographies of super-elite and elite athletes from Olympic sports. In V. Walsh, M. Wilson, & B. Parkin (Eds.), *Sport and the brain: The science of preparing, enduring and winning, Part A* (pp. 1–119). London, UK: Academic Press.

Hardy, L., Jones, G., & Gould, D. (1996). *Understanding psychological preparation for sport: Theory and practice of elite performers.* Chichester, UK: John Wiley & Sons.

Hargrove, M. B., Quick, J. C., Nelson, D. L., & Quick, J. D. (2011). The theory of preventative stress management: A 33-year review and evaluation. *Stress and Health, 27,* 182–193. Doi:10.1002/smi.1417

Harkness, K. L., & Hayden, E. P. (Eds.). (2020a). *The Oxford handbook of stress and mental health.* Oxford, UK: Oxford University Press.

Harkness, K. L., & Hayden, E. P. (2020b). Introduction. In K. L. Harkness & E. P. Hayden (Eds.), *The Oxford handbook of stress and mental health* (pp. 1–6). Oxford, UK: Oxford University Press.

Harwood, C., & Knight, C. (2009). Understanding parental stressors: An investigation of British tennis-players. *Journal of Sports Sciences, 27,* 339–351. Doi:10.1080/02640410802603871

Holmes, T. H., & Rahe, R. H. (1967). The social readjustment rating scale. *Journal of Psychosomatic Research, 11,* 213–218. Doi:10.1016/0022-3999(67)90010-4

Holt, N. L., & Hogg, J. M. (2002). Perceptions of stress and coping during preparations for the 1999 women's soccer world cup finals. *The Sport Psychologist, 16,* 251–271. Doi:10.1123/tsp.16.3.251

Howells, K., & Fletcher, D. (2015). Sink or swim: Adversity- and growth-related experiences in Olympic swimming champions. *Psychology of Sport and Exercise, 16,* 37–48. Doi:10.1016/j.psychsport.2014.08.004

Howells, K., Sarkar, M., & Fletcher, D. (2017). Can athletes benefit from adversity? A systematic review of growth following adversity in competitive sport. *Progress in Brain Research, 234,* 117–159. Doi:10.1016/bs.pbr.2017.06.002

Impellizzeri, F. M., Marcora, S. M., & Coutts, A. J. (2019). Internal and external training load: 15 years on. *International Journal of Sports Physiology and Performance, 14,* 270–273. Doi:10.1123/jspp.2018-0935

Ivarsson, A., Johnson, U., Andersen, M. B., Tranaeus, U., Stenling, A., & Lindwall, M. (2017). Psychosocial factors and sports injuries: Meta-analyses for prediction and prevention. *Sports Medicine, 47,* 353–365. Doi:10.1007/s40279-016-0578-x

James, B., & Collins, D. (1997). Self-presentational sources of competitive stress during performance. *Journal of Sport and Exercise Psychology, 19*, 17–35. Doi:10.1123/jsep.19.1.17

Johnson, U. (2007). Psychosocial antecedents of sport injury, prevention, and intervention: An overview of theoretical approaches and empirical findings. *International Journal of Sport and Exercise Psychology, 5*, 352–369. Doi:10.1080/1 612197X.2007.9671841

Jones, G. (2002). Performance excellence: A personal perspective on the link between sport and business. *Journal of Applied Sport Psychology, 14*, 268–281. Doi:10.1080/10413200290103554

Juster, R-P., McEwen, B. S., & Lupien, S. J. (2010). Allostatic load biomarkers of chronic stress and impact on health and cognition. *Neuroscience and Biobehavioral Reviews, 35*, 2–16. Doi:10.1016/j.neubiorev.2009.10.002

Kanner, A. D., Coyne, J. C., Schaefer, C., & Lazarus, R. S. (1981). Comparison of two modes of stress measurement: Daily hassles and uplifts versus major life events. *Journal of Behavioral Medicine, 4*, 1–39. Doi:10.1007/bf00844845

Katz, D. A., Sprang, G., & Cooke, C. (2012). The cost of chronic stress in childhood: Understanding and applying the concept of allostatic load. *Psychodynamic Psychiatry, 40*, 469–480. Doi:10.1521/pdps.2012.40.3.469

Kellman, M., Bertollo, M., Bosquet, L., Brink, M., Coutts, A. J., Duffield, R., . . Beckmann, J. (2018). Recovery and performance in sport: Consensus statement. *International Journal of Sports Physiology and Performance, 13*, 240–245. Doi:10.1123/ijspp.2017-0759

Kim, M., & Beehr, T. A. (2018). Challenge and hindrance demands lead to employees' health and behaviours through intrinsic motivation. *Stress and Health, 34*, 367–378. Doi:10.1002/smi.2796

Kim, M., & Beehr, T. A. (2020). Thriving on demand: Challenging work results in employee flourishing through appraisals and resources. *International Journal of Stress Management, 27*, 111–125. Doi:10.1037/str0000135

Kristiansen, E. (2017). Walking the line: How young athletes balance academic studies and sport in international competition. *Sport in Society, 20*, 47–65. Doi: 10.1080/17430437.2015.1124563

Kristiansen, E., Halvari, H., & Roberts, G. C. (2012). Organizational and media stress among professional football players: Testing an achievement goal theory model. *Scandinavian Journal of Medicine & Science in Sports, 22*, 569–579. Doi:10.1111/j.1600-0838.2010.01259.x

Krupnik, V. (2019). Trauma or adversity? *Traumatology, 25*, 256–261. Doi:10.1037% 2Ftrm0000169

Krupnik, V. (2020). Trauma or drama: A predicative processing perspective on the continuum of stress. *Frontiers in Psychology, 11*, 1248. Doi:10.3389/ fpsyg.2020.01248

Laethem, M. V., Beckers, D. G. J., de Bloom, J., Sianoja, M., & Kinnunen, U. (2019). Challenge and hindrance demands in relation to self-reported job performance and the role of restoration, sleep quality, and affective rumination. *Journal of Occupational and Organizational Psychology, 92*, 225–254. Doi:10.1111/ joop.12239

Larner, R. J., Wagstaff, C. R. D., Thelwell, R. C., & Corbett, J. (2016). A multistudy examination of organizational stressors, emotional labor, burnout, and turnover in sport organizations. *Scandinavian Journal of Medicine and Science in Sports, 27*, 2103–2115. Doi:10.1111/sms.12833

Lazarus, R. S. (1999). *Stress and emotion: A new synthesis.* London, UK: Springer.

Lazarus, R. S. (2000). Emotions and interpersonal relationships: Towards a person-centred conceptualization of emotions and coping. *Journal of Personality, 74*, 9–46. Doi:10.1111/j.1467-6494.2005.00368.x

Lazarus, R. S., & DeLongis, A. (1983). Psychological stress and coping in aging. *American Psychologist, 38*, 245–254. Doi:10.1037/0003-066x.38.3.245

Lazarus, R. S., & Folkman, S. (1984). *Stress, appraisal and coping.* New York: Springer.

LePine, J. A., Podsakoff, N. P., & LePine, M. A. (2005). A meta-analytic test of the challenge stressor-hindrance stressor framework: An explanation for inconsistent relationships among stressors and performance. *Academy of Management Journal, 48*, 764–775. Doi:10.5465/amj.2005.18803921

Lepore, S. J. (1995). Measurement of chronic stressors. In S. Cohen, R. Kessler, & L. Underwood-Gordon (Eds.), *Measuring stress: A guide for health and social scientists* (pp. 102–120). New York: Oxford University Press.

Lu, F. J-H., Hsu, Y-W., Chan, Y-S., Cheen, J-R., & Kao, K-T. (2012). Assessing college student-athletes' life stress: Initial measurement development and validation. *Measurement in Physical Education and Exercise Science, 16*, 254–267. Doi:10.1080/1091367X.2012.693371

Luhmann, M., Hofmann, W., Eid, M., & Lucas, R. E. (2012). Subjective well-being and adaptation to life events: A meta-analysis. *Journal of Personality and Social Psychology, 102*, 592–615. Doi:10.1037/a0025948

Luthar, S. S., & Cicchetti, D. (2000). The construct of resilience: Implications for interventions and social policies. *Development and Psychopathology, 12*, 857–885. Doi:10.1017/s0954579400004156

Marchant, D. B., Andersen, M. B., & Morris, T. (1997). Perceived uncertainty of outcome as a contributing factor to competitive state anxiety. *Australian Journal of Science and Medicine in Sport, 29*, 41–46.

McEwen, B. S. (2006). Stress, adaptation, and disease. *Annals of the New York Academy of Sciences, 840*, 33–44. Doi:10.1111/j.1749-6632.1998.tb09546.x

McKay, J., Niven, A. G., Lavallee, D., & White, A. (2008). Sources of strain among UK elite athletes. *The Sport Psychologist, 22*, 143–163. Doi:10.1123/tsp.22.2.143

McLaughlin, K. A. (2020). Early life stress and psychopathology. In K. L. Harkness & E. P. Hayden (Eds.), *The Oxford handbook of stress and mental health* (pp. 45–74). Oxford, UK: Oxford University Press.

McLoughlin, E., Fletcher, D., Slavich, G. M., Arnold, R., & Moore, L. J. (2021). Cumulative lifetime stress exposure, depression, anxiety, and well-being in elite athletes: A mixed-method study. *Psychology of Sport and Exercise, 52*, 101823. Doi:10.1016/j.psychsport.2020.101823

Mellalieu, S. D., Hanton, S., & Fletcher, D. (2006). A competitive anxiety review: Recent directions in sport psychology research. In S. Hanton & S. D. Mellalieu (Eds.), *Literature reviews in sport psychology* (pp. 1–45). Hauppauge, NY: Nova Science Publishers.

Mellalieu, S. D., Neil, R., Hanton, S., & Fletcher, D. (2009). Competition stress in sport performers: Stressors experienced in the competition environment. *Journal of Sports Sciences, 27*, 729–744. Doi:10.1080/02640410902889834

Miller, G. A. (1956). The magical number seven, plus or minus two: Some limits on our capacity to process information. *Psychological Review, 63*, 81–97. Doi:10.1037/h0043158

Min, H., Kim, H. J., & Lee, S-B. (2015). Extending the challenge-hindrance stressor framework: The role of psychological capital. *International Journal of Hospitality Management, 50*, 105–114. Doi:10.1016/j.ijhm.2015.07.006

Monroe, S. M., & Simons, A. D. (1991). Diathesis-stress theories in the context of life stress research: Implications for the depressive disorders. *Psychological Bulletin, 110*, 406–425. Doi:10.1037/0033-2909.110.3.406

Monroe, S. M., & Slavich, G. M. (2020). Major life events: A review of conceptual, definitional, measurement issues, and practices. In K. Harkness & E. P. Hayden (Eds.), *The Oxford handbook of stress and mental health* (pp. 1–34). New York: Oxford University Press.

Morales, J., Garcia, V., García-Massó, X., Salvá, P., Escobar, R., & Buscá, B. (2013). The use of heart rate variability in assessing precompetitive stress in high-standard judo athletes. *International Journal of Sports Medicine, 34*, 144–151. Doi:10.1055/s-0032-1323719

Moran, A. (2012). Thinking in action: Some insights from cognitive sport psychology. *Thinking Skills and Creativity, 7*, 85–92. Doi:10.1016/j.tsc.2012.03.005

Neil, R., Hanton, S., Mellalieu, S. D., & Fletcher, D. (2011). Competition stress and emotions in sport performers: The role of further appraisals. *Psychology of Sport and Exercise, 12*, 460–470. Doi:10.1016/j.psychsport.2011.02.001

Newman, H. J. H., Howells, K. L., & Fletcher, D. (2016). The dark side of top level sport: An autobiographic study of depressive experiences in elite sport performers. *Frontiers in Psychology, 7*, 1–12. Doi:10.3389/psyg-2016.00868

Nicholls, A. R., Holt, N. L., Polman, R. C. J., & Bloomfield, J. (2006). Stressors, coping, and coping effectiveness among professional rugby union players. *The Sport Psychologist, 20*, 314–329. Doi:10.1123/tsp.20.3.314

Nicholls, A. R., & Polman, R. C. J. (2008). Think aloud: Acute stress and coping strategies during golf performances. *Anxiety, Stress and Coping: An International Journal, 21*, 283–294. Doi:10.1080/10615800701609207

Noblet, A. J., & Gifford, S. M. (2002). The sources of stress experienced by professional Australian footballers. *Journal of Applied Sport Psychology, 14*, 1–13. Doi:10.1080/104132002753403799

Ntwanano, A., Toriola, A., & Didymus, F. (2017). Development and initial validation of an instrument to assess stressors among South African sports coaches. *Journal of Sports Sciences, 36*, 1378–1384. Doi:10.1080/02640414.2017.1385264

Pearsall, M. J., Ellis, A. P. J., & Stein, J. H. (2009). Coping with challenge and hindrance stressors in teams: Behavioral, cognitive, and affective outcomes. *Organizational Behavior and Human Decision Processes, 109*, 18–28. Doi:10.1016/j.obhdp.2009.02.002

Pillow, D. R., Zautra, A. J., & Sandler, I. (1996). Major life events and minor stressors: Identifying mediational links in the stress process. *Journal of Personality and Social Psychology, 70*, 381–394. Doi:10.1037/0022-3514.70.2.381

Podsakoff, N. P., LePine, J. A., & LePine, M. A. (2007). Differential challenge stressor-hindrance stressor relationships with job attitudes, turnover intentions, turnover, and withdrawal behavior: A meta-analysis. *Journal of Applied Psychology, 92*, 438–454. Doi:10.1037/0021-9010.92.2.438

Pratt, L. I., & Barling, J. (1988). Differentiating between daily events, acute and chronic stressors: A framework and its implications. In J. Hurrell, L. Murphy, S. Sauter, & C. Cooper (Eds.), *Occupational stress: Issues and developments in research* (pp. 41–53). New York: Taylor & Francis.

Prem, R., Ohly, S., Kubicek, B., & Korunka, C. (2017). Thriving on challenge stressors? Exploring time pressure and learning demands as antecedents of thriving at work. *Journal of Organizational Behavior, 38*, 108–123. Doi:10.1002/job.2115

Quick, J. C., & Quick, J. D. (1979). Reducing stress through preventative management. *Human Resource Management, 18*, 15–22. Doi:10.1002/hrm.3930180304

Raedeke, T. D., & Smith, A. L. (2004). Coping resources and athlete burnout: An examination of stress mediated and moderation hypotheses. *Journal of Sport and Exercise Psychology, 26*, 525–541. Doi:10.1123/jsep.26.4.525

Ravizza, K. (1988). Gaining entry with athletic personnel for season-long consulting. *The Sport Psychologist, 2*, 234–274. Doi:10.1123/tsp.2.3.243

Roberts, G., Arnold, R., Bilzon, J., Turner, J., & Colclough, M. (2019). A longitudinal examination of military veterans' Invictus Games stress experiences. *Frontiers in Psychology, 10*, 1–15. Doi:10.3389/fpsyg.2019.01934

Roberts, G., Arnold, R., Gillison, F., Colclough, M., & Bilzon, J. (2020). Military veteran athletes' experiences of competing at the 2016 Invictus Games: A qualitative study. *Disability and Rehabilitation.* Advance online publication. Doi:10.1080/09638288.2020.1725655

Rodell, J. B., & Judge, T. A. (2009). Can "good" stressors spark "bad" behaviours? The mediating role of emotions in links of challenge and hindrance stressors with citizenship and counterproductive behaviours. *Journal of Applied Psychology, 94*, 1438–1451. Doi:10.1037/a0016752

Rumbold, J. L., Fletcher, D., & Daniels, K. (2012). A systematic review of stress management interventions with sport performers. *Sport, Exercise and Performance Psychology, 1*, 173–193. Doi:10.1037/a0026628

Rumbold, J. L., Fletcher, D., & Daniels, K. (2018). Using a mixed method audit to inform organizational stress management interventions in sport. *Psychology of Sport and Exercise, 35*, 27–38. Doi:10.1016/j.psychsport.2017.10.010

Sarkar, M., & Fletcher, D. (2013). How should we measure psychological resilience in sport performers? *Measurement in Physical Education and Exercise Science, 17*, 264–280. Doi:10.1080/1091367X.2013.805141

Sarkar, M., & Fletcher, D. (2014). Psychological resilience in sport performers: A review of stressors and protective factors. *Journal of Sports Sciences, 32*, 1419–1434. Doi:10.1080/026404.14.2014.901551

Sarkar, M., & Fletcher, D. (2017). Adversity-related experiences are essential for Olympic success: Additional evidence and considerations. In V. Walsh, M. Wilson, & B. Parkin (Eds.), *Sport and the brain: The science of preparing, enduring and winning, Part A* (pp. 159–165). London, UK: Academic Press.

Sarkar, M., Fletcher, D., & Brown, D. J. (2015). What doesn't kill me . . . : Adversity-related experiences are vital in the development of superior Olympic performance. *Journal of Science and Medicine in Sport, 18*, 475–479. Doi:10.1016/j.jsams.2014.06.010

Savage, J., Collins, D., & Cruickshank, A. (2016). Exploring traumas in the development of talent: What are they, what do they do, and what do they require?

Journal of Applied Sport Psychology, 29, 101–117. Doi:10.1080/10413200.2016.1 194910

Scanlan, T. K., & Passer, M. W. (1979). Sources of competitive stress in young female athletes. *Journal of Sport Psychology, 1,* 151–159. Doi:10.1123/jsp.1.2.151

Scanlan, T. K., Ravizza, K., & Stein, G. L. (1989). An in-depth study of former elite figure skaters: I. Introduction to the project. *Journal of Sport and Exercise Psychology, 11,* 54–64. Doi:10.1123/jsep.11.1.54

Scanlan, T. K., Stein, G. L., & Ravizza, K. (1991). An in-depth study of former elite figure skaters: III. Sources of stress. *Journal of Sport and Exercise Psychology, 1,* 102–120. Doi:10.1123/jsep.13.2.103

Schinke, R. J., Battochio, R. C., Dube, T. V., Lidor, R., Tenenbaum, G., & Lane, A. M. (2012). Adaptation processes affecting performance in elite sport. *Journal of Clinical Sport Psychology, 6,* 180–195. Doi:10.1123/jcsp.6.2.180

Serido, J., Almeida, D. M., & Wethington, E. (2004). Chronic stressors and daily hassles: Unique and interactive relationships with psychological distress. *Journal of Health and Social Behavior, 45,* 17–33. Doi:10.1177/002214650404500102

Simms, M., Arnold, R., Turner, J., & Hays, K. (2020). A repeated-measures examination of organizational stressors, perceived psychological and physical health, and perceived performance in semi-elite athletes. *Journal of Sport Sciences.* Advance online publication. Doi:10.1080/02640414.2020.1804801

Slavich, G. M., & Shields, G. S. (2018). Assessing lifetime stress exposure using the stress and adversity inventory for adults (adult STRAIN). *Psychosomatic Medicine, 80,* 17–27. Doi:10.1097/psy.0000000000000534

Smith, M., Arnold, R., & Thelwell, R. (2018). There's no place to hide: Exploring the stressors encountered by elite sporting captains. *Journal of Applied Sport Psychology, 30,* 150–170. Doi:10.1080/10413200.2017.1349845

Smyth, J., Zawadzki, M., & Gerin, W. (2013). Stress and disease: A structural and functional analysis. *Social and Personality Psychology Compass, 7,* 217–227. Doi:10.1111/spc3.12020

Sohal, D., Gervis, M., & Rhind, D. (2013). Exploration of organizational stressors in Indian elite female athletes. *International Journal of Sport Psychology, 44,* 565–585. Doi:10.7532/IJSP.2013.44.565

Somerfield, M. R., & McCrae, R. R. (2000). Stress and coping research: Methodological challenges, theoretical advances, and clinical applications. *American Psychologist, 55,* 620–625. Doi: 10.1037/0003-066X.55.6.620

Suinn, R. M. (2005). Behavioral intervention for stress management in sports. *International Journal of Stress Management, 12,* 343–362. Doi:10.1037/1072-5245.12.4.34

Sweller, J. (1988). Cognitive load during problem solving: Effects on learning. *Cognitive Science, 12,* 257–285. Doi:10.1207/s15516709cog1202_4

Tabei, Y., Fletcher, D., & Goodger, K. (2012). The relationship between organizational stressors and athlete burnout in soccer players. *Journal of Clinical Sport Psychology, 6,* 146–165. Doi:10.1123/jcsp.6.2.146

Tamminen, K. A., Sabiston, C. M., & Crocker, P. R. E. (2019). Perceived esteem support predicts competition appraisals and performance satisfaction among varsity athletes: A test of organizational stressors as moderators. *Journal of Applied Sport Psychology, 31,* 27–46. Doi:10.1080/10413200.2018.1468363

Tedeschi, R. G., Shakespeare-Finch, J., Taku, K., & Calhoun, L. G. (2018). *Posttraumatic growth: Theory, research, and applications.* Abingdon, UK: Routledge.

Tenenbaum, G., Jones, C. M., Kitsantas, A., Sacks, D. N., & Berwick, J. P. (2003). Failure adaptation: An investigation of the stress response process in sport. *International Journal of Sport Psychology, 34*, 27–62.

Tennant, C. (2001). Life events, stress and depression: A review of recent findings. *Australian and New Zealand Journal of Psychiatry, 36*, 173–182. Doi:10.1046/j.1440-1614.2002.01007.x

Thatcher, J., & Day, M. C. (2008). Re-appraising stress appraisals: The underlying properties of stress in sport. *Psychology of Sport and Exercise, 9*, 318–335. Doi:10.1016/j-psychsport.2007.04.005

Thelwell, R. C., Weston, N. J. V., & Greenlees, I. A. (2007). Batting on a sticky wicket: Identifying sources of stress and associated coping strategies for professional cricket batsmen. *Psychology of Sport and Exercise, 8*, 219–232. Doi:10.1016/j.psychsport.2006.04.002

Tosevski, D. L., & Milovancevic, M. P. (2006). Stressful life events and physical health. *Current Opinion in Psychiatry, 19*, 184–189. Doi:10.1097/01. yco.0000214346.44625.57

Vagg, P. R., & Spielberger, C. D. (1999). The Job Stress Survey: Assessing perceived severity and frequency of occurrence of generic sources of stress in the workplace. *Journal of Occupational Health Psychology, 4*, 288–292. Doi:10.1037/1076-8998.4.3.288

Van den Broeck, A., De Cuyper, N. D., De Witte, H., & Vansteenkiste, M. (2010). Not all job demands are equal: Differentiating job hindrances and job challenges in the job demands-resources model. *European Journal of Work and Organizational Psychology, 19*, 735–759.

Voight, M. (2009). Sources of stress and coping strategies of US soccer officials. *Stress and Health, 25*, 92–202. Doi:10.1002/smi.1231

Wagstaff, C. R. D., Hings, R., Larner, R., & Fletcher, D. (2018). Psychological resilience's moderation of the relationship between the frequency of organizational stressors and burnout in athletes and coaches. *The Sport Psychologist, 32*, 178–188. Doi:10.1123/tsp.2016-0068

Webster, J. R., Beehr, T. A., & Christiansen, N. D. (2010). Toward a better understanding of the effects of hindrance and challenge stressors on work behavior. *Journal of Vocational Behavior, 76*, 68–77. Doi:10.1016/j.jvb.2009.06.012

Whittingham, J., Barker, J. B., Slater, M. J., & Arnold, R. (2020). An exploration of the organizational stressors encountered by international disability footballers. *Journal of Sports Sciences.* Advance online publication. Doi:10.1080/02640 414.2020.1815956

Williams, J. M., & Andersen, M. B. (1998). Psychosocial antecedents of sport injury: Review and critique of the stress and injury model. *Journal of Applied Sport Psychology, 10*, 5–25. Doi:10.1080/10413209808406375

Williams, J. M., Hudson, J., & Lawson, R. L. (1999). Self-presentation in sport: Initial development of a scale for measuring athletes' competitive self-presentation concerns. *Social Behavior and Personality, 27*, 487–502. Doi:10.2224/ sbp.1999.27.5.487

Wine, J. (1971). Test anxiety and direction of attention. *Psychological Bulletin, 76*, 92–104. Doi:10.1037/h0031332

Woodman, T., & Hardy, L. (2001a). A case study of organizational stress in elite sport. *Journal of Applied Sport Psychology, 13*, 207–238. Doi:10.1080/104132001753149892

Woodman, T., & Hardy, L. (2001b). Stress and anxiety. In R. N. Singer, H. A. Hausenblas, & C. M. Janelle (Eds.), *Handbook of sport psychology* (pp. 290–318). New York: John Wiley & Sons.

Wrenn, L. J. (2003). Trauma: Conscious and unconscious meaning. *Clinical Social Work Journal*, *31*, 123–137.

Wright, A. G. C., Aslinger, E. N., Bellamy, B., Edershile, E. A., & Woods, W. C. (2020). Daily stress and hassles. In K. L. Harkness & E. P. Hayden (Eds.), *The Oxford handbook of stress and mental health* (pp. 27–44). Oxford, UK: Oxford University Press.

2 Cognitive Appraisals

Faye F. Didymus and Marc V. Jones

All sport performers, with rare exception, will experience psychological stress at some point during their careers (Scanlan, Stein, & Ravizza, 1991). Experiences of stress are idiosyncratic and the extent to which stress is helpful or detrimental for an athlete depends largely on the ways that he or she appraises stressors (viz. Lazarus & Folkman, 1984). The notion of appraising is perhaps most famously brought to life by Shakespeare when writing for his character Hamlet: "there is nothing either good or bad, but thinking makes it so". To understand the nuances of athletes' experiences of stress, attention must be paid to meaning-focused stress research, which postulates that athletes' appraisals lie at the heart of stress transactions (e.g., Didymus & Fletcher, 2012; Lazarus, 2000). Appraisals also pave the way for psychological (e.g., Bartholomew, Arnold, Hampson, & Fletcher, 2017), physiological (e.g., Jones, Meijen, McCarthy, & Sheffield, 2009), emotional (e.g., Uphill & Jones, 2007), and behavioral (e.g., Blascovich, Mendes, Hunter, Lickel, & Kowai-Bell, 2001) outcomes, and have important ramifications for health, well-being, and performance (e.g., Didymus & Fletcher, 2017a; Moore, Vine, Wilson, & Freeman, 2012).

Lazarus and Folkman (1984) were some of the first scholars to focus on meaning-focused stress research and, in doing so, developed transactional stress theory to explain stress in this way. This approach focuses on the cognitive activity stemming from any event that an individual perceives as taxing or exceeding his or her resources, and has been widely recognized, tested, and developed (see, e.g., the cognitive-motivational-relational theory [CMRT] of emotion: Lazarus, 1999) over the past four decades. According to transactional stress theorists, appraising (see Table 2.1) includes a set of cognitive actions that consists of at least two discrete but interdependent constructs: primary and secondary appraising (e.g., Lazarus, 1999). While the terms *primary* and *secondary* suggest that one process occurs before the other, it is not entirely clear when the two processes occur during stress transactions; how they interact with each other; or whether any given appraisal is purely primary, secondary, or a combination of the two. The term *appraisal* refers to the evaluative

Table 2.1 Key Terms Used in the Chapter and Conceptualizations of Them

Term	Conceptualization
Appraising	The evaluative process by which stressors are evaluated and relational meanings are constructed
Appraisal	The evaluative product of appraising
Relational meaning	The meaning a person constructs from relationships with the environment
Core relational themes	Expressions of the relational meaning underlying different emotions. Includes a summary of up to six appraisal judgments
Primary appraising	Evaluations of whether a stressor is relevant or significant to one's beliefs, values, goal commitments, and situational intentions
Centrality	The perceived importance of a stressor in relation to one's well-being
Secondary appraising	An evaluation of one's available coping resources in relation to the stressor encountered
Coping self-efficacy	The degree of confidence a person has in his or her ability to cope effectively
Situation factors	Formal properties of situations
Person factors	Characteristics of a person that have the potential to define what is salient for well-being in any given encounter, or mediate or moderate appraising
Cardiovascular reactivity	The difference in measures of cardiovascular function (e.g., heart rate and blood pressure) observed between rest and exposure to a stressor
Sympathetic nervous system	Stimulates activities associated with the body's fight-or-flight response
Cardiac output	Liters of blood pumped from the heart per minute
Total peripheral resistance	Sum of the resistance of all peripheral vasculature

product of *appraising* and we advocate using these two terms for their distinct purposes (see also Lazarus, 1999). This distinction is rarely made in sport psychology literature and incorrect use of the different terms has led to confusion and inconsistency. Such discrepancies are unfortunately not limited to these fundamental terms but are also apparent in the ways that various appraisal-related terminologies have been applied. One such example relates to the notion of centrality, which is widely accepted as a part of primary appraising (Lazarus, 1999) and is positively associated with threat and challenge relational meanings (Nicholls, Polman, & Levy, 2012). Despite this knowledge, some researchers erroneously refer to "the secondary appraisal, centrality" (Gan & Anshel, 2006, p. 224). Inconsistencies such as these have, over decades of research, led to a body of literature that is disjointed in parts and difficult for the novice to grasp.

Primary Appraising

Researchers have suggested that there are three primary appraisal components that influence the appraisals made and the emotions experienced during stress transactions: *goal relevance, goal congruence,* and *type of ego involvement* (e.g., Lazarus, 1999). Further to these components, there are thought to be three different types of primary appraisals: *irrelevant, benign-positive,* and *stressful.* Irrelevant appraisals occur when the individual evaluates the situation as having no implication for well-being and, thus, there is no potential for loss or gain. Benign-positive appraisals are made when a situation has the potential to enhance the individual's well-being, and stressful appraisals occur when the situation is evaluated as being significant to the individual's well-being (see also Chapter 6).

If an encounter is appraised as stressful, there are four possible transactional alternatives that may be experienced: *challenge, benefit, harm/loss,* and *threat* (Lazarus, 1999; Lazarus & Folkman, 1984). Challenge appraisals arise when personal significance of the stressor is in proportion to the available coping resources and, thus, gain may result from the situation. Benefit and harm/loss appraisals occur when an individual perceives that enhancement of, or damage to, well-being has already occurred. Threat appraisals arise when personal significance outweighs coping resources and, thus, damage to the individual's well-being is anticipated. These transactional alternatives are important because they represent the essence of appraising and have implications for individuals' health, well-being, and performance. Indeed, an individual who typically appraises stressful situations as a challenge is more likely to have higher morale, quality of functioning, creativity, and proactive behavior compared to an individual who typically makes threat appraisals (e.g., Ohly & Fritz, 2010). Challenge appraisals are also related to elevated confidence, reduced emotional strain, and increased capability to use coping resources during stressful encounters (Lazarus & Folkman, 1984).

Although threat and challenge appraisals differ in their cognitive and affective components, they can occur simultaneously (e.g., Lazarus, 1999; Lazarus & Folkman, 1984; Moore, Freeman, Hase, Solomon-Moore, & Arnold, 2019). Thus, transactional alternatives are not necessarily mutually exclusive and the relationship between them can shift as a situation evolves. Appraising can also occur either as part of conscious processing or as a subconscious activity (Lazarus, 1991). This raises the possibility that individuals can be unaware of how their thoughts influence stress transactions and, in turn, their emotional and physiological experiences. Subconscious appraisals also have implications for the effectiveness of reappraisal techniques (e.g., reframing) because such techniques may change the conscious but not the subconscious appraisal of a stressor (see Jones, 2003). Practitioners should, therefore, remain aware of the potential influence of automatic thoughts and work with individuals to change both conscious thoughts and those that lie below the normal level of waking consciousness (e.g., with visualization or binaural beats; Padmanabhan, Hildreth, & Laws, 2005).

In sport, research on primary appraising among athletes has highlighted various associations between this process and other psychological constructs. For example, studies have provided insight to the relationship between stressors and appraisals (e.g., Didymus & Fletcher, 2012; see also Chapter 1) and appraisals and anxiety (see also Chapter 4). Some of the more recent research in this area suggests that threat appraisals mediate the relationship between basic psychological need satisfaction and anxiety intensity (Quested et al., 2012), are positively related to emotion-focused and avoidance coping and negatively related to problem-focused coping (Dias, Cruz, & Fonseca, 2012), and mediate the relationship between trait anxiety and burnout (Gomes, Faria, & Vilela, 2017; see also Chapter 7). Other researchers have focused more specifically on primary appraisals and coping and reported that there were no clear patterns in appraisal-coping associations among a sample of high standard swimmers (Didymus & Fletcher, 2014; see also Chapter 3). This speaks to the idiosyncrasies of appraising, coping, and the associations between them, and highlights the need to use sophisticated methods to capture the ways in which these concepts manifest to influence well-being and performance (e.g., Didymus & Fletcher, 2014).

Researchers have also examined the relationships between primary appraisals and various outcomes of stress transactions. These include mastery-based goals (Adie, Duda, & Ntoumanis, 2008), emotions (see also Chapter 4), performance (e.g., Didymus & Fletcher, 2017a, 2017b), and burnout (Gomes et al., 2017; see also Chapter 7). When considering the collective contribution of sport psychology literature in this area, it seems that challenge appraisals are related to adaptive outcomes that have the potential to be interpreted as facilitative for sport performance. It also seems that threat appraisals can be reappraised and or manipulated (e.g., with imagery [Williams & Cumming, 2012] or cognitive restructuring [Didymus & Fletcher, 2017b]) to generate more adaptive emotions, enhanced well-being, and superior performance. Although research has become more sophisticated in recent years by incorporating various person and situation factors into the study of appraising (e.g., Delahaij, Gaillard, & van Dam, 2010), by using more refined methods (e.g., diaries; Didymus & Fletcher, 2012, 2014), and by beginning to examine the interpersonal nature of appraising (e.g., Staff, Didymus, & Backhouse, 2017), many questions remain unanswered (e.g., about how appraising changes over time). Furthermore, limited attention has been paid to harm/loss and benefit appraisals that, alongside threat and challenge appraisals, influence athletes' health, well-being, and performance.

Secondary Appraising

If an athlete appraises a situation as relevant to his or her well-being during primary appraising and, thus, a stressful appraisal is made (i.e., an appraisal of challenge, benefit, threat, or harm/loss) he or she will engage in secondary appraising (see Table 2.1). Secondary appraising is more than an intellectual activity in evaluating what could be done to manage a given encounter; it is a complex process that considers the degree of control over the stressor, what coping resources are available, the likelihood of a given coping strategy effectively dealing with the situation, and the possibility that one can employ a particular strategy effectively (Lazarus & Folkman, 1984). It can be seen, therefore, that secondary appraising is important for determining the coping options that will be deployed, at least in theory (see also Chapter 3). Empirical research (e.g., Nicholls, Perry, & Calmeiro, 2014) has suggested that emotions may be equally important for shaping coping among athletes but further work is needed to substantiate this claim.

Sport psychology researchers have examined athletes' secondary appraisals in a number of ways (e.g., by assessing perceived control over stressors). In one such study, Kaiseler, Polman, and Nicholls (2009) found that being in control of one's emotions may be beneficial because higher emotional control contributed to less perceived stress among a sample of 482 athletes. In two other studies, Nicholls et al. (2012) and Williams and Cumming (2012) found that threat appraisals were associated with significantly less perceived control than challenge appraisals. It appears, therefore, that practitioners should educate athletes and coaches about the importance of challenge appraisals for perceptions of control and about the helpfulness of perceived control for perceptions of stressor intensity (see also Chapter 1).

Another approach that researchers have taken to examining secondary appraising has been to explore some of the person factors (e.g., culture, personality, gender, and mental toughness) that are influential in performers' perceptions of control. To illustrate, Puente-Díaz and Anshel (2005) suggested that culture can predict stressor controllability, and Kaiseler, Polman, and Nicholls (2012a) highlighted that neuroticism and conscientiousness can predict lower and higher perceived stressor control respectively (see also Chapter 10). Kaiseler, Polman, and Nicholls (2012b) focused on the role of gender in secondary appraising and concluded that female soccer players perceived less control over the same stressors than males. Gender, therefore, seems to influence secondary appraising and it may be that other factors (e.g., age and skill level) mediate and or moderate the relationship between the two. Also worth considering is the link between mental toughness and secondary appraising. This is because mental toughness has been shown to be associated with control appraisals (Kaiseler et al., 2009) and higher levels of coping self-efficacy (see Table 2.1; Nicholls, Levy, Polman, & Crust, 2011). Further research in this area and on related constructs (e.g., psychological resilience) would help to better understand how these psychological abilities may (or may not) facilitate more adaptive appraisals.

We have discussed primary and secondary appraising separately in this chapter because little research has examined the complete appraising process. One example of work that has examined appraising more comprehensively is a qualitative study in which the association between appraisals and emotions were explored among 12 elite athletes (Uphill & Jones, 2007). Because emotions are thought to arise from a core relational theme (see Table 2.1), this study can be considered one that examines primary and secondary appraising, albeit indirectly. Eight emotions (anger, anxiety, guilt, happiness, pride, relief, sadness, and shame) considered by Lazarus (2000) to be applicable to sport were reported by athletes to have occurred while competing, and some athletes reported experiencing other emotions (e.g., excitement) as well (Uphill & Jones, 2007; see also Chapter 4). While there was some support for aspects of the CMRT of stress and emotion (Lazarus, 1999), there were notable exceptions. For example, pride was not solely associated with taking credit for an achievement as outlined by CMRT but also with perceptions of individual achievement and with being a member of an elite few.

Situation Factors That Influence Appraising

When considered in relation to various person factors, situation factors (see Table 2.1) help to determine the potential for a stressful appraisal. Lazarus and Folkman (1984) suggested that it is not the situation (i.e., stressor) per se that influences appraising but the situational properties that underpin them. Situational properties are important because it is the individual's perception of the relevance of the properties to his or her well-being that leads to a stressful appraisal. Eight situational properties were originally proposed by Lazarus and Folkman (1984): novelty, predictability, event uncertainty, imminence, duration, temporal uncertainty, timing in relation to life cycle, and ambiguity (see also Chapter 1). Despite seminal works (e.g., Lazarus, 1999; Lazarus & Folkman, 1984) highlighting the importance of these properties rather than stressors themselves, the majority of literature, particularly in sport psychology, has focused on listing and categorizing the infinite number of stressors that athletes and coaches may encounter. We suggest that, instead, researchers' attention should focus on the finite number of situational properties and their influences on stress transactions (see also Chapter 1).

Most of the limited research that has explored situational properties of stressors in sport has focused on a single property and its influence on appraising. However, Didymus and Fletcher (2012, 2017a) and Didymus (2017), for example, took aggregate approaches by examining the relevance of each of the properties to various samples of athletes and coaches. Each of these studies found support for the notion that stressors may be underpinned by situational properties, and the work by Didymus and Fletcher (2012) highlighted that imminence and duration were most likely to be associated with maladaptive appraisals among a sample of high standard swimmers. Thus, the imminence and duration of stressors may be red flags during athletes' stress transactions because they have the potential to generate threat and harm/loss appraisals and, in turn, negatively valenced emotions and inferior performance (e.g., Lazarus, 2000). If this is indeed the case, practitioners would need to consider the timing of their interventions with athletes and coaches, and how an intervention may need to change as stressors become chronic (see also Chapter 1). Further research is needed to substantiate these claims and to allow robust recommendations to be made.

Person Factors That Influence Appraising

Person factors (see Table 2.1) incorporate the individual differences that mediate or moderate appraising. In addition to the aforementioned factors (i.e., culture, personality, gender, and mental toughness) that have been examined in relation to secondary appraising, many other person factors exist that effect how an individual appraises stressors. These include commitments and beliefs (Lazarus & Folkman, 1984), hardiness (e.g., Delahaij et al., 2010), optimism and hostility (Power & Hill, 2010), and self-concept clarity (e.g., Lee-Flynn, Pomaki, DeLongis, Biesanz, & Puterman, 2011). In sport, the influence of person factors on appraising has been more widely researched than situational influences but the literature remains in a relatively infantile state when compared to the relevant general psychology literature. Commitments and beliefs are the two key person factors that are highlighted in transactional stress theory (Lazarus & Folkman, 1984). Interestingly, these factors have not been explored in any depth in sport, which may be due to the difficulty in measuring their influences on appraising.

Commitments are a motivation factor that helps individuals to establish whether an event is important to their well-being and what is at stake in any given situation (Hilton, 1989). An encounter that involves strong commitments will be appraised as meaningful and, thus, the situation will influence an individual's well-being (Lazarus & Folkman, 1984). In sport, the relationships between commitments and appraising are not yet clear. In one study in this area, Ben-Ari, Tsur, and Har-Even (2006) found that higher procedural justice was associated with more positive appraisals and greater team commitment, and that the association between procedural justice and team commitment was mediated by appraisals. Beliefs have been defined as "cognitive configurations (e.g., schemas or scripts) that convey perceptions of reality" (Tomaka & Blascovich, 1994, p. 732) and are thought to affect appraising in at least two ways. First, they act as a perceptual lens that determines "what is fact, that is, 'how things are' in the environment" (Lazarus & Folkman, 1984, p. 63). Second, beliefs help an individual to shape their understanding of the meaning of a particular encounter. For example, a sport coach's autocratic behavior will mean something different to an athlete with high personal control beliefs when compared to his or her counterpart with low personal control beliefs. The links between beliefs and appraising do, however, need further examination with athletes and coaches to better understand how the aforementioned theoretical assumptions manifest.

The situation and person factors that have been outlined in this chapter will influence stress transactions concurrently. It is likely to be a complex and idiosyncratic combination of situation and person factors that influences appraising during any given stress transaction. This is one of the reasons why appraising is difficult to study and is poorly understood in sport. The majority of the findings that relate to situation and person factors have not been discussed or replicated extensively, which makes it difficult to draw firm conclusions about the various influences of them. We can, however, be confident that appraising is not only a complex process in itself but one that is mediated and moderated by many interdependent factors that generate psychological and psychophysiological outcomes (Fletcher, Hanton, & Mellalieu, 2006).

Appraisals and Psychophysiological Outcomes of Stress

One approach that has gathered recent research interest is that which explores the relationship between challenge and threat appraisals and psychophysiological outcomes (see Blascovich & Mendes, 2000; Jones et al., 2009; Vine, Moore, & Wilson, 2016; see also Chapter 5). We focus on this approach in the current chapter but recognize that other explanatory approaches to appraisals and physiological responses do exist (see, e.g., Hudson, Davison, & Robinson, 2013). The biopsychosocial (BPS) model of challenge and threat proposed by Blascovich and colleagues (Blascovich & Mendes, 2000; Blascovich & Tomaka, 1996) built on the concept of physiological toughness (Dienstbier, 1989) and Lazarus and Folkman's (1984) transactional stress theory to describe how psychophysiological outcomes of motivated performance situations are either helpful or unhelpful. According to the BPS model, the motivational states of challenge and threat are reflected in distinct patterns of cardiovascular reactivity. As both challenge and threat states result from activation of the sympathetic nervous system (SNS), both show increased heart rate. However, in a challenge state it is proposed that the sympathetic adreno-medullary (SAM) system and the resultant catecholamine output (epinephrine and norepinephrine) increases cardiac output (CO; see Table 2.1) and decreases vascular resistance (total peripheral resistance [TPR]; see Table 2.1). A threat state is marked by increased activation of the SAM system but is also accompanied by increased pituitary adreno-cortical (PAC) activity and increased levels of cortisol, which inhibits catecholamine output as reflected by little or no change in CO and an increase in TPR (Blascovich & Tomaka, 1996; Dienstbier, 1989).

The mechanisms behind the cardiovascular patterns of challenge and threat and the relative contribution of the SAM and PAC systems have been debated (e.g., Wright & Kirby, 2003). Some of the most recent explanations have focused on the temporal aspects of the SNS response, proposing that challenge states result from a quick SNS response that speedily habituates, whereas threat states have a slower rise in SNS activity that tends to stay elevated for a longer period of time (Epel et al., 2018). It is this response that is thought to be reflected in the differing patterns of challenge and threat cardiovascular reactivity. There is consistent evidence linking patterns of cardiovascular reactivity to performance outcomes in sport and other settings, with a challenge state being associated with better performance than a threat state (see, for a review, Hase, O'Brien, Moore, & Freeman, 2018).

The Theory of Challenge and Threat States in Athletes (TCTSA; Jones et al., 2009; Meijen, Turner, Jones, Sheffield, & McCarthy, 2020) sought to build on the work of Blascovich and colleagues by describing the cognitive, emotional, and physiological aspects of challenge and threat along with potential performance consequences in sport. In the TCTSA it was proposed that a unique combination of psychological constructs (self-efficacy, perceived control, and an approach focus) interact to determine challenge and threat states. Specifically, in a challenge state an individual has high self-efficacy, high perceived control, and an approach focus. In a threat state, however, there is low self-efficacy, low perceived control, and an avoidance focus. Despite the propositions of the TCTSA, there is mixed evidence to support the proposed relationships between the resource appraisals, cardiovascular indices of challenge and threat, and emotions. Some published studies support the proposed relationships (e.g., Trotman, Williams, Quinton, & Veldhuijzen van Zanten, 2018) while others do not (e.g., Meijen, Jones, McCarthy, & Sheffield, 2014). The findings of Trotman et al. (2018) are pertinent because there was support for the central tenets of the TCTSA during competitive stress but not social stress, suggesting that the type of task may have an impact on the relationship between appraisals and cardiovascular reactivity.

While there is mixed evidence on the link between resource appraisals and physiological outcomes, there is more consistent evidence that improving resource appraisals (e.g., with imagery; Williams, Veldhuijzen van Zanten, Trotman, Quinton, & Ginty, 2017) can impact challenge states. This research shows that cardiovascular reactivity indicating challenge and threat states can be successfully manipulated using instructional sets that focus either on altering perceived demands of an upcoming task or on altering perceived task importance, perceived demands, and perceived resources (e.g., Moore, Wilson, Vine, Coussens, & Freeman, 2013). In a similar study, Turner, Jones, Sheffield, Barker, and Coffee (2014) manipulated task instructions to alter only the perceptions of personal resources. By using only resource appraisals to manipulate challenge and threat cardiovascular reactivity, Turner et al. (2014) attempted to enhance the perceived resources of the participant while recognizing that the demands of the situation may remain high. This approach may be particularly useful in situations that are clearly demanding and personally relevant to an individual (e.g., when an athlete has an important trial game coming up). By emphasizing high self-efficacy, high perceived control, and an approach focus, participants reported cardiovascular reactivity indicative of a challenge state in competitive and physically demanding tasks (Turner et al., 2014).

Physiological outcomes of stress can also be changed by reappraising the value and potential performance benefits of the stress experience. There is evidence that reappraisal can facilitate challenge perceptions in both examinations (Jamieson, Mendes, Blackstock, & Schmader, 2010) and speech tasks (Jamieson, Nock, & Mendes, 2012), and that trait reappraisal is linked to stress resilience (Carlson, Dikecligil, Greenberg, & Mujica-Parodi, 2012). Reappraisal may also have utility in helping people change from a threat to a challenge state in a sports task. For example, Moore, Vine, Wilson, and Freeman (2015) showed that a reappraisal intervention shifted cardiovascular patterns from that which is indicative of a threat state to that which suggests a challenge state during a golf putting task. Although this shift was not statistically significant, the reappraisal group did outperform a control group.

Conclusion

This chapter has briefly explored stress, appraising, and appraisals using a transactional lens. In doing so, it has highlighted the pivotal roles of primary and secondary appraising, has directed attention to some of the influential situation and person factors, and has shed light on the links between appraisals and psychophysiological outcomes. Researchers are encouraged to address some of the research priorities that are raised by the discussions in this chapter. For example, situational properties of stressors could be prioritized over a focus on stressors themselves; more research should examine the complete appraising process in sport, including appraisals of emotions (Fletcher et al., 2006) and links between appraising and performance; we need to know more about the underlying mechanisms of appraising and cardiovascular patterns of challenge and threat; and much work is to be done before we fully understand the influence of situation and person factors. Researchers and practitioners should keep in mind the practical significance of appraisals for health, well-being, and performance. Practitioners would do well to educate athletes about the importance of challenge appraisals for fostering adaptive outcomes of stress and should work with clients to change both conscious and subconscious thoughts about stressors. The dynamic nature of transactions means that practitioners must implement stress optimization interventions in a timely and proactive manner (see also Chapter 12).

To make progress with research on appraising, methodological advances are required. While scales such as the Perceived Stress Scale (Cohen, Kamarck, & Mermelstein, 1983) have been developed to measure how stressful an encounter is, and others including the Stress Appraisal Measure (Peacock & Wong, 1990) and the Appraisal of Life Events Scale (Ferguson, Matthews, & Cox, 1999) examine how stressful encounters are appraised, the normative measurement of appraising is yet to be standardized. Other measurement approaches such as interviews (e.g., Didymus & Fletcher, 2017a) and scenario cards (Guillet, Hermand, & Mullet, 2002) have been used but these methods usually only capture snapshots of stress transactions. Methodological advances (e.g., diaries, event sequence analysis, and think aloud protocols) are required to capture the complex, evaluative nature of appraising. By making these advances and forging new lines of enquiry, more robust recommendations about how best to optimize appraising and bolster well-being and performance can be made.

References

Adie, J. W., Duda, J. L., & Ntoumanis, N. (2008). Achievement goals, competition appraisals, and the psychological and emotional welfare of sport participants. *Journal of Sport and Exercise Psychology, 30*, 302–322. Doi:10.1123/jsep.30.3.302

Bartholomew, K. J., Arnold, R., Hampson, R. J., & Fletcher, D. (2017). Organizational stressors and basic psychological needs: The mediating role of athletes' appraisal mechanisms. *Scandinavian Journal of Medicine and Science in Sports, 27*, 2127–2139. Doi:10.1111/sms.12851

Ben-Ari, R., Tsur, Y., & Har-Even, D. (2006). Procedural justice, stress appraisal, and athletes' attitudes. *International Journal of Stress Management, 13*, 23–44. Doi:10.1037/1072-5245.13.1.23

Blascovich, J., & Mendes, W. B. (2000). Challenge and threat appraisals: The role of affective cues. In J. P. Forgas (Ed.), *Feeling and thinking: The role of affect in social cognition* (pp. 59–82). Paris, France: Cambridge University Press.

Blascovich, J., Mendes, W. B., Hunter, S. B., Lickel, B., & Kowai-Bell, N. (2001). Perceiver threat in social interactions with stigmatized others. *Journal of Personality and Social Psychology, 80*, 253–267. Doi:10.1037//0022-3514.80.2.253

Blascovich, J., & Tomaka, J. (1996). The biopsychosocial model of arousal regulation. *Advances in Experimental Social Psychology, 28*, 1–51. Doi:10.1016/S0065-2601(08)60235-X

Carlson, J. M., Dikecligil, G. N., Greenberg, T., & Mujica-Parodi, L. R. (2012). Trait reappraisal is associated with resilience to acute psychological stress. *Journal of Research in Personality, 46*, 609–613. Doi:10.1016/j.jrp.2012.05.003

Cohen, S., Kamarck, T., & Mermelstein, R. (1983). A global measure of perceived stress. *Journal of Health and Social Behavior, 24*, 385–396. Retrieved from http://hsb.sagepub.com/

Delahaij, R., Gaillard, A. W. K., & van Dam, K. (2010). Hardiness and the response to stressful situations: Investigating mediating processes. *Personality and Individual Differences, 49*, 386–390. Doi:10.1016/j.paid.2010.04.002

Dias, C., Cruz, J. F., & Fonseca, M. (2012). The relationship between multidimensional competitive anxiety, cognitive threat appraisal, and coping strategies: A multi-sport study. *International Journal of Sport and Exercise Psychology, 10*, 52–65. Doi:10.1080/1612197X.2012.645131

Didymus, F. F. (2017). Olympic and international level sports coaches' experiences of stressors, appraisals, and coping. *Qualitative Research in Sport, Exercise and Health, 2*, 214–232. Doi:10.1080/2159676X.2016.1261364

Didymus, F. F., & Fletcher, D. (2012). Getting to the heart of the matter: A diary study of swimmers' appraisals of organisational stressors. *Journal of Sports Sciences, 30*, 1375–1385. Doi:10.1080/02640414.2012.709263

Didymus, F. F., & Fletcher, D. (2014). Swimmers' experiences of organizational stress: Exploring the role of cognitive appraisal and coping strategies. *Journal of Clinical Sport Psychology, 8*, 159–183. Doi:10.1123/jcsp.2014-0020

Didymus, F. F., & Fletcher, D. (2017a). Organizational stress in high-level field hockey: Examining transactional pathways between stressors, appraisals, coping and performance satisfaction. *International Journal of Sports Science & Coaching, 12*, 252–263. Doi:10.1177/1747954117694737

Didymus, F. F., & Fletcher, D. (2017b). Effects of a cognitive-behavioral intervention on field hockey players' appraisals of organizational stressors. *Psychology of Sport and Exercise, 30*, 173–185. Doi:10.1016/j.psychsport.2017.03.005

Dienstbier, R. A. (1989). Arousal and physiological toughness: Implications for mental and physical health. *Psychological Review, 96*, 84–100. Doi:10.1037/0033-295X.96.1.84

Epel, E. S., Crosswell, A. D., Mayer, S. E., Prather, A. A., Slavich, G. M., Puterman, E., & Mendes, W. B. (2018). More than a feeling: A unified view of stress measurement for population science. *Frontiers in Neuroendocrinology, 49*, 146–169. Doi:10.1016/j.yfrne.2018.03.001

Ferguson, E., Matthews, G., & Cox, T. (1999). The Appraisal of Life Events (ALE) scale: Reliability and validity. *British Journal of Health Psychology, 4*, 97–116. Doi:10.1348/135910799168506

Fletcher, D., Hanton, S., & Mellalieu, S. D. (2006). An organizational stress review: Conceptual and theoretical issues in competitive sport. In S. Hanton & S. D. Mellalieu (Eds.), *Literature reviews in sport psychology* (pp. 321–374). Hauppauge, NY: Nova Science Publishers.

Gan, Q., & Anshel, M. H. (2006). Differences between elite and non-elite, male and female Chinese athletes on cognitive appraisal of stressful events in competitive sport. *Journal of Sport Behavior, 29*, 213–228. Retrieved from http://southalabama.edu/psychology/journal.html

Gomes, A. R., Faria, S., & Vilela, C. (2017). Anxiety and burnout in young athletes: The mediating role of cognitive appraisal. *Scandinavian Journal of Medicine and Science in Sports, 27*, 2116–2126. Doi:10.1111/sms.12841

Guillet, L., Hermand, D., & Mullet, E. (2002). Cognitive processes involved in the appraisal of stress. *Stress & Health: Journal of the International Society for the Investigation of Stress, 18*, 91–102. Doi:10.1002/smi.927

Hase, A., O'Brien, J., Moore, L., & Freeman, P. (2018). The relationship between challenge and threat states and performance: A systematic review. *Sport, Exercise, and Performance Psychology, 8*, 123–144. Doi:10.1037/spy0000132

Hilton, B. A. (1989). The relationship of uncertainty, control, commitment, and threat of recurrence to coping strategies used by women diagnosed with breast cancer. *Journal of Behavioral Medicine, 12*, 39–54. Doi:10.1007/BF00844748

Hudson, J., Davison, G., & Robinson, P. (2013). Psychophysiological and stress responses to competition in team sport coaches: An exploratory study. *Scandinavian Journal of Medicine & Science in Sports, 3*, 279–285. Doi:10.1111/sms.12075

Jamieson, J. P., Mendes, W. B., Blackstock, E., & Schmader, T. (2010). Turning the knots in your stomach into bows: Reappraising arousal improves performance on the GRE. *Journal of Experimental Social Psychology, 46*, 208–212. Doi:10.1016/j.jesp.2009.08.015

Jamieson, J. P., Nock, M. K., & Mendes, W. B. (2012). Mind over matter: Reappraising arousal improves cardiovascular and cognitive responses to stress. *Journal of Experimental Psychology: General, 141*, 417–422. Doi:10.1037/a0025719.

Jones, M. V. (2003). Controlling emotions in sport. *The Sport Psychologist, 17*, 471–486. Doi:10.1123/tsp.17.4.471

Jones, M. V., Meijen, C., McCarthy, P. J., & Sheffield, D. (2009). A theory of challenge and threat states in athletes. *International Review of Sport and Exercise Psychology, 2*, 161–180. Doi:10.1080/17509840902829331

Kaiseler, M., Polman, R. C. J., & Nicholls, A. R. (2009). Mental toughness, stress, stress appraisal, coping, and coping effectiveness in sport. *Personality and Individual Differences, 47*, 728–733. Doi:10.1016/j.paid.2009.06.012

Kaiseler, M., Polman, R. C. J., & Nicholls, A. R. (2012a). Effects of the big five personality dimensions on appraisal, coping, and coping effectiveness in sport. *European Journal of Sport Science, 12*, 62–72. Doi:10.1080/17461391.2010.551410

Kaiseler, M., Polman, R. C. J., & Nicholls, A. R. (2012b). Gender differences in appraisal and coping: An examination of the situational and dispositional hypothesis. *International Journal of Sport Psychology, 43*, 1–14. Retrieved from http://ijsp-online.com

Lazarus, R. S. (1991). *Emotion and adaptation.* New York: Oxford University Press.

Lazarus, R. S. (1999). *Stress and emotion: A new synthesis.* New York: Springer.

Lazarus, R. S. (2000). How emotions influence performance in competitive sports. *The Sport Psychologist, 14*, 229–252. Doi:10.1123/tsp.14.3.229

Lazarus, R. S., & Folkman, S. (1984). *Stress, appraisal, and coping.* New York: Springer.

Lee-Flynn, S. C., Pomaki, G., DeLongis, A., Biesanz, J. C., & Puterman, E. (2011). Daily cognitive appraisals, daily affect, and long-term depressive symptoms: The role of self-esteem and self-concept clarity in the stress process. *Personality and Social Psychology Bulletin, 37*, 255–268. Doi:10.1177/0146167210394204

Meijen, C., Jones, M. V., McCarthy, P. J., & Sheffield, D. (2014). Challenge and threat states: Cardiovascular, affective and cognitive responses to a sports-related speech task. *Motivation and Emotion*, *38*, 252–262. Doi:10.1007/s11031-013-9370-5

Meijen, C., Turner, M., Jones, M. V., Sheffield, D., & McCarthy, P. (2020). A Theory of Challenge and Threat States in Athletes: A revised conceptualization. *Frontiers in Psychology*, *11*, 126. Doi:10.3389/fpsyg.2020.00126

Moore, L. J., Freeman, P., Hase, A., Solomon-Moore, E., & Arnold, A. (2019). How consistent are challenge and threat evaluations? A generalizability analysis. *Frontiers in Psychology*, *10*, 1778. Doi:10.3389/fpsyg.2019.01778

Moore, L. J., Vine, S. J., Wilson, M. R., & Freeman, P. (2012). The effect of challenge and threat states on performance: An examination of potential mechanisms. *Psychophysiology*, *49*, 1417–1425. Doi:10.1111/j.1469-8986.2012.01449.x

Moore, L. J., Vine, S. J., Wilson, M. R., & Freeman, P. (2015). Reappraising threat: How to optimize performance under pressure. *Journal of Sport and Exercise Psychology*, *37*, 339–343. Doi:10.1123/jsep.2014-0186

Moore, L. J., Wilson, M. R., Vine, S. J., Coussens, A. H., & Freeman, P. (2013). Champ or chump?: Challenge and threat states during pressurized competition. *Journal of Sport and Exercise Psychology*, *35*, 551–562. Doi:10.1123/jsep.35.6.551

Nicholls, A. R., Levy, A. R., Polman, R. C. J., & Crust, L. (2011). Mental toughness, coping self-efficacy, and coping effectiveness among athletes. *International Journal of Sport Psychology*, *42*, 513–524. Retrieved from http://ijsp-online.com/

Nicholls, A. R., Perry, J. L., & Calmeiro, L. (2014). Precompetitive achievement goals, stress appraisals, emotions, and coping among athletes. *Journal of Sport and Exercise Psychology*, *36*, 433–445. Doi:10.1123/jsep.2013-0266

Nicholls, A. R., Polman, R. C. J., & Levy, A. R. (2012). A path analysis of stress appraisals, emotions, coping, and performance satisfaction among athletes. *Psychology of Sport and Exercise*, *13*, 263–270. Doi:10.1016/j.psychsport.2011.12.003

Ohly, S., & Fritz, C. (2010). Work characteristics, challenge appraisal, creativity, and proactive behavior: A multi-level study. *Journal of Organizational Behavior*, *31*, 543–565. Doi:10.1002/job.633

Padmanabhan, R., Hildreth, A. J., & Laws, D. (2005). A prospective, randomised, controlled study examining binaural beat audio and pre-operative anxiety in patients undergoing general anaesthesia for day case surgery. *Anaesthesia: Peri-operative Medicine, Critical Care and Pain*, *60*, 874–877. Doi:10.1111/j.1365-2044.2005.04287.x

Peacock, E. J., & Wong, P. T. P. (1990). The Stress Appraisal Measure (SAM): A multidimensional approach to cognitive appraisal. *Stress Medicine*, *6*, 227–236. Doi:10.1002/smi.2460060308

Power, T. G., & Hill, L. G. (2010). Individual differences in appraisal of minor, potentially stressful events: A cluster analytic approach. *Cognition and Emotion*, *24*, 1081–1094. Doi:10.1080/02699930903122463

Puente-Díaz, R., & Anshel, M. H. (2005). Sources of acute stress, cognitive appraisal, and coping strategies among highly skilled Mexican and U.S. competitive tennis players. *The Journal of Social Psychology*, *145*, 429–446. Doi:10.3200/SOCP.145.4.429-446

Quested, E., Bosch, J. A., Burns, V. E., Cumming, J., Ntoumanis, N., & Duda, J. L. (2012). Basic psychological need satisfaction, stress-related appraisals, and dancers' cortisol and anxiety responses. *Journal of Sport and Exercise Psychology,* *33*, 828–846. Doi:10.1123/jsep.33.6.828

Scanlan, T. K., Stein, G. L., & Ravizza, K. (1991). An in-depth study of former elite figure skaters: III. Sources of stress. *Journal of Sport and Exercise Psychology,* *13*, 103–120. Doi:10.1123/jsep.13.2.103

Staff, H. R., Didymus, F. F., & Backhouse, S. H. (2017). Coping rarely takes place in a social vacuum: Exploring antecedents and outcomes of dyadic coping in coach-athlete relationships. *Psychology of Sport and Exercise, 30,* 91–100. Doi:10.1016/j.psychsport.2017.02.009

Tomaka, J., & Blascovich, J. (1994). Effects of justice beliefs on cognitive appraisal of and subjective, physiological, and behavioral responses to potential stress. *Journal of Personality and Social Psychology, 67,* 732–740. Doi:10.1037/0022-3514.67.4.732

Trotman, G. P., Williams, S. E., Quinton, M. L., & Veldhuijzen van Zanten, J. J. C. S. (2018). Challenge and threat states: Examining cardiovascular, cognitive and affective responses to two distinct laboratory stress tasks. *International Journal of Psychophysiology, 126,* 42–51. Doi:10.1016/J.IJPSYCHO.2018.02.004

Turner, M. J., Jones, M. V., Sheffield, D., Barker, J. B., & Coffee, P. (2014). Manipulating cardiovascular indices of challenge and threat using resource appraisals. *International Journal of Psychophysiology, 94,* 9–18. Doi:10.1016/j.ijpsycho.2014.07.004

Uphill, M. A., & Jones, M. V. (2007). The antecedents of emotions in elite athletes. *Research Quarterly for Sport and Exercise, 78,* 79–89. Doi:10.1080/0270136 7.2007.10599406

Vine, S. J., Moore, L. J., & Wilson, M. R. (2016). An integrative framework of stress, attention, and visuomotor performance. *Frontiers in Psychology, 7,* 1671. Doi:10.3389/fpsyg.2016.01671

Williams, S. E., & Cumming, J. (2012). Sport imagery ability predicts trait confidence, and challenge and threat appraisal tendencies. *European Journal of Sport Science, 6,* 499–508. Doi:10.1080/17461391.2011.630102

Williams, S. E., Veldhuijzen van Zanten, J. J. C. S., Trotman, G. P., Quinton, M. L., & Ginty, A. T. (2017). Challenge and threat imagery manipulates heart rate and anxiety responses to stress. *International Journal of Psychophysiology, 117,* 111–118. Doi:10.1016/j.ijpsycho.2017.04.011

Wright, R. A., & Kirby, L. D. (2003). Cardiovascular correlates of challenge and threat appraisals: A critical examination of the biopsychosocial analysis. *Personality and Social Psychology Review, 7,* 216–233. Doi:10.1207/ S15327957PSPR0703_02

3 Coping

Katherine A. Tamminen

Introduction

Whether the aim is to help athletes deal with specific performance-related stressors, to achieve success in competition, or to develop and maintain productive relationships with others, many sport psychology practitioners and researchers share a common focus of seeking to help athletes cope with the demands of their sport and adapt to the changing conditions they face in relation to their sport participation. Thus, fundamentally, coping is at the core of much of the research and practice within the field of sport psychology.

Coping is defined as "constantly changing cognitive and behavioural efforts to manage specific external and/or internal demands that are appraised as taxing or exceeding the resource of the person" (Lazarus & Folkman, 1984, p. 141). It is also important to note that coping is inseparable from appraisals of stressors, hassles, and adversities that athletes face in the course of their daily lives, and the emotions that arise within these situations. This dynamic perspective of coping helps to explain findings suggesting that, on the one hand, coping is a mediator of the association between appraisals and emotions (Doron & Martinent, 2017), and on the other hand that emotions and affect are antecedents of coping efforts (Martinent & Nicolas, 2017). The coping process is also described as transactional, which means that there are ongoing transactions between the individual and their environment that influence the person's stressor appraisals, their experience and emotions within the situation, and their coping efforts (Lazarus, 1999). Therefore, coping is one aspect of an ongoing, transactional process whereby individuals are continually appraising, responding, adjusting, and then reappraising and readjusting to their environment (see also Chapters 1, 2, and 4).

Classifying Coping Strategies

There have been multiple attempts to create measures and surveys to capture the ways that athletes deal with stressors in competitive performance settings. Some examples of these are the Athletic Coping Skills Inventory 28 (ACS-28; Smith, Schultz, Smoll, & Ptacek, 1995), the Modified COPE (MCOPE; Crocker & Graham, 1995), and the Coping Style in Sport Survey (CSSS; Anshel, William, & Williams, 2000). Beyond the development of these measures to capture the specific strategies that athletes use to cope with stressors in sport, theorists have proposed different perspectives to try and classify coping strategies according to the purpose or function that they serve. The following section presents two common frameworks that are used to categorize the strategies that individuals use to cope with stressors in sport contexts, followed by a review of research using these frameworks in sport.

Task-, Disengagement-, and Distraction-Oriented Coping

One popular approach to conceptualizing and classifying coping strategies among athletes was proposed by Gaudreau and Blondin (2002), who developed the Coping Inventory for Competitive Sport (CICS). This measure of coping provides a synthesis and classification of multiple coping strategies commonly used by athletes in dealing with stressors in competitive sport situations. The CICS contains 10 scales within three overarching categories. The first category of coping strategies is task-oriented coping, and it refers to "actions that are employed in order to change or master some aspects of a situation that is perceived as stressful" (Gaudreau & Blondin, 2002, p. 2). The second category of coping strategies is distraction-oriented coping, which concerns efforts to distract oneself or avoid the stressful situation. The final category, disengagement-oriented coping, includes strategies aimed at disengaging oneself from the task (see Table 3.1).

Problem-Focused, Emotion-Focused, and Avoidance Coping

A second popular approach to classifying coping strategies was proposed by Lazarus and Folkman (1984) and has been adapted for use in sport settings. This framework classifies coping strategies into two categories depending on their function to deal with the situation directly (problem-focused coping) or to try and manage the emotions arising from the situation (emotion-focused coping). Within sport, avoidance coping is also suggested as a category of coping strategies, although within Lazarus' (1999) original classification, strategies to avoid a stressor or to avoid thinking about a stressor would fall under the category of emotion-focused coping. However, the development of the Coping Function Questionnaire to measure coping among adolescent athletes provided evidence for a three-factor model that considers problem-focused coping, emotion-focused coping, and avoidance coping as separate dimensions (Kowalski & Crocker, 2001; see Table 3.1).

Table 3.1 Categories of Coping Strategies Within the Coping Inventory for Competitive Sport and the Coping Function Questionnaire

Category	Coping Strategy
Coping Inventory for Competitive Sport (Gaudreau & Blondin, 2002)	
Task-oriented coping	Mental imagery
	Relaxation
	Thought control
	Logical analysis
	Effort expenditure
	Seeking social support
Distraction-oriented coping	Mental distraction
	Distancing
Disengagement-oriented coping	Disengagement
	Resignation
	Venting of unpleasant emotions
Coping Function Questionnaire (Kowalski & Crocker, 2001; Lazarus, 1999)	
Problem-focused coping	Obtaining information about a problem
	Determining a plan of action
	Increasing effort
	Trying to change the situation
Emotion-focused coping	Positive reappraisal of the situation
	Seeing the situation in a favorable light
	Emotional control
	Relaxation
Avoidance coping	Mentally avoiding thinking about the situation
	Physically avoiding the situation

Research Findings on Coping in Sport

Coping and Performance

Coping plays a significant role in predicting objective and subjective assessments of performance outcomes in sport. For example, golfers' average performance over the course of a season was significantly predicted by their psychological coping resources, even when statistically controlling for the impact of their physical and technical skills on performance outcome (Christensen & Smith, 2018). These findings echo previous research demonstrating that baseball players' performance and career survival (i.e., length of time playing professional baseball) was significantly predicted by the athletes' coping resources (Smith & Christensen, 1995). Research among golfers also demonstrates that task-oriented coping strategy use was positively associated with subjective and objective measures of performance achievement, while disengagement-oriented coping strategy use was associated with poor performance outcomes (Gaudreau, Nicholls, & Levy, 2010). Additional evidence from a wide range of team and individual sport athletes indicated that the use of task-oriented coping strategies was associated with athletes' subjective assessments of their satisfaction with performance in competition (Nicholls, Perry, Jones, Morley, & Carson, 2013). Researchers using Lazarus' framework to classify coping strategies have also demonstrated that elite athletes appear to use more problem-focused coping and less emotion-focused coping compared to non-elite athletes, although elite athletes may demonstrate more flexibility in their choice of coping strategy (e.g., Calmeiro, Tenenbaum, & Eccles, 2014). Although athletes often use a combination of coping strategies to deal with the demands of a situation (Gaudreau & Blondin; 2004; Gould, Eklund, & Jackson, 1993; Martinent & Decret, 2015; Nicholls, Levy, & Perry, 2005; Tamminen & Holt, 2010), it is clear that having coping resources and deploying them appropriately is important for sport performance.

Coping and Well-Being

Athletes' coping is also associated with psychological well-being. For example, task-oriented coping strategies to deal with competitive stressors has been positively associated with athletes' well-being following competition, while disengagement-oriented coping was negatively associated with well-being (Nicholls, Levy, Carson, Thompson, & Perry, 2016). However, in this study, distraction-oriented coping was positively associated with well-being, suggesting that some athletes may find it useful to distract themselves from thinking about upcoming competitions to improve their well-being (Nicholls et al., 2016). Additional evidence from a longitudinal study of competitive adolescent table-tennis players demonstrated that athletes who tended to use high levels of task-oriented coping and low levels of disengagement- and distraction-oriented coping displayed the highest scores of general well-being, sleep quality, personal accomplishment, self-efficacy, and physical recovery (Martinent & Decret, 2015). Conversely, athletes who displayed high levels of distraction- or disengagement-oriented coping along with low levels of task-oriented coping had the highest scores for indicators of burnout (e.g., reduced accomplishment and sport devaluation) as well as higher general and sport-specific stress (see also Chapters 6 and 7).

Coping With Stressors Is Dynamic and Involves Multiple Strategies

Several studies have provided evidence in support of theoretical propositions that coping is a dynamic and changing process, and that athletes use multiple strategies to cope with stressors. Within competitive contexts, athletes' coping has been found to fluctuate over the course of a competition in response to their stressor appraisals and the emotions that arise during competition (Martinent & Nicolas, 2017; see also

Chapters 2 and 4). Furthermore, athletes' coping is also influenced by their achievement goals, stressor appraisals, and emotions in the lead-up to competition (Miles, Neil, & Barker, 2016), and athletes' coping strategy use also changes or fluctuates over longer periods of time. For example, longitudinal studies of rugby players (Nicholls, Holt, Polman, & Bloomfield, 2006), youth golfers (Nicholls, Holt, Polman, & James, 2005), table-tennis players (Martinent & Decret, 2015), and basketball athletes (Tamminen & Holt, 2012) have all demonstrated fluctuations in athletes' use of coping strategies over time across their competitive seasons.

Evidence from qualitative studies indicates that athletes use multiple strategies in combination to cope with stressors (Gould et al., 1993; Nicholls et al., 2005; Tamminen & Holt, 2010), and these coping strategies are selectively applied depending on the specific nature of the situation, the athlete's appraisals of the situation, and the resources he or she has to deal with the situation (Dale, 2000; Holt & Hogg, 2002). In support of these qualitative findings, researchers have provided further quantitative evidence that athletes display different combinations of coping strategies to cope with stressors. For example, Gaudreau and Blondin (2004) reported four different profiles of coping and demonstrated associations between these profiles of coping with athletes' affective states, perceptions of control, and goal attainment. Athletes who reported high levels of task-oriented coping and low levels of disengagement-oriented coping had significantly lower levels of negative affect and higher levels of positive affect, higher subjective goal achievement, and greater experience of control when dealing with competitive stressors compared to athletes who reported high levels of disengagement-oriented coping and low levels of task-oriented coping.

Coping and Personality, Gender, and Culture

Personality factors have been associated with the use of different types of coping strategies to deal with sport-related stressors. For example, problem-focused coping appears to be more likely to be used by athletes with high levels of extraversion as well as higher openness and emotional stability; emotion-focused coping is predicted by greater conscientiousness, openness, and agreeableness; and avoidance coping is associated with low openness and low emotional stability (Allen, Greenlees, & Jones, 2011). Additional research findings have demonstrated that task-oriented coping is associated with higher levels of neuroticism in combination with higher openness to new experiences, while athletes with lower neuroticism and low extraversion were less likely to use task-oriented coping (Kaiseler, Levy, Nicholls, & Madigan, 2019). Additionally, athletes with lower levels of agreeableness and lower conscientiousness were more likely to report using distraction-oriented coping to deal with sport stressors. Overall, these findings suggest that some athletes may tend to use particular types of coping strategies depending on their personality traits (see also Chapter 10). There is also evidence that athletes may adopt particular "styles" of coping with stressors (e.g., trait approach). In a systematic review of coping studies in sport, 11 out of 64 studies provided evidence that athletes demonstrated consistency in their approach to coping with stressors (Nicholls & Polman, 2007). Although the majority of studies provided evidence for a process approach to coping (e.g., athletes used different coping strategies depending on the stressor they encountered), further research is required to examine the consistency and stability of athletes' approaches to coping with stressors, as well as the development of adaptive and maladaptive styles or profiles of coping (see Gaudreau & Blondin, 2004; Hurst, Thompson, Visek, Fisher, & Gaudreau, 2011).

Of the studies that have examined gender differences in coping, the findings have been equivocal: some studies suggest that female athletes use more emotion-focused and avoidant coping, whereas male athletes use more problem-focused and approach-oriented coping (e.g., Gan, Anshel, & Kim, 2009); conversely, other studies have found no gender differences that males use more problem-focused coping than females (e.g., Bolgar, Janelle, & Giacobbi, 2008; Crocker & Graham, 1995), and recent research suggests that female athletes may use more problem-focused coping than males (Nicholls, Polman, Levy, Taylor, & Cobley, 2007). These conflicting findings are further complicated by the idea that different athletes will use different combinations of coping strategies to deal with different stressors, based on their appraisals of the situation and their coping resources.

Cultural differences in coping might also be expected between athletes, as culture is thought to influence all aspects of the coping process and contribute to the socialization of coping strategies that individuals might use (Chun, Moos, & Cronkite, 2006). However, there is limited research that has investigated cultural differences in coping among athletes. Kim and Duda (2003) found considerable similarity in the coping strategies reported by U.S. and Korean athletes: these participants used emotion regulation, problem-focused, and seeking social support coping strategies to deal with controllable stressors. However, the Korean athletes also reported a greater likelihood to use behavioral risk (a type of approach- or task-oriented coping) when facing controllable stressors, and they also reported turning to religion to cope with controllable and uncontrollable stressors. Some studies have also demonstrated differences in the use of coping strategies between U.S. and Australian (Anshel, Williams, & Hodge, 1997) and between Australian and Dutch athletes (Dollen, Grove, & Pepping, 2015). Overall, there is some evidence for differences in coping due to personality, gender, and cultural differences; however, given the complexity of coping processes, researchers have called for further examination of these differences in response to particular stressors and as a function of athletes' stressor appraisals (Gan et al., 2009; Hoar, Crocker, Holt, & Tamminen, 2010; Nicholls et al., 2007).

Development of Coping Across the Lifespan

Coping strategy use also differs among athletes of different ages and developmental status, which reflects changes in athletes' capacity for coping with stressors in sport. A review of research on coping in youth sport (Holt, Hoar, & Fraser, 2005) suggested that young athletes tend to rely on primarily behavioral strategies to deal with stressors (as opposed to cognitive strategies), including actions such as seeking social support, active problem-solving, isolation, and withdrawal. Subsequent research has provided evidence that middle adolescent athletes (aged 15–18 years) appear to use a wider range of coping strategies compared to early adolescents (aged 12–14 years), and middle adolescents appear to use more problem- and emotion-focused coping and less avoidance coping than early adolescents (Reeves, Nicholls, & McKenna, 2009). Older adolescent athletes have also been found to report less use of mental imagery (a type of task-oriented coping), and more venting of negative emotions (a type of disengagement-oriented coping) when dealing with stressors in sport compared to younger athletes (Nicholls, Polman, Morley, & Taylor, 2009). The differences observed in athletes' coping may be related to their emotional and social-cognitive maturity, as athletes between the ages of 12 and 18 years who exhibited greater emotional maturity reported greater use of task-oriented coping when dealing with competitive stressors, although emotional maturity was unrelated to disengagement- and distraction-oriented coping strategy use (Nicholls et al., 2015).

While there are studies documenting differences in coping among athletes at different ages and developmental levels, there is relatively little research that has explored exactly how coping skills develop among young athletes. Tamminen and Holt (2012) suggested that young athletes learn to cope with stressors in sport through a process of trial and error that occurs through exposure to various sport experiences and by engaging in reflective practice. Furthermore, coping skill development was facilitated by parents and coaches, which emphasizes the role of socialization processes and the influence of supportive adults in the development of young athletes' coping (Tamminen & Holt, 2012). The findings from this research suggest several approaches to help develop coping skills among young athletes, including: (i) developing a supportive, trusting context for learning about coping; (ii) asking questions of the athlete in a supportive manner to prompt reflection on the ways they have coped with stressors in the past; (iii) reminding athletes about past situations and coping strategies; (iv) providing perspective and sharing experiences with the athlete; (v) initiating informal conversations about coping; and (vi) creating learning opportunities and providing structured or scaffolded exposure to stressors that enable opportunities for athletes to try and cope with the situation and to reflect upon their efforts (see also Chapter 12).

Collectively, these findings suggest that athletes at different developmental levels should not be expected to cope in the same ways, and that athletes' approaches to coping with stressors are likely to change as they grow and mature. A further implication of these findings is that it is important to consider the developmental stage of the athlete when teaching athletes about coping in sport, and that more research is required to examine optimal developmentally appropriate strategies for teaching young athletes about coping in sport.

Social Influences on Coping

Athletes' efforts to cope with stressors do not occur in a social vacuum: athletes' appraisals of stressors frequently concern other people (e.g., coaches, teammates, opponents, and parents), and athletes' coping actions also frequently involve others (Kerdijk, van der Kamp, & Polman, 2016; Tamminen & Bennett, 2016). For example, seeking support is often cited as a strategy for dealing with sport-related stressors, either to seek advice or information about the problem or to seek emotional support to deal with the emotions arising within the situation (Nicholls & Polman, 2007; see also Chapter 11). Additional evidence supports the idea that athletes' coping is influenced by their perceptions of coaches and parents. For example, athletes' perceptions of supportive coach behaviors were associated with greater use of task-oriented coping in competition and performance achievement, whereas perceptions of unsupportive coach behaviors were associated with greater use of disengagement-oriented coping in competition (Nicolas, Gaudreau, & Franche, 2011). Similarly, perceptions of parental pressure are also associated with greater use of disengagement-oriented coping, while perceptions of parental support are associated with less use of disengagement-oriented coping strategies in sport (Tamminen, McEwen, & Crocker, 2016). Athletes have also indicated that teammates provide communication and encouragement that helped them to cope with the stressful situation (Kerdijk et al., 2016). A future line of inquiry in this area could include examining whether athletes demonstrate coordinated patterns of coping to deal with shared stressors—approaches to examining patterns of coping in teams may involve video-assisted recall (e.g., Doron & Bourbousson, 2017), diary methods (e.g., Tamminen & Holt, 2010), interviews, and social network approaches to analyze how the coping efforts of athletes are influenced by their teammates' coping efforts.

Coping Effectiveness

Coping effectiveness has been described as one of the "most perplexing" issues in the field of coping research (Folkman & Moskowitz, 2004), as it must take into account the individual's goals, appraisals, emotions, coping efforts, and various outcomes of the coping process. Definitions of coping effectiveness frequently center on the degree to which individuals' coping efforts help them to adapt to their environment and reduce the negative emotions related to the stressful encounter; for example, Lazarus (1999) noted that "when coping is ineffective, the level of stress is high; however, when coping is effective, the level of stress is apt to be low" (p. 102). In a review of coping effectiveness in sport, Nicholls (2010) offered a similar definition: "coping effectiveness refers to the degree in which a coping strategy or combination of coping strategies is or are effective in alleviating stress" (p. 264).

In sport, coping effectiveness is often considered in relation to performance outcomes; that is, coping efforts might be considered effective if they help athletes to win in competition, perform well in practice, or achieve continued success in sport. However, any determination of coping effectiveness must take into consideration the short- and long-term effects of coping efforts on the stressor or emotions that the athlete is trying to manage, as well as possible indirect effects on other outcomes that may occur (Lazarus & Folkman, 1984). Thus, some coping efforts may not have a direct impact on athletes' performance, but they may be helpful in maintaining health and well-being, which is critical for sustained sport participation and to avoid burnout and withdrawal (see also Chapters 6 and 7).

One of the key principles of Lazarus' (1999) cognitive–motivational–relational theory of emotion and coping is that no coping strategy is universally effective or ineffective. Strategies that may be effective in coping with some stressors may be ineffective in coping with other stressors, and strategies that are considered "effective" in helping the athlete to achieve one goal (i.e., performance success) may be considered ineffective in relation to other outcomes (i.e., maintaining good physical and mental health). Furthermore, some coping strategies may help athletes attain short-term outcomes, but these may occur at the expense of long-term outcomes. For example, using avoidance coping to deal with competitive stressors has been shown to be effective in reducing immediate psychological or performance problems, although this form of coping was negatively associated with long-term desire to continue sport involvement (Kim & Duda, 2003).

One approach to assessing coping effectiveness is the goodness-of-fit approach (Folkman, 1984; Lazarus & Folkman, 1984), which suggests that effective coping depends on a fit between the situation and the person's appraisal of the situation, and a fit between the situation and the person's resources to cope with it. Thus, applying the goodness-of-fit approach to coping in sport, effective coping depends on athletes being able to accurately appraise the situation and determine which coping strategies are likely to be useful in dealing with the demands of the situation, and it also requires that the athlete has the appropriate resources and is able to apply the most appropriate coping strategy from the resources available to them.

An alternative approach to explain coping effectiveness suggests that some athletes may cope more effectively because their attempts to cope are more "automatic" compared to athletes who cope less effectively with stressors in sport (Gould et al., 1993; Dugdale, Eklund, & Gordon, 2002). Here, it is important to clarify that coping automaticity is not the same as coping effectiveness. That is, the ability to apply a coping strategy "automatically" does not necessarily indicate how effective the strategy will be in coping with the demands of the situation. Dugdale et al. (2002) reported that athletes' reports of coping automaticity were moderately correlated with perceived effectiveness, but coping automaticity was not correlated with goal attainment. However, it is plausible that coping strategies that are well used and have been found to be effective in the past are more likely to be used with relative ease in a wide variety of situations. McCrae and Costa (1986) found that individuals' most frequently used coping strategies were also the strategies rated as most effective in problem solving and distress reduction, and a similar pattern of results has been reported by athletes (Kaiseler, Polman, & Nicholls, 2011). McCrae and Costa (1986) also cautioned that some coping strategies such as wishful thinking could be used frequently but may rarely be considered "useful" or effective.

Appraisals of control are also important for determining which coping strategies are useful to apply in a particular situation (Folkman, 1984; Lazarus & Folkman, 1984; see also Chapter 2). For stressors that are controllable, problem-focused coping strategies are likely to prove effective in dealing with the stressor. Conversely, when facing stressors that are uncontrollable, emotion-focused coping strategies are likely to be more effective in helping the individual manage the emotions arising from the situation. Within sport, athletes typically report using more problem-focused coping strategies to deal with stressors that are perceived as controllable, and they also report the use of emotion-focused or avoidance/withdrawal coping to deal with uncontrollable stressors (Anshel & Kaissidis, 1997; Kim & Duda, 2003). From a practical perspective, these findings suggest it would be prudent for athletes to learn, practice, and reflect on how to apply a range of coping strategies, so that they are able to use them more easily when stressful situations arise.

Future Directions: Proactive and Communal Coping Models

Proactive Coping

Proactive coping refers to efforts that are undertaken to deal with stressors to prevent or modify their occurrence (Aspinwall & Taylor, 1997). In contrast to most other models of coping that have been used in sport, proactive coping explicitly focuses on an individual's efforts to plan ahead, anticipate, and manage future stressors rather than focusing on reactive efforts to deal with stressors as they arise (see also Chapter 12). Although this model has not been extensively used in sport psychology research, there is evidence that athletes who engaged in more proactive coping over the course of a season used more reflection and planning to deal with subsequent stressors in the future (Tamminen & Holt, 2010). To help athletes develop more proactive approaches to coping with stressors in sport, practitioners can support them through a coping-oriented, personal disclosure mutualsharing intervention, as has been implemented in youth soccer (Evans et al., 2018). Because the model of proactive coping considers how athletes reflect on and build their capacity for coping in the future in a recursive, ongoing process, this model could be useful for longitudinally examining the development of coping resources among athletes.

Communal Coping

Communal coping considers how individuals engage in various coping strategies to deal with stressors collectively rather than individually (Lyons, Mickelson, Sullivan, & Coyne, 1998). This framework is novel because it reconceptualizes how some stressors in sport may be appraised as "our problems" to be managed collectively or in coordination with others, rather than conceptualizing stressors as "my problem" to deal with individually. Shared sources of stress may include social pressure issues (e.g., coaches, referees, opponents, and media), teammate relationship issues (e.g., negative teammate behaviors and social interactions), team expectations and team performance issues, and logistical and organizational issues that affect the entire team (Leprince, D'Arripe-Longueville, & Doron, 2018; Tamminen, Palmateer, et al., 2016). To deal with these stressors, athletes may engage in problem-focused communal coping, relationship-focused coping, communal management of emotions, and communal goal withdrawal (e.g., giving up and collectively expressing negative emotions; Leprince et al., 2018). Communal coping may be a useful model for studying and teaching "team approaches" to coping with stressors and emotions in sport, helping to integrate research on coping with group dynamics.

Conclusion

No single coping strategy can be applied to deal with the wide range of stressors that athletes face in sport; therefore, athletes often use multiple coping strategies to manage stressors. When considering how to help improve coping among athletes, it is important to consider the combinations of coping strategies that athletes use, and to reflect on whether these profiles of coping are likely to be associated with better or worse outcomes (e.g., performance, distress, and well-being). Generally, coping profiles that involve task-oriented or problem-focused coping strategies are viewed as being effective for managing stressors that are controllable. However, if stressors are uncontrollable or unlikely to change, then emotion-focused coping strategies may be more effective for managing the emotions arising within the situation. Distraction- and disengagement-oriented coping strategies may be effective for athletes in the short term (e.g., managing pre-competitive anxiety in the moments before a race), although these strategies may have negative consequences if they are repeatedly employed over time (Kim & Duda, 2003).

Some additional principles appear to show promise in helping athletes to improve their coping in sport (see also Chapter 12). One key principle for helping athletes improve their capacity to cope is to focus on developing self-awareness through systematic self-reflection (Aspinwall & Taylor, 1997; Tamminen & Holt, 2012). In doing so, athletes should develop the capacity to assess the demands of a situation and the resources they have to deal with the situation. A second key principle is to help athletes develop flexibility in their coping, so that they can apply a range of coping strategies across various situations rather than rigidly using the same coping strategies to deal with every stressor they face (Folkman & Moskowitz, 2004). Thus, approaches to improving coping in sport should involve opportunities for athletes to reflect on their experiences and learn a broad range of strategies that can help them achieve performance outcomes, make progress toward their goals, reduce negative emotions, or maintain positive relationships with others. Finally, athletes' coping appears to benefit from supportive relationships and positive influence from parents, coaches, and peers (Nicolas et al., 2011; Tamminen & Holt, 2012; Tamminen, McEwen, & Crocker, 2016). Fostering improved communication and empathy with athletes can contribute to perceptions of available support to deal with stressors should they arise, which is important for predicting positive outcomes in sport (Freeman & Rees, 2009; see also Chapter 11).

In conclusion, coping is contextual, it is related to subjective appraisals of ongoing, dynamic situations, and coping efforts can be considered in relation to short- and long-term outcomes related to performance, emotions, distress, and overall well-being. Researchers have documented the wide variety of coping strategies that athletes use to deal with stressors and emotions in sport, as well as the impact of coping on various outcomes including performance, well-being, and burnout. Coping changes with age and development, and athletes can learn to develop greater capacity to cope effectively with stressors in sport. The complexity of this topic, as well as its connections to a broad range of areas in sport psychology, makes coping a vital area of research and one that is fundamental to the practice of sport psychology.

References

Allen, M. S., Greenlees, I., & Jones, M. (2011). An investigation of the five-factor model of personality and coping behaviour in sport. *Journal of Sports Sciences, 29*, 841–850. Doi:10.1080/02640414.2011.565064

Anshel, M. H., & Kaissidis, A. N. (1997). Coping style and situational appraisals as predictors of coping strategies following stressful events in sports as a function of gender and skill level. *British Journal of Psychology, 88*, 263–276. Doi:10.1111/j.2044-8295.1997.tb02634.x

Anshel, M. H., Williams, L. R. T., & Hodge, K. (1997). Cross-cultural and gender differences on coping style in sport. *International Journal of Sport Psychology, 28*, 141–156.

Anshel, M. H., William, L. R. T., & Williams, S. M. (2000). Coping style following acute stress in competitive sport. *The Journal of Social Psychology, 140*, 751–773.

Aspinwall, L. G., & Taylor, S. E. (1997). A stitch in time: Self-regulation and proactive coping. *Psychological Bulletin, 121*, 417–436. Doi:10.1037/0033-2909.121.3.417

Bolgar, M. R., Janelle, C., & Giacobbi, P. R. (2008). Trait anger, appraisal, and coping differences among adolescent tennis players. *Journal of Applied Sport Psychology, 20*, 73–87. Doi:10.1080/10413200701790566

Calmeiro, L., Tenenbaum, G., & Eccles, D. W. (2014). Managing pressure: Patterns of appraisals and coping strategies of non-elite and elite athletes during competition. *Journal of Sports Sciences, 32*(19), 1813–1820. Doi:10.1080/02640 414.2014.922692

Christensen, D. S., & Smith, R. E. (2018). Leveling the playing field: Can psychological coping resources reduce the influence of physical and technical skills on athletic performance? *Anxiety, Stress, & Coping, 31*, 626–638. Doi:10.1080/ 10615806.2018.1506646

Chun, C. A., Moos, R. H., & Cronkite, R. C. (2006). Culture: A fundamental context for the stress and coping paradigm. In P. T. P. Wong & L. C. J. Wong (Eds.), *Handbook of multicultural perspectives on stress and coping* (pp. 29–54). New York: Springer.

Crocker, P. R. E., & Graham, T. R. (1995). Coping by competitive athletes with performance stress: Gender differences and relationships with affect. *The Sport Psychologist, 9*, 325–338.

Dale, G. A. (2000). Distractions and coping strategies of elite decathletes during their most memorable performances. *The Sport Psychologist, 14*, 17–41.

Dollen, M., Grove, J. R., & Pepping, G. J. (2015). A comparison of coping-styles of individual and team athletes of Australia and the Netherlands. *International Sports Studies, 37*, 36–48.

Doron, J., & Bourbousson, J. (2017). How stressors are dynamically appraised within a team during a game: An exploratory study in basketball. *Scandinavian Journal of Medicine & Science in Sports, 27,* 2080–2090.

Doron, J., & Martinent, G. (2017). Appraisal, coping, emotion, and performance during elite fencing matches: A random coefficient regression model approach. *Scandinavian Journal of Medicine & Science in Sports, 27,* 1015–1025. Doi:10.1111/sms.12711

Dugdale, J. R., Eklund, R. C., & Gordon, S. (2002). Expected and unexpected stressors in major international competition: Appraisal, coping, and performance. *The Sport Psychologist, 16,* 20–33.

Evans, A. L., Morris, R., Barker, J., Johnson, T., Brenan, Z., & Warner, B. (2018). Athlete and practitioner insights regarding a novel coping oriented Personal-Disclosure Mutual-Sharing (COPDMS) intervention in youth soccer. *The Sport Psychologist, 33,* 64–74. Doi:10.1123/tsp.2017-0125

Folkman, S. (1984). Personal control and stress and coping processes: A theoretical analysis. *Journal of Personality and Social Psychology, 46,* 839–852.

Folkman, S., & Moskowitz, J. T. (2004). Coping: Pitfalls and promise. *Annual Review of Psychology, 55,* 745–774.

Freeman, P., & Rees, T. (2009). How does perceived support lead to better performance? An examination of potential mechanisms. *Journal of Applied Sport Psychology, 21,* 429–441. Doi:10.1080/10413200903222913

Gan, Q., Anshel, M. H., & Kim, J. K. (2009). Sources and cognitive appraisals of acute stress as predictors of coping style among male and female Chinese athletes. *International Journal of Sport and Exercise Psychology, 7,* 68–88. Doi:10.1 080/1612197X.2009.9671893

Gaudreau, P., & Blondin, J. P. (2002). Development of a questionnaire for the assessment of coping strategies employed by athletes in competitive sport settings. *Psychology of Sport and Exercise, 3,* 1–34.

Gaudreau, P., & Blondin, J. P. (2004). Different athletes cope differently: A cluster analysis of coping. *Personality and Individual Differences, 36,* 1865–1877.

Gaudreau, P., Nicholls, A. R., & Levy, A. R. (2010). The ups and downs of sports performance: An episodic process analysis of within-person associations. *Journal of Sport & Exercise Psychology, 32,* 298–311.

Gould, D., Eklund, R. C., & Jackson, S. A. (1993). Coping strategies used by US Olympic wrestlers. *Research Quarterly for Exercise and Sport, 64,* 83–93.

Hoar, S. D., Crocker, P. R., Holt, N. L., & Tamminen, K. A. (2010). Gender differences in adolescent athletes' coping with interpersonal stressors in sport: More similarities than differences? *Journal of Applied Sport Psychology, 22,* 134–149. Doi:10.1080/10413201003664640

Holt, N. L., Hoar, S., & Fraser, S. N. (2005). How does coping change with development? A review of childhood and adolescence sport coping research. *European Journal of Sport Science, 5,* 25–39.

Holt, N. L., & Hogg, J. M. (2002). Perceptions of stress and coping during preparations for the 1999 women's soccer World Cup finals. *The Sport Psychologist, 16,* 251–271.

Hurst, J. F., Thompson, A., Visek, A. J., Fisher, B., & Gaudreau, P. (2011). Towards a dispositional version of the coping inventory for competitive sport. *International Journal of Sport Psychology, 42,* 167–185.

Kaiseler, M., Levy, A., Nicholls, A. R., & Madigan, D. J. (2019). The independent and interactive effects of the Big-Five personality dimensions upon dispositional coping and coping effectiveness in sport. *International Journal of Sport and Exercise Psychology, 17*, 410–426. Doi:10.1080/1612197X.2017.1362459

Kaiseler, M., Polman, R. C. J., & Nicholls, A. R. (2011). Effects of the Big Five personality dimensions on appraisal coping, and coping effectiveness in sport. *European Journal of Sport Science, 12*, 62–72. Doi:10.1080/17461391.20 10.551410

Kerdijk, C., van der Kamp, J., & Polman, R. (2016). The influence of the social environment context in stress and coping in sport. *Frontiers in Psychology, 7*, 875. Doi:10.3389/fpsyg.2016.00875

Kim, M. S., & Duda, J. L. (2003). The coping process: Cognitive appraisals of stress, coping strategies, and coping effectiveness. *The Sport Psychologist, 17*, 406–425.

Kowalski, K. C., & Crocker, P. R. E. (2001). Development and validation of the Coping Function Questionnaire for adolescents in sport. *Journal of Sport and Exercise Psychology, 23*, 136–155.

Lazarus, R. S. (1999). *Stress and emotion: A new synthesis.* New York: Springer.

Lazarus, R. S., & Folkman, S. (1984). *Stress, appraisal and coping.* New York: Springer.

Leprince, C., D'Arripe-Longueville, F., & Doron, J. (2018). Coping in teams: Exploring athletes' communal coping strategies to deal with shared stressors. *Frontiers in Psychology, 9*, 1908. Doi:10.3389/fpsyg.2018.01908

Lyons, R. F., Mickelson, K. D., Sullivan, M. J., & Coyne, J. C. (1998). Coping as a communal process. *Journal of Social and Personal Relationships, 15*, 579–605. Doi:10.1177/0265407598155001

Martinent, G., & Decret, J. C. (2015). Coping profiles of young athletes in their everyday life: A three-wave two-month study. *European Journal of Sport Science, 15*, 736–747. Doi:10.1080/17461391.201531051131

Martinent, G., & Nicolas, M. (2017). Temporal ordering of affective states and coping within a naturalistic achievement-related demanding situation. *International Journal of Stress Management, 24*(S1), 29–51. Doi:10.1037/str0000024

McCrae, R. R., & Costa Jr, P. T. (1986). Personality, coping, and coping effectiveness in an adult sample. *Journal of Personality, 54*(2), 385–404. Doi:10.1111/j.1467-6494.1986.tb00401.x

Miles, A., Neil, R., & Barker, J. (2016). Preparing to take the field: A temporal exploration of stress, emotion, and coping in elite cricket. *The Sport Psychologist, 30*, 101–112. Doi:10.1123/tsp.2014-0142

Nicholls, A. R. (2010). Effective versus ineffective coping in sport. In A. R. Nicholls (Ed.), *Coping in sport: Theory, methods, and related constructs* (pp. 263–276). New York: Nova Science Publishers.

Nicholls, A. R., Holt, N. L., Polman, R. C. J., & Bloomfield, J. (2006). Stressors, coping, and coping effectiveness among professional rugby union players. *The Sport Psychologist, 20*, 314–329.

Nicholls, A. R., Holt, N. L., Polman, R. C. J., & James, D. W. G. (2005). Stress, coping, and coping effectiveness among international adolescent golfers. *Journal of Applied Sport Psychology, 17*, 333–340.

Nicholls, A. R., Levy, A. R., Carson, F., Thompson, M. A., & Perry, J. L. (2016). The applicability of self-regulation theories in sport: Goal adjustment capacities, stress appraisals, coping, and well-being among athletes. *Psychology of Sport and Exercise, 27*, 47–55. Doi:10.1016/j.psychsport.2016.07.011

Nicholls, A. R., Levy, A. R., & Perry, J. L. (2015). Emotional maturity, dispositional coping, and coping effectiveness among adolescent athletes. *Psychology of Sport and Exercise, 17*, 32–39. Doi:10.1016/j.psychsport.2014.11.004

Nicholls, A. R., Perry, J. L., Jones, L., Morley, D., & Carson, F. (2013). Dispositional coping, coping effectiveness, and cognitive social maturity among adolescent athletes. *Journal of Sport and Exercise Psychology, 35*, 229–238. Doi:10.1123/jsep.35.3.229

Nicholls, A. R., & Polman, R. C. (2007). Coping in sport: A systematic review. *Journal of Sports Sciences, 25*, 11–31.

Nicholls, A. R., Polman, R. C., Levy, A. R., Taylor, N. J., & Cobley, S. (2007). Stressors, coping, and coping effectiveness: Gender, type of sport, and skill differences. *Journal of Sports Sciences, 25*, 1521–1530. Doi:10.1080/02640410701230479

Nicholls, A. R., Polman, R. C., Morley, D., & Taylor, N. J. (2009). Coping and coping effectiveness in relation to a competitive sport event: Pubertal status, chronological age, and gender among adolescent athletes. *Journal of Sport and Exercise Psychology, 31*, 299–317.

Nicolas, M., Gaudreau, P., & Franche, V. (2011). Perception of coaching behaviors, coping, and achievement in a sport competition. *Journal of Sport and Exercise Psychology, 33*, 460–468.

Reeves, C. W., Nicholls, A. R., & McKenna, J. (2009). Stressors and coping strategies among early and middle adolescent premier league academy soccer players: Differences according to age. *Journal of Applied Sport Psychology, 21*, 31–48. Doi:10.1080/10413200802443768.

Smith, R. E., & Christensen, D. S. (1995). Psychological skills as predictors of performance and survival in professional baseball. *Journal of Sport and Exercise Psychology, 17*, 399–415. Doi:10.1123/jsep.17.4.399

Smith, R. E., Schultz, R. W., Smoll, F. L., & Ptacek, J. T. (1995). Development and validation of a multidimensional measure of sport-specific psychological skills: The athletic coping skills inventory-28. *Journal of Sport and Exercise Psychology, 17*, 379–398.

Tamminen, K. A., & Bennett, E. (2016). No emotion is an island: An overview of theoretical perspectives and narrative research on emotions in sport and physical activity. *Qualitative Research in Sport, Exercise, and Health, 9*, 183–199. Doi:10.1080/2159676X.2016.1254109

Tamminen, K. A., & Holt, N. L. (2010). Female adolescent athletes' coping: A season-long investigation. *Journal of Sports Sciences, 28*, 101–114. Doi:10.1080/02640410903406182

Tamminen, K. A., & Holt, N. L. (2012). Adolescent athletes' learning about coping and the roles of parents and coaches. *Psychology of Sport & Exercise, 13*, 69–79. Doi:10.1016/j.psychsport.2011.07.006

Tamminen, K. A., McEwen, C. E., & Crocker, P. R. E. (2016). Perceptions matter: Parental support, pressure, and the socialization of adolescent athletes' coping. *International Journal of Sport Psychology, 47*, 335–354. Doi:10.7352/IJSP2016.47.000

Tamminen, K. A., Palmateer, T. M., Denton, M., Sabiston, C., Crocker, P. R. E., Eys, M., . . . Smith, B. (2016). Exploring emotions as social phenomena among Canadian varsity athletes. *Psychology of Sport and Exercise, 27*, 28–38. Doi:10.1016/j.psychsport.2016.07.010

Section II

Responses to and Outcomes of Stress in Sport

4   Emotions

Christopher R. D. Wagstaff and
Katherine A. Tamminen

Emotions are a universally experienced core aspect of human existence and most people tend to think they know emotion when they feel or see it. Yet despite this ubiquity, researchers have consistently failed to reach consensus on a definition of emotions. Perhaps the most widely held view is that emotions are a relatively brief episode of coordinated responses by all or most organismic subsystems to the evaluation of an external or internal event being of major significance (cf. Ekman, 1992; Frijda, 1988; Scherer, 1984; Smith & Ellsworth, 1985). The challenge with such definitions is their limited utility for understanding the complexity of the emotion generation, experience, and regulation process. Indeed, what makes emotions a unique and challenging variable to study in sport is their dynamic nature; they are experienced differently from day-to-day and moment-to-moment, and even differ greatly in response to similar stimuli. Given the lack of global consensus on conceptual and definitional issues relating to the study of emotions, sport psychology scholars have more frequently merely differentiated between emotions from the similar but distinct concepts of mood and affect. If emotions typically refer to discrete, intense, and short-lived experiences, moods are typically characterized as experiences that are longer and more diffuse, where individuals may lack awareness of a focal or eliciting stimuli. Moods can be created by stimuli of relatively low intensity, or can be supplanted by emotions that fade, so that the initial antecedent is no longer salient (e.g., Cropanzano, Weiss, Hale, & Reb, 2003; Schwarz, 1990). Affect is an umbrella term encompassing mood and emotion (Forgas, 1995). In this chapter, we focus on emotions.

Emotion Theory: A Brief Overview

As alluded earlier, there remains conceptual debate regarding the definition and role of emotions in human life. Nevertheless, there are some areas of convergence among emotion scholars. For example, many psychologists stress the episodic nature of emotion (e.g., Ekman, 1992; Frijda & Mesquita, 1994; Scherer, 1993). The foundation of this perspective is that a triggering event results in a noticeable change in the functioning of the individual, which can be observed externally (e.g., expressions and behavior) or internally (e.g., thoughts, sensations, memories, and physiological arousal). From this episodic perspective, emotions are experienced with decreasing intensity, as the intensity of the experience dissipates over a short period of time. Another commonly agreed aspect of emotion theory relates to the so-called necessity of a "reaction triad" of physiological arousal, motor expression, and subjective feeling to legitimize the existence of an emotion. Some theorists extend the necessary facets of an emotion to include motivational factors such as action tendencies, and the cognitive processes that are involved in the evaluation of eliciting events (cf. Frijda, 1986; Scherer, 1993). A further point of definitional convergence is the assumption that emotions are normally triggered by an internal or external stimuli or events of substantial significance to an individual. For instance, Frijda (1986) characterized emotions as relevance detectors, which require a priori evaluation of stimuli with respect to their meaning (see also Chapters 1 and 2). Following this line of relational meaning, it is generally agreed that emotions serve some functional role for adaptation or mastery for individuals.

Historical Roots of Emotion in Sport

Research on emotion in sport has generally adopted a *within-person* view, focusing primarily on an individual's emotional response to competitive sport. For example, a wealth of research has been dedicated to the study of competitive anxiety (see, for a comprehensive review, Wagstaff, Neil, Mellalieu, & Hanton, 2012). The foundation of this work lies in the assumption that emotions are experienced by an *individual* prior to, or during, a competition by the same *individual*. Indeed, using this approach to examine competitive anxiety in sport, researchers have amassed a body of over 100 research articles, making this concept one of the most prolifically studied within the field of sport psychology (see Wagstaff et al., 2012; see also Introduction chapter). This body of work has also been fruitful; it has illustrated the importance of appraisal in the anxiety response process (see also Chapter 2) and distinguished a significant number of antecedent and mechanistic variables that influence the anxiety-performance relationship (see, for reviews, Jones, 1995; Mellalieu, Hanton, & Fletcher, 2006; Wagstaff et al., 2012; Woodman & Hardy, 2001).

The substantial research dedicated to emotional experience at the within-person level in sport has prompted the development of numerous associated models. For instance, general approaches to the emotion-performance relationship at the within-person level in sport have been developed, including inter alia: cognitive-motivational-relational theory (CMR: Lazarus, 2000), individual zone of optimal functioning (IZOF;

Hanin, 2000), and the meta-model of stress, emotions, and performance (Fletcher & Fletcher, 2005; Fletcher, Hanton, & Mellalieu, 2006). There have also been numerous perspectives offered on the anxiety-performance relationship specifically, including, for example: Multi-dimensional Anxiety Theory (see Martens, Burton, Vealey, Bump, & Smith, 1990), Jones' (1995) Control Model, Catastrophe Model (Hardy, 1990), Theory of Reinvestment (see Masters, 1992), Attentional Control Theory (see Eysenck & Calvo, 1992; see also Chapter 5), Biopsychosocial Model of Challenge and Threat (see Blascovich et al., 2004; see also Chapters 2 and 5), and the Theory of Challenge and Threat States in Athletes (Jones, Meijen, McCarthy, & Sheffield, 2009; see also Chapter 2). While a review of each of these and their allied research is beyond the scope of this chapter, the number is indicative of the extent of research dedicated to the examination of emotional experience in sport performers.

As alluded earlier and considering the variety of theoretical approaches adopted to examine intrapersonal emotion experience in sport, a breadth of research exists which illuminates a wide spectrum of emotions (e.g., anxiety) with different study designs (e.g., Jones & Uphill, 2011; Mullen, Hardy, & Tattersall, 2005; Robazza & Bortoli, 2007; Séve, Ria, Poizat, Saury, & Durand, 2007; Woodman et al., 2009) and different measures to assess emotions in sport (e.g., Jones, Lane, Bray, Uphill, & Catlin, 2005; see, for a review, Ekkekakis, 2012). Nevertheless, anxiety has primarily been the emotion of interest to sport psychologists (see Wagstaff et al., 2012), with researchers mostly highlighting the negative impact of anxiety on sport performance (e.g., Woodman & Hardy, 2003). Indeed, there is substantial evidence that anxiety can impair performance in soccer penalty kicks (e.g., Jordet, 2009; Wilson, Wood, & Vine, 2009), table tennis (e.g., Williams, Vickers, & Rodrigues, 2002), golf putting (e.g., Vine, Moore, & Wilson, 2011), and rock climbing (e.g., Nieuwenhuys, Pijpers, Oudejans, & Bakker, 2008). In addition, Nibbeling, Daanen, Gerritsma, Hofland, and Oudejans (2012) found several indications that efficiency in running in an aerobic task was reduced by anxiety. In contrast to these results, there also exists a body of research that has found anxiety to be associated with positive outcomes. Specifically, substantial research has been dedicated to examining whether anxiety symptoms can be perceived as either facilitative or debilitative to performance; that is, when an individual reports experiencing cognitive or somatic anxiety symptoms, whether they believe that these feelings will be helpful or harmful to their performance. Numerous studies have found that when the directional scale of anxiety is considered, the variance predicted by anxiety increases; that is, scores on the directional scale of anxiety (i.e., facilitative vs. debilitative interpretations) appear to be effective predictors of performance (see, for reviews, Jones, 1995; Mellalieu et al., 2006; Raglin & Hanin, 2000; Wagstaff et al., 2012).

While the study of performers' emotional experience is firmly established in sport psychology, almost all this research has focused on the examination of negative emotions in competitive environments such as anxiety (Fletcher et al., 2006). Indeed, there is a relative dearth of research examining the daily affective experiences of sport performers within their dyads, teams, and organizations or the value of emotion-based interventions to improve psychological well-being and organizational performance. McCarthy (2011) argued that the benefits of positive emotions (e.g., happiness and excitement) have hitherto not been wholly realized in sport, especially in their capacity to result in greater self-efficacy, motivation, attention, problem-solving, and coping with adversity. Subsequent work (e.g., Stenseng, Forest, & Curran, 2015) has pointed to predictive associations between harmonious—but not obsessive—passion and the experience of positive emotions and belongingness in recreational sport. The authors concluded that athletes with harmonious passion are more likely to feel socially connected in sport and, therefore, exhibit higher levels of positive emotions. Furthermore, a body of research has emerged examining the role of a range of discrete emotional experiences on sport performance (e.g., Baron, Guilloux, Begue, & Uriac, 2015; Lane et al., 2015; Rathschlag & Memmert, 2015).

While the previous examples reflect a shift to adopt a more holistic research agenda for within-person emotion experience in sport, there remains much to be examined at this level relevant to sport performance. For example, with some notable exceptions (e.g., Cerin, Szabo Hunt, & Williams, 2000; Hanton, Thomas, & Maynard, 2004; Thomas, Hanton, & Maynard, 2007) substantially less within-person emotion research has been conducted examining the daily and within-competition fluctuations of emotional experience and its influence on attitudes, motivation, well-being, and performance. Indeed, despite several notable exceptions (e.g., Doron & Martinent, 2016; Martinent, Campo, & Ferrand, 2012; Martinent, Gareau, Lienhart, Nicaise, & Guillet-Descas, 2018; Saby, Pupier, Guillet-Descas, Nicolas, & Martinent, 2019), only minimal gains have been made to examine complex within-competition and longitudinal emotion profiles among athletes. Additionally, there remain many potential benefits to be made through a greater understanding of athletes' emotions—both negative and positive—in competitive and non-competitive situations.

The "Interpersonal Turn": Social Perspectives of Emotion in Sport

Adopting an interpersonal perspective of emotions in sport explicitly considers the social and interpersonal dynamics related to emotions. The historical focus of research in sport examining emotions from an individualistic perspective is understandable, particularly regarding the effects of anxiety on sport performance: as an applied field, sport psychology researchers and practitioners have long sought ways to help athletes improve their personal performance and well-being through improved coping and emotion regulation (see, e.g., Jones, 2003). Yet, while Vallerand and Blanchard (2000) and Hanin (2007) noted the lack of research on interpersonal aspects of emotions, it is only in recent years that researchers have made significant advances that have shed light on the occurrence, experience, and effects of emotions within groups and teams, and the factors that may influence emotions within groups. Broadly, these advances are seen in research examining the social functions of emotions in sport, the experience and spread of emotions within groups and teams, as well as conceptualizations of emotions in relation to one's social identity (e.g., group-based emotions; see also Chapter 11).

Social Functions of Emotions in Teams and Organizations

A key focus of examining emotions in teams and organizations within sport is to understand the functions that these emotions serve and their impact on various performance and psychosocial processes. Accordingly, researchers have also begun to explore the social functions that emotions serve within sport settings. One perspective suggests that emotions serve multiple functions across four levels that have implications for interpersonal interactions (Keltner & Haidt, 1999). First, at the individual level, emotional experiences are thought to inform the individual about the social situation and prepare them to respond. At the dyadic level, emotions help individuals infer the emotions, beliefs, intentions, and likely actions of others, they evoke complementary emotions, and they may serve as incentives of deterrents for the behaviors of others. At the group level, emotions may strengthen group membership and define group boundaries, and they may help individuals navigate group-related roles and interpersonal problems. Finally, at the cultural level, emotions may play a role in the adoption of cultural identities and engagement in culturally accepted behaviors, and emotions also serve to build and maintain power structures (Keltner & Haidt, 1999).

In alignment with this perspective, Wagstaff and colleagues (e.g., Wagstaff, Fletcher, & Hanton, 2012a, 2012b; Wagstaff, Hanton, & Fletcher, 2013) and Friesen, Devonport, Sellars, and Lane (2013) have explored/examined emotion-related phenomena (e.g., emotion regulation and abilities) within sport groups and organizations. To elaborate, Wagstaff et al.'s (2012a) ethnography of organizational functioning in a national sport organization illustrated the pivotal importance of interpersonal relationships and emotion-related abilities as highly influential in successful person-organization dynamics. Specifically, individuals managed conflict, communicated emotion, managed emotional expression for the psychological contract, and engaged in contagious emotion regulation for building strong relationships, all of which were important emotion-related factors relevant for organizational functioning. Indeed, those individuals better able to monitor and manage their own emotions and those of others were able to develop and maintain more successful interpersonal relationships during a period of organizational change. Wagstaff et al. (2012b) found such emotion "abilities" to be highly contextualized and influenced regulation strategy selection through sociocultural norms present within the sport environment. Based on these findings, Wagstaff et al. (2013) developed and evaluated an intervention to develop emotion abilities and regulation strategies to facilitate organizational functioning by assisting individuals to perceive, process, comprehend, and manage emotions intelligently within their interpersonal relationships in sport. Friesen et al. (2013) described the ways that two ice hockey captains perceived the emotions of their teammates influenced their attention to the demands of competitive situations, triggered interpersonal emotion regulation efforts, helped teammates focus on the shared goals of the team, and established values related to winning, positivity, and productivity within the team.

Building on the work of Wagstaff and colleagues, and in the social functioning vein, Tamminen, Palmateer, et al. (2016) described several social functions of emotions among varsity athletes and their impacts on athletes' perceptions of the group environment in team and individual varsity sports. Athletes said that positive and negative expressions of emotions influenced their teammates' effort and performance, and that emotional expressions communicated one's values and commitment to the team: for example, laughing or joking around after a loss was viewed as communicating a lack of commitment to the team, suggesting that some athletes did not value their team or thought the competition was not important to them. Athletes also described affiliative and distancing functions of emotions, whereby expressions of positive and negative emotions served to motivate athletes to seek out others to share their experiences. Nevertheless, some athletes also indicated that expressions of negative emotions may function to isolate others or communicate messages to "stay away" from teammates, thus further segregating athletes from the team.

Another perspective concerning the social functions of emotions that has been adopted by some researchers in sport is the Emotions as Social Information (EASI) model, which similarly suggests that emotions provide individuals with information about one another's experiences that influences subsequent cognitions, emotions, and actions (van Kleef, 2009; van Kleef, Cheshin, Koning, & Wolf, 2019). Recently, van Kleef et al. (2019) provided evidence that coaches' emotional expressions influenced athletes' experiences of happiness and anger during competition. Furthermore, team performance was also influenced by the coaches' emotional expressions—coaches' expressions of happiness predicted team success, whereas coaches' expressions of anger were negatively associated with team success.

The Experience and Spread of Emotions Within Teams and Organizations

Early research in sport examining the spread of affective phenomena within teams demonstrated that athletes' positive, happy moods were linked to the collective mood of their teammates, which was also associated with players' subjective performances (Totterdell, 2000). Players who were older, more committed to the team, and more susceptible to emotional contagion showed greater associations between their own mood and that of their teammates. Totterdell (2000) suggested that associations between individual-team moods may be related to athletes' emotional expressiveness and affective communication via deliberate and non-deliberate facial, verbal, and behavioral expressions. Emotional contagion has also been examined using video analysis of the celebratory behaviors of soccer players following penalty kicks, with athletes' displays of pride (e.g., arms in the air, smiling) after a successful goal being associated with their team's eventual success in the penalty shootout (see Moll, Jordet, & Pepping, 2010).

Additional research suggests that emotions "spread" within teams and that athletes are also affected by the emotional displays of their coaches. For example, athletes (Thelwell, Wagstaff, Rayner, Chapman, & Barker, 2017) and coaches (Thelwell, Wagstaff, Chapman, & Kenttä, 2017) have described the impact of coaches' stress on athletes' cognitions, emotions, and behaviors in elite sport environments. To elaborate, coaches perceived that athletes were negatively impacted when they were experiencing and displaying signs of strain as coaches, including effects on athletes' performance and development, psychological and emotional responses, and on behaviors and interpersonal interactions (see Thelwell, Wagstaff, Chapman, et al., 2017). Athletes reported that the impact of coaches' stress resulted in reduced confidence, increased negativity related to self-worth, decreased motivation, as well as potential negative impacts on performance (Thelwell, Wagstaff, Rayner, et al., 2017). These findings build on early research by Gallmeier (1987), who highlighted how teammates, fans, and coaches influenced the emotions of ice hockey players, who then altered their expressions and behaviors to respond in appropriate accordance with the expected norms of hockey culture.

Group-Based and Collective Emotions

Another way of considering emotions in groups and teams is to examine group-based emotions that are experienced as a function of one's affiliation or identity as a member of a group (Goldenberg, Saguy, &

Halperin, 2014). A similar concept is collective emotions (Von Scheve & Ismer, 2013), which refers to the collective experience of emotions in the presence of others belonging to the same groups (e.g., celebrations among a team of athletes following a win). Group-based and collective emotions are thought to arise as a function of appraisals that explicitly involve elements of individuals' social relationships and their identification as a member of a group or team (Kuppens & Yzerbyt, 2012, see also Chapter 2).

Preliminary qualitative research has revealed that athletes report experiencing group-based and collective emotions such as pride or happiness on behalf of their teammates and as a function of their identities as athletes (Tamminen, Gaudreau, McEwen, & Crocker, 2016). Similarly, Uphill and Jones (2007) provided evidence that athletes' sense of belonging to an "elite" group was associated with their emotional experience of pride. Subsequent experimental research has provided evidence that athletes whose personal identities were manipulated or primed, such that they identified more strongly with their team, reported more positive emotions (and a greater intensity of them) during a rugby match than athletes who identified more strongly as individuals (Campo et al., 2019).

While the experience and expression of emotion has been largely examined as an individualistic phenomenon, there is emerging evidence regarding the impact of emotions and emotion regulation efforts on the appraisals, cognitions, emotions, and behaviors of others. This "interpersonal turn" in the study of emotions in sport is an exciting one that promises to shed light on the ways that emotions and affective phenomena are intertwined with research on group dynamics and social identity. Beyond these studies of interpersonal emotional experiences and the social functions of emotions, there is also an emerging body of research examining processes of interpersonal emotion regulation between teammates (Friesen et al., 2013; Palmateer & Tamminen, 2017; Tamminen & Crocker, 2013; Tamminen et al., 2016; Wagstaff & Weston, 2014), between coaches and athletes (Braun & Tamminen, 2019), and among those operating within the breadth of the same sport organization (e.g., Wagstaff et al., 2012a, 2012b; Wagstaff, Hanton, & Fletcher, 2013). Moreover, research has been conducted examining dyadic (Nicholls & Perry, 2016) and communal coping in sport (Leprince, D'Arripe-Longueville, & Doron, 2018; Neely, McHugh, Dunn, & Holt, 2017; see also Chapter 3). Given the increasing attention to these topics in the field of sport psychology, these promise to be fruitful areas for future research.

Future Research Directions

In sport, emotion has typically been studied as a within-person, one-direction, non-repetitive phenomenon, which, although contributory, is a somewhat narrow focus and does not allow for a full appreciation of emotion phenomena in sport organizations. Hence, much stands to be gained from extending the prevailing examination of emotion phenomena at the individual-level in sport by considering an inclusive, multilevel model that spans micro (i.e., individual), meso (e.g., dyadic and team), and macro (i.e., organizational and cultural) dimensions. Given dyads, groups, teams, and organizations are witness to instances of individual influence through emotion experience and expression, there is a potentially fruitful future for the research on interpersonal emotion-related phenomena in sport.

Sociocultural norms distinct to each sport are evident in both research and applied contexts within sport psychology. Research is required to further illuminate the dynamics surrounding self and interpersonal emotional regulation in teams and organizations. Moreover, it would be valuable to explore the role that environment-related factors (e.g., organizational culture, climate, and change) play in influencing these sociocultural norms regarding emotions. Wagstaff and Hanton (2017) noted that such work might benefit from the use of ecological momentary analysis, diary, and experience sampling methods while also attempting to address issues of aggregation across levels of analysis.

While we have argued for a more multilevel, and in particular, an interpersonal and social functioning perspective on emotions in sport, we are mindful that the intrapersonal level of analysis retains interest for many scientist-practitioners. Hence, we would call on such scholars to direct their efforts toward longitudinal, in-competition, post-competition, and complex modeling of multiple emotional experiences at the intraindividual level of emotion. Such work may require the use of psychophysiological testing (e.g., variable heart rate monitoring and hormonal stress markers) and more useable in-competition emotion psychometrics (e.g., very brief emotion self-report measures).

Applied Considerations

It is important to educate individuals fulfilling a variety of roles within sport organizations (i.e., athletes, coaches, managers, and support staff) that they are vulnerable to and influence the emotions of those they transact with (see also Chapter 12). Hence, sport psychologists must be better prepared for working within the "emotional cauldron" of sport and support individuals to use emotions wisely to prepare for and respond to circumstances that transcend multiple levels of the organizational hierarchy. Moreover, the requirement for emotion regulation and emotional intelligence abilities have been underestimated in sport and reflect a pervasive necessity of organizational life. It would be valuable for sport psychologists to incorporate the ability to develop such competencies into their skillset. By reflecting on and better preparing for the contexts in which they must practice, practitioners will likely become more self- and culturally aware, and develop richer working alliances with clients.

Additional implications are evident from the emerging interpersonal emotion regulation literature. Although reported as a necessary emotion regulation strategy within sport organizations, suppressing one's emotional expression appears to have undesirable implications for relationships and sport performance (see Wagstaff, 2014; Wagstaff & Weston, 2014). That is, Hings and colleagues (see Hings, Wagstaff, Anderson, Gilmore, & Thelwell, 2018, 2019; Hings, Wagstaff, Thelwell, Gilmore, & Anderson, 2018), recently observed emotional labor to be an essential professional act in sport science and medicine practitioners, albeit associated with poor well-being and intention to leave the profession. Moreover, Hings et al. (2019) made a number of recommendations regarding the emotional educational—training—practice gap in the professional formation of sport and exercise psychologists through the theoretical lens of emotional labor. These recommendations would benefit practitioners at all stages of professional advancement but might also be adapted—following further exploration—for use with clients. Additionally, given the emerging evidence that emotional expressiveness and affective communication via deliberate facial, verbal, and behavioral expressions might have utility in sport environments, practitioners should work closely with individuals in sport to optimize their use of emotions, while remaining conscious not to commodify or deauthenticate emotions within these domains.

Finally, enabling the discovery of emotional information that would otherwise remain private might facilitate empathy, shared understanding, and common experiences of problems and issues that serve to promote socioemotional bonds between others within one's sport environment (cf. Hägglund, Kenttä, Thelwell, & Wagstaff, 2019). Hence, practitioners stand to foster substantial social and cultural capital among the teams and organizations with whom they work, should they be able to act in a facilitative and constructive manner to nudge the emotional fabric of the environment. We would go so far as to suggest that sport psychologists are perfectly placed and must develop the competence to act as emotion advisors, handlers, and supporters to influence the sociocultural setting of sport organizations; working behind the scenes to facilitate interpersonal emotion regulation among others. This role is not dissimilar to that of a cultural architect (see Wagstaff & Burton-Wylie, 2018).

Conclusion

To conclude, we return to reflect on the present status of emotion research in sport. We would argue that the study of emotion in sport is generally viewed as a mature research area and one that represents a ubiquitous area of applied sport psychology practice with individuals, dyads, teams, and organizations. Yet, we are both surprised and excited to highlight in this review how much remains to be systematically examined within this domain. Given leading contemporary emotion theorists (e.g., van Kleef, 2010) have specifically identified the sport domain as one of great potential for research, and that sport environments offer such vibrant contexts for studying and influencing human well-being and performance, there remains much valuable work to be completed.

References

Baron, B., Guilloux, B., Begue, M., & Uriac, S. (2015). Emotional responses during repeated sprint intervals performed on level, downhill and uphill surfaces. *Journal of Sports Sciences, 33*, 476–486.

Blascovich, J., Seery, M. D., Mugridge, C. A., Norris, R. K., & Weisbuch, M. D. (2004). Predicting athletic performance from cardiovascular indexes of challenge and threat. *Journal of Experimental Social Psychology, 40*, 683–688.

Braun, C., & Tamminen, K. A. (2019). Coaches' interpersonal emotion regulation and the coach-athlete relationship. *Movement Sport Sciences, 3*, 37–51.

Campo, M., Champely, S., Louvet, B., Rosnet, E., Ferrand, C., Pauketat, J. V. T., & Mackie, D. M. (2019). Group-based emotions: Evidence for emotion-performance relationships in team sports. *Research Quarterly for Exercise and Sport, 90*, 54–63. Doi:10.1080/02701367.2018.1563274

Cerin, E., Szabo, A., Hunt, N., & Williams, C. (2000). Temporal patterning of competitive emotions: A critical review. *Journal of Sports Sciences, 18*, 605–626.

Cropanzano, R., Weiss, H. M., Hale, J. M., & Reb, J. (2003). The structure of affect: Reconsidering the relationship between negative and positive affectivity. *Journal of Management, 29*, 831–857.

Doron, J., & Martinent, G. (2016). Trajectories of psychological states of women elite fencers during the final stages of international matches. *Journal of Sports Science, 34*, 836–842.

Ekkekakis, P. (2012). The measurement of affect, mood, and emotion in exercise psychology. In G. Tenenbaum, R. C. Eklund, & A. Kamata (Eds.), *Measurement in sport and exercise psychology* (pp. 321–332). Champaign; IL: Human Kinetics.

Ekman, P. (1992). An argument for basic emotions. *Cognition & Emotion, 6*, 169–200.

Eysenck, M. W., & Calvo, M. G. (1992). Anxiety and performance: The processing efficiency theory. *Cognition & Emotion, 6*, 409–434.

Fletcher, D., & Fletcher, J. (2005). A meta-model of stress, emotions and performance: Conceptual foundations, theoretical framework, and research directions. *Journal of Sports Sciences, 23*, 157–158.

Fletcher, D., Hanton, S., & Mellalieu, S. D. (2006). An organisational stress review: Conceptual and theoretical issues in competitive sport. In S. Hanton & S. D. Mellalieu (Eds.), *Literature reviews in sport psychology* (pp. 321–374). Hauppauge, NY: Nova Science Publishers.

Forgas, J. P. (1995). Mood and judgment: The affect infusion model (AIM). *Psychological Bulletin, 117*, 39–66.

Friesen, A. P., Devonport, T. J., Sellars, C. N., & Lane, A. M. (2013). A narrative account of decision-making and interpersonal emotion regulation using a social-functional approach to emotions. *International Journal of Sport and Exercise Psychology, 11*(2), 203–214.

Friesen, A. P., Lane, A. M., Devonport, T. J., Sellars, C. N., Stanley, D. N., & Beedie, C. J. (2013). Emotion in sport: Considering interpersonal regulation strategies. *International Review of Sport and Exercise Psychology, 6*, 139–154.

Frijda, N. H. (1986). *The emotions.* Cambridge, UK: Cambridge University Press.

Frijda, N. H. (1988). The laws of emotion. *American Psychologist, 43*, 349–358.

Frijda, N. H., & Mesquita, B. (1994). The social roles and functions of emotions. In S. Kitayama & H. R. Markus (Eds.), *Emotion and culture: Empirical studies of mutual influence* (pp. 51–87). Washington, DC: American Psychological Association.

Gallmeier, C. P. (1987). Putting on the game face: The staging of emotions in professional hockey. *Sociology of Sport Journal, 4*, 347–362.

Goldenberg, A., Saguy, T., & Halperin, E. (2014). How group-based emotions are shaped by collective emotions: Evidence for emotional transfer and emotional burden. *Journal of Personality and Social Psychology, 107*, 581–596.

Hägglund, K., Kenttä, G., Thelwell, R., & Wagstaff, C. R. (2019). Is there an upside of vulnerability in sport? A mindfulness approach applied in the pursuit of psychological strength. *Journal of Sport Psychology in Action, 10*, 220–226. Doi:10.1080/21520704.2018.1549642

Hanin, Y. L. (2000). Individual zones of optimal functioning (IZOF) model. In Y. L. Hanin (Ed.), *Emotions in sport* (pp. 65–89). Champaign, IL: Human Kinetics.

Hanin, Y. L. (2007). Emotions in sport: Current issues and perspectives. In G. Tenenbaum & R. Eklund (Eds.), *Handbook of sport psychology* (3rd ed., pp. 31–58). New York: John Wiley & Sons.

Hanton, S., Thomas, O., & Maynard, I. (2004). Competitive anxiety responses in the week leading up to competition: The role of intensity, direction and frequency dimensions. *Psychology of Sport and Exercise, 5*, 169–181.

Hardy, L. (1990). A catastrophe model of performance in sport. In G. Jones & L. Hardy (Eds.), *Stress and performance in sport* (pp. 81–106). Chichester, UK: John Wiley & Sons.

Hings, R. F., Wagstaff, C. R. D., Anderson, V., Gilmore, S., & Thelwell, R. C. (2018). Professional challenges in elite sports medicine and science: Composite vignettes of practitioner emotional labor. *Psychology of Sport and Exercise, 35*, 66–73. Doi:10.1016/j.psychsport.2017.11.007

Hings, R. F., Wagstaff, C. R. D., Anderson, V., Gilmore, S., & Thelwell, R. C. (2019). Better preparing sports psychologists for the demands of applied practice: The emotional labor training gap. *Journal of Applied Sport Psychology, 1–22.* Doi:10.1080/10413200.2018.1560373

Hings, R. F., Wagstaff, C. R. D., Thelwell, R. C., Gilmore, S., & Anderson, V. (2018). Emotional labor and professional practice in sports medicine and science. *Scandinavian Journal of Medicine & Science in Sports, 28*, 704–716. Doi:10.1111/sms.12941

Jones, G. (1995). More than just a game: Research developments and issues in competitive anxiety in sport. *British Journal of Psychology, 86*, 449–478.

Jones, M. V. (2003). Controlling emotions in sport. *The Sport Psychologist, 17*, 471–486.

Jones, M. V., Lane, A. M., Bray, S. R., Uphill, M., & Catlin, J. (2005). Development and validation of the sport emotion questionnaire. *Journal of Sport and Exercise Psychology, 27*, 407–431.

Jones, M. V., Meijen, C., McCarthy, P. J., & Sheffield, D. (2009). A theory of challenge and threat states in athletes. *International Review of Sport and Exercise Psychology, 2*, 161–180.

Jones, M. V., & Uphill, M. (2011). Emotion in sport: Antecedents and performance consequences. In J. Thatcher, M. V. Jones, & D. Lavallee (Eds.), *Coping and emotion in sport* (2nd ed., pp. 33–61). Hove, UK: Routledge.

Jordet, G. (2009). Why do English players fail in soccer penalty shootouts? A study of team status, self-regulation, and choking under pressure. *Journal of Sports Sciences, 27*, 97–106.

Keltner, D., & Haidt, J. (1999). Social functions of emotions at four levels of analysis. *Cognition & Emotion, 13*, 505–521.

Kuppens, T., & Yzerbyt, V. Y. (2012). Group-based emotions: The impact of social identity on appraisals, emotions, and behaviors. *Basic and Applied Social Psychology, 34*, 20–33.

Lane, A. M., Devonport, T. J., Friesen, A. P., Beedie, C. J., Fullerton, C. L., & Stanley, D. M. (2015). How should I regulate my emotions if I want to run faster? *European Journal of Sport Science, 11*, 1–8.

Lazarus, R. S. (2000). How emotions influence performance in competitive sports. *The Sport Psychologist, 14*, 229–252.

Leprince, C., D'Arripe-Longueville, F., & Doron, J. (2018). Coping in teams: Exploring athletes' communal coping strategies to deal with shared stressors. *Frontiers in Psychology, 9*, 1908. Doi:10.3389/fpsyg.2018.01908

Martens, R., Burton, D., Vealey, R. S., Bump, L. A., & Smith, D. E. (1990). Development and validation of the Competitive State Anxiety Inventory-2. In R. Martens, R. S. Vealey, & D. Burton (Eds.), *Competitive anxiety in sport* (pp. 117–190). Champaign, IL: Human Kinetics.

Martinent, G., Campo, M., & Ferrand, C. (2012). A descriptive study of emotional process during competition: Nature, frequency, direction, duration and co-occurrence of discrete emotions. *Psychology of Sport and Exercise, 13*, 142–151.

Martinent, G., Gareau, A., Lienhart, N., Nicaise, V., & Guillet-Descas, E. (2018). Emotion profiles and their motivational antecedents among adolescent athletes in intensive training settings. *Psychology of Sport and Exercise, 35*, 198–206.

Masters, R. S. (1992). Knowledge, knerves and know-how: The role of explicit versus implicit knowledge in the breakdown of a complex motor skill under pressure. *British Journal of Psychology, 83*, 343–358.

McCarthy, P. J. (2011). Positive emotion in sport performance: Current status and future directions. *International Review of Sport and Exercise Psychology, 4*, 50–69.

Mellalieu, S. D., Hanton, S., & Fletcher, D. (2006). A competitive anxiety review: Recent directions in sport psychology research. In S. Hanton & S. D. Mellalieu (Eds.), *Literature reviews in sport psychology* (pp. 1–45). Hauppage, NY: Nova.

Moll, T., Jordet, G., & Pepping, G. J. (2010). Emotional contagion in soccer penalty shootouts: Celebration of individual success is associated with ultimate team success. *Journal of Sports Sciences, 28*, 983–992.

Mullen, R., Hardy, L., & Tattersall, A. (2005). The effects of anxiety on motor performance: A test of the conscious processing hypothesis. *Journal of Sport & Exercise Psychology, 27,* 212–225.

Neely, K. C., McHugh, T. L. F., Dunn, J. G., & Holt, N. L. (2017). Athletes and parents coping with deselection in competitive youth sport: A communal coping perspective. *Psychology of Sport and Exercise, 30,* 1–9. Doi:10.1016/j. psychsport.2017.01.004

Nibbeling, N., Daanen, H. A., Gerritsma, R. M., Hofland, R. M., & Oudejans, R. R. (2012). Effects of anxiety on running with and without an aiming task. *Journal of Sports Sciences, 30,* 11–19.

Nicholls, A. R., & Perry, J. L. (2016). Perceptions of coach—athlete relationship are more important to coaches than athletes in predicting dyadic coping and stress appraisals: An actor—partner independence mediation model. *Frontiers in Psychology, 7,* 447. Doi:10.3389/fpsyg.2016.00447

Nieuwenhuys, A., Pijpers, J. R., Oudejans, R. R., & Bakker, F. C. (2008). The influence of anxiety on visual attention in climbing. *Journal of Sport & Exercise Psychology, 30,* 171–185.

Palmateer, T., & Tamminen, K. A. (2017). A case study of interpersonal emotion regulation among a varsity volleyball team. *Journal of Applied Sport Psychology, 30,* 321–340. Doi:10.1080/10413200.2017.1367335

Raglin, J. S., & Hanin, Y. L. (2000). Competitive anxiety. In Y. L. Hanin (Ed.), *Emotions in sport* (pp. 93–111). Champaign, IL: Human Kinetics.

Rathschlag, M., & Memmert, D. (2015). Self-generated emotions and their influence on sprint performance: An investigation of happiness and anxiety. *Journal of Applied Sport Psychology, 27,* 186–199.

Robazza, C., & Bortoli, L. (2007). Perceived impact of anger and anxiety on sporting performance in rugby players. *Psychology of Sport and Exercise, 8,* 875–896.

Saby, Y., Pupier, Y., Guillet-Descas, E., Nicolas, M., & Martinent, G. (2019). Longitudinal emotional process among adolescent soccer player in intensive training centre. *Journal of Sports Sciences,* 1–12. Doi:10.1080/02640414.2019. 1662538

Scherer, K. R. (1984). Emotion as a multicomponent process: A model and some cross-cultural data. In P. Shaver (Ed.), *Review of personality and social psychology* (5th ed., pp. 37–63). Beverly Hills, CA: Sage.

Scherer, K. R. (1993). Studying the emotion-antecedent appraisal process: An expert system approach. *Cognition & Emotion, 7,* 325–355.

Schwarz, N. (1990). *Feelings as information: Informational and motivational functions of affective states.* New York: Guilford Press.

Sève, C., Ria, L., Poizat, G., Saury, J., & Durand, M. (2007). Performance-induced emotions experienced during high-stakes table tennis matches. *Psychology of Sport and Exercise, 8*(1), 25–46.

Smith, C. A., & Ellsworth, P. C. (1985). Patterns of cognitive appraisal in emotion. *Journal of Personality and Social Psychology, 48,* 813–838.

Stenseng, F., Forest, J., & Curran, T. (2015). Positive emotions in recreational sport activities: The role of passion and belongingness. *Journal of Happiness Studies, 16,* 1117–1129.

Tamminen, K. A., & Crocker, P. R. (2013). "I control my own emotions for the sake of the team": Emotional self-regulation and interpersonal emotion regulation among female high-performance curlers. *Psychology of Sport and Exercise, 14,* 737–747.

Tamminen, K. A., Gaudreau, P., McEwen, C. E., & Crocker, P. R. E. (2016). Interpersonal emotional regulation among adolescent athletes and their teammates: A Bayesian multilevel model of sport enjoyment and commitment. *Journal of Sport & Exercise Psychology, 38,* 541–555. Doi:10.1123/jsep.2015-0189

Tamminen, K. A., Palmateer, T. M., Denton, M., Sabiston, C., Crocker, P. R. E., Eys, M., & Smith, B. (2016). Exploring emotions as social phenomena among Canadian varsity athletes. *Psychology of Sport and Exercise, 27,* 28–38. Doi:10.1016/j.psychsport.2016.07.010

Thelwell, R. C., Wagstaff, C. R. D., Chapman, M. T., & Kenttä, G. (2017). Examining coaches' perceptions of how their stress influences the coach-athlete relationship. *Journal of Sports Sciences, 35,* 1928–1939. Doi:10.1080/02640414. 2016.1241422

Thelwell, R. C., Wagstaff, C. R. D., Rayner, A., Chapman, M., & Barker, J. (2017). Exploring athletes' perceptions of coach stress in elite sport environments. *Journal of Sports Sciences, 35,* 44–55.

Thomas, O., Hanton, S., & Maynard, I. (2007). Anxiety responses and psychological skill use during the time leading up to competition: Theory to practice I. *Journal of Applied Sport Psychology, 19,* 379–397.

Totterdell, P. (2000). Catching moods and hitting runs: Mood linkage and subjective performance in professional sport teams. *Journal of Applied Psychology, 85,* 848.

Uphill, M. A., & Jones, M. V. (2007). Antecedents of emotions in elite athletes: A cognitive motivational relational theory perspective. *Research Quarterly for Exercise and Sport, 78*(2), 79–89.

Vallerand, R. J., & Blanchard, C. M. (2000). The study of emotion in sport and exercise: Historical, definitional, and conceptual perspectives. In Y. L. Hanin (Ed.), *Emotions in sport* (pp. 3–38). Champaign, IL: Human Kinetics.

Van Kleef, G. A. (2009). How emotions regulate social life: The emotions as social information (EASI) model. *Current Directions in Psychological Science, 18,* 184–188.

Van Kleef, G. A. (2010). The emerging view of emotion as social information. *Social and Personality Psychology Compass, 4,* 331–343.

Van Kleef, G. A., Cheshin, A., Koning, L. F., & Wolf, S. A. (2019). Emotional games: How coaches' emotional expressions shape players' emotions, inferences, and team performance. *Psychology of Sport and Exercise, 41,* 1–11.

Vine, S. J., Moore, L. J., & Wilson, M. R. (2011). Quiet eye training facilitates competitive putting performance in elite golfers. *Frontiers in Psychology, 2,* 1–9.

Von Scheve, C., & Ismer, S. (2013). Towards a theory of collective emotions. *Emotion Review, 5*(4), 406–413.

Wagstaff, C. R. D. (2014). Emotion regulation and sport performance. *Journal of Sport and Exercise Psychology, 36,* 401–412.

Wagstaff, C. R. D., & Burton-Wylie, S. (2018). Organisational culture in sport: A conceptual, definitional and methodological review. *Sport & Exercise Psychology Review, 14,* 32–52.

Wagstaff, C. R. D., Fletcher, D., & Hanton, S. (2012a). Positive organizational psychology in sport: An ethnography of organizational functioning in a national sport organization. *Journal of Applied Sport Psychology, 24,* 26–47.

Wagstaff, C. R. D., Fletcher, D., & Hanton, S. (2012b). Exploring emotion abilities and regulation strategies in sport organizations. *Sport, Exercise, and Performance Psychology, 1*, 268–282.

Wagstaff, C. R. D., & Hanton, S. (2017). Emotions in sport organizations. In C. R. D. Wagstaff (Ed.), *The organizational psychology of sport: Key issues and practical applications* (pp. 33–61). Abingdon, UK: Routledge.

Wagstaff, C. R. D., Hanton, S., & Fletcher, D. (2013). Developing emotion abilities and regulation strategies in a sport organization: An action research intervention. *Psychology of Sport & Exercise, 14*, 476–487.

Wagstaff, C. R. D., Neil, R., Mellalieu, S. D., & Hanton, S. (2012). Key movements in directional research in competitive anxiety. *Routledge Online Studies on the Olympic and Paralympic Games, 53*, 143–166. Doi:10.4324/9780203852293

Wagstaff, C. R. D., & Weston, N. J. (2014). Examining emotion regulation in an isolated performance team in Antarctica. *Sport, Exercise, and Performance Psychology, 3*, 273–287.

Williams, A. M., Vickers, J., & Rodrigues, S. (2002). The effects of anxiety on visual search, movement kinematics, and performance in table tennis: A test of Eysenck and Calvo's processing efficiency theory. *Journal of Sport and Exercise Psychology, 24*, 438–455.

Wilson, M. R., Wood, G., & Vine, S. J. (2009). Anxiety, attentional control, and performance impairment in penalty kicks. *Journal of Sport and Exercise Psychology, 31*, 761–775.

Woodman, T., Davis, P. A., Hardy, L., Callow, N., Glasscock, I., & Yuill-Proctor, J. (2009). Emotions and sport performance: An exploration of happiness, hope, and anger. *Journal of Sport & Exercise Psychology, 31*, 169–188.

Woodman, T., & Hardy, L. (2001). Stress and anxiety. In R. Singer, H. A. Hausenblas, & C. M. Janelle (Eds.), *Handbook of research on sport psychology* (pp. 290–318). New York: Wiley.

Woodman, T., & Hardy, L. (2003). The relative impact of cognitive anxiety and self-confidence upon sport performance: A meta-analysis. *Journal of Sports Sciences, 21*, 443–457.

5 Attention and Visuomotor Performance Under Pressure

Lee J. Moore, Samuel J. Vine, and Mark R. Wilson

Research has shown that concentration is a key skill that enables world-class athletes (e.g., Olympic medalists) to produce high levels of performance during stressful competition (e.g., Gould, Eklund, & Jackson, 1993; Orlick & Partington, 1988; Robazza & Bortoli, 1998). For instance, Gould, Dieffenbach, and Moffett (2002) found that, alongside other psychological characteristics (e.g., coping with anxiety and mental toughness), Olympic champions attributed their success to their ability to focus attention and block out distractions. Attention is widely accepted as the process of concentrating mental activity on environmental, sensory, or cognitive events (Moran, 2009), and can be split into two main dimensions, namely selective and divided attention. While selective attention allows athletes to "zoom in" on task-relevant information and ignore less-relevant information (e.g., block out the crowd when hitting a golf shot), divided attention enables athletes to focus on multiple stimuli and complete two or more actions simultaneously (e.g., monitor a goalkeepers' movements while taking a soccer penalty; Moran, 1996). Stress is proposed to influence the performance of visually guided sports skills via its effects on attention, a process that will be explored in this chapter using the Integrative Framework of Stress, Attention, and Visuomotor Performance as a guide (Vine, Moore, & Wilson, 2016).

Integrative Framework of Stress, Attention, and Visuomotor Performance

To explain the effects of stress on visually guided motor (visuomotor) performance, and inter- and intra-individual variability in performance during potentially stressful situations, Vine et al. (2016) developed a conceptual framework (see Figure 5.1). This framework was developed from existing evidence and integrated the core predictions of the Biopsychosocial Model (BPSM) of Challenge and Threat (Blascovich & Tomaka, 1996) and Attentional Control Theory (ACT; Eysenck, Derakshan, Santos, & Calvo, 2007). In the following sections, the BPSM and ACT are briefly summarized before the predictions of the Integrative Framework of Stress, Attention, and Visuomotor Performance are outlined.

Biopsychosocial Model of Challenge and Threat

The BPSM helps explain why athletes respond and perform differently during potentially stressful competition (Blascovich, 2008). The BPSM applies to motivated performance situations, or contexts in which individuals must perform instrumental responses (cognitive and/or physical) to attain important and self-relevant goals (e.g., sporting competition, tests, interviews, and public speaking; Seery, 2013). Inspired by the work of Lazarus and Folkman (1984), the BPSM contends that how an athlete reacts to a stressful competition is determined by their evaluations of situational demands and personal coping resources (Blascovich, 2008). If an athlete perceives that they have sufficient resources to cope with the demands of the competition, they evaluate it as a challenge. Conversely, if an athlete judges that they lack the necessary resources, they evaluate it as a threat (Seery, 2011; see also Chapter 2). The BPSM argues that these demand and resource evaluations occur at a more subconscious and automatic, rather than conscious and deliberate, level (Blascovich & Mendes, 2000). Additionally, these evaluations are thought to be relatively dynamic (Blascovich, 2008), meaning that while an athlete might initially evaluate a competition as a threat, after a few minutes, they might re-evaluate it as a challenge.

Drawing on the work of Dienstbier (1989), the BPSM predicts that varying psychological evaluations trigger distinct physiological responses (Blascovich, 2008). If an athlete evaluates a stressful competition as a challenge, sympathetic-adrenomedullary activation increases and catecholamines are released (e.g., adrenaline), causing blood vessels to dilate and blood flow to increase (Seery, 2011). In contrast, if an athlete evaluates a competition as a threat, pituitary-adrenocortical activation increases, attenuating sympathetic-adrenomedullary activity and releasing cortisol, resulting in little change in or constriction of the blood vessels, and little change in or decreased blood flow (Seery, 2011). Thus, compared to a threat state, a challenge state is marked by greater reductions in total peripheral resistance (TPR; net constriction vs. dilation in the arterial system) and increases in cardiac output (CO; amount of blood pumped by the heart per minute) from rest (Blascovich, 2008). Importantly, this cardiovascular response is considered to be more efficient because it quickly mobilizes energy for the brain and muscles, preparing the body for immediate action (Mendes & Park, 2014). The cardiovascular responses marking challenge and threat are argued to provide an indirect and objective (relatively bias-free) measure of underlying demand and resource evaluations, offering a window into an athletes' mind (Seery, 2013; see also Chapter 2).

The BPSM predicts that an athlete who responds to a stressful competition with a challenge state will outperform an athlete who reacts with a threat state (Blascovich, 2008). Research has supported this assertion, with a challenge state associated with better performance in baseball batting (Blascovich, Seery, Mugridge, Norris, & Weisbuch, 2004), netball shooting (Turner, Jones, Sheffield, & Cross, 2012), golf putting (Moore, Vine, Wilson, & Freeman, 2012), cricket batting (Turner et al., 2013), dart throwing (Moore, Young, Freeman, & Sarkar, 2018), sprint cycling (Wood, Parker, Freeman, Black, & Moore, 2018), simulated car racing (Trotman, Williams, Quinton, & Van Zanten, 2018), and soccer penalty taking (Brimmell, Parker, Wilson, Vine, & Moore, 2019). As well as predicting performance in laboratory-based tasks, a challenge state has also been linked to superior performance in real-world sporting competition (Dixon, Jones, & Turner, 2019; Moore, Wilson, Vine, Coussens, & Freeman, 2013). To summarize work in this area, Hase, O'Brien, Moore, and Freeman (2019) conducted a systematic review of 38 studies (3257 participants), revealing that a challenge state was related to better performance in 74% of studies (see Behnke & Kaczmarek, 2018 for a meta-analysis).

Despite ample research demonstrating that challenge and threat states have divergent effects on sports performance (Hase, O'Brien, et al., 2019; see also Chapter 2), relatively little is known about the potential mechanisms underlying these effects (e.g., emotional; see Jones, Meijen, McCarthy, & Sheffield, 2009). Although the BPSM can explain athletes' psychological and physiological responses to potentially stressful competition, and why these responses might vary between athletes and across situations, it does not specify precisely how these responses influence sports performance. Thus, to better elucidate how challenge and threat states impact the performance of visually guided sports skills, Vine et al. (2016) integrated the predictions of the BPSM with the core assumptions of ACT (Eysenck et al., 2007).

Attentional Control Theory

Like its predecessor, Processing Efficiency Theory (Eysenck & Calvo, 1992), ACT has been used to explain how anxiety affects sports performance via its impact on attentional control (Wilson, 2008)—defined as the ability to flexibly focus and shift attention (Muris, Mayer, Van Lint, & Hofman, 2008). While other mechanistic explanations argue that performance deteriorates because highly anxious athletes direct attention inward to consciously control movements (e.g., Theory of Reinvestment; Masters & Maxwell, 2008), ACT contends that performance suffers because anxious athletes become less focused and more distractible (Eysenck & Wilson, 2016). ACT was originally developed in relation to trait anxiety or one's general propensity to experience anxiety; however, in sport, it has mostly been applied to state anxiety, defined as a negative transient emotional state evoked during stressful situations (Eysenck et al., 2007; see also Chapter 4). ACT has three main assumptions, which have received empirical support (see, for a review, Shi, Sharpe, & Abbott, 2019). First, ACT predicts that anxiety impairs processing efficiency (ratio between performance effectiveness and effort) more than performance effectiveness or quality (e.g., dart throwing accuracy; Eysenck & Derakshan, 2011), such that anxious athletes can offset the negative effects of anxiety by using extra processing resources or effort (Wilson, 2008).

Second, ACT predicts that anxiety disrupts the balance of two attentional systems, increasing the influence of the stimulus-driven (bottom-up) system at the expense of the goal-directed (top-down) system (Eysenck et al., 2007). The goal-directed system is located in the dorsal posterior parietal and frontal cortex, and directs attention based on knowledge, expectations, and current goals (Corbetta & Shulman, 2002). In contrast, the stimulus-driven system is located in the temporo-parietal and ventral frontal cortex, and helps detect salient and threatening environmental stimuli (Corbetta, Patel, & Shulman, 2008). The most notable effect of the anxiety-induced imbalance in these attentional systems is that athletes become more distractible by task-irrelevant and threatening stimuli (e.g., crowd or negative thoughts during a basketball free throw). Third, in explaining this imbalance, ACT predicts that anxiety impairs the inhibition and shifting functions of the central executive of working memory (Eysenck et al., 2007). While the inhibition function stops interference or disruptions from task-irrelevant stimuli (negative attentional control), the shifting function allocates attention flexibly to remain focused on task-relevant cues (positive attentional control; Miyake, Friedman, Emerson, Witzki, Howerter, & Wager, 2000). Studies in cognitive psychology have supported these disruptions to inhibition and shifting (Shi et al., 2019).

Beyond controlled cognitive tasks, research in sport psychology has also supported the assumptions of ACT (Payne, Wilson, & Vine, 2019; Roberts, Jackson, & Grundy, 2019). In particular, anxiety has been shown to disrupt attentional control in studies using eye-tracking technology, which allows the location and duration of visual attention (via fixations— when the eyes rest steady on a location or object) to be recorded during skill execution (Kredel, Vater, Klostermann, & Hossner, 2017). Optimal attentional control in many sports skills (e.g., rifle shooting) involves fewer fixations of a longer duration, or lower search rates (Mann, Williams, Ward, & Janelle, 2007), and longer fixations immediately before skill execution, also known as extended quiet eye durations (Lebeau et al., 2016; Vickers, 2016). However, highly anxious athletes tend to display less efficient attentional control characterized by higher search rates and shorter quiet eye durations (Behan & Wilson, 2008; Causer,

Holmes, Smith, & Williams, 2011; Nibbeling, Oudejans, & Daanen, 2012; Nieuwenhuys, Pijpers, Oudejans, & Bakker, 2008; Vickers & Williams, 2007; Williams, Vickers, & Rodrigues, 2002; Wilson, Wood, & Vine, 2009). For example, Wilson, Vine, and Wood (2009) found that during free throws under high anxiety, basketball players displayed more erratic visual search, including more fixations of a shorter duration to various locations (e.g., hoop, backboard, and net), owing to the increased influence of the stimulus-driven system, and shorter quiet eye durations, due to the reduced impact of the goal-directed system.

Although considerable research has supported the attentional disruptions proposed by ACT in sports skills, the theory is not without its limitations (see Eysenck & Wilson, 2016). Indeed, while ACT provides a mechanistic explanation for how maladaptive stress responses (i.e., heightened anxiety) can disrupt attentional processes that are critical in supplying the visual information needed to plan and execute accurate sports skills, it fails to explain precisely how psychophysiological responses to stress arise, and why these responses might vary between athletes and across situations (Vine et al., 2016). Indeed, this limitation is also relevant to other models that explain the anxiety-performance relationship (e.g., Integrated Model of Anxiety and Perceptual-Motor Performance; Nieuwenhuys & Oudejans, 2012, 2017). Thus, the integrative conceptual framework by Vine et al. (2016) aimed to align the strengths and weaknesses of the BPSM and ACT to better explain how athletes respond to stress, and the impact of these stress responses on attentional control and sports performance.

Predictions of Integrative Framework and Supporting Evidence

The Integrative Framework of Stress, Attention, and Visuomotor Performance applies to stressful situations, in which individuals must perform visually guided skills to achieve important and meaningful goals (e.g., sporting competition; Vine et al., 2016; see Figure 5.1). Consistent with the BPSM, this framework predicts that during stressful competition, an athlete will evaluate situational demands and if they have the resources to cope with these demands (see also Chapters 1–3). An athlete who believes that they have the coping resources will evaluate the competition as a challenge, and respond with lower TPR and higher CO reactivity. In contrast, an athlete who believes that they lack the coping resources will evaluate the competition as a threat and respond with higher TPR and lower CO reactivity. Next, inspired by ACT, the integrative framework proposes that challenge and threat evaluations effect attentional control differently. Specifically, a challenge evaluation leads an athlete to optimally pick up visual information from task-relevant stimuli, because the goal-directed and stimulus-driven attentional systems are balanced. Conversely, a threat evaluation causes an athlete to become more distractible

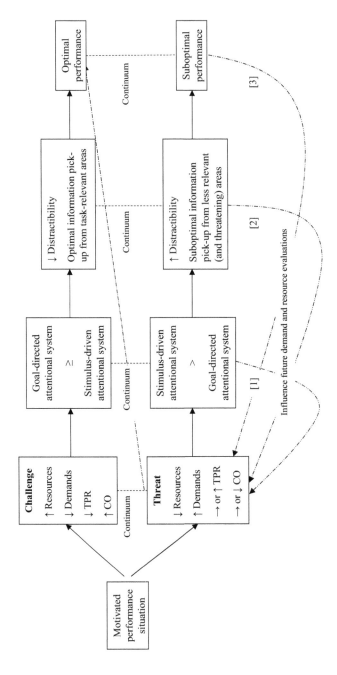

Figure 5.1 The Integrative Framework of Stress, Attention, and Visuomotor Performance (Adapted From Vine et al., 2016)

Notes: **TPR** = total peripheral resistance, **CO** = cardiac output, Diagonal dash dot line = compensatory strategies (e.g., increased effort), Curved dash dot lines = feedback loops by task-irrelevant and threatening stimuli, resulting in the suboptimal pickup of information due to the stimulus-driven system dominating the goal-directed system. In the integrative framework, this imbalance is attributed to the greater anxiety commonly accompanying a threat evaluation, which ultimately causes disruptions in attentional control that degrade performance quality during visually guided sports skills, unless additional processing resources are mobilized (e.g., effort; Vine et al., 2016).

Research has supported the core predictions of the integrative framework in the sport psychology literature, demonstrating that the goal-directed system predominately controls attention during a challenge state, while the stimulus-driven system largely directs attention during a threat state (Vine et al., 2016). For example, Moore, Vine, Wilson, et al. (2012) manipulated novice golfers into either a challenge or threat state before a stressful golf putting task and found that golfers who were manipulated into a challenge state performed better, reported less anxiety, and displayed longer quiet eye durations reflecting superior goal-directed attentional control. These findings were replicated by Moore, Wilson, et al. (2013), who found that experienced golfers who were manipulated into a threat state performed worse, reported more anxiety, and exhibited shorter quiet eye durations during a stressful golf putting task. More recently, Brimmell et al. (2019) found that soccer players who responded to a stressful penalty task with a challenge state (lower TPR and higher CO) performed better and displayed gaze behavior more indicative of goal-directed attentional control, including longer quiet eye durations, lower search rates, more fixations toward the goal and ball, and more time spent fixating on the goal (see Figure 5.2). Similar results have been found outside of sport (e.g., surgery; Vine, Freeman, Moore, Chandra-Ramanan, & Wilson, 2013). For example, Vine et al. (2015) found that pilots who evaluated a stressful aviation task as a threat displayed higher search rates and spent more time fixating on less-relevant areas of the cockpit, reflecting greater stimulus-driven attentional control.

In addition to the core predictions noted previously, three feedback loops were also outlined in the integrative framework, suggesting that athletes are more likely to evaluate similar stressful competitions as a threat in the future if they, (i) experience more threat-like cardiovascular reactivity (higher TPR and lower CO), (ii) overly attend to task-irrelevant and potentially threatening stimuli, and (iii) perform poorly, during a current stressful competition (Vine et al., 2016; see Figure 5.1). To date, few studies have tested these feedback loops, with evidence only offering mixed support. For example, Brimmell et al. (2019) asked experienced soccer players to complete two trials on a stressful penalty task and found that players who took a more accurate penalty during the first trial were more likely to evaluate the second trial as a challenge. However,

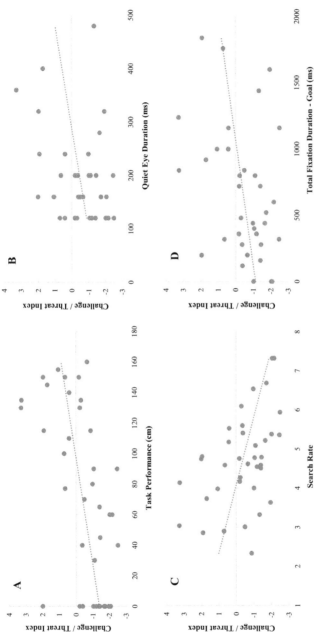

Figure 5.2 The Relationship Between Challenge and Threat States (Challenge/Threat Index) and Task Performance (Soccer Penalty Accuracy) and Attentional Control (Quiet Eye Duration, Search Rate, and Total Fixation Duration on the Goal) Using Data From Brimmell et al. (2019)

Notes: Panel A = challenge/threat index and task performance (cm), Panel B = challenge/threat index and quiet eye duration (ms), Panel C = challenge/threat index and search rate, and Panel D = challenge/threat index and total fixation duration on the goal (ms). A positive challenge/threat index reflects a challenge state (relatively lower TPR and higher CO reactivity), and a negative index reflects a threat state (relatively higher TPR and lower CO reactivity) neither cardiovascular reactivity nor time spent fixating on threatening stimuli (goalkeeper) during the first trial predicted challenge and threat evaluations during the second trial (Brimmell et al., 2019). Studies in social psychology have also provided mixed results. For instance, while Rith-Najarian, McLaughlin, Sheridan, and Nock (2014) found that participants who performed poorly during a stressful speech task were more likely to evaluate the task as a threat in the future, Quigley, Feldman Barrett, and Weinstein (2002) found that prior performance in a stressful mental arithmetic task did not predict future challenge and threat evaluations. Although the feedback loops proposed by the integrative framework require further testing, practitioners can use the core predictions of the framework to develop interventions that help athletes perform better during stressful competition.

Optimizing Attention and Performance Under Pressure

The assumptions of the Integrative Framework of Stress, Attention, and Visuomotor Performance highlight several evidence-based interventions that could help athletes improve their attentional control and performance during stressful competition (Vine et al., 2016). First, given that a challenge state is associated with superior attentional control and sports performance (Hase, O'Brien, et al., 2019), interventions that encourage athletes to view stressful competition as a challenge rather than a threat could be beneficial. While research into challenge-promoting interventions is still growing, some strategies have been shown to foster a challenge state, including imagery (e.g., Williams, Van Zanten, Trotman, Quinton, & Ginty, 2017), self-talk (e.g., Hase, Hood, Moore, and Freeman, 2019), and verbal instructions that promote self-efficacy, perceived control, and a focus on approach goals (e.g., Turner, Jones, Sheffield, Barker, & Coffee, 2014; see also Chapters 2 and 12). Another promising intervention is arousal reappraisal, which helps athletes reinterpret stress-induced increases in physiological arousal (e.g., racing heart) as a tool that can aid performance (Jamieson, Mendes, & Nock, 2013; Sammy et al., 2017). For example, Moore, Vine, Wilson, and Freeman (2015) found that during a stressful golf putting task, novice golfers who received an arousal reappraisal intervention displayed a challenge state and better performance compared to golfers assigned to a control group.

Second, the integrative framework suggests that if disruptions in attentional control can be prevented, then athletes may be able to produce performance that is resilient to stress. One evidence-based intervention that has been shown to accomplish this is quiet eye training (Vine, Moore, & Wilson, 2014). Indeed, as well as being indicative of skilled sports performance and a marker of optimal goal-directed attention control, research has shown that the quiet eye is trainable (Wilson, Wood, &

Vine, 2016). Training athletes to display longer quiet eye durations has been found to counteract the negative effects of anxiety on attentional control and performance (Moore, Vine, Cooke, Ring, & Wilson, 2012; Vine & Wilson, 2011; Wood & Wilson, 2011). For example, Vine and Wilson (2010) found that novice golfers who received quiet eye training maintained effective quiet eye durations and performance under high anxiety, while golfers in a control group exhibited shorter quiet eye durations and poorer performance. Crucially, the benefits of quiet eye training transfer to real-world sporting competition (e.g., Causer, Holmes, & Williams, 2011; Vine, Moore, & Wilson, 2011). While it is still unclear precisely how quiet eye training works, it might provide a pre-performance routine that promotes perceptions of control and helps athletes view stressful competition as a challenge (Moore, Vine, Freeman, & Wilson, 2013; Wood & Wilson, 2012).

Beyond quiet eye training, cognitive training that improves inhibitory attentional control has also been shown to create sports skills that are robust under stress (e.g., Ducrocq, Wilson, Vine, & Derakshan, 2016). Interestingly, this form of attentional control training has also been used with vulnerable individuals affected by anxiety and depression, helping them to become less sensitive to threatening stimuli (e.g., Owens, Koster, & Derakshan, 2013; Sari, Koster, Pourtois, & Derakshan, 2015). Another intervention that has shown promise in helping athletes optimize attentional control and performance during stressful competition is pressure training, or training with anxiety (Gropel & Mesagno, 2017; see also Chapter 12). For example, Alder, Ford, Causer, and Williams (2016) found that elite badminton players who trained under high anxiety made longer final fixations and better anticipatory judgments during a stressful serve reception task, compared to players assigned to a control group or trained under low anxiety. Similar findings have also been reported outside of sport in other domains (e.g., law enforcement; Low et al., 2020). For instance, Nieuwenhuys and Oudejans (2011) found that police officers that trained under high anxiety displayed lower search rates and superior shooting accuracy relative to police officers in a control group. Undoubtedly, other interventions could help athletes optimize attentional control and performance during stressful competition (e.g., pre-performance routines; Mesagno, Hill, & Larkin, 2015); however, many of these require further investigation using objective measures of attention (e.g., eye-tracking metrics).

Future Research

There are several potential avenues for future research. First, most of the research examining stress-related disruptions in attentional control has used objective measurements, such as eye movements (e.g., fixations) recorded via eye-tracking technology (Moran, Campbell, &

Ranieri, 2018). However, according to ACT (Eysenck et al., 2007), the elevated anxiety experienced during potentially stressful situations not only makes athletes more distractible by task-irrelevant environmental stimuli (e.g., crowd during a basketball free throw), but also internal thoughts (e.g., concerns about poor performance; Eysenck & Wilson, 2016). Thus, to offer a more complete test of theoretical predictions (e.g., Vine et al., 2016), future research is encouraged to employ multiple measures of attentional control, including trait-like indices before (e.g., Attentional Control Scale; Derryberry & Reed, 2002), eye-tracking metrics (e.g., quiet eye; Vickers, 2016) and think-aloud protocols (Eccles & Arsal, 2017) during, and retrospective self-report measures after (e.g., Thought Occurrence Questionnaire for Sport; Hatzigeorgi-adis & Biddle, 2000), highly stressful competition. Second, despite being developed from existing evidence, some predictions of the integrative framework require further testing (e.g., elevated state anxiety triggers imbalance in goal-directed and stimulus-driven attentional systems; Vine et al., 2016). In particular, the framework proposes that athletes who evaluate a stressful competition as a threat can still perform well, particularly if they use additional processing resources (e.g., effort). Indeed, this notion fits with the results of Turner et al. (2013), who found that a small subset of cricketers responded to a stressful batting task with a threat state (higher TPR and lower CO), still performed well, possibly due to higher self-efficacy.

Third, while a recent study highlighted that challenge and threat evaluations are mostly situation-specific, it also revealed that athletes have general tendencies to evaluate all stressful situations as a challenge or threat (Moore, Freeman, Hase, Solomon-Moore, & Arnold, 2019). Given that frequently appraising stressors as a threat has been linked to poorer mental and physical health (e.g., social anxiety and cellular aging; O'Donovan et al., 2012; Tomaka, Palacios, Champion, & Monks, 2018), future research is encouraged to move beyond athletic performance and examine the long-term effects of challenge and threat states on athlete health and well-being (see also Chapters 6–8). Specific to the focus of this chapter, this research could also explore if challenge and threat states impact health via their effects on attention (e.g., depression is linked with greater attentional bias toward negative stimuli; Peck-ham, McHugh, & Otto, 2010). Finally, although some interventions have shown promise in helping athletes optimize attentional control and performance during stressful competition (e.g., quiet eye training; Vine et al., 2014), more techniques should be evaluated (e.g., breathing; Zaccaro et al., 2018). For instance, mindfulness and acceptance interventions fit neatly with the predictions of the integrative framework, as they are thought to help athletes sustain task-focused attention by training open, non-reactive, and present-moment awareness (Noetel, Ciar-rochi, Van Zanden, & Lonsdale, 2017). While qualitative studies have supported this proposition (e.g., Bernier, Thienot, Pelosse, & Fournier, 2014), few studies have supported it using objective measures of attentional control (e.g., eye tracking indices).

Conclusion

According to the Integrative Framework of Stress, Attention, and Visuomotor Performance, an athlete who evaluates a potentially stressful competition as a challenge (coping resources exceed situational demands) will react with a cardiovascular response marked by lower TPR and higher CO, which benefits sports performance by keeping attention goal-directed and optimally focused on important task-relevant stimuli. In contrast, an athlete who evaluates a potentially stressful competition as a threat (situational demands exceed coping resources) will react with a cardiovascular response marked by higher TPR and lower CO, which hampers sports performance by increasing distractibility and shifting attention to less-relevant and potentially threatening stimuli. Therefore, to help athletes perform better during stressful competition, practitioners are encouraged to help their athletes view competition as a challenge, not a threat, and to maintain optimal attentional control.

References

Alder, D., Ford, P. R., Causer, C., & Williams, A. M. (2016). The effects of high- and low-anxiety training on the anticipation judgments of elite performers. *Journal of Sport and Exercise Psychology, 38*, 93–104. Doi:10.1123/jsep.2015-0145.

Behan, M., & Wilson, M. (2008). State anxiety and visual attention: The role of the quiet eye period in aiming to a far target. *Journal of Sports Sciences, 26*, 207–215. Doi:10.1080/02640410701446919.

Behnke, M., & Kaczmarek, L. D. (2018). Successful performance and cardiovascular markers of challenge and threat: A meta-analysis. *International Journal of Psychophysiology, 130*, 73–79. Doi:10.1016/j.ijpsycho.2018.04.007.

Bernier, M., Thienot, E., Pelosse, E., & Fournier, J. F. (2014). Effects and underlying processes of a mindfulness-based intervention with young elite figure skaters: Two case studies. *The Sport Psychologist, 28*, 302–315. Doi:10.1123/tsp.2013-0006.

Blascovich, J. (2008). Challenge and threat. In A. J. Elliot (Ed.), *Handbook of approach and avoidance motivation* (pp. 431–445). New York: Psychology Press.

Blascovich, J., & Mendes, W. B. (2000). Challenge and threat appraisals: The role of affective cues. In J. P. Forgas (Ed.), *Feeling and thinking: The role of affect in social cognition* (pp. 59–82). Cambridge, UK: Cambridge University Press.

Blascovich, J., Seery, M. D., Mugridge, C. A., Norris, R. K., & Weisbuch, M. (2004). Predicting athletic performance from cardiovascular indexes of challenge and threat. *Journal of Experimental Social Psychology, 40*, 683–688. Doi:10.1016/j.jesp.2003.10.007.

Blascovich, J., & Tomaka, J. (1996). The biopsychosocial model of arousal regulation. In M. Zanna (Ed.), *Advances in experimental social psychology* (pp. 1–51). New York: Academic Press.

Brimmell, J., Parker, J., Wilson, M. R., Vine, S. J., & Moore, L. J. (2019). Challenge and threat states, performance, and attentional control during a pressurized soccer penalty task. *Sport, Exercise, and Performance Psychology, 8*, 63–79. Doi:10.1037/spy0000147.

Causer, J., Holmes, P. S., Smith, N. C., & Williams, A. M. (2011). Anxiety, movement kinematics, and visual attention in elite-level performers. *Emotion, 11*, 595–602. Doi:10.1037/a0023225.

Causer, J., Holmes, P. S., & Williams, A. M. (2011). Quiet eye training in a visuomotor control task. *Medicine and Science in Sports and Exercise, 43*, 1042–1049. Doi:10.1249/MSS.0b013e3182035de6.

Corbetta, M., Patel, G., & Shulman, G. L. (2008). The reorienting system of the human brain: From environment to theory of mind. *Neuron, 58*, 306–324. Doi:10.1016/j.neuron.2008.04.017.

Corbetta, M., & Shulman, G. L. (2002). Control of goal-directed and stimulus-driven attention in the brain. *Nature Reviews and Neuroscience, 3*, 201–215. Doi:10.1038/nrn755.

Derryberry, D., & Reed, M. A. (2002). Anxiety-related attentional biases and their regulation by attentional control. *Journal of Abnormal Psychology, 111*, 225–236. Doi:10.1037/0021-843X.111.2.225.

Dienstbier, R. A. (1989). Arousal and physiological toughness: Implications for mental and physical health. *Psychological Review, 96*, 84–100. Doi:10.1037/0033-295X.96.1.84.

Dixon, J. G., Jones, M. V., & Turner, M. J. (2019). The benefits of a challenge approach on match day: Investigating cardiovascular reactivity in professional academy soccer players. *European Journal of Sport Science*. Advance online publication. Doi:10.1080/17461391.2019.1629179.

Ducrocq, E., Wilson, M. R., Vine, S. J., & Derakshan, N. (2016). Training attentional control improves cognitive and motor task performance. *Journal of Sport and Exercise Psychology, 38*, 521–533. Doi:10.1123/jsep.2016-0052.

Eccles, D. W., & Arsal, G. (2017). The think aloud method: What is it and how do I use it? *Qualitative Research in Sport, Exercise and Health, 9*, 514–531. Doi:10.1080/2159676X.2017.1331501.

Eysenck, M. W., & Calvo, M. G. (1992). Anxiety and performance: The processing efficiency theory. *Cognition and Emotion, 6*, 409–434. Doi:10.1080/02699939208409696.

Eysenck, M. W., & Derakshan, N. (2011). New perspectives in attentional control theory. *Personality and Individual Differences, 50*, 955–960. Doi:10.1016/j.paid.2010.08.019.

Eysenck, M. W., Derakshan, N., Santos, R., & Calvo, M. G. (2007). Anxiety and cognitive performance: Attentional control theory. *Emotion, 7*, 336–353. Doi:10.1037/1528-3542.7.2.336.

Eysenck, M. W., & Wilson, M. R. (2016). Sporting performance, pressure and cognition: Introducing attentional control theory: Sport. In D. Groome & M. Eysenck (Eds.), *An introduction to applied cognitive psychology* (pp. 329–350). London, UK: Routledge.

Gould, D., Dieffenbach, K., & Moffett, A. (2002). Psychological characteristics and their development in Olympic champions. *Journal of Applied Sport Psychology, 14*, 172–204. Doi:10.1080/10413200290103482.

Gould, D., Eklund, R. C., & Jackson, S. A. (1993). Coping strategies used by US Olympic wrestlers. *Research Quarterly for Sport and Exercise, 64*, 83–93. Doi:10.1080/02701367.1993.10608782.

Gropel, P., & Mesagno, C. (2017). Choking interventions in sports: A systematic review. *International Review of Sport and Exercise Psychology, 12*, 176–201. Doi:10.1080/1750984X.2017.1408134.

Hase, A., Hood, J., Moore, L. J., & Freeman, P. (2019). The influence of self-talk on challenge and threat states and performance. *Psychology of Sport and Exercise.* Advance online publication. Doi:10.1016/j.psychsport.2019.101550.

Hase, A., O'Brien, J., Moore, L. J., & Freeman, P. (2019). The relationship between challenge and threat states and performance: A systematic review. *Sport, Exercise, and Performance Psychology, 8*, 123–144. Doi:10.1037/spy0000132.

Hatzigeorgiadis, A., & Biddle, S. J. H. (2000). Assessing cognitive interference in sport: Development of the thought occurrence questionnaire for sport. *Anxiety, Stress, and Coping, 13*, 65–86. Doi:10.1080/10615800008248334.

Jamieson, J. P., Mendes, W. B., & Nock, M. K. (2013). Improving acute stress responses: The power of reappraisal. *Current Directions in Psychological Science, 22*, 51–56. Doi:10.1177/0963721412461500.

Jones, M., Meijen, C., McCarthy, P. J., & Sheffield, D. (2009). A theory of challenge and threat states in athletes. *International Review of Sport and Exercise Psychology, 2*, 161–180. Doi:10.1080/17509840902829331.

Kredel, R., Vater, C., Klostermann, A., & Hossner, E. J. (2017). Eye-tracking technology and the dynamics of natural gaze behavior in sports: A systematic review of 40 years of research. *Frontiers in Psychology, 8*, 1845. Doi:10.3389/fpsyg.2017.01845.

Lazarus, R. S., & Folkman, S. (1984). *Stress, appraisal, and coping.* New York: Springer.

Lebeau, J. C., Liu, S., Saenz-Moncaleano, C., Sanduvete-Chaves, S., Chacon-Moscoso, S., Becker, B. J., & Tenenbaum, G. (2016). Quiet eye and performance in sport: A meta-analysis. *Journal of Sport and Exercise Psychology, 38*, 441–457. Doi:10.1123/jsep.2015-0123.

Low, W. R., Sandercock, G. R. H., Freeman, P., Winter, M. E., Butt, J., & Maynard, I. (2020). Pressure training for performance domains: A meta-analysis. *Sport, Exercise, and Performance Psychology.* Doi:10.1037/spy0000202.

Mann, D. T. Y., Williams, M. A., Ward, P., & Janelle, C. M. (2007). Perceptual-cognitive expertise in sport: A meta-analysis. *Journal of Sport and Exercise Psychology, 29*, 457–478. Doi:10.1123/jsep.29.4.457.

Masters, R. S. W., & Maxwell, J. P. (2008). The theory of reinvestment. *International Review of Sports and Exercise Psychology, 1*, 160–183. Doi:10.1080/17509840802287218.

Mendes, W. B., & Park, J. (2014). Neurobiological concomitants of motivational states. *Advances in Motivational Science, 1*, 233–270. Doi:10.1016/bs.adms.2014.09.001.

Mesagno, C., Hill, D. M., & Larkin, P. (2015). Examining the accuracy and in-game performance effects of pre- and post-performance routines: A mixed methods study. *Psychology of Sport and Exercise, 19*, 85–94. Doi:10.1016/j. psychsport.2015.03.005.

Miyake, A., Friedman, N. P., Emerson, M. J., Witzki, A. H., Howerter, A., & Wager, T. D. (2000). The unity and diversity of executive functions and their contributions to complex 'frontal lobe' tasks: A latent variable analysis. *Cognitive Psychology, 41*, 49–100. Doi:10.1006/cogp.1999.0734.

Moore, L. J., Freeman, P., Hase, A., Solomon-Moore, E., & Arnold, R. (2019). How consistent are challenge and threat evaluations? A generalizability analysis. *Frontiers in Psychology.* Advance online publication. Doi:10.3389/fpsyg.2019.01778.

Moore, L. J., Vine, S. J., Cooke, A., Ring, C., & Wilson, M. R. (2012). Quiet eye training expedites motor learning and aids performance under heightened anxiety: The roles of response programming and external attention. *Psychophysiology, 49*, 1005–1015. Doi:10.1111/j.1469-8986.2012.01379.x.

Moore, L. J., Vine, S. J., Freeman, P., & Wilson, M. R. (2013). Quiet eye training promotes challenge appraisals and aids performance under elevated anxiety. *International Journal of Sport and Exercise Psychology, 11*, 169–183. Doi:10.1080/1612197X.2013.773688.

Moore, L. J., Vine, S. J., Wilson, M. R., & Freeman, P. (2012). The effect of challenge and threat states on performance: An examination of potential mechanisms. *Psychophysiology, 49*, 1417–1425. Doi:10.1111/j.1469-8986.2012.01449.x.

Moore, L. J., Vine, S. J., Wilson, M. R., & Freeman, P. (2015). Reappraising threat: How to optimize performance under pressure. *Journal of Sport and Exercise Psychology, 37*, 339–343. Doi:10.1123/jsep.2014-0186.

Moore, L. J., Wilson, M. R., Vine, S. J., Coussens, A. H., & Freeman, P. (2013). Champ or chump? Challenge and threat states during pressurized competition. *Journal of Sport and Exercise Psychology, 35*, 551–562. Doi:10.1123/jsep.35.6.551.

Moore, L. J., Young, T., Freeman, P., & Sarkar, M. (2018). Adverse life events, cardiovascular responses, and sports performance under pressure. *Scandinavian Journal of Medicine and Science in Sports, 28*, 340–347. Doi:10.1111/sms.12928.

Moran, A. P. (1996). *The psychology of concentration in sport performers: A cognitive analysis.* London, UK: Routledge.

Moran, A. P. (2009). Attention in sport. In S. Mellalieu & S. Hanton (Eds.), *Advances in applied sport psychology: A review* (pp. 195–220). London, UK: Routledge.

Moran, A. P., Campbell, M., & Ranieri, D. (2018). Implications of eye-tracking technology for applied sport psychology. *Journal of Sport Psychology in Action, 9*, 249–259. Doi:10.1080/21520704.2018.1511660.

Muris, P., Mayer, B., Van Lint, C., & Hofman, S. (2008). Attentional control and psychopathological symptoms in children. *Personality and Individual Differences, 44*, 1495–1505. Doi:10.1016/j.paid.2008.01.006.

Nibbeling, N., Oudejans, R. R. D., & Daanen, H. A. M. (2012). Effects of anxiety, a cognitive secondary task, and expertise on gaze behavior and performance in a far aiming task. *Psychology of Sport and Exercise, 13*, 427–435. Doi:10.1016/j.psychsport.2012.02.002.

Nieuwenhuys, A., & Oudejans, R. R. D. (2011). Training with anxiety: Short- and long-term effects on police officers' shooting behavior under pressure. *Cognitive Processing, 12*, 277–288. Doi:10.1007/s10339-011-0396-x.

Nieuwenhuys, A., & Oudejans, R. R. D. (2012). Anxiety and perceptual-motor performance: Toward an integrated model of concepts, mechanisms, and processes. *Psychological Research, 76,* 747–759. Doi:10.1007/s00426-011-0384-x.

Nieuwenhuys, A., & Oudejans, R. R. D. (2017). Anxiety and performance: Perceptual-motor behavior in high-pressure contexts. *Current Opinion in Psychology, 16,* 28–33. Doi:10.1016/j.copsyc.2017.03.019.

Nieuwenhuys, A., Pijpers, J. R., Oudejans, R. R. D., & Bakker, F. C. (2008). The influence of anxiety on visual attention in climbing. *Journal of Sport and Exercise Psychology, 30,* 171–185. Doi:10.1123/jsep.30.2.171.

Noetel, M., Ciarrochi, J., Van Zanden, B., & Lonsdale, C. (2017). Mindfulness and acceptance approaches to sporting performance enhancement: A systematic review. *International Review of Sport and Exercise Psychology, 12,* 139–175. Doi: 10.1080/1750984X.2017.1387803.

O'Donovan, A., Tomiyama, A. J., Lin, J., Puterman, E., Adler, N. E., Kemeny, M., & Epel, E. S. (2012). Stress appraisals and cellular aging: A key role for anticipatory threat in the relationship between psychological stress and telomere length. *Brain, Behaviour, and Immunity, 26,* 573–579. Doi:10.1016/j.bbi.2012.01.007.

Orlick, T., & Partington, J. (1988). Mental links to excellence. *The Sport Psychologist, 2,* 105–130. Doi:10.1123/tsp.2.2.105.

Owens, M., Koster, E. H. W., & Derakshan, N. (2013). Improving attention control in dysphoria through cognitive training: Transfer effects on working memory capacity and filtering efficiency. *Psychophysiology, 50,* 297–307. Doi:10.1111/psyp.12010.

Payne, K. L., Wilson, M. R., & Vine, S. J. (2019). A systematic review of the anxiety-performance relationship in far-aiming tasks. *International Review of Sport and Exercise Psychology, 12,* 325–355. Doi:10.1080/1750984X.2018.1499796.

Peckham, A. D., McHugh, R. C., & Otto, M. W. (2010). A meta-analysis of the magnitude of biased attention in depression. *Depression and Anxiety, 27,* 1135–1142. Doi:10.1002/da.20755

Quigley, K. S., Feldman Barrett, L., & Weinstein, S. (2002). Cardiovascular patterns associated with threat and challenge appraisals: A within-subjects analysis. *Psychophysiology, 39,* 292–302. Doi:10.1017.S0048577201393046

Rith-Najarian, L. R., McLaughlin, K. A., Sheridan, M. A., & Nock, M. K. (2014). The biopsychosocial model of stress in adolescence: Self-awareness of performance versus stress reactivity. *Stress, 17,* 193–203. Doi:10.3109/10253890.2014.891102

Robazza, C., & Bortoli, L. (1998). Mental preparation strategies of Olympic archers during competition: An exploratory investigation. *High Ability Studies, 9,* 219–235. Doi:10.1080/1359813980090207

Roberts, L. J., Jackson, M. S., & Grundy, I. H. (2019). Choking under pressure: Illuminating the role of distraction and self-focus. *International Review of Sport and Exercise Psychology, 12,* 49–69. Doi:10.1080/1750984X.2017.1374432

Sammy, N., Anstiss, P. A., Moore, L. J., Freeman, P., Wilson, M. R., & Vine, S. J. (2017). The effects of arousal reappraisal on stress responses, performance, and attention. *Anxiety, Stress, and Coping: An International Journal, 30,* 619–629. Doi:10.1080/10615806.2017.1330952

Sari, B. A., Koster, E. H. W., Pourtois, G., & Derakshan, N. (2015). Training working memory to improve attentional control in anxiety: A proof-of-principle study using behavioural and electrophysiological measures. *Biological Psychology, 121,* 203–212. Doi:10.1016/j.biopsycho.2015.09.008

Seery, M. D. (2011). Challenge or threat? Cardiovascular indexes of resilience and vulnerability to potential stress in humans. *Neuroscience and Biobehavioural Reviews, 35,* 1603–1610. Doi:10.1016/j.neubiorev.2011.03.003.

Seery, M. D. (2013). The biopsychosocial model of challenge and threat: Using the heart to measure the mind. *Social and Personality Psychology Compass, 7,* 637–653. Doi:10.1111/spc3.12052

Shi, R., Sharpe, L., & Abbott, M. (2019). A meta-analysis of the relationship between anxiety and attentional control. *Clinical Psychology Review, 72,* 101754. Doi:10.1016/j.cpr.2019.101754

Tomaka, J., Palacios, R. L., Champion, C., & Monks, S. (2018). Development and validation of an instrument that assesses individual differences in threat and challenge appraisal. *Journal of Depression and Anxiety, 7,* 1–10. Doi:10.4172/2167-1044.1000313

Trotman, G. P., Williams, S. E., Quinton, M. L., & Van Zanten, J. J. C. S. (2018). Challenge and threat states: Examining cardiovascular, cognitive and affective responses to two distinct laboratory stress tasks. *International Journal of Psychophysiology, 126,* 42–51. Doi:10.1016/j.ijpsycho.2018.02.004

Turner, M. J., Jones, M. V., Sheffield, D., Barker, J. B., & Coffee, P. (2014). Manipulating cardiovascular indices of challenge and threat using resource appraisals. *International Journal of Psychophysiology, 94,* 9–18. Doi:10.1016/j.ijpsycho.2014.07.004

Turner, M. J., Jones, M. V., Sheffield, D., & Cross, S. L. (2012). Cardiovascular indices of challenge and threat states predict competitive performance. *International Journal of Psychophysiology, 86,* 48–57. Doi:10.1016/j.ijpsycho.2012.08.004

Turner, M. J., Jones, M. V., Sheffield, D., Slater, M. J., Barker, J. B., & Bell, J. J. (2013). Who thrives under pressure? Predicting the performance of elite academy cricketers using the cardiovascular indicators of challenge and threat states. *Journal of Sport and Exercise Psychology, 35,* 387–397. Doi:10.1123/jsep.35.4.387

Vickers, J. N. (2016). Origins and current issues in quiet eye research. *Current Issues in Sports Science, 1,* 101. Doi:10.15203/CISS_2016.101

Vickers, J. N., & Williams, A. M. (2007). Performing under pressure: The effects of physiological arousal, cognitive anxiety, and gaze control in biathlon. *Journal of Motor Behavior, 39,* 381–394. Doi:10.3200/JMBR.39.5.381-394

Vine, S. J., Freeman, P., Moore, L. J., Chandra-Ramanan, R., & Wilson, M. R. (2013). Evaluating stress as a challenge is associated with superior attentional control and motor skill performance: Testing the predictions of the biopsychosocial model of challenge and threat. *Journal of Experimental Psychology, 19,* 185–194. Doi:10.1037/a0034106

Vine, S. J., Moore, L. J., & Wilson, M. R. (2011). Quiet eye training facilitates competitive putting performance in elite golfers. *Frontiers in Psychology, 2*(8), 1–9. Doi:10.3389/fpsyg.2011.00008.

Vine, S. J., Moore, L. J., & Wilson, M. R. (2014). Quiet eye training: The acquisition, refinement and resilient performance of targeting skills. *European Journal of Sport Science, 14,* S235–S242. Doi:10.1080/17461391.2012.683815.

Vine, S. J., Moore, L. J., & Wilson, M. R. (2016). An integrative framework of stress, attention, and visuomotor performance. *Frontiers in Psychology, 7*(1671), 1–10. Doi:10.3389/fpsyg.2016.01671.

Vine, S. J., Uiga, L., Lavric, A., Moore, L. J., Tsaneva-Atanasova, K., & Wilson, M. R. (2015). Individual reactions to stress predict performance during a critical aviation incident. *Anxiety, Stress, & Coping, 28*, 467–477. Doi:10.1080/106158 06.2014.986722.

Vine, S. J., & Wilson, M. R. (2010). Quiet eye training: Effects on learning and performance under pressure. *Journal of Applied Sport Psychology, 22*, 361–376. Doi:10.1080/10413200.2010.495106.

Vine, S. J., & Wilson, M. R. (2011). The influence of quiet eye training and pressure on attention and visuo-motor control. *Acta Psychologica, 136*, 340–346. Doi:10.1016/j.actpsy.2010.12.008.

Williams, A. M., Vickers, J., & Rodrigues, S. (2002). The effects of anxiety on visual search, movement kinematics, and performance in table tennis: A test of Eysenck and Calvo's processing efficiency theory. *Journal of Sport & Exercise Psychology, 24*, 438–455. Doi:10.1123/jsep.24.4.438.

Williams, S. E., Van Zanten, J. J. C. S., Trotman, G. P., Quinton, M. L., & Ginty, A. T. (2017). Challenge and threat imagery manipulates heart rate and anxiety responses to stress. *International Journal of Psychophysiology, 117*, 111–118. Doi:10.1016/j.ijpsycho.2017.04.011.

Wilson, M. R. (2008). From processing efficiency to attentional control: A mechanistic account of the anxiety-performance relationship. *International Review of Sport and Exercise Psychology, 1*, 184–201. Doi:10.1080/17509840802400787.

Wilson, M. R., Vine, S. J., & Wood, G. (2009). The influence of anxiety on visual attentional control in basketball free throw shooting. *Journal of Sport and Exercise Psychology, 31*, 152–168. Doi:10.1123/jsep.31.2.152.

Wilson, M. R., Wood, G., & Vine, S. J. (2009). Anxiety, attentional control, and performance impairment in penalty kicks. *Journal of Sport and Exercise Psychology, 31*, 761–775. Doi:10.1123/jsep.31.6.761.

Wilson, M. R., Wood, G., & Vine, S. J. (2016). Say it quietly, but we still do not know how quiet eye training works—Comment on Vickers. *Current Issues in Sport Science, 1*, 117. Doi:10.15203/CISS_2016.117.

Wood, G., & Wilson, M. R. (2011). Quiet-eye training for soccer penalty kicks. *Cognitive Processing, 12*, 257–266. Doi:10.1007/s10339-011-0393-0.

Wood, G., & Wilson, M. R. (2012). Quiet-eye training, perceived control and performing under pressure. *Psychology of Sport and Exercise, 13*, 721–728. Doi:10.1016/j.psychsport.2012.05.003.

Wood, N., Parker, J., Freeman, P., Black, M., & Moore, L. J. (2018). The relationship between challenge and threat states, anaerobic power, core affect, perceived exertion, and self-focused attention during a competitive sprint cycling task. *Progress in Brain Research, 240*, 1–17. Doi:10.1016/bs.pbr.2018.08.006.

Zaccaro, A., Piarulli, A., Laurino, M., Garbella, E., Menicucci, D., Neri, B., & Gemigani, A. (2018). How breath-control can change your life: A systematic review of the psycho-physiological correlates of slow breathing. *Frontiers in Human Neuroscience, 12*, 353. Doi:10.3389/fnhum.2018.00353

6 Well-Being and Quality of Life

Carolina Lundqvist

The Challenging Nature of Competitive Sport

Competitive sport, particularly at the elite level, is an exclusive area where athletes get the possibility to challenge themselves, test their limits, and seek to pursue dreams of personally significant goals. A natural part of an elite sports journey is also that athletes are likely to face both success and failures and are exposed to stressors that may evoke distress or other aversive emotional states both in the moment and sometimes over time (see also Chapter 1). An athlete's experience of the athletic life and satisfaction with outcomes in relation to the amount of effort invested may vary both during the competitive season and across different phases in their sport career (e.g., Amorose, Anderson-Butcher, & Cooper, 2009). Moreover, the view athletes hold of themselves about their performance also influences the experiences of their sports life; an inner view dominated by concerns over mistakes, fear of failure, and a self-worth fully dependent on results is likely to evoke distress, whereas an inner view where sport participation is regarded as an avenue for development and purpose in life may relate more strongly to life satisfaction (Houltberg, Wang, Qi, & Nelson, 2018).

This chapter emphasizes the benefits of stimulating well-being and quality of life (QOL) among athletes. The reader is introduced to the historical development of this research field, and scientific definitions, models, and frameworks of well-being and QOL are presented. The protection of athletes' mental health in elite sports settings has over recent years received considerable attention in the research literature (e.g., Kuettel & Larsen, 2019; see also Chapter 8), and this chapter therefore particularly considers well-being and QOL research performed on elite athletes. Examples of studies are provided, together with future research directions and applied implications for practitioners interested in well-being and QOL promotion.

Well-Being Research: A Historical Perspective

Philosophers have pondered "what a good life is" for centuries (Diener, 1984; Ryan & Deci, 2001). The ways that humans evaluate "the good life" have also changed over time, influenced by, for example, prevailing values, norms, and language in contemporary society, as well as politics and culture (e.g., Kinderman, Allsopp, & Cooke, 2017). Empirical research of well-being as we know the construct today slowly developed after the 1960s (Diener, Oishi, & Lucas, 2005). For example, Wilson (1967) published a review of early studies where various correlates were investigated in relation to well-being (e.g., IQ, age, health, marriage, and leisure-time activities). The happy person was concluded to be a highly privileged person in life—for example, well-educated with a good salary, married, optimistic, extroverted, free of worries, healthy, and with high self-esteem. By the 1980s, well-being as a research field had developed into an established science and the focus changed to definitions of well-being, measurement, and attempts to understand various psychological causes of happiness (Diener, 1984).

While anxiety and various stress-related conditions in competitive sports were common research themes during the 1980s and 1990s (Raglin, 1992; see also Introduction chapter), well-being research on athletes was still relatively invisible (Lundqvist, 2011). At this time, Morgan (1985) introduced the Mental Health Model (MHM) of sports performance. The MHM was an early endeavor to understand mental health among athletes and suggested that psychopathology, empirically investigated by personality and mood assessments (see also Chapter 10), inversely correlated to successful sports performance. The MHM should be acknowledged for introducing a new perspective in sport psychology, in which psychological health was emphasized as important both for sports performance and wellness among elite athletes (Raglin, 2001; see also Chapter 13). The main variables of interest in sport psychology research at this point were nevertheless various problematic aspects or aversive emotional states among sports participants rather than well-being per se (Brady & Grenville-Cleave, 2018).

The Increase of Well-Being Research in the Sports Domain

At the beginning of the 21st century, an increase in curiosity about competitive athletes' well-being was notable among researchers (Lundqvist, 2011). The increase was likely influenced both by the World Health Organization's (WHO's) call for attention to mental health (WHO, 2004; see also Chapter 8) and the introduction of positive psychology as a pronounced scientific discipline in psychology (Seligman & Csikszentmihalyi, 2000). The WHO (2004) stressed well-being in their definition of mental health, explained to be "a state of well-being in which the individual realizes his or her abilities, can cope with the normal stresses of life, can work productively and fruitfully, and is able to make a contribution to his or her community" (WHO, 2004, p. 12). Introducing positive psychology, Seligman and Csikszentmihalyi (2000) strongly criticized psychological research for relying on a disease model with a pronounced focus on the healing of psychopathology, and repairment of negative and deviating psychological functioning, where human unhappiness was emphasized. The positive psychology movement explicitly aimed to acknowledge human qualities and strengths as well as happiness and flourishing in life, and therefore challenged the one-sided "impaired psychological health" focus in the literature (Seligman & Csikszentmihalyi, 2000). Thus, both the WHO definition and the incipient positive psychology movement stressed well-being as a valuable concept to seriously consider in research and society overall.

Definitions and Theoretical Perspectives of Well-Being and Quality of Life

Well-being and QOL research have struggled with the ambiguity of definitions and assessments over the years. Numerous labels are used rather interchangeably, for example, wellness, welfare, happiness, subjective well-being, emotional well-being, psychological well-being, eudaimonic well-being, and QOL (Greenville-Cleave & Brady, 2018; Lundqvist, 2011). Thus, there is no universally accepted definition of well-being or QOL across all scientific traditions and disciplines (Cooke, Melchert, & Connor, 2016; Huta & Waterman, 2014). Two main theoretical orientations of well-being rooted in different underlying philosophies nevertheless dominate the psychological literature: the hedonic and the eudaimonic perspectives. QOL relates closely to well-being but is generally viewed as a broader concept, accounting for more holistic life evaluations.

Hedonic Well-Being

The hedonic tradition emphasizes pleasure, happiness, and comfort as essential for human well-being (e.g., Diener, 2009; Huta & Ryan, 2010) and adopts the label subjective well-being (e.g., Diener, 2009) or emotional well-being (e.g., Keyes, 2005). Positive affect (or happiness) and life satisfaction are two central components: (i) happiness refers to a state where positive affect is dominating in the presence of a relative absence of negative affect and (ii) life satisfaction refers to the person's cognitive evaluation of life and overall judgments of perceived discrepancies between actual and desired life (Diener, 2009; Diener et al., 2005). Assessments of athletes' well-being would according to this perspective focus on the e᙭ ᙗtion-oriented content of experiences.

A great number of factors (e.g., health behaviors, physiological systems, and stress) are likely to mediate relationships between emotional indicators of subjective well-being and various health-related outcomes

(Diener & Pressman, 2017), and the specific function of happiness is still not fully established in the literature. For example, episodic happiness—that is, the momentary emotional response of a specific activity—may not endure over activities and does not necessarily correspond to perceived life satisfaction or a meaningful life (Huta & Ryan, 2010; Raibley, 2012). The primary function of short-term happiness or pleasure may therefore be emotion regulation and a temporary release from concerns and worries (Huta & Ryan, 2010; see also Chapter 4). Fredrickson and colleagues (e.g., Fredrickson, 2001; Fredrickson & Levenson, 1998) contend on the other hand in the Broaden-and-Build Theory that positive emotions not only make people "feel good" in the moment, but also act to develop long-term resources that are helpful in building resilience and in adaptively coping with challenges or stressful circumstances over time (Cohn, Fredrickson, Brown, Mikels, & Conway, 2009).

Eudaimonic Well-Being

The eudaimonic perspective accentuates effective and positive functionality in subjectively valued activities and life, not only in situations when life runs smoothly but also when life challenges are confronted (Keyes & Annas, 2009). Well-being from the eudaimonic perspective is rooted in humanistic and developmental ideas of self-realization. Moreover, an existential perspective is prominent, whereby eudaimonia also accounts for the meaning people make of adversity or of living in a non-perfect world (Ryff, 2014; Ryff, Singer, & Dienberg Love, 2004). Thus, the eudaimonic perspective considers growth, development, meaningfulness in life, and positive functionality as essential components of well-being. Positive and pleasurable affective states are acknowledged to be plausible outcomes when persons are successful in their strivings toward growth and development of unique talents. However, the primary goal is not positive affect per se, but instead the pursuit and personal growth itself (Huta & Waterman, 2014).

Ryff's (1989, 2014) conceptualization of the eudaimonic perspective, labeled as psychological well-being, is commonly adopted in the psychological literature. Psychological well-being describes six key dimensions of private and personal aspects of positive functioning: autonomy, environmental mastery, personal growth, positive relations with others, purpose in life, and self-acceptance. Keyes (1998) later introduced the label social well-being to refer to five dimensions of functionality and flourishing in social life: social acceptance, social actualization, social contribution, social coherence, and social integration. A summary of the main content of these psychological and social well-being dimensions is shown in Table 6.1.

Table 6.1 Summary of Main Content in Dimensions of Psychological Well-Being (Ryff, 2014) and Social Well-Being (Keyes, 1998)

Well-Being Dimension	*Main Content of Well-Being Dimension ("The person . . .")*
Psychological well-being	
Autonomy	. . . is self-determined, independent, can resist social pressure, uses self-referenced standards for self-evaluations and behavior regulation
Environmental mastery	. . . can effectively manage the environment and complex external activities. Chooses, creates, or uses opportunities in the surrounding environment to fulfill personal needs or goals
Personal growth	. . . shows openness to new experiences, perceives continued development and growth with increased effectiveness and self-knowledge
Positive relations with others	. . . has sincere, intimate, empathetic, and trusting relationships. Shows concern about others' welfare
Purpose in life	. . . perceives directedness, meaning, and goals that give life a purpose
Self-acceptance	. . . feels positive about the past life. Has a positive and accepting view of multiple aspects of self and own qualities (good and bad)
Social well-being	
Social acceptance	. . . trusts and feels comfortable with others. Holds a positive view of human nature and others' kindness
Social actualization	. . . believes evolution of society has potential, is hopeful about the future, and perceives citizens as beneficiaries of progress in society
Social contribution	. . . has a belief of being a vital and valuable member of society who can contribute important things to the world
Social coherence	. . . perceives the world around as understandable and organized and, although the world might not be perfect, maintains an aspiration to make sense of things that happen
Social integration	. . . has relationship quality toward society and community, and the perception of being part of and having things in common with others in the social reality

Self-Determination Theory as a Eudaimonic Framework

The self-determination theory (SDT) has been adopted as a framework in sport psychology to understand well-being among competitive athletes. This theory is rooted in the eudaimonic philosophy of well-being (Lambert, Passmore, & Holder, 2015). The framework was originally established by Ryan and Deci (2000) and over the years has evolved into six interrelated sub-theories (see, for a comprehensive review, Standage, Curran, & Rouse, 2019). The SDT particularly emphasizes the three basic psychological needs of autonomy, competence, and relatedness as central for well-being (Ryan & Deci, 2002). The basic needs in the SDT framework resemble, to some extent, certain key dimensions suggested by Ryff (1989, 2014) but with one essential difference: Ryff's conceptualization defined well-being as a construct, whereas SDT regards well-being as an outcome nurtured by the individual's level of need satisfaction in life (Lambert et al., 2015). Sport psychology well-being studies using SDT as a framework have commonly focused on outcomes of perceived coach autonomy support. Results from studies generally support a positive relationship between need satisfaction and various well-being indicators (e.g., Adie, Duda, & Ntoumanis, 2008; Cheval, Chalabaev, Quested, Courvoisier, & Sarrazin, 2017; Felton & Jowett, 2017).

The Hedonic-Eudaimonic Well-Being Distinction

A question discussed in the literature is whether hedonic and eudaimonic well-being represent distinct or overlapping constructs (e.g., Kashdan, Biswas-Diener, & King, 2008). Keyes and Annas (2009) conclude that our level of functioning and experienced feelings can overlap; positive feelings are often, but not always, a result of having a well-functioning life. Moreover, hedonia is often treated in research as an outcome (i.e., how the person feels), whereas eudaimonia is commonly considered as a predictor (i.e., how the person lives or behaves) (Ryan, Huta, & Deci, 2008). Hedonia and eudaimonia appears therefore to be distinct but related constructs, where a combination of both may be beneficial because people have various goals, needs, and motives relating to their engagement in activities (Huta & Ryan, 2010). For example, competitive athletes who strive to pursue personally valued eudaimonic sports goals often voluntarily expose themselves to challenging situations which may be linked not only to positive emotional outcomes (e.g., feeling of satisfaction or experiences of a "rush") but also to negative emotional experiences (e.g., disappointment, distress, disharmony, and pain).

Models That Combine Hedonic and Eudaimonic Perspectives

Various models have combined essential parts of hedonic and eudaimonic well-being. Two of them are the PERMA model (Seligman, 2011) and Lundqvist's (2011) Integrated Model of Global and Sport-Specific Well-Being.

The PERMA Model

As a further development of Seligman's (2002) authentic happiness framework, the PERMA model (Seligman, 2011) suggests five pathways to happiness: positive emotions, engagement, relationships, meaning, and accomplishment. Butler and Kern (2016) developed a brief measure called the PERMA-profiler to enable the assessment of Seligman's PERMA model. The combination of the five PERMA pillars is argued to lead to human flourishing. Seligman (2018) contends that PERMA includes essential well-being components and building blocks of well-being rather than constituting a new or alternative form of well-being. Some studies have provided at least partial support for the usefulness and relevance of the proposed well-being components (e.g., Coffey, Wray-Lake, Mashek, & Branand, 2016; Iasiello, Bartholomaeus, Jarden, & Kelly, 2017), but scholars have also questioned the model's usefulness, claiming it to be redundant and overlapping in conceptual content with Diener's (1984) Subjective Well-Being Model (Goodman, Disabato, Kashdan, & Kauffman, 2018). There is presently limited sport psychology research that has directly validated the complete PERMA model among athletes.

Lundqvist's (2011) Integrated Model of Global and Sport-Specific Well-Being

Lundqvist's (2011) model builds on established hedonic and eudaimonic well-being conceptualizations as shown in Table 6.1 and distinguishes between well-being at a global level (i.e., in life in general) and well-being in the sport context. Global and context-specific levels of well-being are suggested as being related but also as constituting separate dimensions; well-being assessed in specific domains is argued to provide more specific information, whereas global well-being scores would represent an average and undefined estimation of the broader life context. The relevance of the model has been supported in qualitative studies on elite orienteers (Lundqvist & Sandin, 2014) and Parasport athletes (MacDougall, O'Halloran, Sherry, & Shields, 2016). The latter study suggested that an additional dimension of physical health and well-being could be suitable when the model is applied to Parasport athletes. Both studies questioned, however, the usefulness of separate social well-being dimensions in the sport context.

Quality of Life

The label QOL is adopted in several scientific disciplines (e.g., economics, medicine, sociology, and psychology) with various meanings and purposes of inquiry. Some disciplines (e.g., economics) may use objective indicators of external life conditions to estimate QOL at the population level, building on assumptions that external life conditions can be favorable or unfavorable in comparison to normative levels (Cummins, 2000; Rapley, 2003). Other disciplines, for example, psychology or medicine, more commonly use subjective indicators to investigate an individual's internal evaluations of their life (e.g., Green-Shortridge & Odle-Dusseau, 2009; Post, 2014).

QOL was discussed early on in medical literature (Elkington, 1966); the development of successful treatment methods increased survival and life expectancy from serious diseases, but sometimes left the patient suffering in life. The construct of health-related QOL (HRQOL) was increasingly brought into focus in the 1980s and is used to describe the dimension of QOL that specifically relates to various health aspects, for example of experienced symptoms; physical, emotional and social functioning; pain; and various well-being indicators (Guyatt, Feeny, & Patrick, 1993; Post, 2014).

In psychology, QOL is often discussed in relation to mental health. From this perspective, QOL describes a person's evaluations of life dimensions such as goals, values, expectations and concerns, social and environmental relationships and culture, as well as psychological states of life satisfaction and happiness (e.g., Green-Shortridge & Odle-Dusseau, 2009). The WHO (1999) suggests QOL to be defined as:

> an individual's perception of their position in life in the context of the culture and value systems in which they live and in relation to their goals, expectations, standards and concerns. It is a broad ranging concept affected in a complex way by the person's physical health, psychological state, personal beliefs, social relationships and their relationship to salient features of their environment.
>
> (WHO, 1999, p. 3)

Although QOL includes well-being as an essential component, according to definitions it is not fully equated with well-being or other health-related concepts (e.g., life satisfaction, health, or general lifestyle; Cooke et al., 2016; WHO, 1999).

Research on Well-Being, QOL, and Elite Sport

Well-Being Research

Lundqvist (2011) reviewed well-being studies in competitive sport and concluded that well-being at that time was treated as an unspecific "feel-good factor" and that researchers rarely adopted established well-being frameworks or concordant assessments. Similar conclusions were described by Kuettel and Larsen (2020) in a scoping review of 20 years of mental health research in elite sport; only a limited number of studies that targeted well-being as a core construct utilized established theoretical frameworks or models to guide the investigation.

Some examples of studies that have utilized hedonic and eudaimonic frameworks to investigate elite athletes' well-being are described subsequently. Jowett and Cramer (2009) studied relationship qualities among national and international level athletes. They found that spillover (i.e., the transfer of negative feelings, attitudes, or behaviors between a romantic relationship and elite sport) was negatively associated with athletes' subjective well-being (i.e., lowered sport satisfaction and increased levels of negative mood/affect). Lundqvist and Raglin (2015) investigated various personality and motivational variables and their association with elite orienteers' profiles of well-being (hedonic and eudaimonic) and perceived stress. Results showed a mastery-oriented climate, need satisfaction, need dissatisfaction, perfectionistic concerns, and self-esteem to significantly differentiate athletes with low well-being/high stress scores from athletes displaying the opposite pattern (i.e., high well-being/low stress).

Using a qualitative approach, Lundqvist and Sandin (2014) further explored elite orienteers' experiences of well-being and the findings revealed essential factors for well-being to consist of value-driven behaviors, functional relationships, self-regulated autonomy, an ability to organize and obtain life-sport balance, as well as functional strategies to protect the self when setbacks occurred. Investigating Paralympic athletes' well-being needs and strengths, MacDougall and colleagues (2016) found that well-being needs consisted of various interacting factors (e.g., physical pain, emotional regulation, a low purpose outside sport, and low self-acceptance). Perceived well-being strengths (e.g., personal growth, optimism, social support networks, and perceived contribution to multiple communities) increased with higher competition levels. MacDougall, O'Halloran, Sherry, and Shields (2019) further performed a pilot randomized control trial (RCT) to investigate the feasibility of a mindfulness-acceptance-commitment program (MAC; Gardner & Moore, 2007) to improve Paralympic athletes' well-being. The MAC interventions group showed significant increases in dimensions of hedonic, eudaimonic, and physical well-being compared to the wait list control group.

QOL Research

Exploring the essence of elite athletes' idiosyncratic perceptions of QOL by use of a qualitative approach, Lundqvist, Träff, and Brady (2020) identified athletes' inner striving to move forward in their athletic development (i.e., inner motivation) as a superordinate category for their experienced QOL. Other categories included, for example, perceived gratitude and good prerequisites for the sports investment, value-driven behaviors, relief from stressors in sport and life, as well as emotional states linked to sports execution. Quantitative research further suggests that QOL may be positively related to the ability to cope with stress and anxiety among young elite athletes (Ledochowski, Unterrainer, Ruedl, Schnitzer, & Kopp, 2012). In a systematic review and meta-analysis of former professional and collegiate athletes' HRQOL and life satisfaction, it was found that involuntary retirement, higher BMI, collision or high contact sport, concussions, and osteoarthritis were factors associated with decreased physical HRQOL, but not necessarily with decreased mental HRQOL and life satisfaction (Filbay et al., 2019). Studies have also shown both current and former athletes to report better mental HRQOL than the general population (Bullock, Collins, Peirce, Arden, & Filbay, 2020; Filbay et al., 2019) and professional cricketers to perceive high satisfaction with their QOL despite experiences of pain and musculoskeletal limitations after retirement (Filbay, Bishop, Peirce, Jones, & Arden, 2017). Overall, studies suggest that psychological attributes (e.g., resilience, a positive attitude, awareness of the body's capability, self-management skills, and gratefulness of the elite sport career) acquired through elite sport participation plausibly could act to enhance athletes' QOL and flourishing also after the elite sport career has ended (Bullock et al., 2020; Filbay et al., 2017, 2019).

Assessment of Well-Being and QOL

A limiting factor for the progress of research is the general lack of conceptually and psychometrically sound measures to assess well-being and QOL among athletes (Giles, Fletcher, Arnold, Ashfield, & Harrison, 2020; Lundqvist, 2011). A great number of well-being or QOL assessments have nevertheless been developed in both mainstream and clinical psychology literature. For example, Cooke and colleagues (2016) found 42 self-rating instruments that assessed well-being (hedonic and eudaimonic), QOL, or wellness, whereas Linton, Dieppe, and Medina-Lara (2016) identified a total of 99 different well-being measures. In the latter study, the measurements were found to include a total of 196 separate well-being dimensions (for a comprehensive review of all measures, see Linton et al., 2016). Thus, great variability of well-being or QOL content is today evident in available measurements, and the scales have therefore also been criticized as displaying insufficient or varied operationalizations and low precision of item content (Cooke et al., 2016; Linton et al., 2016). A challenge thus remains in research to develop measurement approaches that adequately and with precision can capture clearly defined aspects of well-being and QOL adapted for the defined populations under study.

Future Research Directions and Applied Implications

The promotion of well-being is today accepted as a viable approach to obtain sustained health over time (e.g., Davidson & Schuyler, 2015; Diener & Pressman, 2017; WHO, 2004). Proactively helping athletes to develop psychosocial resources to stay functional and flourishing is also preferable to a mere focus on the treatment of already developed concerns (see also Chapters 12 and 13). Protective factors that could be related to well-being or QOL in high-level competitive sport environments have nevertheless received significantly less attention in the research literature compared to risk factors or problematic outcomes (Kuettel & Larsen, 2020). Further research is therefore warranted that aims to (i) increase the empirical knowledge of essential factors that act to promote athletes' well-being and QOL and (ii) develop tailored and evidence-based well-being and QOL-promoting interventions for use with competitive athletes at different stages of their sports careers.

To help guide and stimulate future research and applied work on well-being and QOL in sport, Figure 6.1 summarizes some complexities and the interplay between various factors that may be related to athletes' well-being and QOL evaluations at different levels. In the center of the model, well-being (hedonic and eudaimonic) and ill-being symptoms are shown. Symptoms of well-being and ill-being are known not to be mutually exclusive but can occur simultaneously (Keyes, 2005), which calls for a holistic evaluation of their interactions and relative importance, with consideration also of the situational context in which they occur and the athletes' subjective goals and values. Several biological (e.g., genetic vulnerability and stress reactivity), psychological (e.g., attitudes, beliefs, behaviors, and coping skills), and social factors (e.g., family background, relationships, and social support) are also proposed in the general literature to interact and impact on individuals' health, well-being, and QOL (e.g., Diener & Pressman, 2017; Engel, 1980; Suls & Rothman, 2004; see also Chapters 2, 3, and 11). In addition, researchers and practitioners need to keep in mind that well-being evaluations expressed by athletes might sometimes relate specifically to sport participation (the sport-specific domain) and may at other times represent experiences in life at a global level having little to do with the individual being an athlete (Lundqvist, 2011; Lundqvist & Sandin, 2014). Various life domains may also postulate different norms and cultural elements which additionally might influence participants' views of what characterizes well-being and QOL under certain circumstances or in specific contexts (e.g., Kinderman et al., 2017; Lundqvist et al., 2020). Thus, researchers and practitioners are encouraged to consider that both generic and sport-related factors may promote or prevent experienced well-being and QOL, and to strive to obtain a detailed level of investigation that can help to increase the understanding of individual

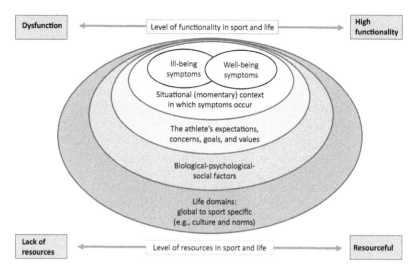

Figure 6.1 A Multilevel Model of Factors Related to Athletes' Well-Being and QOL Evaluations

and contextual variations that may be present among athletes. Interacting factors summarized and exemplified in Figure 6.1, together with each athlete's individual learning history, make it probable that athletes will exhibit a great variety in the availability of internal and external resources needed to stay functional and cope with demands and challenges in sport and life.

Conclusion

In this chapter, various well-being and QOL definitions, frameworks, and models were reviewed together with examples of well-being and QOL studies conducted with elite athletes. To enable a more comprehensive and empirical understanding of the complexity of athletes' well-being and QOL, in which both mental health and performance are accounted for (see also Chapters 8 and 13), studies with quantitative assessments as well as idiographic research approaches are warranted. As has been noted throughout this chapter, the subject of well-being and QOL in high-level competitive sport settings is not just about athletes "feeling momentarily good". Rather the focus is on how athletes' psychological functionality in relation to goals and values that provide purposeful lives can be sustained or increased while accounting for a great number of interacting factors both within and outside the context of sport.

References

Adie, J. W., Duda, J. L., & Ntoumanis, N. (2008). Autonomy support, basic need satisfaction and the optimal functioning of adult male and female sport participants: A test of basic needs theory. *Motivation and Emotion, 32,* 189–199. Doi:10.1007/s11031-008-9095-z

Amorose, A. J., Anderson-Butcher, D., & Cooper, J. (2009). Predicting changes in athletes' wellbeing from changes in need satisfaction over the course of a competitive season. *Research Quarterly for Exercise and Sport, 80,* 386–392. Doi:10.1080/02701367.2009.10599575

Brady, A., & Grenville-Cleave, B. (2018). Introducing positive psychology and its value for sport and physical activity. In A. Brady & B. Grenville-Cleave (Eds.), *Positive psychology in sport and physical activity: An introduction* (pp. 7–19). London, UK: Routledge.

Bullock, G. S., Collins, G. S., Peirce, N., Arden, N. K., & Filbay, S. R. (2020). Health-related quality of life and flourishing in current and former recreational and elite cricketers. *Health and Quality of Life Outcomes, 18,* 1–12. Doi:10.1186/s12955-020-01301-7

Butler, J., & Kern, M. L. (2016). The PERMA-Profiler: A brief multidimensional measure of flourishing. *International Journal of Wellbeing, 6,* 1–48. Doi:10.5502/ijw.v6i3.526

Cheval, B., Chalabaev, A., Quested, E., Courvoisier, D. S., & Sarrazin, P. (2017). How perceived autonomy support and controlling coach behaviors are related to well- and ill-being in elite soccer players: A within-person changes and between-person differences analysis. *Psychology of Sport and Exercise, 28,* 68–77. Doi:10.1016/j.psychsport.2016.10.006

Coffey, J. K., Wray-Lake, L., Mashek, D., & Branand, B. (2016). A multi-study examination of well-being theory in college and community samples. *Journal of Happiness Studies: An International Forum on Subjective Well-Being, 17,* 187–211. Doi:10.1007/s10902-014-9590-8

Cohn, M. A., Fredrickson, B. L., Brown, S. L., Mikels, J. A., & Conway, A. M. (2009). Happiness unpacked: Positive emotions increase life satisfaction by building resilience. *Emotion, 9,* 361–368. Doi:10.1037/a0015952

Cooke, P. J., Melchert, T. P., & Connor, K. (2016). Measuring well-being: A review of instruments. *The Counseling Psychologist, 44,* 730–757. Doi:10.1177/0011000016633507

Cummins, R. A. (2000). Objective and subjective quality of life: An interactive model. *Social Indicators Research, 52,* 55–72. Doi:10.1023/A:1007027822521

Davidson, R. J., & Schuyler, B. S. (2015). Neuroscience and happiness. In J. F. Helliwell, R. Lyard, & J. Sachs (Eds.), *World happiness report 2015* (pp. 88–105). New York: Sustainable Development Solutions Network.

Diener, E. (1984). Subjective well-being. *Psychological Bulletin, 93,* 542–575. Doi:10.1037/0033-2909.95.3.542

Diener, E. (2009). Subjective well-being. In E. Diener (Ed.), *Social indicators of research series. The science of well-being* (Vol. 37, pp. 11–58). New York: Springer.

Diener, E., Oishi, S., & Lucas, R. E. (2005). Subjective well-being: The science of happiness and life satisfaction. In S. J. Lopez & C. R. Snyder (Eds.), *Oxford handbook of positive psychology* (pp. 63–73). Oxford, UK: Oxford University Press.

Diener, E., & Pressman, S. D. (2017). If, why, and when subjective well-being influences health, and future needed research. *Applied Psychology: Health and Well-Being, 9*, 133–167. Doi:10.1111/aphw.12090

Elkington, J. R. (1966). Medicine and quality of life. *Annals of Internal Medicine, 64*, 711–714. Doi:10.7326/0003-4819-64-3-711

Engel, G. L. (1980). The clinical application of the biopsychosocial model. *American Journal of Psychiatry, 137*, 535–544. Doi:10.1176/ajp.137.5.535

Felton, L., & Jowett, S. (2017). A self-determination theory perspective on attachment, need satisfaction, and well-being in a sample of athletes: A longitudinal study. *Journal of Clinical Sport Psychology, 11*, 304–323. Doi:10.1123/jcsp.2016-0013

Filbay, S. R., Bishop, F., Peirce, N., Jones, M. E., & Arden, N. K. (2017). Common attributes in retired professional cricketers that may enhance or hinder quality of life after retirement: A qualitative study. *BMJ Open, 7*, e016541. Doi:10.1136/bmjopen-2017-016541

Filbay, S. R., Pandya, T., Thomas, B., McKay, C., Adams, J., & Arden, N. (2019). Quality of life and life satisfaction in former athletes: A systematic review and meta-analysis. *Sports Medicine, 49*, 1723–1738. Doi:10.1007/s40279-019-01163-0

Fredrickson, B. L. (2001). The role of positive emotions in positive psychology: The Broaden-and-Build Theory of positive emotions. *American Psychologist, 56*, 218–226. Doi:10.1037/0003-066X.56.3.218

Fredrickson, B. L., & Levenson, R. W. (1998). Positive emotions speed recovery from the cardiovascular sequelae of negative emotions. *Cognition and Emotion, 12*, 191–220. Doi:10.1080/026999398379718

Gardner, F. L., & Moore, Z. E. (2007). *The psychology of enhancing human performance: The mindfulness-acceptance-commitment (MAC) approach.* New York: Springer.

Giles, S., Fletcher, D., Arnold, R., Ashfield, A., & Harrison, J. (2020). Measuring well-being in sport performers: Where are we now and how do we progress? *Sports Medicine, 50*, 1255–1270. Doi:10.1007/s40279-020-01274-z

Goodman, F. R., Disabato, D. J., Kashdan, T. B., & Kauffman, S. B. (2018). Measuring well-being: A comparison of subjective wellbeing and PERMA. *The Journal of Positive Psychology, 13*, 321–332. Doi:10.1080/17439760.2017.1388434

Green-Shortridge, T. M., & Odle-Dusseau, H. N. (2009). Quality of life. In S. J. Lopez (Ed.), *The encyclopedia of positive psychology* (pp. 817–821). West Sussex, UK: John Wiley & Sons.

Greenville-Cleave, B., & Brady, A. (2018). The components of well-being. In A. Brady & B. Grenville-Cleave (Eds.), *Positive psychology in sport and physical activity: An introduction* (pp. 20–34). London, UK: Routledge.

Guyatt, G. H., Feeny, D. H., & Patrick, D. L. (1993). Measuring health-related quality of life. *Annals of Internal Medicine, 118*, 622–629. Doi:10.7326/0003-4819-118-8-199304150-00009

Houltberg, B. J., Wang, K. T., Qi, W., & Nelson, C. S. (2018). Self-narrative profiles of elite athletes and comparisons on psychological well-being. *Research Quarterly for Exercise and Sport, 89*, 354–360. Doi:10.1080/02701367.2018.1481919

Huta, V., & Ryan, R. M. (2010). Pursuing pleasure or virtue: The differential and overlapping well-being benefits of hedonic and eudaimonic motives. *Journal of Happiness Studies, 11*, 735–762. Doi:10.1007/s10902-009-9171-4

Huta, V., & Waterman, A. S. (2014). Eudaimonia and its distinction from hedonia: Developing a classification and terminology for understanding conceptual and operational definitions. *Journal of Happiness Studies, 15*, 1425–1456. Doi:10.1007/s10902-013-9485-0

Iasiello, M., Bartholomaeus, J., Jarden, A., & Kelly, G. (2017). Measuring PERMA+ in South Australia, the state of wellbeing: A comparison with national and international norms. *Journal of Positive Psychology and Wellbeing, 1*, 53–72. Retrieved from http://journalppw.com/index.php/JPPW/article/view/12

Jowett, S., & Cramer, D. (2009). The role of romantic relationships on athletes' performance and wellbeing. *Journal of Clinical Sport Psychology, 3*, 58–72. Doi:10.1123/jcsp.3.1.58

Kashdan, T. B., Biswas-Diener, R., & King, L. A (2008). Reconsidering happiness: The costs of distinguishing between hedonics and eudaimonia. *The Journal of Positive Psychology, 3*, 219–233. Doi:10.1080/17439760802303044

Keyes, C. L. M. (1998). Social well-being. *Social Psychological Quarterly, 61*, 121–140. Doi:10.2307/2787065

Keyes, C. L. M. (2005). Mental illness and/or mental health? Investigating axioms of the complete state model of health. *Journal of Consulting and Clinical Psychology, 73*, 539–548. Doi:10.1037/0022-006X.73.3.539

Keyes, C. L. M., & Annas, J. (2009). Feeling good and functioning well: Distinctive concepts in ancient philosophy and contemporary science. *The Journal of Positive Psychology, 4*, 197–201. Doi:10.1080/17439760902844228

Kinderman, P., Allsopp, K., & Cooke, A. (2017). Responses to the publication of the American Psychiatric Association's *DSM-5*. *Journal of Humanistic Psychology, 57*, 625–649. Doi:10.1177/0022167817698262

Kuettel, A., & Larsen, C. H. (2020). Risk and protective factors for mental health in elite athletes: A scoping review. *International Review of Sport and Exercise Psychology, 13*, 231–265. Doi:10.1080/1750984X.2019.1689574

Lambert, L., Passmore, H- A., & Holder, M. D. (2015). Foundational frameworks of positive psychology: Mapping well-being orientations. *Canadian Psychology, 56*, 311–321. Doi:10.1037/cap0000033

Ledochowski, L., Unterrainer, C., Ruedl, G., Schnitzer, M., & Kopp, M. (2012). Quality of life, coach behaviour and competitive anxiety in Winter Youth Olympic Games participants. *British Journal of Sports Medicine, 46*, 1044–1047. Doi:10.1136/bjsports-2012-091539

Linton, M. J., Dieppe, P., & Medina-Lara, A. (2016). Review of 99 self-report measures for assessing well-being in adults: Exploring dimensions of well-being and developments over time. *British Medical Journal Open, 6*, 1–17. Doi:10.1136/bmjop en-2015–010641

Lundqvist, C. (2011). Well-being in competitive sports—The feel-good factor? A review of conceptual considerations of well-being. *International Review of Sport and Exercise Psychology, 4*, 109–127. Doi:10.1080/1750984X.2011.584067

Lundqvist, C., & Raglin, J. (2015). The relationship of basic need satisfaction, motivational climate and personality to well-being and stress patterns among elite athletes: An explorative study. *Motivation and Emotion, 39*, 237–246. Doi:10.1007/s11031-014-9444-z

Lundqvist, C., & Sandin, F. (2014). Well-being in elite sport: Dimensions of hedonic and eudaimonic well-being among elite orienteers. *The Sport Psychologist, 28*, 245–254. Doi:10.1123/tsp.2013-0024

Lundqvist, C., Träff, M., & Brady, A. (2020). "Not everyone gets the opportunity to experience this": Swedish elite athletes' perceptions of quality of life. *International Journal of Sport Psychology*. Manuscript accepted for publication.

MacDougall, H., O'Halloran, P., Sherry, E., & Shields, N. (2016). Needs and strengths of Australian Para athletes: Identifying the subjective, psychological, social, and physical health and well-being. *The Sport Psychologist, 30*, 1–12. Doi:10.1123/tsp.2015-0006

MacDougall, H., O'Halloran, P., Sherry, E., & Shields, N. (2019). A pilot randomised controlled trial to enhance well-being and performance of athletes in para sports. *European Journal of Adapted Physical Activity, 12*, 1–19. Doi:10.5507/euj.2019.006

Morgan, W. P. (1985). Selected psychological factors limiting performance: A mental health model. In D. H. Clarke & H. M Eckert (Eds.), *Limits of human performance* (pp. 70–80). Champaign, IL: Human Kinetics.

Post, M. W. M. (2014). Definitions of quality of life: What has happened and how to move on. *Topics in Spinal Cord Injury Rehabilitation, 20*, 167–180. Doi:10.1310/sci2003-167.

Raglin, J. S. (1992). Anxiety and sport performance. In J. O. Holloszy (Ed.), *Exercise and sport sciences reviews* (Vol. 20, pp. 243–274). New York: Williams & Wilkins.

Raglin, J. S. (2001). Psychological factors in sport performance: The mental health model revisited. *Sports Medicine, 31*, 875–890. Doi:10.2165/00007256-200131120-00004

Raibley, J. R. (2012). Happiness is not well-being. *Journal of Happiness Studies, 13*, 1105–1129. Doi:10.1007/s10902-011-9309-z

Rapley, M. (2003). *Quality of life research: A critical introduction.* London, UK: Sage.

Ryan, R. M., & Deci, E. L. (2000). Self-determination and the facilitation of intrinsic motivation, social development, and well-being. *American Psychologist, 55*, 68–78. Doi:10.1037//0003-066x.55.1.68

Ryan, R. M., & Deci, E. L. (2001). On happiness and human potentials: A review of research on hedonic and eudaimonic well-being. *Annual Review of Psychology, 52*, 141–166. Doi:10.1146/annurev.psych.52.1.141

Ryan, R. M., & Deci, E. L. (2002). An overview of self-determination theory: An organismic-dialectical perspective. In E. L. Deci & R. M. Ryan (Eds.), *Handbook of self-determination research* (pp. 3–33). Rochester, NY: University of Rochester Press.

Ryan, R. M., Huta, V., & Deci, E. L. (2008). Living well: A self-determination theory perspective on eudaimonia. *Journal of Happiness Studies, 9*, 139–170. Doi:10.1007/s10902-006-9023-4

Ryff, C. D. (1989). Happiness is everything, or is it? Exploration on the meaning of psychological well-being. *Journal of Personality and Social Psychology, 57*, 1069–1081. Doi:10.1037/0022-3514.57.6.1069

Ryff, C. D. (2014). Psychological well-being revisited: Advances in the science and practice of eudaimonia. *Psychotherapy and Psychosomatics, 83*, 10–28. Doi:10.1159/000353263

Ryff, C. D., Singer, B. H., & Dienberg Love, G. (2004). Positive health: Connecting well-being with biology. *Philosophical Transactions of the Royal Society B: Biological Sciences, 359*, 1383–1394. Doi:10.1098/rstb.2004.1521

Seligman, M. E. P. (2002). *Authentic happiness: Using the new positive psychology to realize your potential for lasting fulfillment.* New York: Free Press.

Seligman, M. E. P. (2011). *Flourish: A visionary new understanding of happiness and well-being.* New York: Free Press.

Seligman, M. E. P. (2018). PERMA and the building blocks of well-being. *The Journal of Positive Psychology, 13,* 333–335. Doi:10.1080/17439760.2018.1437466

Seligman, M. E. P., & Csikszentmihalyi, M. (2000). Positive psychology. An introduction. *American Psychologist, 55,* 5–14. Doi:10.1037/0003-066X.55.1.5

Standage, M., Curran, T., & Rouse, P. C. (2019). Self-determination-based theories of sport, exercise, and physical activity motivation. In T. S. Horn, & A. L. Smith (Eds.), *Advances in sport and exercise psychology* (4th ed., pp. 289–311). Champaign, IL: Human Kinetics.

Suls, J., & Rothman, A. (2004). Evolution of the biopsychosocial model: Prospects and challenges for health psychology. *Health Psychology, 23,* 119–125. Doi:10.1037/0278-6133.23.2.119

WHO (1999). *WHOQOL annotated bibliography.* Geneva, Switzerland: WHO Department of Mental Health. Retrieved from www.who.int/healthinfo/survey/whoqol-qualityoflife/en/

WHO (2004). *Promoting mental health: Concepts, emerging evidence, practice.* Geneva, Switzerland: World Health Organization. Retrieved from www.who.int/mental_health/evidence/en/promoting_mhh.pdf

Wilson, W. (1967). Correlates of avowed happiness. *Psychological Bulletin, 67,* 294–306. Doi:10.1037/h0024431

7 Burnout

J. D. DeFreese and Robert C. Eklund

Introduction

Burnout is a complex psychological phenomenon relevant to multiple actors in sport including athletes. With the goal to provide a synthesis of the sport-based literature on burnout, this chapter highlights the most up to date research and theory on burnout using a stress and coping perspective. With a focus on its development as a response to chronic exposure to stress, athlete burnout is discussed primarily but what is known about burnout in coaches and officials is also reviewed. The four sections of the chapter focus on: (i) defining and describing athlete burnout within the psychological stress and coping model, (ii) describing how other prominent burnout processes work synergistically with the stress and coping model in explaining burnout in sport, (iii) describing evidence of burnout in coaches and other non-athlete populations, and (iv) highlighting potential practical implications of the current evidence on burnout in sport as they relate to prevention and symptom mitigation. We begin by defining the athlete burnout construct in sport relative to stress and coping processes.

Athlete Burnout Within the Psychological Stress and Coping Model

Following its conceptualization as a phenomenon of concern in the workplace (Freudenberger, 1974; Maslach, 1982, 2001), burnout was recognized as a concern in the sporting arena for those being chronically exposed to sport-related stressors (Dale & Weinberg, 1990; Rotella, Hanson, & Coop, 1991; Smith, 1986; see also Chapter 1). Commentaries on burnout highlighted the important need to more clearly and carefully define the burnout syndrome in sport particularly with regard to athlete populations. Early on, researchers attempted to define burnout based primarily upon anecdotal accounts, even suggesting that distinct "physical" and "psychological" pathways to burnout from various sport-based stressors merited consideration (Gould, 1996). However, a call was made for a clearly defined sport-based conceptualization of burnout, with Raedeke (1997; Raedeke & Smith, 2001) most commonly credited with adapting Maslach's (1982, 2001) work-based burnout definition to sport. Accordingly, athlete burnout was defined as a cognitive-affective syndrome characterized by the enduring experience of symptoms relating to emotional and physical exhaustion, sport devaluation, and reduced accomplishment. *Emotional and physical exhaustion* is characterized by psychological and physical fatigue resulting from the individual's response to training and competition demands. *Sport devaluation* is characterized by a cynical attitude toward the value of sport. This is in contrast to the work-based burnout definition in which this dimension was depersonalization and characterized by cynicism toward the workplace patient/client (Maslach, 2001). Finally, *reduced accomplishment* is characterized by an inefficacy and tendency to evaluate one's competence and accomplishment in sport more negatively regardless of objective performance quality. This definitional adaptation of burnout from work to sport was based on the notion that there are commonalities in the experience of burnout as a stress response which transcend both environments (Schaufeli & Enzman, 1998). Specifically, individuals in both workplace and sport environments undergo exposure to chronic psychosocial stress resulting in the common aversive experiential state of burnout even if the roles and the specific implicated ongoing demands differ substantially across the environments (Cresswell & Eklund, 2006c, 2007; Dale & Weinberg, 1990; Gould, Tuffey, Udry, & Loehr, 1996; Rotella et al., 1991; see also Chapter 1). The adaptation of the workplace conceptualization of burnout to be relevant to athletes was a crucial facilitating step in the development of reliable and valid psychometric assessment of the construct to support the development and testing of coherent theorical explanations to advance understanding of this aversive chronic experiential state.

Measurement of Athlete Burnout

Early studies of athlete burnout were undermined by measurement difficulties (Eklund & DeFreese, 2020). Minor adjustments to the "gold standard" Maslach Burnout Inventory (Maslach & Jackson, 1986) for measuring burnout in the helping professions proved fruitless because, for example, the depersonalization symptom dimension had no relevance to the athlete role. The amorphously and eclectically conceptualized Eades Athlete Burnout Inventory (Eades, 1990) fared a little better but did provide an imperative for the development of the Athlete Burnout Questionnaire (Raedeke, 1997; Raedeke & Smith, 2001), which is now the most widely and commonly used measure of athlete burnout. This 15-item Likert scale measure assesses three dimensions of burnout symptoms including emotional and physical exhaustion, reduced accomplishment, and sport devaluation. Participants endorse the degree to which they experience each item on a 5-point Likert scale ranging from one (not at all) to five (most of the time). This measure has been found to consistently provide reliable and valid data when used with athlete populations across age groups and competitive levels (Raedeke & Smith, 2009) and has been an essential measurement tool in many studies advancing knowledge in the area. In the next section, we discuss some of the foundational commentaries and studies to showcase the progression of theoretical/conceptual developments in the exploration of burnout in sport from a stress and coping perspective.

Early Key Studies on Athlete Burnout

A primary theoretical conceptualization of burnout development was posited by Smith (1986) who specified that athlete burnout was implicated in the "psychological, emotional, and at times a physical withdrawal from a formerly pursued and enjoyable activity" (p. 37). This idea was grounded in Maslach and Jackson's (1986) conceptualization of burnout and built on Lazarus's (1966) positions on emotion and the stress and coping process as well as Thibaut and Kelley's (1959) Social Exchange Theory. As a broad description, burnout was posited to result from sport-related appraisals resulting from the demands-resources trade-off made by athletes in the intensive competitive sport environment (see also Chapters 1 and 2). This appraisal is partially based on (albeit not necessarily objectively grounded in) one's actual physical training load and also other stressors importantly including those of a psychosocial nature. While the appraisal of stress is important, the potential for coping efforts to mitigate athlete perceived stress exists along with potential for mitigation of the development of athlete burnout as opposed to more adaptive or well-being related outcomes (see also Chapters 3 and 6). This dynamic and transactional process, therefore, has the potential to result in adaptive (i.e., well-being and positive affect) or maladaptive (i.e., distress, ineffective coping, and burnout) responses. Athlete dispositions (i.e., perfectionism, optimism, and motivation; see also Chapter 10), as well as the sport-based social environment also have the potential to impact whether or not athlete burnout is experienced along with implications for outcomes of athlete psychosocial health and performance. Essentially, as indicated in Goodger, Gorely, Lavallee, and Harwood's (2007) systematic review of athlete burnout, it is posited in this conceptualization that perceived stress exacerbates the possibility of an athlete experiencing burnout as do deficits/mismatches in athlete resources and coping skills. Thus, a review of key individual studies of athlete burnout and stress and/or coping can provide a solid foundation for understanding of this knowledge base.

Smith's (1986) conceptualization was not the only early conceptualization of processes involved in athlete burnout. Silva (1990), for example, posited burnout as the final phase in his "training stress syndrome" being a maladaptive psychophysiological response, including psychological symptoms consistent with Maslach and Jackson's (1986) syndrome, that was largely attributable to overtraining. Retrospective data from a small convenience sample ($n = 68$) provided some support for his contentions. The prevalence of burnout based upon these retrospective data was purported to be as high as 46.9% of participants. The conceptualization of burnout in this study was imprecise and symptomatically confounded; however, the prevalence reported certainly provided impetus for more carefully conceptualized continued investigation of this important problem in sport.

The United States Tennis Association (USTA) funded some of the earliest systematic research on athlete burnout (Gould et al., 1996; Gould, Tuffey, Udry, & Loehr, 1997; Gould, Udry, Tuffey, & Loehr, 1996) precisely because of concerns about the prevalence and management of burnout and dropout in their developmental programs. Using a mixed methods approach in conducting a series of largely retrospective cross-sectional studies, Gould and his colleagues identified decreases in sport motivation, less adaptive forms of motivation (i.e., amotivation), high levels of perfectionism, social pressures from parents and coaches, and chronic exposure to sport as key factors preceding the development of athlete burnout. Although highly influential in its seminal influence on the understanding of burnout in sport, this work was largely atheoretical in nature and limited by its use of the conceptually troubled, as previously mentioned, Eades Athlete Burnout Inventory.

As is apparent in the preceding commentary, the salience of conceptual and measurement challenges to the advancement of knowledge in the study of athlete burnout had been progressively growing across early research efforts. Raedeke's (Raedeke, 1997; Raedeke & Smith, 2001, 2004) efforts to develop and validate a conceptually well-grounded measurement tool (i.e., Athlete Burnout Questionnaire—ABQ) represented an important step forward as previously mentioned. As a part of the initial process of development of the ABQ, Raedeke and Smith (2001) obtained data from 244 senior age-group swimmers (M_{age} = 15.8 years, SD = 13.3) on outcomes of perceived psychological stress, general coping resources, and athlete burnout as part of a larger survey battery. Within this sample, the individual dimensions of athlete burnout were all found to be significantly positively associated with perceived stress and negatively associated with coping. These researchers further questioned the potential sequencing of burnout, stress, and coping and investigated this model in an additional cross-sectional modeling study (Raedeke & Smith, 2004). In this sample of senior age-group swimmers, the authors replicated the aforementioned associations of perceived stress (positive) and coping (negative) with burnout as well and also found, using structural equation modeling, that coping was a potential mediator of the relationship between perceived stress and burnout, consistent with

Smith's (1986) conceptualization. Cumulatively, these early studies provided initial support for the psychological stress and coping perspective in describing athlete burnout and formed a basis from which continuing work was built upon.

A series of studies, funded by the New Zealand Rugby Union (NZRU), continued to add to the knowledge base on athlete burnout as a psychosocial stress and coping response to athletic training and participation. Interviews with 15 rugby athletes endorsing burnout symptoms (Cresswell & Eklund, 2006c) highlighted many key stress-based burnout antecedents within rugby including transition across competitive teams and seasons, heavy physical training and competition demands, and social pressures to comply with these demands despite physical or mental fatigue. An additional study (Cresswell & Eklund, 2006b) established the psychometric reliability and validity of the ABQ within this population for its use in other studies. This series of studies included intensive examination of burnout development in relation to motivation; these studies highlighted athlete burnout to be negatively associated with more self-determined forms of motivation (Cresswell & Eklund, 2004, 2005b, 2005c, 2006a). Additionally, a longitudinal qualitative study of NZRU professional athletes (Cresswell & Eklund, 2007) further emphasized the dynamic nature of the burnout response. Specifically, study results showcased changes in burnout to be associated with periods of positive and negative change over time in motivational, stress, and coping (or the lack thereof) responses within the competitive training environment of the elite athletes sampled.

Beyond direct links to psychological stress and coping (see also Chapters 1–4), the findings of a systematic review highlighted that athlete burnout is positively associated with amotivation, anxiety, and mood disturbance, and negatively associated with adaptive motivation types, perceived control, enjoyment, recovery, and social support (Goodger et al., 2007). Social relationships also clearly fit within the stress and coping model as negative relationships can place stressful demands upon individuals while the social support in positive relationships can function to buffer stress and/or serve as coping resources promotive of well-being outcomes (see also Chapter 11). In a recent meta-analytic review of 20 studies of burnout in athletes, for example, Pacewicz, Mellano, and Smith (2019) observed low-to-moderate positive associations of burnout dimensions with negative social interactions and also low-to-moderate negative associations of burnout dimensions with social support and relatedness. Notably, relatively few studies of positive social constructs (i.e., social support and relatedness) exist to date suggesting a need for further study in this area. Overall, the psychosocial stress and coping model has been studied extensively with cross-sectional data, with findings being overwhelmingly supportive of its use as a model to understand burnout antecedents. These findings have been relied upon extensively to inform research and practice efforts.

More Recent Longitudinal Studies of Athlete Burnout

Building on early athlete burnout research, more recent longitudinal investigations grounded in Smith's (1986) model have also been informed by the work of Lazarus and Folkman (1984). Herein, a selection of longitudinal studies germane to the understanding of athlete burnout as an outcome of heightened stress and/or inability to adequately cope with sport-based stress are overviewed (see also Chapters 1–4).

Firstly, DeFreese and Smith (2014) examined temporal associations of social support and negative social interactions with athlete burnout and life satisfaction across a competitive season in a sample of American collegiate swimming and track and field athletes ($N = 465$). Participants completed self-report assessments of athlete burnout, social support, negative social interactions, and life satisfaction (an outcome representative of psychological well-being; see also Chapter 6) along with assessments of perceived stress, sport motivation, and dispositional measures of optimism and negative affect at four equally spaced seasonal time points. Study results showcased the importance of social support (negative relationship) and negative social interactions (positive relationship) as significant predictors of athlete burnout when accounting for empirically specified covariates (i.e., perceived stress and sport motivation). Notably, this was the first longitudinal study to our knowledge to examine a negative social predictor of athlete burnout.

Schellenberg, Gaudreau, and Crocker (2013) also provided longitudinal evidence in a study of passionate involvement in sport supporting earlier cross-sectional findings on links between coping and athlete burnout. In a sample of 421 volleyball athletes, obsessive passion positively predicted changes in athlete burnout over time. This relationship was then found to be mediated by disengagement-oriented coping behaviors (see also Chapter 3). More recently, Madigan and Nicholls (2017) examined the coping-related variable of mental toughness as a potential predictor of athlete burnout in a sample of English junior athletes ($n = 93$) using a two-time-point longitudinal study design. After controlling for burnout at Time 1, mental toughness was a negative predictor of Time 2 athlete burnout at both global and dimensional levels. These two longitudinal studies are important as they began to build the knowledge base on the complexity of other psychological constructs relevant to relationships among burnout, stress, and coping.

Dispositional traits are also relevant to burnout as explained by the stress and coping model (see also Chapter 10). Madigan, Stoeber, and Passfield (2015) examined associations among perfectionistic strivings, perfectionistic concerns, and athlete burnout across three active training months in a junior athlete sample ($n = 101$). Using a two-wave, cross-lagged panel design, structural equation modelling results revealed perfectionistic strivings predicted decreases in athlete burnout while perfectionistic concerns predicted increases in athlete burnout. Moreover, in a follow-up study using a three-time-point multilevel structural model (Madigan, Stoeber, & Passfield, 2016), autonomous motivation was found to mediate the negative perfectionistic strivings-burnout relationship at both between- and within-person levels while controlled motivation was found to mediate the positive perfectionistic concerns-burnout relationship at the between-person level only.

Overall, the psychological stress and coping model has provided a useful conceptual framework for advancing understanding of athlete burnout. Research using this perspective indicates that perceived stress tends to exacerbate the possibility of an athlete experiencing burnout as do athlete ineffectiveness and/or mismatches in coping skills/resources. Longitudinal research on burnout in sport has shed further light on the complex development of this maladaptive syndrome by highlighting social perceptions, mental toughness, passion, and perfectionism as variables of potential influence on stress and coping processes resulting in burnout. Continued development of theoretically informed and methodologically sound longitudinal studies is needed to further unearth knowledge about burnout development in sport. Gender has already been identified as a potentially meaningful moderator variable in the development of burnout in multiyear studies of athletes (Isoard-Gautheur, Guillet-Descas, Gaudreau, & Chanal, 2015) but other potential conjunctive or disjunctive moderators (e.g., competition level, training load, markers of recovery, and therapeutic resource utilization) also warrant consideration in future longitudinal investigations. The psychological stress and coping model perspective continues to offer a potentially fruitful empirical and practical avenue for advancement of the sport-based burnout knowledge base.

Other Prominent Burnout Processes Synergistic With the Stress and Coping Model

Athlete burnout research has also been focused on the influence of maladaptive patterns of sport commitment, sport motivation, unidimensional sport identity, and perceived lack of control in sport. A primary aim of this section is to discuss how these additional explanations add to understanding of burnout as a potential stress response. Accordingly, these additional explanations are reviewed and discussed subsequently.

Sport Commitment Theory and Burnout

Schmidt and Stein (1991) first proposed a commitment-based framework for sport participation which has informed the study of athlete burnout as well. Building on this framework, Raedeke (1997) conceptualized burnout as an experience emanating from an *entrapped* pattern of sport commitment—a type of commitment inherently laden with potential for perceived stress—that is characterized by high levels of perceived costs, investments, and social constraints combined with few participation barriers or attractive alternatives to sport participation. This position was supported by one of the seminal studies examining burnout in sport. First, as expected, Raedeke (1997) found burnout to be positively associated with psychological stress among youth and adolescent swimmers ($n = 236$, $M_{age} = 15.5$ years, $SD = 1.5$). More interestingly, cluster analyses of the swimmers based upon their patterns of commitment revealed, as hypothesized, the highest levels of burnout symptoms were observed among athletes reporting *entrapped* sport commitment. This sport commitment perspective on athlete burnout has contributed to both athlete burnout research design and interpretation. Specifically, this study involved the examination of multiple variables (i.e., enjoyment, identity, commitment stress, and social constraints) simultaneously and, importantly, resulted in the conclusion that not all athletes experiencing burnout leave sport, as those sampled reporting the highest burnout levels also reported the highest levels of sport commitment and the lowest levels of sport enjoyment.

Identity and Control Theory Burnout

Not entirely satisfied with stress process perspectives on athlete burnout, Jay Coakley (1992, 2009), a prominent American sport sociologist, posited that young athletes' "burnout" (i.e., drop out) of sport because the social structure of youth sport is controlled by adults which leaves young athletes with little latitude or influence over the nature of their participation while also producing identities that are uncomfortably sport-centric. His contention, albeit formulated on the basis of a relatively small number of informal interviews with youth sport athletes ($n = 15$), was that stress is the result of burning out of the aversive sport environment rather than its cause. A good argument can be made, however, that Coakley's (1992, 2009) perspective is a complimentary (rather than contrary) explanation to the stress and coping model of burnout in so much that the environment is fundamental to the stress experience (see also Chapters 1, 8, and 14) and that identity is a crucial component of the appraisal process (see also Chapter 2). Little research has directly examined Coakley's perspective with the exception of a study of elite swimmers by Black and Smith (2007) which found partial support. Regardless, the practical message of Coakley's (1992, 2009) argument is important and should remain salient in efforts to understand this aversive experiential state; organizational structures within sport may contribute to burnout— perhaps even in parallel to athletes' stress and coping responses.

Self-Determination Theory and Burnout

Self-Determination Theory (SDT) has also been useful in better understanding multiple questions germane to athlete burnout including: (i) how are multiple types of motivation related to burnout? And (ii) what is the directional nature of the burnout-motivation association in sport? In SDT (Deci & Ryan, 1985), behavior is broadly proposed to be most adaptively influenced by intrinsic motives, resulting in the greatest behavioral persistence and positive outcomes of psychological health/well-being over time. Within SDT, moreover, behaviors are qualified as being more or less self-determined, or performed as a result of differing degrees of individual choice relative to external demands. Intrinsic behavior represents the most self-determined form of motivation, while extrinsic motivation can be characterized as involving varying degrees of self-determination. Thus, SDT proposes a continuum of motivational regulations based on their level of self-determination (see Ryan & Deci, 2000a, 2000b, for reviews). External regulation is the least self-determined form of extrinsic motivation as it involves performing a behavior purely to respond to an external demand or contingency. It is followed on the continuum of increasingly more self-determined extrinsic regulations (i.e., introjected, identified, and integrated regulations). Conceptually, social contextual factors within an environment are posited to influence satisfaction of the fundamental psychological needs of autonomy, competence, and relatedness. The extent to which individuals experience need satisfaction in their behavioral engagements is then proposed to influence where that individual falls on the continuum of motivational regulation and, ultimately, the extent to which there are benefits to their psychosocial health/well-being. More specifically, from a self-determination theory perspective, athlete burnout results from basic psychological needs not being satisfied (perhaps even thwarted) in sport involvement which also results in less self-determined forms of sport motivational engagement. Researchers have examined hypotheses on these theoretically anticipated relationships in sport accordingly.

In general, athlete burnout has been found to be robustly associated with both amotivation and more self-determined (i.e., autonomous) forms of sport motivation (albeit in, respectively, positive and negative directions). More controlled forms of motivation have also tended to be inconsistently and, at best, weakly associated with athlete burnout (see, for a review, Li, Wang, Pyun, & Kee, 2013). In addition, motivational quality and overtraining have been observed to contribute to the emergence of athlete burnout (Lemyre, Roberts, & Stay-Gunderson, 2007) with shifts away from more self-determined forms of motivation over time being predictive of the development of burnout symptoms among elite athletes (Lemyre, Hall, & Roberts, 2007; Lemyre, Treasure, & Roberts, 2006). Nonetheless, descriptive analyses of longitudinal data cannot fully disentangle whether decreases in self-determined motivation lead to the experience of athlete burnout, increases in burnout lead to negative shifts in self-determined motivation, or if the process involves reciprocal effects among constructs (Cresswell & Eklund, 2005a). This represents an important area for continued research relative to burnout in sport.

More fine-grained analyses of SDT theoretical contentions have indicated that deficits in psychological need satisfaction (and thwarting) are likely implicated in athlete burnout while satisfaction of needs tend to be associated with more adaptive outcomes including psychological well-being (see also Chapters 6 and 8). For example, research has shown a negative relationship between psychological need satisfaction and athlete burnout, as well as at least partial support for self-determined motivation as a mediator of the relationship between need satisfaction and burnout-related perceptions (Lonsdale, Hodge, & Rose, 2009). Furthermore, elite rugby players classified as "high-burnouts" have reported lower perceptions of need fulfillment compared to players classified as "low burnouts" (Hodge, Lonsdale, & Ng, 2008). Evidence also exists to suggest that the extent of simultaneous satisfaction of fundamental psychological needs contributes to the predication of athlete burnout above and beyond the contribution of the satisfaction of individual needs (Perreault, Gaudreau, Lapointe, & Lacroix, 2007). Finally, a three time-point longitudinal study of a sample of dancers enrolled in vocational training (n = 219) also supports the impact of psychological needs on athlete burnout. Specifically, Quested and Duda (2011) found that self-reported perceptions of autonomy support positively predicted changes in dancers' basic need satisfaction over a year with adverse changes in need satisfaction being subsequently predictive of increases in global burnout scores. The three needs also fully mediated the relationship between perceived autonomy support and global athlete burnout scores.

SDT has been useful in explaining athlete burnout but other motivational frameworks, largely compatible with SDT, have also shown promise as well. Lemyre, Hall, and Roberts (2008), for example, utilized Achievement Goal Theory to examine burnout. They found burnout to be negatively predicted by task goal involvement (i.e., a more adaptive and autonomously oriented motivational typology) and positively predicted by ego goal involvement (i.e., a less adaptive and more externally oriented motivational typology). Given the commonalities in the theories, it is not surprising that both have proven useful in efforts to understand burnout in sport.

Integrated Model of Athlete Burnout

Finally, Gustafsson, Kenttä, and Hassmén (2011) proposed an eclectically Integrated Model of Burnout combining variables identified across a variety of burnout process conceptualizations. Athlete burnout antecedents in their model include excessive training, school/work demands, stressful social situations, negative performance demands, insufficient recovery, and early age sport success. Specific theoretically informed variables were also integrated within this model including perceived sport entrapment, unidimensional athlete identity, high sport investment, constraints on non-sport social activities, performance-contingent self-esteem and other salient (to sport) personality, coping skills, and environmental factors (e.g., social support and motivational climate). Maladaptive burnout consequences proposed in this model include sport withdrawal, impaired immune system function, over-use impairment symptoms, and long-term performance impairment. Although this model has potential for pedagogical and practical utility in serving as a broad orienting heuristic for sports scientists and practitioners alike on the breadth of constructs germane to understanding sport burnout, the absence of overarching and integrating theory means that it has little utility as a model for hypothesis generation.

Cumulatively, research utilizing these aforementioned models and theories is additive, rather than subtractive, such that all aforementioned theories add to our ability to better understand athlete burnout as a maladaptive stress and coping response, albeit with unique conceptual interpretations which highlight unique stress-adjacent psychosocial factors. Sport scientists, practitioners, and participants alike should be well versed in all burnout theories so as to best understand the development of this potentially complex syndromic experience. Certainly, the conceptualizations described herein have been extremely helpful to building the sport-based burnout knowledge base and will continue to inform research and practice efforts designed to positively impact athlete performance and well-being.

Burnout in Coaches and Other Non-Athlete Populations

A good place to begin an understanding of burnout in non-athlete populations is by reviewing the work on sport coaches. Hjälm, Kentta, Hassmén, and Gustafsson (2007), for example, reported experiences of moderate-to-high levels of emotional exhaustion using the Maslach Burnout Inventory in a sample of elite Swedish club level soccer coaches (n = 47), highlighting the presence of burnout among coaches. In the aforementioned systematic review of burnout in sport, Goodger and colleagues (2007) also examined key antecedents of burnout among sport coaches. Coach burnout was observed to have positive associations with perceived stress, sport commitment, coaching issues, and role conflict and role ambiguity as well as negative associations with coach support. Perceived coaching success and coach behaviors were also found to have mixed associations with coach burnout with some studies exhibiting positive associations and others a negative association. Measurement has also been an issue in this domain as the ABQ is not appropriate for assessment of burnout in non-athlete populations, and some have suggested that perhaps the MBI may have deficits (Lundkvist, Stenling, Gustafsson, & Hassmén, 2014). Ultimately, the area of research on burnout in sport coaches in still in its infancy, but advancing understanding of the prevalence, antecedents, and measurement of coach burnout may have important implications for this sport-based population as well as potential impact upon the athletes that they serve.

Indeed, some early research supports the idea that the experience of burnout among coaches may be implicated in the experience of burnout among the athletes they coach (Price & Weiss, 2000; Vealey, Armstrong, Comar, & Greenleaf, 1998). Moreover, coach knowledge and insight about athlete burnout may be an important consideration in the link between coaches' and athletes' burnout experiences. For example, Raedeke, Lunney, and Venables (2002) interviewed U.S. senior swimming coaches ($n = 13$) who endorsed the relevance of the burnout syndrome to the experiences of their swimmers. Coaches further endorsed the saliency of athlete burnout to stress- and coping-related factors as well as suggested strategies for prevention. Notably, coaches in the study endorsed support (from parents, teammates, and coaches), having a supportive training environment conducive to improvement and long-term development, and keeping the program exciting as key intervention strategies. Replicating and extending this work, Kroshus and DeFreese (2017) investigated coaches self-reported burnout prevention strategies for their athletes via a content analysis of short answer responses provided by a large sample of collegiate soccer coaches ($n = 933$). The most frequently endorsed prevention strategies involved efforts to manage and/or limit athlete exposure to physical stressors (see also Chapter 1). Coaches' acknowledgement of their role in athlete burnout prevention is important to their potential impact on athletes. That said, going forward, it would be helpful for coaches to receive additional psychoeducational training regarding how strategies beyond training load management (e.g., psychosocial stress and coping strategies, and monitoring of markers of recovery) may also represent fruitful athlete burnout prevention strategies.

A few historical studies have examined other individuals involved in sport, including referees. Although less detailed in nature, this work highlights the association of burnout with factors such as stress, time pressure, and performance concerns in basketball referees (Rainey, 1999). Additional work in rugby union referees found burnout to be predicted by time pressure and interpersonal conflict and, in turn, referee burnout and age to predict intention to terminate officiating (Rainey & Hardy, 1999). Overall, research on burnout in coaches and referees supports the stress and coping model and provides impetus for future longitudinal and interventional efforts to prevent and/or mitigate burnout in these populations.

Ultimately, a deeper understanding of burnout among "performers" in sport beyond the athletes themselves, including its relationship to stress and coping, has potential to deepen practitioners' abilities to intervene and offer aid to these individuals (e.g., coaches and referees). One goal of such work could be to facilitate the development of appropriate and effective avenues of coping with stressors emanating from demands of their professional responsibilities (see also Chapter 3). Such work would benefit from looking to the knowledge bases in both the sport- and work-based burnout literatures to design and implement interventions which could be carefully evaluated for effectiveness (see also Chapter 12).

Practical Implications of the Current Evidence on Burnout in Sport

This chapter concludes with a few practical considerations for how understanding of burnout theory and research can positively impact burnout prevention and treatment in sport. Extant research reviewed herein highlights the potential importance of considering stress and coping strategies which target the individual (i.e., athlete, coach) as well as the environmental demands and resources which may render athletes vulnerable to this maladaptive stress response (see also Chapters 1, 12, and 14). Accordingly, we subscribe to Coakley's (1992) position that burnout is not solely the problem of the individual but is also an issue of the environment that impacts participants' stress and coping responses, performance, and well-being outcomes.

First, organizational stress reduction and/or management strategies should be considered for burnout prevention and treatment because helping to equip athletes (and coaches or referees) to effectively manage and/or cope with their sport-based stress has potential utility as a means to deter burnout and potentially enhance performance (see also Chapters 1 and 12). Appraisal strategies to lower the perceived demands-resources trade-off balance could be beneficial (see also Chapter 2). Specifically, enhancing participants' knowledge of resources and support may be helpful in stress reduction and, ultimately, burnout prevention and well-being promotion. Individual coping strategies (i.e., goal setting and self-regulation) can also mitigate stress and prevent burnout via successful adaptation to sport-based stressors (see also Chapter 3). For example, Dubuc-Charbonneau and Durand-Bush (2015) implemented a person-centered self-regulation intervention relating to athlete outcomes of stress, burnout, well-being, and capacity for self-regulation in a sample of eight Canadian university student-athletes. Results showed decreases in athlete stress and burnout levels as well as increases in well-being and self-regulation following the intervention protocol. Their results suggest that intervention strategies designed to teach athletes to self-regulate more effectively may have benefits in terms of burnout prevention and performance as well as well-being enhancement.

Second, clinicians can help participants to lower burnout-related perceptions by teaching strategies to manage/cope with psychosocial stress in training and/or competition (see also Chapters 3 and 12). A variety of psychological skills (e.g., imagery, relaxation training, and mindfulness) may represent effective options as coping resources for individuals in sport with a potential dual benefit of also enhancing their performance despite the often unavoidable stress associated with intensive training and competition within sport. Ultimately, any appropriate strategy that may minimize the initial stress response and/or help the individual cope with the resulting stress could have a long-term effect in preventing and treating burnout symptoms as well as enhancing performance and well-being outcomes (see also Chapters 3, 12, and 13). Third, clinical therapeutic interventions guided by licensed mental health professionals or trainees under the guidance of said professional also represent another way to help participants build general- and sport-specific coping skills and potentially prevent burnout. Cognitive-behavioral therapy (CBT; Gustafsson, DeFreese, & Madigan, 2017) is a therapeutic strategy which has been examined as an option for treating burnout in workers. Accordingly, the design and evaluation of sport-based CBT may prove fruitful for sport-based burnout prevention (see also Chapter 8).

Finally, as outlined by Lonsdale, Hodge, and Jackson (2007), sport organizations may benefit from working to promote sport engagement as a positive psychological experience characterized by confidence (in contrast to a reduced sense of accomplishment), dedication (in contrast to devaluation), and vigor and enthusiasm (in contrast to exhaustion). Such prevention and well-being strategies have been described in detail in organizational psychology. For example, research on worker burnout has used the job-person fit model of burnout/engagement (see Maslach & Leiter, 1997, 1999; Leiter & Maslach, 2004). This model emphasizes individual perceptions of the six areas of worklife (i.e., workload, control, reward, community, fairness, and values). The perceived congruence of individuals' needs and organizational resources in these worklife areas is thought to predicate engagement while less congruence is thought to increase the likelihood of burnout. Accordingly, athlete endorsement of athlete-team congruence on workload, control, reward, community, fairness, and values has been shown to be positively associated with athlete engagement and negatively associated with athlete burnout (DeFreese & Smith, 2013). Thus, fostering individual-organizational congruence on these domains may be innovative for enhancing engagement, preventing burnout, and potentially enhancing performance. Altogether, the worklife model provides areas where organizations could intervene to minimize stress and/or provide coping resources on behalf of participants.

Continued theoretical and applied research examining burnout as a stress-based experiential concern represents an important area for future study as sport scientists and practitioners alike seek to better understand and ultimately deter burnout as a means to promote more adaptive coping, well-being, and performance responses. A deeper understanding of its link to psychological stress and coping at both individual and organizational levels represents a future empirical and practical pathway fruitful for future sport science inquiry.

Conclusion

This chapter highlights key considerations relative to the growing knowledge base on burnout in sport. The past 30-plus years have seen important theoretical and applied advancements in the understanding of this maladaptive psychological response. However, continued longitudinal (observational and theoretical) and intervention (applied) research efforts are needed. We hope the theory and research synthesized in the current chapter serves to catalyze such important future work.

References

Black, J. M., & Smith, A. L. (2007). An examination of Coakley's perspective on identity, control, and burnout among adolescent athletes. *International Journal of Sport Psychology, 38*, 417–436.

Coakley, J. (1992). Burnout among adolescent athletes: A personal failure or social problem? *Sociology of Sport Journal, 9*, 271–285. Doi:10.1123/ssj.9.3.271

Coakley, J. (2009). From the outside in: Burnout as an organizational issue. *Journal of Intercollegiate Sports, 2*, 35–41. Doi:10.1123/jis.2.1.35

Cresswell, S. L., & Eklund, R. C. (2004). The athlete burnout syndrome: Possible early signs. *Journal of Science and Medicine in Sport, 7*, 481–487. Doi:10.1016/S1440-2440(04)80267-6

Cresswell, S. L., & Eklund, R. C. (2005a). Changes in athlete burnout and motivation over a 12-week league tournament. *Medicine and Science in Sports and Exercise, 37*, 1957–1966. Doi:10.1249/01.mss.0000176304.14675.32

Cresswell, S. L., & Eklund, R. C. (2005b). Motivation and burnout among top amateur rugby players. *Medicine and Science in Sports and Exercise, 37*, 469–477. Doi:10.1249/01.MSS.0000155398.71387.C2

Cresswell, S. L., & Eklund, R. C. (2005c). Motivation and burnout in professional rugby players. *Research Quarterly for Exercise and Sport, 76*, 370–376. Doi:10.108 0/02701367.2005.10599309

Cresswell, S. L., & Eklund, R. C. (2006a). Changes in athlete burnout over a 30-wk "rugby year". *Journal of Science and Medicine in Sport, 9*, 125–134. Doi:10.1016/j.jsams.2006.03.017

Cresswell, S. L., & Eklund, R. C. (2006b). The convergent and discriminant validity of burnout measures in sport: A multi-trait/multi-method analysis. *Journal of Sports Sciences, 24*, 209–220. Doi:10.1080/02640410500131431

Cresswell, S. L., & Eklund, R. C. (2006c). The nature of player burnout in rugby: Key characteristics and attributions. *Journal of Applied Sport Psychology, 18*, 219–239. Doi:10.1080/10413200600830299

Cresswell, S. L., & Eklund, R. C. (2007). Athlete burnout: A longitudinal qualitative study. *The Sport Psychologist, 21*, 1–20. Doi:10.1123/tsp.21.1.1

Dale, J., & Weinberg, R. (1990). Burnout in sport: A review and critique. *Journal of Applied Sport Psychology, 2*, 67–83. Doi:10.1080/10413209008406421

Deci, E. L., & Ryan, R. M. (1985). *Intrinsic motivation and self-determined human behavior.* New York: Plenum Press.

DeFreese, J. D., & Smith, A. L. (2013). Areas of worklife and the athlete burnout—Engagement relationship. *Journal of Applied Sport Psychology, 25*, 180–196. Doi: 10.1080/10413200.2012.705414

DeFreese, J. D., & Smith, A. L. (2014). Athlete social support, negative social interactions, and psychological health across a competitive sport season. *Journal of Sport & Exercise Psychology, 36*, 619–630. Doi:10.1080/10413200.2012.705414

Dubuc-Charbonneau, N., & Durand-Bush, N. (2015). Moving to action: The effects of self-regulation intervention on the stress, burnout, well-being, and self-regulation capacity levels of university student-athletes. *Journal of Clinical Sport Psychology, 9*, 173–192. Doi:10.1123/jcsp.2014-0036

Eades, A. M. (1990). *An investigation of burnout of intercollegiate athletes: The development of the Eades athlete burnout inventory* (Unpublished master's thesis). University of California, Berkeley.

Eklund, R. C., & DeFreese, J. D. (2020). Athlete burnout. In G. Tenenbaum & R. C. Eklund (Eds.), *Handbook of sport psychology* (4th ed., pp. 1220–1240). Hoboken, NJ: John Wiley & Sons.

Freudenberger, H. J. (1974). Staff burnout. *Journal of Social Issues, 30*, 159–165. Doi:10.1111/j.1540-4560.1974.tb00706.x

Goodger, K., Gorely, T., Lavallee, D., & Harwood, C. (2007). Burnout in sport: A systematic review. *The Sport Psychologist, 21*, 127–151.

Gould, D. (1996). Personal motivation gone awry: Burnout in competitive athletes. *Quest, 48*, 275–289. Doi:10.1123/tsp.21.2.127

Gould, D., Tuffey, S., Udry, E., & Loehr, J. (1996). Burnout in competitive junior tennis players: II. Qualitative analysis. *The Sport Psychologist, 10*, 341–366. Doi:10.1123/tsp.10.4.341

Gould, D., Tuffey, S., Udry, E., & Loehr, J. (1997). Burnout in competitive junior tennis players: III. Individual differences in the burnout experience. *The Sport Psychologist, 11*, 257–276. Doi:10.1123/tsp.11.3.257

Gould, D., Udry, E., Tuffey, S., & Loehr, J. (1996). Burnout in competitive junior tennis players: I. A quantitative psychological assessment. *The Sport Psychologist, 10*, 322–340. Doi:10.1123/tsp.10.4.322

Gustafsson, H., DeFreese, J. D., & Madigan, D. J. (2017). Athlete burnout: Review and recommendations. *Current Opinion in Psychology, 16*, 109–113. Doi:10.1016/j.copsyc.2017.05.002

Gustafsson, H., Kenttä, G., & Hassmén, P. (2011). Athlete burnout: An integrated model and future research directions. *International Review of Sport and Exercise Psychology, 4*, 3–24. Doi:10.1080/1750984X.2010.541927

Hjälm, S., Kentta, G., Hassmén, P., & Gustafsson, H. (2007). Burnout among elite soccer coaches. *Journal of Sport Behavior, 30*, 415–427. Doi:10.1037/e548052012-669

Hodge, K., Lonsdale, C., & Ng, J. Y. (2008). Burnout in elite rugby: Relationships with basic psychological needs fulfillment. *Journal of Sports Sciences, 26*, 835–844. Doi:10.1080/02640410701784525

Isoard-Gautheur, S., Guillet-Descas, E., Gaudreau, P., & Chanal, J. (2015). Development of burnout perceptions during adolescence among high level athletes: A developmental and gendered perspective. *Journal of Sport & Exercise Psychology, 37*, 436–448. Doi:10.1123/jsep.2014-0251

Kroshus, E., & DeFreese, J. D. (2017). Athlete burnout prevention strategies used by U.S. collegiate soccer coaches. *The Sport Psychologist, 31*, 332–343. Doi:10.1123.tsp.2016-0067

Lazarus, R. S. (1966). *Psychological stress and the coping process.* New York: McGraw-Hill.

Lazarus, R. S., & Folkman, S. (1984). *Stress, appraisal and coping.* New York: Springer.

Leiter, M. P., & Maslach, C. (2004). Areas of worklife: A structured approach to organizational predictors of job burnout. In P. L. Perrewe & D. C. Ganster (Eds.), *Research in occupational stress and well-being.* Oxford, UK: Elsevier.

Lemyre, P.-N., Hall, H. K., & Roberts, G. C. (2007). Influence of variability in motivation and affect on elite athlete burnout susceptibility. *Journal of Sport & Exercise Psychology, 28*, 32–48. Doi:10.1123/jsep.28.1.32

Lemyre, P.-N., Hall, H. K., & Roberts, G. C. (2008). A social cognitive approach to burnout in elite athletes. *Scandinavian Journal of Medicine & Science in Sports, 18*, 221–234. Doi:10.1111/j.1600-0838.2007.00671.x

Lemyre, P.-N., Roberts, G. C., & Stay-Gunderson, J. (2007). Motivation, overtraining, and burnout: Can self-determined motivation predict overtraining and burnout in elite athletes? *European Journal of Sport Science, 7*, 115–126. Doi:10.1080/17461390701302607

Lemyre, P.-N., Treasure, D. C., & Roberts, G. C. (2006). Influence of variability in motivation and affect on elite athlete burnout susceptibility. *Journal of Sport & Exercise Psychology, 28*, 32–48. Doi:10.1111/j.1600-0838.2007.00671.x

Li, C., Wang, C. K. J., Pyun, D. Y., & Kee, Y. H. (2013). Burnout and its relations with basic psychological needs and motivation among athletes: A systematic review and meta-analysis. *Psychology of Sport & Exercise, 14*, 692–700. Doi:10.1016/j.psychsport.2013.04.009

Lonsdale, C., Hodge, K., & Jackson, S. A. (2007). Athlete engagement: II. Development and initial validation of the athlete engagement questionnaire. *International Journal of Sport Psychology, 38*, 471–492. Doi:10.1037/t50268-000

Lonsdale, C., Hodge, K., & Rose, E. (2009). Athlete burnout in elite sport: A self-determination perspective. *Journal of Sport Sciences, 27*, 785–795. Doi:10.1080/02640410902929366

Lundkvist, E., Stenling, A., Gustafsson, H., & Hassmén, P. (2014). How to measure coach burnout: An evaluation of three burnout measures. *Measurement in Physical Education and Exercise Science, 18,* 209–226. Doi:10.1080/10913 67X.2014.925455

Madigan, D. J., & Nicholls, A. R. (2017). Mental toughness and burnout in junior athletes: A longitudinal investigation. *Psychology of Sport and Exercise, 32,* 138–142. Doi:10.1016/j.psychsport.2017.07.002

Madigan, D. J., Stoeber, J., & Passfield, L. (2015). Perfectionism and burnout in junior athletes: A three-month longitudinal study. *Journal of Sport & Exercise Psychology, 37,* 305–315. Doi:10.1123/jsep.2014-0266

Madigan, D. J., Stoeber, J., & Passfield, L. (2016). Motivation mediates the perfectionism-burnout relationship: A three-wave longitudinal study with junior athletes. *Journal of Sport & Exercise Psychology, 38,* 341–354. Doi:10.1123/jsep.2015-0238

Maslach, C. (1982). *Burnout: The cost of caring.* London, UK: Prentice Hall.

Maslach, C. (2001). What have we learned about burnout and health? *Psychology and Health, 16,* 607–611. Doi:10.1080/08870440108405530

Maslach, C., & Jackson, S. E. (1986). *Maslach burnout inventory manual* (2nd ed.). Palo Alto, CA: Consulting Psychologists Press.

Maslach, C., & Leiter, M. P. (1997). *The truth about burnout: How organizations cause personal stress and what to do about it.* San Francisco, CA: Josey-Bass.

Maslach, C., & Leiter, M. P. (1999). Burnout and engagement in the workplace: A contextual analysis. *Advances in Motivation and Achievement, 11,* 275–302.

Pacewicz, C. E., Mellano, K. T., & Smith, A. L. (2019). A meta-analytic review of the relationship between social constructs and athlete burnout. *Psychology of Sport & Exercise, 43,* 155–164. Doi:10.1016/j.psychsport.2019.02.002

Perreault, S., Gaudreau, P., Lapointe, M.-C., & Lacroix, C. (2007). Does it take three to tango? Psychological need satisfaction and athlete burnout. *International Journal of Sport Psychology, 38,* 437–450.

Price, M. S., & Weiss, M. R. (2000). Relationships among coach burnout, coach behaviors, and athletes' psychological responses. *The Sport Psychologist, 14,* 391–409. Doi:10.1123/tsp.14.4.391

Quested, E., & Duda, J. L. (2011). Antecedents of burnout among elite dancers: A longitudinal test of basic needs theory. *Psychology of Sport & Exercise, 12,* 159–167. Doi:10.1016/j.psychsport.2010.09.003

Raedeke, T. D. (1997). Is athlete burnout more than just stress? A sport commitment perspective. *Journal of Sport & Exercise Psychology, 19,* 396–417. Doi:10.1123/jsep.19.4.396

Raedeke, T. D., Lunney, K., & Venables, K. (2002). Understanding athlete burnout: Coach perspectives. *Journal of Sport Behavior, 25,* 181–206.

Raedeke, T. D., & Smith, A. L. (2001). Development and preliminary validation of an athlete burnout measure. *Journal of Sport & Exercise Psychology, 23,* 281–306. Doi:10.1123/jsep.23.4.281

Raedeke, T. D., & Smith, A. L. (2004). Coping resources and athlete burnout: An examination of stress mediated and moderation hypotheses. *Journal of Sport & Exercise Psychology, 26,* 525–541. Doi:10.1123/jsep.26.4.525

Raedeke, T. D., & Smith, A. L. (2009). *The athlete burnout questionnaire manual.* Morgantown, WV: Fitness Information Technology.

Rainey, D. W. (1999). Sources of stress, burnout, and intention to terminate among basketball referees. *Journal of Sport Behavior, 22,* 578–590.

Rainey, D. W., & Hardy, L. (1999). Sources of stress, burnout, and intention to terminate among rugby union referees. *Journal of Sport Sciences, 17*, 797–806. Doi:10.1080/026404199365515

Rotella, R. J., Hanson, T., & Coop, R. H. (1991). Burnout in youth sport. *The Elementary School Journal, 91*, 421–428. Doi:10.1086/461664

Ryan, R. M., & Deci, E. L. (2000a). The darker and brighter sides of human existence: Basic psychological needs as a unifying concept. *Psychological Inquiry, 11*, 319–338. Doi:10.1207/S15327965PLI1104_03

Ryan, R. M., & Deci, E. L. (2000b). Self-determination theory and the facilitation of intrinsic motivation, social development, and well-being. *American Psychologist, 55*, 68–78. Doi:10.1037/0003-066X.55.1.68

Schaufeli, W. B., & Enzmann, D. (1998). *The burnout companion to study and practice: A critical analysis*. Philadelphia, PA: Taylor & Francis.

Schellenberg, B. J. I., Gaudreau, P., & Crocker, P. R. E. (2013). Passion and coping: Relationships with changes in burnout and goal attainment in collegiate volleyball players. *Journal of Sport and Exercise Psychology, 35*, 270–280. Doi:10.1123/jsep.35.3.270

Schmidt, G. W., & Stein, G. L. (1991). Sport commitment: A model integrating enjoyment, dropout, and burnout. *Journal of Sport & Exercise Psychology, 13*, 254–265. Doi:10.1123/jsep.13.3.254

Silva, J. M. (1990). An analysis of the training stress syndrome in competitive athletics. *Journal of Applied Sport Psychology, 2*, 5–20. Doi:10.1080/10413209008406417

Smith, R. E. (1986). Toward a cognitive-affective model of athletic burnout. *Journal of Sport Psychology, 8*, 36–50. Doi:10.1123/jsp.8.1.36

Thibaut, J. W., & Kelley, H. H. (1959). *The social psychology of groups*. New York: John Wiley & Sons.

Vealey, R. S., Armstrong, L., Comar, W., & Greenleaf, C. A. (1998). Influence of perceived coaching behaviors on burnout and competitive anxiety in female college athletes. *Journal of Applied Sport Psychology, 10*, 297–318. Doi:10.1080/10413209808406395

8 Mental Health

*Simon Rice, Courtney C. Walton, Kate Gwyther,
and Rosemary Purcell*

Athlete Mental Health—Rationale for Greater Focus

The global burden of disease attributable to mental disorders has risen—
across all countries globally—in line with major shifts in demographic,
environmental, and sociopolitical factors (Patel et al., 2018). Given this
alarming trend, it is critical that approaches to addressing mental ill-
health are appropriately targeted and sensitized to sub-populations with
particular needs. One such group who have historically been ignored
from mental health programming are athletes. Given the unique stressors and experiences associated with a high-performing athletic career
(see also Chapter 1), a focused approach to the management of mental
health concerns in this group is warranted (Breslin & Leavey, 2019). The
World Health Organization (WHO) identifies positive health as a state
of complete physical, mental, and social well-being, and not merely the
absence of disease (WHO, 2006). Accordingly, positive mental health
can be characterized by a state of well-being in which an individual is able
to realize their own abilities, cope and respond to the normal stresses of
life, work and achieve productively, and make a meaningful contribution
to their community (WHO, 2014; see also Chapter 6).

It is useful to conceptualize mental health states as being part of a
continuum instead of binary classifications. Rather than mental health
and mental illness sitting on opposite ends of one spectrum, however,
they have been proposed as two distinct but correlated axes (Keyes,
2002, 2005). In such a model, an individual could maintain good mental health even *with* mental illness, or conversely, poor mental health
without mental illness. While diagnostic criteria for mental disorders are
outlined in detail in the *Diagnostic and Statistical Manual of Mental Disorders* (*DSM-5*; American Psychiatric Association, 2013), these may not be
the crucial factor in defining if an athlete (or individual) is experiencing positive mental health and functioning. As an illustration, an athlete
may experience excessive and intermittent worry that they are not able
to control (which is the core symptom of generalized anxiety disorder).
However, without any other accompanying symptoms of anxiety such as

restlessness, fatigue, concentration problems, irritability, or sleep disturbance, they would not meet criteria for a diagnosis of generalized anxiety disorder. While in the sub-clinical range and not meeting criteria for
an anxiety diagnosis, there is still a likelihood of significant psychological
distress for the individual.

The promotion and maintenance of mental health is a vital concern for individuals and communities, given mental disorders account
for close to one-in-six deaths globally (Walker, McGee, & Druss, 2015).
Physical activity, potentially achieved through athletic and sports participation, is an important aspect of preventing mental ill-health, as
well as being a potential vehicle for symptom management and recovery (Chekroud et al., 2018; Knapen, Vancampfort, Moriën, & Marchal,
2015; Rosenbaum, Tiedemann, & Ward, 2014). Research into the nature
and impact of physical injury among athletes has led to major advances
in how these injuries are optimally managed and prevented. For example, the field of sports medicine has seen significant progress into the
way that injuries (including brain injury and concussion) are now dealt
with (e.g., McCrory et al., 2017). There is however comparatively less
research, though a growing interest, in the mental health and psychological well-being of athletes (Rice et al., 2016; see also Chapter 6). While
prevalence rates of clinician diagnosed psychiatric disorders in this population are yet to be definitively established, notions that elite athletes
are devoid of mental health problems have been increasingly scrutinized
by sports medicine practitioners (Reardon, 2017), with recent evidence
suggesting otherwise (Gulliver, Griffiths, Mackinnon, Batterham, & Stanimirovic, 2015; Junge & Feddermann-Demont, 2016; Rice et al., 2016).
Indeed, recent meta-analytic data suggest that mental health symptoms among population-based studies of elite athletes range from 20%
for psychological distress to 34% for anxiety/depression (Gouttebarge,
Castaldelli-Maia, et al., 2019). To place into context, symptom prevalence
in the general population is estimated as 9.5% for psychological distress
(Slade, Grove, & Burgess, 2011) and 19% for anxiety/depression (Gouttebarge, Castaldelli-Maia, et al., 2019). Furthermore, some research
has suggested that athlete populations have an increased risk of mental
health problems, including eating disorders (Sundgot-Borgen & Torstveit, 2004), with these factors in turn elevating an individual's risk for suicide (Baum, 2005). A national survey of elite athletes in Australia found
that almost half endorsed symptoms of at least one of the mental health
problems assessed, with prevalence rates similar to those reported in the
community (Gulliver et al., 2015). Accurately comparing population
rates remains challenging, given differences between assessment tools,
scoring criterion, and population demographics. Another challenge
faced is that the peak competitive years for athletes at the elite level overlap substantially with the peak age of onset for emotional and mental
health difficulties (Allen & Hopkins, 2015; Rice et al., 2016). Specifically,

over 50% of mental disorders develop before the age of 15 years and 75% develop by 25 years (Kessler et al., 2005), and in any given year, an estimated 1 in 4, to 1 in 5 young people experience a mental health disorder (Patel, Flisher, Hetrick, & McGorry, 2007). In both developed and less-developed countries, mental ill-health is the most important health issue facing young people (Bloom et al., 2012). While elite and professional athletes comprise a relatively small proportion of the sporting population, they have a range of specific needs.

Elite athletes are susceptible to an array of unique stressors that make them vulnerable to impaired well-being and potential mental health difficulties (Arnold & Fletcher, 2012; Hughes & Leavey, 2012; Simms, Arnold, Turner, & Hays, 2020). These stressors include risk of significant injury (including concussion and repeated sub-concussive exposures), pressures associated with public scrutiny and social media, frequent travel from home and likelihood of missing important life events, performance difficulties and pressures to succeed, and stress associated with transition to a non-competitive or athletic identity (see also Chapter 1). The ways by which athletes appraise and cope with competitive and non-competitive stressors are a powerful determinant of the impact the stressor has on both their mental health and sporting success (see also Chapters 2 and 3). While it is well established that physical activity has a positive effect on mental health, intense physical activity performed at the elite level might instead *compromise* mental well-being, increasing symptoms of anxiety and depression through overtraining, injury, and/or burnout (Peluso & Andrade, 2005; see also Chapters 6 and 7). Symptoms of mental ill-health may be expressed in unique ways. For instance, coping difficulties may be expressed as excessive or increased risk taking on or off the sporting field.

Symptoms of mental ill-health can significantly interfere with social or occupational functioning, resulting in reduced well-being, and lower rates of community participation and social inclusion (Wahlbeck, 2015). For athletes, this interference may actualize as declined athletic performance, isolation from teammates or coaches, poor concentration, or low mood. Indeed, treatment approaches may facilitate engagement by leveraging the potential performance gains that are likely to co-occur with improved mental health (Donohue et al., 2018; Gavrilova, Donohue, & Galante, 2017). While sporting contexts have largely privileged the notion of mental toughness, it has been argued that mental toughness (which emphasizes stoicism and self-reliance) may run contrary to help-seeking for mental health concerns (Bauman, 2016). Somewhat conversely, others have argued that one of the ways to proactively engage athletes in mental health intervention may be through focusing on the benefits to their mental toughness (and therefore performance) that may arise as a result (Gucciardi, Hanton, & Fleming, 2017). That said, any direct link between mental toughness and mental health is yet to be conclusively established (Purcell, Chevroulet, Pilkington, & Rice, 2020). Regardless, early identification and intervention for symptoms of mental ill-health are recommended to avoid unnecessary distress or impairment in athletes, especially in younger populations uniquely sensitive to critical developmental periods (Patel, Flisher, Hetrick, & McGorry, 2007). Moreover, developing a comprehensive understanding of the mental health and psychological well-being factors specific to elite athletes has the potential to advance models of care and management for this population, which may in turn facilitate performance gains or maintenance.

Ensuring athletes, as well as sport practitioners—including coaches, high-performance and medical staff, sport psychologists, and caregivers of young athletes—have an understanding of ways in which positive coping abilities can be developed in elite athletes, will likely improve their emotional well-being and mental health (see also Chapters 3 and 6). Indicating the current gaps between treatment needs and available service provision, recent research indicates that less than half the medical representatives from International Olympic Sport Federations believe that mental health is addressed in a "*fully*" or "*mostly*" sufficient way within each of their Federations (Mountjoy et al., 2019).

Biopsychosocial Factors

Specific factors which can contribute to mental health (or mental ill-health) that are relevant for individuals engaged in community through to elite sports participation should be considered (see Table 8.1). These factors are commonly referred to within the framework of the Biopsychosocial Model (Engel, 1980), which is increasingly being applied to athletic settings (DeFreese, 2017; Solomon & Haase, 2008; von Rosen, Frohm, Kottorp, Fridén, & Heijne, 2017). In contrast to the predominant Biomedical Model of disease whereby ill-health is accounted for

Table 8.1 Biopsychosocial Determinants of Mental Health Within the Context of Sporting Participation

Biological	Psychological	Social
Age	Personality	Support systems
Sex	Behavior	Cultural factors
Sleep	Coping repertoires	Family-based factors
Injury	Help-seeking attitudes	Economic situation
Genetic predisposition to mental illness	Perceived stress (e.g., selection pressures and response to travel)	Education
		Exposure to adverse events and loss
	Burnout (overtraining)	Social media
	Mental health literacy	

by deviation of biological somatic variables (Engel, 1977, 1997), the Biopsychosocial Model incorporates multiple social, psychological, and biological determinants of an individual's mental health functioning at any point of time. Similar to the WHO definition outlined previously, the Biopsychosocial Model of mental ill-health is applied at the within person-level. Hence, the individual, their body, and their surrounding environment are seen as essential components of the total system, with these biopsychosocial factors operating to facilitate, sustain, or modify the course of mental health symptoms (Fava & Sonino, 2007). Biopsychosocial factors relevant to mental health within the context of sport are presented in Table 8.1.

The Biopsychosocial Model has been applied as a framework to better understand athlete-specific presentations including complicated recovery from concussion or repetitive brain trauma in collision sports (Asken et al., 2016; Wäljas et al., 2015), risk of injury (von Rosen et al., 2017), and the development of models of mental health care for elite athletes (Schinke, Stambulova, Si, & Moore, 2018). The Biopsychosocial Model is particularly useful in the process of monitoring, diagnosing, and referring athletes for appropriate mental health treatment as it highlights for practitioners where their attention should be directed (i.e., toward key domains that are known to increase vulnerability to the onset or progression of mental health problems; see Table 8.1). Many of these domains are modifiable and amenable to intervention (e.g., poor mental health literacy, sleep problems, overtraining, maladaptive coping repertoires, and negative help-seeking attitudes; see Breslin, Shannon, Haughey, Donnelly, and Leavey (2017) for a systematic review of athlete-specific mental health awareness programs; see O'Donnell, Beaven, and Driller (2018) for a review on sleep interventions in athletes). An important aspect of implementing a biopsychosocial approach to athlete mental health is the development of an environment where athletes feel safe and supported in disclosing possible symptoms of mental ill-health so that the appropriate diagnostic and treatment decisions can be taken (DeFreese, 2017; see also Chapters 11 and 14).

Athletes and Help-Seeking

There are growing efforts to enhance mental health education and awareness, and advance the prevention, identification, and early treatment of mental health problems in elite athletes (Glick, Stillman, Reardon, & Ritvo, 2012; Gouttebarge, Cowie, et al., 2019). However, there are suggestions that idealization of athletic achievement has historically led healthcare providers (and possibly sporting governing bodies) to incorrectly assume a low prevalence rate of mental illness among high-performing athletes (Reardon & Factor, 2010). This longstanding assumption of athletes supposedly having superior mental health has had important implications. Specifically, if elite athletes within such organizations are not provided with access to timely or adequate mental health care, or do not feel that the culture of the sporting organization is such that they can raise their mental health concerns, they are more likely to self-manage symptoms. Athletes may use maladaptive strategies like substance use (Dunn & Thomas, 2012), which—on top of being potentially dangerous and negatively affecting mental health—can have significant impacts on an athlete's career and public perception (Moston, Skinner, & Engelberg, 2012). As suggested previously, it is critically important that practitioners working to support athlete mental health are able to foster an environment where athletes can experience a sense of safety in disclosing symptoms of mental health (DeFreese, 2017). Specific factors that can inhibit help-seeking among athletes regarding their mental health include concerns in relation to privacy prohibiting disclosure of symptoms (reduced motivation) or behaviors (substance use) which may negatively affect coach or team decision making, viewing mental health intervention (e.g., psychotherapy, counseling, or medication) as a sign of weakness, a mindset for the need to push through pain or discomfort established through elite training, poorly developed coping mechanisms (or being solely reliant on coping through exercise), and a lack of a non-athletic identity that can result in significant experiences of loss where athletic ability is threatened by injury or illness (Doherty, Hannigan, & Campbell, 2016; Gulliver et al., 2015; Putukian, 2016). To address these barriers, approaches should span across the individual to organizational level. For instance, setting and communicating clear practices regarding confidentiality, implementing anti-stigma and mental health literacy campaigns, and addressing maladaptive athlete coping mechanisms or promoting non-athletic identity.

Wherever possible, practitioners should seek to engage athletes in preventive interventions (or early intervention when an initial presentation of symptoms occurs) to reduce the likelihood of the athlete developing chronic symptoms or escalating to crisis (Schinke et al., 2018; see also Chapter 12). Attention to key biopsychosocial factors (see Table 8.1) can help facilitate positive mental health and help-seeking behaviors. For example, the culture toward mental health help-seeking that is developed by sporting organizations has a powerful effect on athletes' attitudes. Normalizing help-seeking in response to distress and promoting psychological safety within sporting environments may foster adaptive mental health practices. In addition, fostering an environment where athletes are encouraged to practice self-compassionate responses within sporting settings may be an effective strategy for reducing mental health problems and psychological distress (Mosewich, Ferguson, McHugh, & Kowalski, 2019; Walton, Baranoff, Gilbert, & Kirby, 2020). These approaches may be particularly important across specific demographic groups. For example, younger male athletes are known to hold especially negative attitudes toward mental health help-seeking due to cultural and societal pressures related to masculinity (Doherty et al., 2016; Rice, Purcell, & McGorry, 2018; Tibbert, Andersen, & Morris, 2015). It is also important to consider the systems of support (or in some cases the "entourage") that accompany athletes (MacIntyre et al., 2017).

The nature of and accessibility to informal support systems necessarily differs by sport and competition level (see also Chapter 11). Elite athletes may have greater accessibility to sport psychologists rather than clinical psychologists. Having sufficient expertise for treating mental health problems differs amongst sport psychologists globally depending on their training program, while clinical psychologists will have varied experiences and understanding of sports contexts. Therefore, neither is overall better or worse suited to dealing with such concerns, and practitioners from both specialty fields must instead rely on using appropriate self-reflection to understand their abilities and limitations in treatment, and refer out where necessary. Unfortunately, junior or sub-elite athletes will often have lesser accessibility to professional psychological support comparative to elite athletes. However, trusted others—such as partners, family, and friends are typically the first sources of support that are sought out by athletes experiencing mental health problems (Gulliver, Griffiths, & Christensen, 2012); therefore, there exists an opportunity to upskill these individuals in relation to mental health awareness and signposting (Rice et al., 2016). In any case, it is imperative that supporting individuals have appropriate expertise and knowledge of referral avenues.

Consensus Perspectives on Athlete Mental Health

The growing focus on improving athlete mental health services, systems, and models is evidenced by the development of major consensus and position statements from key organizational and sporting bodies. Among these are the International Society of Sport Psychology Statement (Henriksen, Schinke, et al., 2019), the European Federation of Sports Psychology Position Statement (Moesch et al., 2018), and the National Collegiate Athletic Association Consensus on Mental Health Best Practices (NCAA, 2017). Each of these documents provide recommendations for the integration of mental health supports and services within athletic settings. These include providing athletes with sufficient mental health education, developing sports-specific approaches to detecting and treating mental health disorders, and ensuring athletes have suitable recognition of local support or treatment pathways and access points to these.

In addition to the previous points, the International Olympic Committee (IOC) has led a major international effort in developing the IOC Expert Consensus Statement on Athlete Mental Health (Reardon et al.,

2019). The IOC statement was underpinned by 20 major systematic reviews and meta-analyses (e.g., Rice, Gwyther, et al., 2019), in addition to a 2.5-day consensus meeting. The IOC statement provides an exhaustive overview of sport-specific presentations of athlete mental health disorders, current prevalence data, and recommendations for management (see Figure 8.1 for an overview)—readers seeking specific guidance on management of mental disorders in athlete populations are encouraged to consult the resource by Reardon et al. (2019).

Athlete-Specific Mental Health Assessment and Screening

Self-report screening tools for mental health problems are commonly used in primary care or sports medicine settings to identify athletes at elevated risk of mental health problems. Given the peak competitive athletic years overlap with youth (Allen & Hopkins, 2015), interested readers may wish to consult the list of youth-appropriate self-report mental health screening tools recommended by the Neurobiology in Youth Mental Health Partnership (Lavoie et al., 2019) for major mental health domains, including assessment of depression (e.g., Quick Inventory of Depression Symptoms—QIDS; Rush et al., 2003), anxiety (e.g., Generalized Anxiety Disorder Scale; GAD-7; Spitzer, Kroenke, Williams, & Löwe, 2006), or psychological distress (e.g., Kessler-10 Psychological Distress Scale, K-10; Kessler et al., 2002). These screening tools are freely available and have been validated across multiple population groups and age ranges. However, the sensitivity of these tools to assessing the range of unique symptom manifestations in athletes is unclear (Reardon et al., 2019), and it is possible that athletes will experience better engagement with mental health screening tools that enquire about daily challenges specific to their sporting role.

Recent work has started to focus on the development and validation of athlete-specific mental health measures (Baron, Baron, Tompkins, & Polat, 2013; Donohue et al., 2018, 2019). To this end, the Athlete Psychological Strain Questionnaire (Rice, Parker, et al., 2019, 2020) was developed as a broad screening tool to identify the potential early onset of mental ill-health in athletes, using items specific to the athletic environment. The scale was developed from a validation sample of 1,007 elite athletes, and includes 10 items, comprising three athlete distress domains of Problems with Self-Regulation ("It was difficult to be around teammates"), Performance Difficulties ("I found it hard to cope with selection pressures"), and Externalized Coping ("I took unusual risks off-field"). Further research developing, validating, and refining these bespoke athlete mental health measures is needed, for instance, tailoring measures for individual or team-sport athletes, or identifying predictive cut-off scores.

Figure 8.1 Mental Health in Elite Athletes: IOC Consensus Statement Infographic

Promising Frameworks for Athlete-Specific Service Provision and Intervention

A highly useful conceptual framework for developing models of athlete mental health service provision is Self-Determination Theory (SDT; Ryan & Deci, 2000). SDT aligns with the Biopsychosocial Model (Williams & Deci, 1996) and has been effectively applied in athlete populations (Amorose & Anderson-Butcher, 2007). SDT is a theory of optimal human motivation and performance, characterized by the fulfillment of three basic psychological needs—autonomy, competence, and relatedness. The theory considers the degree to which an individual's actions are freely chosen and enacted (i.e., self-determined) vs. externally controlled or restricted (Mahoney, Ntoumanis, Mallett, & Gucciardi, 2014). Within an athletic context, autonomy indicates a perception of choice and self-directedness, where an athlete voluntarily decides their actions and performs them in a way that is congruent for them. Competence refers to the experience of having the requisite skill, ability, and opportunity to be effective in one's sport. Relatedness is a sense of mutual caring, connectedness, and safety with others, such as teammates, coaches, and administrative staff (Hodge, Lonsdale, & Ng, 2008). SDT focuses on the processes that enable an individual athlete to acquire the motivation for (i) initiating adaptive mental health promotive and/or protective behaviors and (ii) maintaining these behaviors over time.

There is also a need for the development and evaluation of specific athlete-appropriate intervention models. As highlighted by previous systematic review research, there is an absence of well-designed randomized control trials (RCTs) testing elite athlete mental health interventions (Rice et al., 2016; Stillman et al., 2019). Subsequently, we review the two RCTs we are aware of. First, Gulliver and colleagues (2012) developed and tested an internet-based mental health literacy intervention in an RCT among 59 Australian elite athletes. While the trial was small, results indicated that a brief mental health literacy approach (i.e., online information about prevalence, risk, myths, and treatments for depression and anxiety) had the capacity to improve athlete mental health knowledge (anxiety and depression literacy) and may also decrease stigma, but did not translate to any increase in actual help-seeking behavior relative to the control condition. More recently, an athlete-specific mental health optimization intervention model was tested in an RCT of 74 U.S. college athletes competing at the NCAA level (Donohue et al., 2018). Referred to as The Optimum Performance Program in Sports (TOPPS), the intervention is unique in that it employs an "optimization" approach, whereby the role of increased general well-being is emphasized, and an explicit link made between maintenance of, or recovery to, optimum well-being as positively impacting sporting performance (see also Chapters 6 and 13). This is in contrast to the usual approach of simply reducing mental health psychopathology. In TOPPS model, rather than referring to "therapy sessions" the intervention approach is delivered via "performance meetings", and the program is supported by a visual identity (a gender-neutral athlete emblem) and integrated into attractive marketing paraphernalia (e.g., back packs, T-shirts, pens, water and sport drinks, and energy bars). These products helped to promote, brand, and normalize TOPPS initiative in a stigma-free manner that resonated with athletes. The RCT found that the intervention reduced an array of mental health-based outcomes (i.e., reduced symptoms of anxiety and depression and increased interpersonal relationships with teammates and coaches), and these improvements were maintained over eight months, with the intervention particularly effective for those with more severe mental health problems. Of note, the TOPPS intervention resulted in substantially higher rates of engagement than general counseling sessions on the university campus.

As discussed by Stillman and colleagues (2019), there is a dearth of literature examining *how* to treat mental health disorders in a sporting context using psychological approaches, making suggestions for individual practitioners difficult. While there is a small amount of, but growing, literature on the role of rational emotive behavioral therapy (REBT; Ellis & Dryden, 2007) in sport (Jordana, Turner, Ramis, & Torregrossa, 2020), most evidence for psychological approaches must be inferred from case study examples (e.g., McArdle & Moore, 2012) or the broader psychotherapy literature (see, for a review, Stillman et al., 2019). A number of common approaches to mental health treatment may be appropriate for translation to sport, including cognitive-behavioral therapy (CBT; Beck, 2011), acceptance and commitment therapy (ACT; Hayes, Strosahl, & Wilson, 2011), and compassion-focused therapies (Gilbert, 2010). While less rigorously tested in athletes, using our clinical experience, we propose that these approaches to treating mental health concerns in athletes can be taken and are briefly summarized in Table 8.2.

Future Directions in Athlete Mental Health

Given the nascent stage of development of the field of athlete mental health, it is likely that the next decade will see a rapid rise in research and innovation. Decades of focus on the management of physical injuries have seen major advances in sports medicine as a discipline, and there is scope for corresponding advances for the management of mental ill-health in athletes. Given the inevitable performance gains associated with positive mental health in athletes (Donohue et al., 2018), future investment and expansion in bespoke athlete mental health programs are almost assured. Subsequently, we highlight a number of further important future directions.

Table 8.2 Clinically Informed Treatment Approaches for Practitioners Addressing Mental Health in Athletes

	Cognitive Therapies	Acceptance and Commitment Therapy	Compassion-Focused Therapies
Overview area of focus	• Targets athletes' *beliefs* around activating events that lead to emotional distress • Exercises are implemented which teach athletes to objectively examine their thoughts and feelings	• Involves developing non-judgmental, moment-to-moment awareness of thoughts • This combined with values-driven efforts is suggested to lead to a reduction of the internal psychological conflicts that lead to distress	• Fostering an ability to engage with one's distress in a compassionate manner to activate affiliative processing systems
Suitable for athletes coping with:	• Irrational thought patterns • Low frustration tolerance • Self-criticism and depreciation	• An all-consuming "athlete identity" • Lack of understanding around values and direction • Unchangeable stressors (e.g., injury rehabilitation)	• Self-criticism and depreciation • Shame • Body image • Performance concerns
Suggested sport-specific reading	• McArdle and Moore (2012); • Turner (2016); • Jordana et al. (2020)	• Gardner and Moore (2012); • Henrikson, Hansen, and Larsen (2019)	• Mosewich, Ferguson, McHugh, and Kowalski (2019); • Mosewich (2020)

An area of emerging research interest is exposure to sports-related concussion and the development of subsequent mental health problems (Manley et al., 2017; Rice, Parker, et al., 2018). While some studies have linked the concussion exposure to a heightened risk of subsequent mental health symptoms (Gouttebarge, Aoki, Lambert, Stewart, & Kerkhoffs, 2017; Kerr et al., 2014), a causal relationship is yet to be established. Development of consensus-driven protocols regarding concussion symptom assessment and return to play guidelines (e.g., SCAT5; Echemendia et al., 2017) now contains monitoring of mental health symptoms. These include irritability, sadness, concentration problems, and worry—which overlap with symptoms attributable to anxiety and depression (King, Crawford, Wenden,

Moss, & Wade, 1995; Potter, Leigh, Wade, & Fleminger, 2006). Further policy and practice development is needed to best prevent mental ill-health following concussion. There is evidence that elite athletes have improved performance on measures of processing speed and attention (Voss, Kramer, Basak, Prakash, & Roberts, 2010; see also Chapter 5), but the interaction of these domains with mental health in athletes is unclear. There is potential scope for new approaches in cognitive training (e.g., object tracking to improve decision making accuracy) to be applied amongst athlete populations (Walton, Keegan, Martin, & Hallock, 2018), and there may be specific mental health benefits associated with this field, especially among athletes competing in collision sports with a risk of concussion. Illustrating this, meta-analytic evidence suggests that cognitive training is effective for improving cognitive and functional outcomes in patients following traumatic brain injury (Hallock et al., 2016).

Other areas for development of the field relate to disclosure of information, and the population level impact this may have. As rates of mental health stigma shift, some athletes are becoming increasingly comfortable publicly sharing their lived experience with mental ill-health. In recent times, there has been an increasing presence of high-profile elite athletes using traditional and social media in this way to share their own personal experiences around mental ill-health. We have argued that by such experiences becoming more visible in the public domain, a secondary benefit may occur by which young and vulnerable individuals experiencing psychological distress may become more likely to bypass previously perceived stigma to instigate psychological help-seeking (Walton, Purcell, & Rice, 2019). Indeed, Swann and colleagues (2018) have illustrated how a young male athlete may become more engaged in discussions around mental health when it revolves around a sporting role model. Future research should investigate tangible benefits for both athletes that publicly share their mental health experiences, and community members who engage with them (see also Chapter 9).

Conclusion

Recent shifts have seen sport medicine and sport psychology practice increasingly focus on the role of positive health and mental ill-health in the lives (and sporting performance) of athletes. The field however has much progress to make, particularly in the areas of understanding the most appropriate methods of diagnoses and symptom assessment, and how best to treat mental health problems in the highly unique context of competitive sport. This chapter has provided an overview of current thinking in this area and highlighted key future avenues for exploration through research and practice.

References

Allen, S. V., & Hopkins, W. G. (2015). Age of peak competitive performance of elite athletes: A systematic review. *Sports Medicine, 45*, 1431–1441. Doi:10.1007/s40279-015-0354-3

American Psychiatric Association. (2013). *Diagnostic and statistical manual of mental disorders (DSM-5)*. Washington, DC: American Psychiatric Publishing.

Amorose, A. J., & Anderson-Butcher, D. (2007). Autonomy-supportive coaching and self-determined motivation in high school and college athletes: A test of self-determination theory. *Psychology of Sport and Exercise, 8*, 654–670. Doi:10.1016/j.psychsport.2006.11.003

Arnold, R., & Fletcher, D. (2012). A research synthesis and taxonomic classification of the organizational stressors encountered by sport performers. *Journal of Sport & Exercise Psychology, 34*, 397–429. Doi:10.1123/jsep.34.3.397

Asken, B. M., Sullan, M. J., Snyder, A. R., Houck, Z. M., Bryant, V. E., Hizel, L. P., . . . Bauer, R. M. (2016). Factors influencing clinical correlates of chronic traumatic encephalopathy (CTE): A review. *Neuropsychology Review, 26*, 340–363. Doi:10.1007/s11065-016-9327-z

Baron, D. A., Baron, S. H., Tompkins, J., & Polat, A. (2013). Assessing and treating depression in athletes. In D. A. Baron, C. L. Reardon & S. H. Baron (Eds.), *Clinical sports psychiatry: An international perspective* (pp. 65–78). Chichester, West Sussex: John Wiley & Sons.

Baum, A. L. (2005). Suicide in athletes: A review and commentary. *Clinics in Sports Medicine, 24*, 853–869. Doi:10.1016/j.csm.2005.06.006

Bauman, N. J. (2016). The stigma of mental health in athletes: Are mental toughness and mental health seen as contradictory in elite sport? *British Journal of Sports Medicine, 50*, 135. Doi:10.1136/bjsports-2015-095570

Beck, J. S. (2011). *Cognitive behavior therapy: Basics and beyond*. New York: Guilford Press.

Bloom, D. E., Cafiero, E., Jané-Llopis, E., Abrahams-Gessel, S., Bloom, L. R., Fathima, S., . . . O'Farrell, D. (2012). *The global economic burden of noncommunicable diseases*. Geneva, Switzerland: World Economic Forum.

Breslin, G., & Leavey, G. (Eds.). (2019). *Mental health and well-being interventions in sport: Research, theory and practice*. Abingdon, Oxfordshire: Routledge.

Breslin, G., Shannon, S., Haughey, T., Donnelly, P., & Leavey, G. (2017). A systematic review of interventions to increase awareness of mental health and well-being in athletes, coaches and officials. *Systematic Reviews, 6*, 177. Doi:10.1186/s13643-017-0568-6

Chekroud, S. R., Gueorguieva, R., Zheutlin, A. B., Paulus, M., Krumholz, H. M., Krystal, J. H., & Chekroud, A. M. (2018). Association between physical exercise and mental health in 1–2 million individuals in the USA between 2011 and 2015: A cross-sectional study. *The Lancet Psychiatry, 5*, 739–746. Doi:10.1016/S2215-0366(18)30227-X

DeFreese, J. D. (2017). Athlete mental health care within the biopsychosocial model. *Athletic Training and Sports Health Care, 9*, 243–245. Doi:10.3928/19425864-20170703-03

Doherty, S., Hannigan, B., & Campbell, M. J. (2016). The experience of depression during the careers of elite male athletes. *Frontiers in Psychology, 7*, 1–11. Doi:10.3389/fpsyg.2016.01069

Donohue, B., Galante, M., Hussey, J., Lee, B., Paul, N., Perry, J. E., . . . Allen, D. N. (2019). Empirical development of a screening method to assist mental health referrals in collegiate athletes. *Journal of Clinical Sport Psychology, 13*, 1–28. Doi:10.1123/jcsp.2018-0070

Donohue, B., Gavrilova, Y., Galante, M., Burnstein, B., Aubertin, P., Gavrilova, E., . . . Benning, S. D. (2018). Empirical development of a screening method for mental, social, and physical wellness in amateur and professional circus artists. *Psychology of Aesthetics, Creativity, and the Arts*. Advanced online publication. Doi:10.1037/aca0000199

Dunn, M., & Thomas, J. O. (2012). A risk profile of elite Australian athletes who use illicit drugs. *Addictive Behaviors, 37*, 144–147. Doi:10.1016/j.addbeh.2011.09.008

Echemendia, R. J., Meeuwisse, W., McCrory, P., Davis, G. A., Putukian, M., Leddy, J., . . . Schneider, K. (2017). The sport concussion assessment tool 5th edition (SCAT5): Background and rationale. *British Journal of Sports Medicine, 51*, 848–850. Doi:10.1136/bjsports-2017-097506

Ellis, A., & Dryden, W. (2007). *The practice of rational emotive behavior therapy*. New York: Springer.

Engel, G. L. (1977). The need for a new medical model: A challenge for biomedicine. *Science, 196*, 129–136. Doi:10.1126/science.847460

Engel, G. L. (1980). The clinical application of the biopsychosocial model. *American Journal of Psychiatry, 137*, 535–544.

Engel, G. L. (1997). From biomedical to biopsychosocial: Being scientific in the human domain. *Psychosomatics, 38*, 521–528. Doi:10.1016/S0033-3182(97)71396-3

Fava, G. A., & Sonino, N. (2007). The biopsychosocial model thirty years later. *Psychotherapy and Psychosomatics, 77*, 1–2. Doi:10.1159/000110052

Gardner, F. L., & Moore, Z. E. (2012). Mindfulness and acceptance models in sport psychology: A decade of basic and applied scientific advancements. *Canadian Psychology, 53*, 309–318. Doi:10.1037/a0030220

Gavrilova, Y., Donohue, B., & Galante, M. (2017). Mental health and sport performance programming in athletes who present without pathology: A case examination supporting optimization. *Clinical Case Studies, 16*, 234–253. Doi:10.1177/1534650116689302

Gilbert, P. (2010). *Compassion focused therapy: Distinctive features*. New York: Routledge.

Glick, I. D., Stillman, M. A., Reardon, C. L., & Ritvo, E. C. (2012). Managing psychiatric issues in elite athletes. *The Journal of Clinical Psychiatry, 73*, 640–644. Doi:10.4088/jcp.11r07381

Gouttebarge, V., Aoki, H., Lambert, M., Stewart, W., & Kerkhoffs, G. (2017). A history of concussions is associated with symptoms of common mental disorders in former male professional athletes across a range of sports. *The Physician and Sportsmedicine, 45*, 443–449. Doi:10.1080/00913847.2017.1376572.

Gouttebarge, V., Castaldelli-Maia, J., Gorczynski, P., Hainline, B., Hitchcock, B., Kerkhoffs, G., . . . Reardon, C. (2019). Occurrence of mental health symptoms and disorders in current and former elite athletes: A systematic review and meta-analysis. *British Journal of Sports Medicine. 53*, 700–707. Doi:10.1136/bjsports-2019-100671

Gouttebarge, V., Cowie, C., Goedhart, E., Kemp, S. P., Kerkhoffs, G. M., Patricios, J., . . . Stokes, K. A. (2019). Educational concussion module for professional footballers: From systematic development to feasibility and effect. *BMJ Open Sport & Exercise Medicine, 5*, e000490. Doi:10.1136/bmjsem-2018-000490

Gucciardi, D. F., Hanton, S., & Fleming, S. (2017). Are mental toughness and mental health contradictory concepts in elite sport? A narrative review of theory and evidence. *Journal of Science and Medicine in Sport, 20*, 307–311. Doi:10.1016/j.jsams.2016.08.006

Gulliver, A., Griffiths, K. M., & Christensen, H. (2012). Barriers and facilitators to mental health help-seeking for young elite athletes: A qualitative study. *BMC Psychiatry, 12*, 1–14. Doi:10.1186/1471-244X-12-157

Gulliver, A., Griffiths, K. M., Christensen, H., Mackinnon, A., Calear, A. L., Parsons, A., . . . Stanimirovic, R. (2012). Internet-based interventions to promote mental health help-seeking in elite athletes: An exploratory randomized controlled trial. *Journal of Medical Internet Research, 14*, e69. Doi:10.2196/jmir.1864

Gulliver, A., Griffiths, K. M., Mackinnon, A., Batterham, P. J., & Stanimirovic, R. (2015). The mental health of Australian elite athletes. *Journal of Science and Medicine in Sport, 18*, 255–261. Doi:10.1016/j.jsams.2014.04.006

Hallock, H., Collins, D., Lampit, A., Deol, K., Fleming, J., & Valenzuela, M. (2016). Cognitive training for post-acute traumatic brain injury: A systematic review and meta-analysis. *Frontiers in Human Neuroscience, 10*, 1–16. Doi:10.3389/fnhum.2016.00537

Hayes, S. C., Strosahl, K. D., & Wilson, K. G. (2011). *Acceptance and commitment therapy: The process and practice of mindful change.* New York: Guilford Press.

Henriksen, K., Hansen, J., & Larsen, C. H. (2019). *Mindfulness and acceptance in sport: How to help athletes perform and thrive under pressure.* New York: Routledge. Doi:10.4324/9780429435232

Henriksen, K., Schinke, R., Moesch, K., McCann, S., Parham, W. D., Larsen, C. H., . . . Terry, P. (2019). Consensus statement on improving the mental health of high performance athletes. *International Journal of Sport and Exercise Psychology*. Advance online publication. Doi:10.1080/1612197X.2019.1570473

Hodge, K., Lonsdale, C., & Ng, J. Y. (2008). Burnout in elite rugby: Relationships with basic psychological needs fulfilment. *Journal of Sports Science, 26*, 835–844. Doi:10.1080/02640410701784525

Hughes, L., & Leavey, G. (2012). Setting the bar: Athletes and vulnerability to mental illness. *British Journal of Psychiatry, 200*, 95–96. Doi:10.1192/bjp.bp.111.095976

Jordana, A., Turner, M. J., Ramis, Y., & Torregrossa, M. (2020). A systematic mapping review on the use of rational emotive behavior therapy (REBT) with athletes. *International Review of Sport and Exercise Psychology*, 1–26.

Junge, A., & Feddermann-Demont, N. (2016). Prevalence of depression and anxiety in top-level male and female football players. *BMJ Open Sport & Exercise Medicine, 2*, e000087. Doi:10.1136/bmjsem-2015-000087

Kerr, Z. Y., Evenson, K. R., Rosamond, W. D., Mihalik, J. P., Guskiewicz, K. M., & Marshall, S. W. (2014). Association between concussion and mental health in former collegiate athletes. *Injury Epidemiology, 1*, 1–10. Doi:10.1186/s40621-014-0028-x

Kessler, R. C., Andrews, G., Colpe, L. J., Hiripi, E., Mroczek, D. K., Normand, S. L., . . . Zaslavsky, A. M. (2002). Short screening scales to monitor population prevalences and trends in non-specific psychological distress. *Psychological Medicine, 32*, 959–976. Doi:10.1017/S0033291702006074

Kessler, R. C., Berglund, P., Demler, O., Jin, R., Merikangas, K. R., & Walters, E. E. (2005). Lifetime prevalence and age-of-onset distributions of *DSM-IV* disorders in the National Comorbidity Survey replication. *Archives of General Psychiatry, 62*, 593–602. Doi:10.1001/archpsyc.62.6.593

Keyes, C. L. M. (2002). The mental health continuum: From languishing to flourishing in life. *Journal of Health and Social Behavior, 43*, 207–222. Doi:10.2307/3090197

Keyes, C. L. M. (2005). Mental illness and/or mental health? Investigating axioms of the complete state model of health. *Journal of Consulting and Clinical Psychology, 73*, 539–548. Doi:10.1037/0022-006X.73.3.539

King, N. S., Crawford, S., Wenden, F. J., Moss, N. E. G., & Wade, D. T. (1995). The rivermead post concussion symptoms questionnaire: A measure of symptoms commonly experienced after head injury and its reliability. *Journal of Neurology, 242*, 587–592. Doi:10.1007/BF00868811

Knapen, J., Vancampfort, D., Moriën, Y., & Marchal, Y. (2015). Exercise therapy improves both mental and physical health in patients with major depression. *Disability and Rehabilitation, 37*, 1490–1495. Doi:10.3109/096382 88.2014.972579

Lavoie, S., Allott, K., Amminger, P., Berger, M., Breakspear, M., Henders, H., . . . Wood, S. (2019). Harmonised collection of data in youth mental health: Towards large datasets. *Australian and New Zealand Journal of Psychiatry, 54*, 46–56. Doi:10.1177/0004867419844322

MacIntyre, T. E., Jones, M., Brewer, B. W., Van Raalte, J., O'Shea, D., & McCarthy, P. J. (2017). Mental health challenges in elite sport: Balancing risk with reward. *Frontiers in Psychology, 8*, 1–4. Doi:10.3389/fpsyg.2017.01892

Mahoney, J., Ntoumanis, N., Mallett, C., & Gucciardi, D. (2014). The motivational antecedents of the development of mental toughness: A self-determination theory perspective. *International Review of Sport and Exercise Psychology, 7*, 184–197. Doi:10.1080/1750984X.2014.925951

Manley, G., Gardner, A. J., Schneider, K. J., Guskiewicz, K. M., Bailes, J., Cantu, R. C., . . . Dvořák, J. (2017). A systematic review of potential long-term effects of sport-related concussion. *British Journal of Sports Medicine, 51*, 969–977. Doi:10.1136/bjsports-2017-097791

McArdle, S., & Moore, P. (2012). Applying evidence-based principles from CBT to sport psychology. *The Sport Psychologist, 26*, 299–310. Doi:10.1123/tsp.26.2.299

McCrory, P., Meeuwisse, W., Dvorak, J., Aubry, M., Bailes, J., Broglio, S., . . . Davis, G. A. (2017). Consensus statement on concussion in sport—The 5th International Conference on Concussion in Sport held in Berlin, October 2016. *British Journal of Sports Medicine, 51*, 838–847. Doi:10.1136/bjsports-2017-097699

Moesch, K., Kenttä, G., Kleinert, J., Quignon-Fleuret, C., Cecil, S., & Bertollo, M. (2018). FEPSAC position statement: Mental health disorders in elite athletes and models of service provision. *Psychology of Sport and Exercise, 38*, 61–71. Doi:10.1016/j.psychsport.2018.05.013

Mosewich, A. D. (2020). Self-compassion in sport and exercise. In G. Tenenbaum & R. C. Eklund (Eds.), *Handbook of sport psychology* (pp. 158–176).

Mosewich, A. D., Ferguson, L. J., McHugh, T.-L. F., & Kowalski, K. C. (2019). Enhancing capacity: Integrating self-compassion in sport. *Journal of Sport*

Psychology in Action. Advance online publication. Doi:10.1080/21520704.201 8.1557774

Moston, S., Skinner, J., & Engelberg, T. (2012). Perceived incidence of drug use in Australian sport: A survey of public opinion. *Sport in Society, 15,* 64–77. Doi: 10.1080/03031853.2011.625277

Mountjoy, M., Junge, A., Budgett, R., Doerr, D., Leglise, M., Miller, S., . . . Foster, J. (2019). Health promotion by international Olympic sport federations: Priorities and barriers. *British Journal of Sports Medicine, 53,* 1117–1125. Doi:10.1136/bjsports-2018-100202

National Collegiate Athletic Association. (2017, May). *Interassociation consensus document: Mental health best practices.* Retrieved from www.ncaa.org/sites/default/files/SSI_MentalHealthBestPractices_Web_20170921.pdf

O'Donnell, S., Beaven, C. M., & Driller, M. W. (2018). From pillow to podium: A review on understanding sleep for elite athletes. *Nature and Science of Sleep, 10,* 243–253. Doi:10.2147/NSS.S158598

Patel, V., Flisher, A. J., Hetrick, S., & McGorry, P. (2007). Mental health of young people: A global public-health challenge. *The Lancet, 369,* 1302–1313. Doi:10.1016/S0140-6736(07)60368-7

Patel, V., Saxena, S., Lund, C., Thornicroft, G., Baingana, F., Bolton, P., . . . Herrman, H. (2018). The lancet commission on global mental health and sustainable development. *The Lancet, 392,* 1553–1598. Doi:10.1016/S0140-6736(18)31612-X

Peluso, M. A. M., & Andrade, L. H. S. G. D. (2005). Physical activity and mental health: The association between exercise and mood. *Clinics, 60,* 61–70. Doi:10.1590/S1807-59322005000100012

Potter, S., Leigh, E., Wade, D., & Fleminger, S. (2006). The rivermead post concussion symptoms questionnaire. *Journal of Neurology, 253,* 1603–1614. Doi:10.1007/s00415-006-0275-z

Purcell, R., Chevroulet, C., Pilkington, V., & Rice, S. (2020). *What works for mental health in sporting teams? An evidence guide for best practice in mental health promotion and early intervention.* Melbourne, Australia: Orygen.

Putukian, M. (2016). The psychological response to injury in student athletes: A narrative review with a focus on mental health. *British Journal of Sports Medicine, 50,* 145–148. Doi:10.1136/bjsports-2015-095586

Reardon, C. L. (2017). Psychiatric comorbidities in sports. *Neurologic Clinics, 35,* 537–546. Doi:10.1016/j.ncl.2017.03.007

Reardon, C. L., & Factor, R. M. (2010). Sport psychiatry. *Sports Medicine, 40,* 961–980. Doi:10.2165/11536580-000000000-00000

Reardon, C. L., Hainline, B., Miller Aron, C., Baron, D., Baum, A., Bindra, A., . . . Engebretsen, L. (2019). International Olympic committee consensus statement on mental health in elite athletes. *British Journal of Sports Medicine, 53,* 667–699. Doi:10.1136/bjsports-2019-100715

Rice, S., Gwyther, K., Santesteban-Echarri, O., Baron, D., Gorczynski, P., Gouttebarge, V., . . . Purcell, R. (2019). Determinants of anxiety in elite athletes: A systematic review and meta-analysis. *British Journal of Sports Medicine, 53,* 722–730. Doi:10.1136/bjsports-2019-100620

Rice, S., Olive, L., Gouttebarge, V., Parker, A. G., Clifton, P., Harcourt, P., . . . Purcell, R. (2020). Mental health screening: Severity and cut-off point sensitivity of the Athlete Psychological Strain Questionnaire in male and female elite athletes. *BMJ Open Sport & Exercise Medicine, 6,* e000712. Doi:10.1136/bmjsem-2019-000712

Rice, S. M., Parker, A. G., Mawren, D., Clifton, P., Harcourt, P., Lloyd, M., . . . Purcell, R. (2019). Preliminary psychometric validation of a brief screening tool for athlete mental health among male elite athletes: The athlete psychological strain questionnaire. *International Journal of Sport and Exercise Psychology.* Advance online publication. Doi:10.1080/1612197X.2019.1611900

Rice, S. M., Parker, A. G., Rosenbaum, S., Bailey, A., Mawren, D., & Purcell, R. (2018). Sport-related concussion and mental health outcomes in elite athletes: A systematic review. *Sports Medicine, 48,* 447–465. Doi:10.1007/s40279-017-0810-3

Rice, S. M., Purcell, R., De Silva, S., Mawren, D., McGorry, P. D., & Parker, A. G. (2016). The mental health of elite athletes: A narrative systematic review. *Sports Medicine, 46,* 1333–1353. Doi:10.1007/s40279-016-0492-2

Rice, S. M., Purcell, R., & McGorry, P. D. (2018). Adolescent and young adult male mental health: Transforming system failures into proactive models of engagement. *Journal of Adolescent Health, 62,* S9–S17. Doi:10.1016/j.jadohealth.2017.07.024

Rosenbaum, S., Tiedemann, A., & Ward, P. B. (2014). Meta-analysis physical activity interventions for people with mental illness: A systematic review and meta-analysis. *Journal of Clinical Psychiatry, 75,* 1–11. Doi:10.4088/JCP.13r08765

Ryan, R., & Deci, E. (2000). Self-determination theory and the facilitation of intrinsic motivation, social development, and well-being. *American Psychologist, 55,* 68–78.

Rush, A. J., Trivedi, M. H., Ibrahim, H. M., Carmody, T. J., Arnow, B., Klein, D. N., . . . Thase, M. E. (2003). The 16-item quick inventory of depressive symptomatology (QIDS), clinician rating (QIDS-C), and self-report (QIDS-SR): A psychometric evaluation in patients with chronic major depression. *Biological Psychiatry, 54,* 573–583. Doi:10.1016/S0006-3223(02)01866-8

Schinke, R. J., Stambulova, N. B., Si, G., & Moore, Z. (2018). International society of sport psychology position stand: Athletes' mental health, performance, and development. *International Journal of Sport and Exercise Psychology, 16,* 622–639. Doi:10.1080/1612197X.2017.1295557

Simms, M., Arnold, R., Turner, J., & Hays, K. (2020). A repeated-measures examination of organizational stressors, perceived psychological and physical health, and perceived performance in semi-elite athletes. *Journal of Sport Sciences.* Advance online publication. Doi:10.1080/02640414.2020.1804801

Slade, T., Grove, R., & Burgess, P. (2011). Kessler psychological distress scale: Normative data from the 2007 Australian national survey of mental health and wellbeing. *Australian and New Zealand Journal of Psychiatry, 45,* 308–316. Doi:10.3109/00048674.2010.543653

Solomon, G. S., & Haase, R. F. (2008). Biopsychosocial characteristics and neurocognitive test performance in national football league players: An initial assessment. *Archives of Clinical Neuropsychology, 23,* 563–577. Doi:10.1016/j.acn.2008.05.008

Spitzer, R., Kroenke, K., Williams, J., & Löwe, B. (2006). A brief measure for assessing generalized anxiety disorder: The GAD-7. *Archives of Internal Medicine, 166,* 1092–1097. Doi:10.1001/archinte.166.10.1092

Stillman, M. A., Glick, I. D., McDuff, D., Reardon, C. L., Hitchcock, M. E., Fitch, V. M., . . . Hainline, B. (2019). Psychotherapy for mental health symptoms and disorders in elite athletes: A narrative review. *British Journal of Sports Medicine, 53,* 767–771. Doi:10.1136/bjsports-2019-100654

Sundgot-Borgen, J., & Torstveit, M. K. (2004). Prevalence of eating disorders in elite athletes is higher than in the general population. *Clinical Journal of Sport Medicine, 14,* 25–32.

Swann, C., Telenta, J., Draper, G., Liddle, S., Fogarty, A., Hurley, D., & Vella, S. (2018). Youth sport as a context for supporting mental health: Adolescent male perspectives. *Psychology of Sport and Exercise, 35,* 55–64. Doi:10.1016/j.psychsport.2017.11.008

Tibbert, S. J., Andersen, M. B., & Morris, T. (2015). What a difference a "Mentally Toughening" year makes: The acculturation of a rookie. *Psychology of Sport and Exercise, 17,* 68–78. Doi:10.1016/j.psychsport.2014.10.007

Turner, M. J. (2016). Rational emotive behavior therapy (REBT), irrational and rational beliefs, and the mental health of athletes. *Frontiers in Psychology, 7,* 1–16 Doi:10.3389/fpsyg.2016.01423

von Rosen, P., Frohm, A., Kottorp, A., Fridén, C., & Heijne, A. (2017). Multiple factors explain injury risk in adolescent elite athletes: Applying a biopsychosocial perspective. *Scandinavian Journal of Medicine & Science in Sports, 27,* 2059–2069. Doi:10.1111/sms.12855

Voss, M. W., Kramer, A. F., Basak, C., Prakash, R. S., & Roberts, B. (2010). Are expert athletes 'expert' in the cognitive laboratory? A meta-analytic review of cognition and sport expertise. *Applied Cognitive Psychology, 24,* 812–826. Doi:10.1002/acp.1588

Wahlbeck, K. (2015). Public mental health: The time is ripe for translation of evidence into practice. *World Psychiatry, 14,* 36–42. Doi:10.1002/wps.20178

Wäljas, M., Iverson, G. L., Lange, R. T., Hakulinen, U., Dastidar, P., Huhtala, H., . . . Öhman, J. (2015). A prospective biopsychosocial study of the persistent post-concussion symptoms following mild traumatic brain injury. *Journal of Neurotrauma, 32,* 534–547. Doi:10.1089/neu.2014.3339

Walker, E. R., McGee, R. E., & Druss, B. G. (2015). Mortality in mental disorders and global disease burden implications: A systematic review and meta-analysis. *JAMA Psychiatry, 72,* 334–341. Doi:10.1001/jamapsychiatry.2014.2502

Walton, C. C., Baranoff, J., Gilbert, P., & Kirby, J. (2020). Self-compassion, social rank, and psychological distress in athletes of varying competitive levels. *Psychology of Sport and Exercise, 50,* 101733. Doi:10.1016/j.psychsport.2020.101733

Walton, C. C., Keegan, R. J., Martin, M., & Hallock, H. (2018). The potential role for cognitive training in sport: More research needed. *Frontiers in Psychology, 9,* 1–7. Doi:10.3389/fpsyg.2018.01121

Walton, C. C., Purcell, R., & Rice, S. (2019). Addressing mental health in elite athletes as a vehicle for early detection and intervention in the general community. *Early Intervention in Psychiatry, 13,* 1530–1532. Doi:10.1111/eip.12857

WHO. (2006). *Constitution of the World Health Organization.* Geneva, Switzerland: WHO.

WHO. (2014). *Mental health: A state of well-being.* Geneva, Switzerland: WHO. Retrieved from www.who.int/features/factfiles/mental_health/en/

Williams, G. C., & Deci, E. L. (1996). Internalization of biopsychosocial values by medical students: A test of self-determination theory. *Journal of Personality and Social Psychology, 70,* 767–779. Doi:10.1037/0022-3514.70.4.767

Section III

Moderators of the Stress Process in Sport

9 Stress-Related Growth and Resilience

David Fletcher

To succeed at the top level of sport, athletes must negotiate and overcome a wide range of challenges. Apart from the obvious demands associated with training and competing, higher standards of athletic performance bring with them increasing lifestyle- and organizational-related stressors. These challenges often coincide with one of the most demanding stages of human life; transitioning from adolescence to adulthood. Withstanding and adapting to this array of stressors is necessary if athletes are to fulfill their sporting potential and gain the competitive edge. Notwithstanding the phenomenal levels of resilience required to thrive in elite sport, athletes will inevitably struggle with difficulties at times. Although adversity is usually distressing and sometimes traumatic, the athletes who reach the pinnacle of global sport will also likely find a way to, at least in part, positively change and grow in some way from such hardship. Indeed, it is often the stress-related growth and resilience exhibited by the world's best athletes that separates them from their rivals.

Over the past decade or so, the topics of stress-related growth and resilience in sport have become popular areas of inquiry. Studies have burgeoned to the extent that researchers have reviewed and discussed how sporting activities can facilitate growth and development (Henley, Schweizer, de Gara, & Vetter, 2007; Massey & Williams, 2019; Tamminen & Neely, 2016), how athletes can positively grow following adversity (Howells, Sarkar, & Fletcher, 2017; Tamminen & Neely, 2016), how researchers have studied growth following adversity in sport (Day & Wadey, 2017), how resilience is experienced and developed in sport performers and teams (Brady & Alleyne, 2018; Bryan, O'Shea, & MacIntyre, 2018; Fletcher & Sarkar, 2016a, 2016b; Galli & Gonzalez, 2015; Galli & Pagano, 2018; Hill, Den Hartigh, Meijer, De Jonge, & Van Yperen, 2018a, 2018b; Russell, 2015; Sarkar & Fletcher, 2014b; Wagstaff, Sarkar, Davidson, & Fletcher, 2017; Wood, Barker, & Turner, 2018), and how researchers should measure resilience in sport performers (Sarkar & Fletcher, 2013). This chapter focuses on elite athletes' experiences of stress-related growth and resilience. The emphasis is on how the world's best performers differ in some pivotal psychosocial respects from others competing at the highest level (O'Boyle & Aguinas, 2012; see also Cappelli & Crocker-Hefter, 1997; Simonton, 2014; Walberg, Strykowski, Rovai, & Hung, 1984) in terms of how they grow following adversity, develop their resilience beyond their pretrauma functioning, and deliver superior performance (cf. Fletcher, 2019; Sarkar & Fletcher, 2017).

What Is Stress-Related Growth?

Most people experience hardship during their life; but such difficulties are rarely permanent and individuals may benefit in some way from their experiences. The term stress-related growth refers to positive psychosocial changes experienced following stress-related events and responses (cf. Park, Cohen, & Murch, 1996), such as adversity and trauma. Indeed, scholars in this area often use more specific terminology to conceptually differentiate growth on the basis of the severity of the stressor or distress (cf. Howells et al., 2017; see also Chapter 1). Specifically, growth that occurs following severe circumstances typically associated with adjustment difficulties (i.e., adversity) is referred to as adversarial growth (cf. Linley & Joseph, 2004; Luthar & Cicchetti, 2000), and growth that occurs following an individual's distressed response to adversity or the accumulation of stressors (i.e., trauma) is referred to as posttraumatic growth (cf. Bovin & Marx, 2011; Tedeschi & Calhoun, 1995).

In terms of the main components and outcomes of the growth process, several theoretical models have been developed including the Functional Descriptive Model of Posttraumatic Growth (FDM; Calhoun, Cann, & Tedeschi, 2010; Calhoun & Tedeschi, 1998; Tedeschi & Calhoun, 1995, 2004), the Organismic Valuing Theory of Growth Through Adversity (OVT; Joseph & Linley, 2005), the Affective-Cognitive Processing Model of Posttraumatic Growth (ACPM; Joseph, Murphy, & Regel, 2012), the Janus-Faced Model of Self-Perceived Posttraumatic Growth (Maercker & Zoellner, 2004; Zoellner & Maercker, 2006), and the Theory on Reports of Constructive (Real) and Illusory Posttraumatic Growth (Boerner, Joseph, & Murphy, 2020). Collectively, the theory and research in this area suggest that growth entails an increased appreciation for life, more meaningful relationships, an increased sense of personal strength, a change in priorities, and/or a richer existential and spiritual awareness (Tedeschi, Shakespeare-Finch, Taku, & Calhoun, 2018). Particularly relevant in the context of this chapter is the increased sense of personal strength involving enhanced resilience to subsequent adversity.

Stress-Related Growth in the World's Best Athletes

Over half a century ago, Goertzel and Goertzel (1962) published "a provocative and eye-opening study" (p. 1) of the biographies of men and women who had made a positive contribution to society, including some athletes. What was contentious about their work—and remains so to the present day—was the counterintuitive finding that, as children, three-quarters of these prominent individuals had been burdened by poverty, broken homes, abusive parents, alcoholism, handicaps, illness, or other misfortunes. Comparable findings have since been reported for writers, political leaders, poets, creative children, geniuses, scientists, presidential scholars, professional athletes, and other eminent individuals who appear to suffer a rate of loss (through death or absence) of a parent (and other hardships) in childhood which exceeds that found in the general population (see, for reviews, Cskikszentmihalyi, 1990; Fletcher, 2019; Gardner, 1994; Haynal, 2003; Olszewski-Kubilius, 2000; Piirto, 1992; Rinn & Bishop, 2015). Iremonger (1970) described this phenomenon as the Phaeton Effect, based on Phaeton who, in Greek mythology, was the illegitimate son of Helios, a sun god, and Clymene, a nymph. In compensation for feeling that he did not know his father and the inferiority he felt about the circumstances of his existence, Phaeton became ambitious and vain, taking his father's sun chariot and attempting to drive it across the sky (an endeavor that, ultimately, leads to his death).

A significant finding of the sport psychology research in recent years is that early life, non-sport adversity appears to be a consistent feature of the world's best athletes' lives (Fletcher, 2019; Sarkar & Fletcher, 2017). Adversities that have been reported in the literature include the death or serious illness of a significant family member, parental divorce or serious relationship problems, unstable or unsettled home environment (e.g., witnessing, or undergoing personal experience of, physical or verbal abuse), frequently moving home (with a subsequent loss of friendship groups), the perception of being sent away from parents (e.g., boarding school), difficulty at school (e.g., low achievement, bullying, and loneliness), serious injury or illness, diagnosis of developmental-related disorders (e.g., attention-deficit/hyperactivity disorder [ADHD], speech impediment, and dyslexia), and symptoms of compromised mental health (e.g., obsessive-compulsive disorder, depression, suicidal thoughts, self-harm, substance abuse, and eating disorder) (Hardy et al., 2017a; Howells & Fletcher, 2015; Sarkar, Fletcher, & Brown, 2015; see also Chapter 1). Lower elite-level athletes who, while performing in international competition, do not attain or sustain the highest possible success at this level appear to experience less early life, non-sport adversity (Collins, MacNamara, & McCarthy, 2016; Hardy et al., 2017a; Savage, Collins, & Cruickshank, 2017). Turning back to the world's best athletes, as their careers commence and progress, adversity may originate from sport or non-sport events, including an athlete being told that he or she will never be a world-class performer, not being selected for an Olympic team, perceived underperformance in Olympic competition, illness or injury, personal relationship breakdown, experiencing the death of a close family member, or political unrest (Hardy et al., 2017a; Howells &

Fletcher, 2015; Sarkar et al., 2015). These later career adversities, while appearing to be experienced by the majority of the world's best athletes, do not appear to be universally experienced in the same way that early life adversities are (Hardy et al., 2017a; see also Fletcher, 2019; Sarkar & Fletcher, 2017).

Within the psychology research literature, childhood adversity that precedes adult success has been referred to as a "diversifying experience" (Goclowska, Damian, & Mor, 2018; Simonton, 2000, 2016). Such experiences are "highly unusual and unexpected events or situations" (Goclowska et al., 2018, p. 303) "that help weaken the constraints imposed by conventional socialization" (Simonton, 2000, p. 153) "so that the children do not become 'normal' adults" (Simonton, 2016, p. 7). Research suggests that the role that diversifying experiences play in the development of high performance may vary across domains. More specifically, the frequency and intensity of such developmental events and conditions appear to be higher for literary and artistic geniuses than for scientific geniuses (Berry, 1981; Damian & Simonton, 2014, 2015). It has also been suggested that the relationship between diversifying experiences and adult achievement is best described by a curvilinear inverted-U relationship suggesting an optimal level of adversity for talent development (Damian & Simonton, 2014; Goclowska et al., 2018). According to Goclowska et al.'s (2018) Diversifying Experience Model, this occurs when an individual has appropriate adaptive resources to appraise the diversifying experience as a challenge rather than as a threat (see also Chapters 2 and 5).

Scholars have proposed a number of concepts and theories relating to how individuals can develop following stress-related experiences, including "wise baby", traumatic progression, eustress, systematic desensitization, stress inoculation, steeling, psychophysiological toughness, stress exposure, psychological preparedness, antifragility, discretionary vulnerability, and pressure inurement (see also Chapter 12). Research investigating these concepts has generally found that moderate cumulative lifetime adversity is associated with more positive responses to subsequently encountered stressors (see, for reviews, Chapter 12; Höltge, Mc Gee, Maercker, & Thoma, 2018; Liu, 2015; Seery, 2011; Seery & Quinton, 2016; Updegraff & Taylor, 2000). This body of work indicates that, for some individuals at least, stress-related experiences can stimulate the development of psychosocial resources that individuals can harness for future encounters. According to the Systematic Self-Reflection Model of Resilience Strengthening (Crane, Searle, Kangas, & Nwiran, 2019), this occurs when an individual adaptively reflects on his or her response to stressors encountered.

Turning back to the world's best athletes, research suggests that following their (typically traumatic) initial response to adversity they go through a "transitional process" (Howells & Fletcher, 2015, p. 43) whereby growth is facilitated by ongoing complex interactions of numerous personal and situational factors. Important internal processes appear to be engaging in a process of reflection that tends to focus on the significance of the experience in the athletes' lives (Howells & Fletcher, 2015; Sarkar et al., 2015; see also Day, 2013), questioning the performance narrative (Howells & Fletcher, 2015), and personality traits (Hardy et al., 2017a; Sarkar et al., 2015; see also Crawford, Gayman, & Tracey, 2014; Udry, Gould, Bridges, & Beck, 1997; Chapter 10). Other research with elite athletes has highlighted the importance of cognition and cognitive processing, the thinking that accompanied an acceptance of the adversity, seeking meaning (comprehension) in the adversity (Howells & Fletcher, 2016), and reestablishing a sense of autonomy (Day, 2013). Important external processes appear to be sport playing a significant role in reestablishing identity, empowering the athletes, and/or providing a safe place or sanctuary to escape the impact of the adversity (Howells & Fletcher, 2015; see also Crawford et al., 2014; Tamminen, Holt, & Neely, 2013), the support of others (e.g., families, friends, teammates, coaches, and psychologists; see also Chapter 11) and feelings of relatedness (Howells & Fletcher, 2015; see also Tamminen et al., 2013), and informational resources in the form of cultural scripts or narrative about how adversity could be negotiated (Howells & Fletcher, 2015). Providing further insight into situational factors, Hardy et al. (2017a) emphasized the importance of athletes experiencing a positive sport-related event in close proximity to early life adversity, involving finding a sport in which an individual perceived that he or she could thrive, finding a significant sport coach or mentor, and/or experiencing an inspirational sporting pathway moment (cf. Henley et al., 2007; Massey & Williams, 2019).

As a consequence of this transitional process, a variety of intrapersonal, interpersonal, and physical outcomes has been reported by the world's best athletes, including increased motivation (Hardy et al., 2017a; Howells & Fletcher, 2015; Sarkar et al., 2015), total preparation for competition and increased importance of sport (Hardy et al., 2017a), spiritual change, enhanced relationships, increased altruism or prosocial behavior (Howells & Fletcher, 2015), and better athletic functioning, superior performance, being physically stronger, and/or increased fitness (Hardy et al., 2017a; Howells & Fletcher, 2015; Sarkar et al., 2015; see also Crawford et al., 2014; Day, 2013; Tamminen et al., 2013; Udry et al., 1997). Other research with elite athletes has highlighted the importance of positive reframing of the negative experiences or derogation of adversity-related experiences to allow athletes to perceive their adversities in a different light, developing a positive bias toward the future (Howells & Fletcher, 2016), identification of new possibilities (Day, 2013; Howells & Fletcher, 2016), a greater appreciation of life (Crawford et al., 2014; Day, 2013; Howells & Fletcher, 2016), improved personal strength (Tamminen et al., 2013; Udry et al., 1997), relating to others or positive changes in social relationships, greater appreciation of family and friends (Crawford et al., 2014; Tamminen et al., 2013), being less judgmental (Crawford et al., 2014), and a move toward disclosure and the ability to speak out to others (Howells & Fletcher, 2016). Among the aforementioned growth processes and outcomes, motivational and personality changes appear to be particularly salient psychological aspects of stress-related growth in the world's best athletes.

Motivational Changes

The world's best athletes are extremely driven to the point that their motivation goes beyond simply enjoying competitive sport for the inherent satisfaction of training and performing, to a burning desire to succeed and avoid failure. For top athletes, childhood "adversities represented significant, life-changing events that acted as extreme motivational triggers" (Howells & Fletcher, 2015, p. 45), "adversities [are exploited] to fuel . . . ambition" (Sarkar et al., 2015, p. 477), "adversity and the resultant trauma served to ignite the . . . desire to excel at the highest level" (Sarkar et al., 2015, p. 477), "negative emotions appear to have fueled . . . subsequent effort and application . . . [and] . . . . Increased exertion and execution" (Sarkar et al., 2015, p. 477), "the sense of injustice drove them on to their performance development" (Sarkar et al., 2015, p. 477), and "[an] extreme form of motivation" (Sarkar et al., 2015, p. 478) whereby "the demonstration of high achievement and superiority become fundamental psychological exigencies for that individual" (Sarkar et al., 2015, p. 477). Within elite sport, the intensity of this "deep-seated need to succeed" (Hardy et al., 2017a, p. 65) is borne out in the findings of the Faustian bargain offered by Goldman's dilemma (Goldman, Bush, & Klatz, 1984). In Goldman's dilemma, international athletes are asked if there existed a drug that would make them unbeatable for the next five years, after which they would die, would they take it? The dilemma has been posed to hundreds of international athletes with the results consistently reporting that approximately half of the athletes accept the deal (Connor & Mazanov, 2009). Notwithstanding the methodological limitations of this research, the findings not only underscore the extremely high levels of determination and perseverance of elite athletes but also point to the potentially darker aspects of achievement motivation.

To better understand the fundamental origins and drivers of the motivation of high achievers, McClelland (1965) and colleagues (McClelland, Atkinson, Clark, & Lowell, 1953) argued that a psychodynamic approach is required (see also Beisser, 1967). In resurrecting this line of thought, Hardy et al. (2017a) suggested that, for the world's best athletes, the sense of loss induced by early life adversity creates a strong unconscious need to avoid such experiences in the future.

Hardy et al. (2017a) went on to highlight three core psychodynamic mechanisms: guilt ("the loss was something I could have stopped from happening"), achievement striving ("if I try hard enough it won't happen again"), and a need for success ("so that I can be worthy of the attention/love that I did not get because of the loss"). Ultimately, these unconscious processes manifest themselves in the world's best athletes not only by outperforming others and winning but also through demonstrating complete mastery of one's domain (Fletcher & Sarkar, 2012; Hardy et al., 2017a).

Personality Changes

In terms of the link between adversity and personality, research on the world's best athletes has reported that the "trauma stemming from adversity can leave an indelible impression on an individual's psyche and schema, to the extent that his or her raison d'etre is established or altered" (Sarkar et al., 2015, p. 478; see also Hardy et al., 2017a; Howells & Fletcher, 2015). Contemporary personality theorists recognize the malleability of an individual's character (see, e.g., Caspi, Roberts, & Shiner, 2005; Edmonds, Jackson, Fayard, & Roberts, 2008; see also Chapter 10) and, in particular, the potential role of traumatic experiences in initiating personality change (Blackie et al., 2017; Jayawickreme & Blackie, 2014). Indeed, the concept of adversarial growth is typically grounded in Janoff-Bulman's (1989, 1992) notion of shattered assumptions or schema which suggests that traumatic experiences can lead to changes in how individuals view themselves and the world (see also Bothers & Ulman, 1993).

Personality changes in the world's best athletes following adversity appear to be characterized by "a 'dark side' of core psychological processes" (Sarkar et al., 2015, pp. 477–478), "highly driven mindsets that boarder... on the obsessional" (Howells & Fletcher, 2015, p. 45), "a single-minded, narcissistic desire to prove one's worth" (Sarkar et al., 2015, p. 478), "self-serving indifference and disturbing malevolence" (Sarkar et al., 2015, p. 478), and "*obsessional/perfectionistic*, and *ruthless/selfish*, attitudes to sport" (Hardy et al., 2017a, p. 171). It has been recognized for some time that the motives and personalities of elite athletes may have some darker underpinnings (Beisser, 1967) and that "the 'normal man' [sic] is not a likely candidate for the Hall of Fame" (Goertzel & Goertzel, 1962). Because winning in sport at the highest level is not normal (cf. Bell, 1982), Hardy et al. (2017a) concluded that it is unlikely that sportspersons with "normal" personalities, "normal" relationships, or who fit into a "normal" system will achieve sporting excellence. Rather, the world's best athletes are different and have idiosyncrasies that make them exceptional, but potentially difficult to relate to and communicate with (Hardy et al., 2017a).

What Is Psychological Resilience?

Although by no means the only potential outcome of the growth process, the development of psychological resilience appears to be an important differentiating factor in the emergence of sporting talent (Hardy et al., 2017a; Rees et al., 2016). At an individual level, psychological resilience, occasionally referred to as and used interchangeably with mental fortitude (Bruce et al., 2012; Fletcher & Sarkar, 2016b), is defined as "the role of an individual's mental processes and behaviors in their ability to withstand or adapt to environmental demands" (Fletcher, 2019, p. 733; adapted from Fletcher & Sarkar, 2012, 2013, 2016b). Consistent with contemporary approaches to conceptualizing resilience (see, e.g., Fletcher & Sarkar, 2013; Helmreich et al., 2017; Kalisch, Müller, & Tüscher, 2015; Kent, Davis, & Reich, 2014; Kumar, 2017), Fletcher and Sarkar (2016b) distinguished between the term "robust resilience" to refer to a protective quality (cf. Rutter, 1987) characterized by an individual maintaining their well-being and performance when under pressure (cf. Bonanno, 2004) and the term "rebound resilience" to refer to a bounce back ability (cf. Smith, Tooley, Christopher, & Kay, 2010) characterized by minor or temporary disruptions to an individual's well-being and performance when under pressure (cf. Norris, Tracy, & Galea, 2009) and the quick return to normal functioning (cf. Carver, 1998).

Although the aforementioned inevitably describes the fundamental meaning and usage of the term psychological resilience, this phenomenon is more broadly and best conceived as a dynamic psychosocial process involving ongoing person-situation transactions (Fletcher & Sarkar, 2013). The role of an individual's mental processes and behaviors in their ability to withstand or adapt to environmental demands is not a static capacity (Luthar, Cicchetti, & Becker, 2000) but rather ever-changing and involving complex interactions of personal and environmental factors (Masten, 2001). Akin to other psychosocial processes, this conceptualization emphasizes a variety of component parts (e.g., adversity and adaptation), linking mechanisms (e.g., appraisals and metacognitions), influencing factors (e.g., personality and support), and consequential outcomes (e.g., well-being and performance)—*all* of which are important for conceptualizing, operationalizing, and assessing psychological resilience (Kumar, 2017; Fletcher & Sarkar, 2013). To this end, interactive relationships and temporal dynamics are fundamental to understanding trajectories of functioning (Bonanno, 2004) across different contexts (Rutter, 1981). Bonanno, Romero, and Klein (2015) highlighted four basic considerations: baseline or preadversity adjustment, the actual adverse circumstances themselves, postadversity resilient outcomes, and predictors of resilient outcomes. From a theoretical perspective, three models of psychological resilience in sport performers have been developed: the Conceptual Model of Sport Resilience

(Galli & Vealey, 2008), the Grounded Theory of Psychological Resilience and Optimal Sport Performance (Fletcher & Sarkar, 2012), and the Model of Resilience in Competitive Athletes After Traumatic Injury (Machida, Irwin, & Feltz, 2013).

Psychological Resilience in the World's Best Athletes

Research suggests that the ability to positively evaluate and interpret stressors, together with one's own resources, thoughts, and emotions—processes collectively referred to as challenge appraisal and meta-cognitions—is a pivotal aspect of psychological resilience in the world's best athletes (Fletcher & Sarkar, 2012; see also Chapter 2). This ability is largely predicated on the combined influence of various psychosocial resources that are commonly referred to in the resilience literature as protective and promotive factors (Rutter, 1985, 1987; Sameroff, Gutman, & Peck, 2003).

Psychological Factors

Research findings indicate that there are five main families of psychological factors that are particularly important for the world's best athletes: personality, motivation, confidence, focus, and support (Fletcher & Sarkar, 2012; see, for a review, Sarkar & Fletcher, 2014b). Personality refers to (relatively and typically) enduring characteristics that reflect the tendency to respond in certain ways to events (cf. Cervone & Pervin, 2013; see also Chapter 10) and for athletes' resilience includes perfectionism, optimism, competitiveness, hope, and proactivity traits. Motivation concerns the reason(s) for thinking, feeling, or acting in a particular way (cf. Dweck, 2017) and for athletes' resilience involves optimizing perseverance in the face of hardship and difficulties. Confidence, or the degree of certainty one possesses about his or her ability to be successful (cf. Bandura, 1977), is crucial for athletes' resilience to buffer against potential threats and uncertainty in demanding environments. Focus, or concentration, refers to cognitively attending to what is important in a given situation (cf. Pashler, 1998; see also Chapter 5) and for athletes' resilience needs to be maintained or regained despite distractions and setbacks. Support in this context concerns the assistance that an individual perceives that he or she receives or is able to access if needed (cf. Shumaker & Brownell, 1984; see also Chapter 11) and for athletes' resilience is an important aspect of preparing for and negotiating stressors encountered.

There are (at least) four salient points to consider relating to psychological protective and promotive factors. The first is that because some of these factors, such as psychosocial regulation strategies, are more malleable than others, such as personality character traits, some psychological resources are more amenable to training than others (Fletcher & Sarkar, 2016b). The second is that the relevance and importance of these factors will vary across contexts and time, so some combinations of resources will likely be more effective in withstanding and adapting to certain types of stressors compared to others (Fletcher & Sarkar, 2016b). The third is that although possessing certain characteristics is beneficial for performing under pressure, these same traits may not always have a positive impact on mental health (e.g., obsessional and perfectionistic) or others' evaluations (e.g., ruthlessness and selfishness). With the aforementioned points in mind, the fourth consideration is that training or intervening to enhance resilience should, as much as practically possible, be personalized and contextualized to meet apposite performance- and non-performance-related goals.

Environmental Factors

A persistent straw man's argument in the sport psychology literature is that psychological resilience only relates to cognitive-affective processes manifested in an individuals' behaviors, despite scholars repeatedly emphasizing the importance and impact of environmental factors (see, e.g., Fletcher & Sarkar, 2013; Morgan, Fletcher, & Sarkar, 2015; Sarkar & Fletcher, 2014b). As Fletcher and Sarkar (2016b) remarked, "psychological resilience . . . is profoundly influenced by a wide range of environmental factors . . . [that] may originate from social, cultural, organizational, political, economic, occupational and/or technological sources" (p. 140). Available space precludes a detailed discussion of such factors (see, for a review in the sport domain, Wagstaff et al., 2017) but, in the context of the development of high performance, it is worth discussing the fundamental role of challenge and support in the environment (cf. Arthur, Hardy, & Woodman, 2013; Fletcher & Sarkar, 2016b; Fletcher & Streeter, 2016; Jones, Gittins, & Hardy, 2009; see also Csikszentmihalyi, Rathunde, & Whalen, 1993; Therival, 1999; Chapters 11 and 12).

Educationists have for some time argued that optimum human development and performance occurs when the environment effectively balances the challenge and support presented to those operating within it (see Bower, Diehr, Morzinski, & Simpson, 1998; Cameron-Jone & O'Hara, 1997; Daloz, 1986; Hamrick, Evans, & Schuh, 2002; Martin, 1996; Sanford, 1967; Ward, Trautvetter, & Braskamp, 2005). Challenge involves promoting a culture of high expectations that stretches individuals and groups out of their comfort zones. Support involves promoting a culture that provides individuals and groups with assistance to enable them to operate effectively. In the context of resilience development, Fletcher and Sarkar (2016b) differentiated between four types of environment: stagnant environment, unrelenting environment, comfortable environment, and facilitative environment (see Figure 9.1). In an unrelenting environment, too much challenge and not enough support will compromise well-being (see also Chapter 6); conversely, in a comfortable environment, too much support and not enough challenge will inhibit performance (Fletcher & Sarkar, 2016b). In a facilitative environment, however, high challenge and high support are balanced resulting in resilience being optimally developed.

The facilitative environment is characterized by individuals thriving in a challenging but supportive climate (Fletcher & Sarkar, 2016b; see also Chapter 13). Regarding the challenge, the culture should be imbued with a sense of an aspirational and ambitious vision; that is, a compelling version of the future that inspires people to seek out challenging opportunities to achieve meaningful goals. Developmental feedback is provided in the form of advice outlining how individuals and groups can progress and enhance their resilience. In terms of maintaining functioning and performance under pressure, challenge should also involve some manipulation of the environment to evoke a stress-related response to stimulate desensitization and inoculation, an approach referred to as pressure inurement training in the resilience development literature (see also Chapter 12; Fletcher & Sarkar, 2016b; Low et al., in press). Turning to the support, the culture should present athletes with opportunities to access to different types of assistance that are appropriate to their needs (cf. Cutrona, 1990; see also Chapter 11). Motivational feedback is provided in the form of encouragement outlining how individuals and groups have progressed and enhanced their resilience. Although there

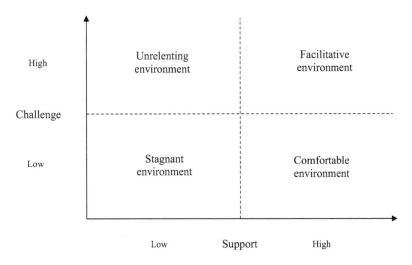

Figure 9.1 A Challenge-Support Matrix for Developing Resilience (Reproduced With Permission From Fletcher and Sarkar, 2016b)

will likely be occasions where more emotional and/or esteem support is appropriate, and other times where more informational and/or tangible support is suitable (cf. Cutrona & Russell, 1990), the environment should be fundamentally created around a nurturing and compassionate culture that facilitates athlete resilience and well-being. Importantly, *both* individuals and organizations should take *shared* responsibility for developing resilience for performance *and* well-being (see also Chapters 6, 8, 13, and 14).

Performance and Well-Being

As noted earlier, there are psychological aspects of resilience that, while being largely beneficial for performing under pressure, may not always have a positive impact on mental health or others' evaluations. Standing and Ringo (2016) emphasized a similar point in the context of high achievers who had experienced childhood adversity:

> We must remember that subsequent outstanding achievements by an orphan do not guarantee that they [sic] will enjoy a happy life overall as an adult (e.g., John Barrymore, John Berryman, Edvard Munch), nor that they will be benign individuals (e.g., Adolf Eichmann, Adolf Hitler, Josef Stalin). The Phaeton effect initially appears surprising, since in the general population early parental loss due to death (or divorce) is associated with so many adverse developmental outcomes in subsequent adult life, but different domains are generally involved, so that someone who is depressed or alcoholic could still become a great artist or politician, for example.
>
> (Standing & Ringo, 2016, p. 148)

In the short-term, the adversities experienced by the world's best athletes can elicit distressing and traumatic responses characterized by intrusive thoughts and ruminations, negative emotions (e.g., anger, shock, frustration, guilt, and helplessness; see also Chapter 4), and impact on their perceptions of identity (Howells & Fletcher, 2015; Sarkar et al., 2015). Other research with elite athletes reinforces these findings (Crawford, Gayman, & Tracey, 2014; Tamminen, Holt, & Neely, 2013) and also suggests that athletes at this level cognitively process the cause of the experience and the implications for the future (Day, 2013; Udry et al., 1997), experience regret and loss (Day, 2013), use denial to suppress negative emotions and as a short-term palliative coping strategy (Howells & Fletcher, 2016), experience disruption of enjoyable activities with others (Crawford et al., 2014), have difficulty completing previously achievable tasks (Day, 2013), are reluctant to disclose information about the adversities (Howells & Fletcher, 2016), and withdraw from others (Tamminen et al., 2013).

The research is less clear about the long-term effects of adversity on elite athletes' mental health, although there is some evidence that suggests perceived underperformance (Hammond, Gialloreto, Kubas, & Hap Davis, 2013) and injury (Gulliver, Griffiths, Mackinnon, Batterham, & Stanimirovic, 2015) may increase the risk of mental ill-health in elite athletes (see also Chapter 8). In the general psychology research, however, it is well-established that individuals who experience childhood adversities tend to have more physical and mental health problems as adults than those who do not experience such hardships (see, for a review, Hughes et al., 2017). In particular, there appears to be an association between childhood adversities and adult mental ill-health (Hughes et al., 2017) and psychotic symptoms (Trotta, Murray, & Fisher, 2015).

When one reflects on the extreme motivation of world's best athletes, it is not difficult to understand how the comic strip character, Dilbert, mischievously concluded: "I would think that a willingness to practice the same thing for 10,000 hours is a mental disorder". Furthermore, it is likely that the resilience required to attain and sustain expert sport performance involves enduring some difficulties and at times pushing oneself to the limit. For the world's best athletes who have experienced childhood adversity, Hardy et al. (2017a) argued that experiencing a positive sport-related event in close proximity to the adversity is probably very important for countering the negative mental health consequences that typically accompany childhood trauma. Although it is quite possible, even probable, that the self-esteem enhancing effects of sport and success (cf. Fox & Lindwall, 2014) can and do mitigate some aspects of adjustment difficulties, Sarkar and Fletcher (2017) suggested that such events may only mask some of the undesirable outcomes associated with early life adversity.

Extremely high levels of determination and perseverance to succeed in the face of hardship and difficulties have been referred to as John Henryism (James, 1994; James, Hartnett, & Kalsbeek, 1983). John Henry was a 19th-century railroad worker from a disadvantaged background who purportedly defeated a steam-powered drill in a steeling-driving contest. In doing so, he displayed three attributes that have come to characterize John Henryism: efficacious mental and physical vigor, a strong commitment to hard work, and a single-minded determination to succeed (James, 1994). Despite his victory, however, John Henry died of exhaustion immediately following the contest—in other words, his greatness came at a price (cf. Ludwig, 1995). Research investigating John Henryism has found that repetitive, high-effort coping with adversity potentiates risk for various indicators of physical ill-health (see, for reviews, Bennett et al., 2004; James, 1994). Notwithstanding that it could be argued that the high levels of physical activity typically associated with most elite athletes' training may counter such negative physical health consequences (cf. Reiner, Niermann, Jekauc, & Woll, 2013), there is some evidence that John Henryism also negatively affects mental health (Brody et al., 2013). Collectively, these findings led Brody, Yu, Miller, and Chen (2016) to suggest that "striving for success may act as a 'double-edged sword'" (p. 2) in that it may enhance performance but undermine health. Although there is no robust evidence to suggest that elite athletes' mental health is any more impaired than the general population (see, for a review, Rice et al., 2016; see also Chapter 8), there is some anecdotal evidence to suggest that some mental health symptoms and disorders may be associated with exceptional athletic performance (Beisser, 1967; Gogarty & Williamson, 2009) which, when considered alongside analogous evidence from other performance domains (Baas, Nijstad, Boot, & De Dreu, 2016; Simonton, 2014), would suggest that for at least some top athletes, "resilience may . . . [sometimes] be only 'skin deep'" (Brody et al., 2013, p. 1285).

The sporting idiom, "winning at all costs" (cf. Gogarty & Williamson, 2009; Watson, 2007) conveys how the deep-seated need to succeed can have baneful ramifications. It is not difficult to appreciate how some potentially darker characteristics associated with the world's best athletes, such as being driven, ruthless, or selfish, can spillover over into less desirable aspects of human nature, such as obduracy, uncaring, or duplicity. One need look no further than the former cyclist, Lance Armstrong, who was stripped of seven Tour de France titles and banned from competitive cycling before admitting to using performance-enhancing drugs (Hamilton & Coyle, 2013; Macur, 2014; O'Reilly, 2014; Walsh, 2012). Armstrong's reflections give pause for thought when seeking to understand resilience in elite sport:

> [My] ruthless desire to . . . win at all costs . . . serves me well on the bike, served me well during [my cancerous] disease, but the level that it went to, for whatever reason, is a flaw. . . . That defiance, that attitude . . . that arrogance . . . —it's not good.
>
> (Jimjoe bobjacktom, 2013)

It is cases like Armstrong's that provide a stark reminder that adversarial growth leading to solitary resilience at its extreme can turn from a virtue to a vice (cf. Friedman & Robbins, 2012; Russell, 2015). Rather than throwing the metaphorical baby out with the bathwater by attempting to derogate or denounce resilience, a more reasoned and realistic approach is to counteract undesirable outcomes via more holistic psychosocial training and support in areas such as ethical awareness, emotional intelligence, performance intelligence, and reflective practice (Fletcher & Sarkar, 2016b; see also Russell, 2015; Chapter 4). Moreover, it is not inconceivable that some of the world's best athletes attenuate the potential darker side of some of their characteristics by developing dissociative identities—a persona that meets their deep-seated need to succeed and another persona that better serves their mental health and societal integration. Interestingly, a contributory factor in the development of dissociative identities is often early life adversity (Howell & Itzkowitz, 2016; Huntjens et al., 2016) and it may be that different identities can, perhaps, be triggered, accessed, and/or expressed within different contexts (cf. Ogawa, Sroufe, Weinfield, Carlson, & Egeland, 1997; Ringrose, 2018; Rodewald, Dell, Wilhelm-Gossling, & Gast, 2011).

When considering performance and mental health in the world's best athletes, it is important to recognize that although psychological resilience is necessary to thrive in elite sport (see also Chapter 13), it would be remiss to suggest that expert athletes must always be resilient in all situations. The greatest sport performers are still human. If even fictional superheroes (e.g., Batman/Bruce Wayne) and movie characters (e.g., Rocky Balboa) have their weaknesses and vulnerabilities, it would be unrealistic (and inaccurate) to expect or portray the world's best athletes as invincible performers with nerves of steel. As should be apparent, athletes—both as people and as performers—are bombarded with a multitude of ever-changing stressors which demand a constellation of qualities to withstand and adapt to them. For those constantly seeking out opportunities to challenge themselves, as is typically the case for high achieving athletes (cf. Sarkar & Fletcher, 2014a), it is inevitable that they will have some flaws and falter at times. As Fletcher and Sarkar (2016b) emphasized, resilience and vulnerability coexist in everyone (cf. Miller et al., 2010). It is the potential resilience that can stem from adversity and vulnerability that is the central focus and thesis of this chapter (cf. Tedeschi & Blevins, 2017). Indeed, vulnerability can have many benefits for re-evaluation and reflection, opening up dialogue and frank communication, enhancing relationships, stimulating learning, gaining perspective, humility, and a new beginning (Fletcher & Sarkar, 2016b; Uphill & Hemmings, 2017).

An Uncomfortable Truth?

An "uncomfortable truth" (Hardy et al., 2017a, p. 29) to emerge from stress-related growth and resilience research with the world's best athletes may be that although adversity-related experiences appear essential to develop the resilience required to attain and sustain success at the highest level of sport, this does not make such athletes immune to the darker aspects of adversity-related experiences that have less desirable effects on mental health and relationships. Drawing on some of the contentious and ethical issues this raises (cf. Sarkar & Fletcher, 2017), a question that is sometimes asked is should adversity be imposed on (aspiring) athletes to be successful? The answer is a resounding "no" because it would be unethical and potentially abusive and harmful to do so. Rather the main implications of the research are threefold: (i) if a child or athlete experiences adversity and trauma he or she may potentially grow and develop following this experience, to the point that it enhances his or her sport performance (Howells & Fletcher, 2015; Sarkar et al., 2015); (ii) that athletes should be exposed to relevant and progressively demanding stressors that, with appropriate support, become surmountable challenges (Howells & Fletcher, 2015; Sarkar et al., 2015); and (iii) that athletes who grow from adversity and cope with stressors will, all things being equal, have a competitive advantage over those who do not (Hardy et al., 2017a).

The second question sometimes posed is should talent be identified and subsequently selected on the basis of experiencing adversity and trauma? Again, the answer is a unequivocal "no" because there is a multitude of psychosocial and non-psychosocial factors that are needed to grow from adversity and also to achieve at the highest levels of sport. Indeed, most people who experience adversity and trauma are not successful at the highest levels. The evidence suggests that a positive sport-related event (Hardy et al., 2017a) and growth-related transitional processes (Howells & Fletcher, 2015; Sarkar et al., 2015) are also essential features of the adversity-related experience. The third question that has been asked is whether pre-existing psychosocial skills are more important than the adversity-related experiences. Although the genetic and pre-existing characteristics that an individual has will contribute to how he or she responds to and potentially grows from adversity, the evidence indicates that it is the adversity-related experience that is essential in the emergence of new psychosocial characteristics (Hardy et al., 2017a; Howells & Fletcher, 2015; Sarkar et al., 2015). The psychosocial skills that athletes already have or bring to the adversity and trauma will not be enough on their own (even if they are further developed) to achieve at the highest levels.

Unfortunately, the research findings in this area have been used on occasions to romanticize hardship in elite sport or, worse still, to justify the imposition of adversity on (or the abuse of) athletes by implying that talent *needs* trauma. The insinuation that aspiring athletes *must* experience trauma or *should* grow from adversity comes in many (explicit and implicit) forms including journalistic misrepresentation, social media provocation, uneducated coaching, academic one-upmanship, cultural narratives, and so on. It is crucial that responsible psychology experts who are knowledgeable about the topic area in elite sport disseminate clear evidence-based implications. Namely, that for athletes who experience adversity they *may* or *can* change in some positive and beneficial ways, such as enhanced resilience and superior performance, but not in others, such as their mental health and relationships. This dialectical observation will likely place coaches and practitioners working with elite athletes in uncomfortable situations that require difficult decisions to be made.

Future Research

The study of stress-related growth and resilience in sport is a relatively recent research endeavor. In terms of better understanding the experiences of the world's best athletes, the findings of nascent research by Fletcher and colleagues (Fletcher & Sarkar, 2012; Howells & Fletcher, 2015; Sarkar et al., 2015) have been advanced by Hardy and colleagues (Hardy et al., 2017a), but there is still much work to do. To date, researchers have predominately utilized retrospective qualitative approaches, which should, in the future, be supplemented with prospective quantitative approaches (cf. Hardt & Rutter, 2004; Infurna & Jayawickreme, 2019) that incorporate objective outcome indicators (Berens, Jensen, & Nelson, 2017; Reuben et al., 2016). Indeed, growth and resilience are multifaceted constructs that necessitate the multidimensional assessment and multilevel analysis of genetic, neural, biological, psychological, and social factors (Cicchetti, 2010; Cicchetti & Blender, 2006; Feder, Nestler, Westphal, & Charney, 2010; Rutten et al., 2013).

Given that growth and resilience are processes that unfold over time (Fletcher & Sarkar, 2013; Howells et al., 2017), researchers should use longitudinal designs that temporally represent dynamic fluctuations within both an individual's psyche and the social environment (Bonanno, Romero, & Klein, 2015; Hayes, Laurenceau, Feldman, Strauss, & Cardaciotto, 2007). Identifying such patterns will require using relatively sophisticated data analytic approaches, such as latent growth mixture modeling, to provide more accurate assessments of growth and resilience over time (Galatzer-Levy & Bonanno, 2016; Galatzer-Levy, Huang, & Bonanno, 2018; Infurna & Luthar, 2016a, 2016b, 2018). Indeed, little is known about athletes' response trajectories following adversity, but pathways of change are fundamental to operationally identify and distinguish between robust resilience (maintenance of well-being and performance under pressure; cf. Bonanno, 2004), rebound resilience (minor or temporary disruptions to well-being and performance under pressure and the quick return to normal functioning; cf. Carver, 1998; Norris et al., 2009), stress-related growth (development of well-being and performance beyond pre-stress functioning; Park et al., 1996), and other related constructs such as coping and recovery (cf. Fletcher & Sarkar, 2013; see also Chapter 3).

Future researchers should pay greater attention to the classification, properties, and dimensions of the adversity encountered (see also Chapter 1; Fletcher, 2019). Of particular importance is how stressors influence one another and accumulate, together with the implications for the overall severity and allostatic load for an athlete (Fletcher, Hanton, & Mellalieu, 2006; Gucciardi, 2017; Howells & Fletcher, 2015; Howells et al., 2017). Other research questions that relate to the experience of adversity include: Does the nature of the adversity and subsequent growth in some way relate to the specific demands and competencies of the sport in which an individual thrives? What effect does early life adversity, such as loss of a parent, have on the attachments that athletes form with others, such as sports coaches, teammates, family and friends, and the development of these relationships? How important (e.g., sufficient, advantageous, and/or necessary) are adversity-related experiences and growth in the development of superior performance and Olympic success (cf. Hardy et al., 2017b; Sarkar & Fletcher, 2017)? Although these questions largely relate to negative events, it is worth emphasizing that positive events can also stimulate growth, a phenomenon referred to as postecstatic growth (Mangelsdorf & Eid, 2015; Roepke, 2013) and appears relevant in elite athletes' development (Hardy et al., 2017a).

In terms of growth and resilience, there are several lines of inquiry that merit further attention. Although not a straightforward task, it would be informative to explore what role psychodynamic factors, such as compensatory mechanisms and counterphobic attitudes (cf. Hardy et al., 2017a), play in the growth and development process of elite athletes. Another intriguing area of research is the veridicality of athletes' accounts of adversity and growth (cf. Howells & Fletcher, 2016). Given the limitations surrounding retrospective recall, survivorship bias, and social desirability, more attention needs to be paid to investigating the extent to which the world's best athletes may be (consciously or unconsciously) deceiving themselves and/or others about their adversity and growth experiences (Howells et al., 2017; Sarkar & Fletcher, 2017). Resilience research in elite sport has been conducted at individual and group levels (see, for reviews, Morgan, Fletcher, & Sarkar, 2017; Sarkar & Fletcher, 2014b) but, as Fletcher and Wagstaff (2009) recognized, the notion of resilience is also relevant at an organizational level and should be investigated in elite sport. Indeed, given the salience of the social and organizational environment in the development of resilience at all levels (Fletcher & Sarkar, 2016b; Wagstaff et al., 2017), it is surprising that organizational resilience in elite sport remains a neglected area of inquiry.

Examining relationships between stress-related growth, psychological resilience, athletic performance, and mental health is a particularly worthwhile area for future research. Given the non-normality of elite athletes (O'Boyle & Aguinas, 2012; see also Cappelli & Crocker-Hefter, 1997; Walberg et al., 1984), researchers should take this into account in their study designs and sampling procedures (see, e.g., Hardy et al., 2017a). From a performance and health perspective, Simonton (2014) found that although creative people appear to be more mentally healthy than the general population, highly creative people appear to be more mentally ill than the general population. Notably, he concluded that his findings:

> . . . could very well apply to many other research questions in psychological science. . . . The factors that distinguish athletes from nonathletes do not have to be equivalent to those that distinguish the rare competitors who won multiple gold medals from those in the same Olympic events who earned only a single bronze medal. Some of those factors might even be antithetical.
>
> (p. 478)

Research is needed to better understand why and under what circumstances some psychosocial characteristics associated with the world's best athletes may compromise mental health and/or social integration. To elaborate, some motivational and personality characteristics (e.g., obsessiveness, perfectionism, ruthlessness, and selfishness) appear to have paradoxical or countervailing effects in terms of the enhancement of performance but the undermining of health (cf. John Henryism). In the context of adversarial growth, Lomas and Ivtzan (2016) argued that growth-related development is "dialectical in that it is an on-going process in which positive and negative are continually intertwined" (p. 1763). Furthermore, if one accepts that human thriving is the "*the joint experience of development and success*" (Brown, Arnold, Fletcher, & Standage, 2017, p. 168; see also Chapter 13), then reconciling the potential antithetically of well-being and performance at their respective high*est* levels may be one of the most challenging but important tasks within the field of sport psychology.

Conclusion

The world's best athletes are supernormal, extraordinary performers. It is, therefore, unlikely that normal and ordinary backgrounds will be sufficient to develop and acquire the phenomenal levels of psychological resilience necessary to thrive in elite sport. Rather, it appears that extreme events, in the form of early life adversity, and responses, characterized by psychosocial growth, are essential to develop the resilience required to attain and sustain success at the highest level of sport. The interrelated experiences of adversity, growth, and resilience involves ongoing complex interactions of numerous personal and situational factors. Although there is a variety of potential beneficial outcomes of this process, it appears that there may also be some darker aspects to the world's best athletes' development and performance that have less desirable effects on their mental health and relationships. The integrative synthesis of stress-related growth and resilience offers one of the most exciting and insightful avenues for future research in sport and performance.

References

Arthur, C. A., Hardy, L., & Woodman, T. (2013). Realising the Olympic dream: Vision, support and challenge. *Reflective Practice: International and Multidisciplinary Perspectives, 13*, 399–406. Doi:10.1080/14623943.2012.670112

Baas, M., Nijstad, B. A., Boot, N. C., & De Dreu, C. K. W. (2016). Mad genius revisited: Vulnerability to psychopathology, biobehavioral approach-avoidance, and creativity. *Psychological Bulletin, 142*, 668–692. Doi:10.1037/bul0000049

Bandura, A. (1977). Self-efficacy: Toward a unifying theory of behavioral change. *Psychological Review, 84*, 191–215. Doi:10.1037/0033-295x.84.2.191

Beisser, A. R. (1967). *The madness in sports: Psychosocial observations on sports.* New York: Appleton-Century-Crofts.

Bell, K. (1982). *Winning isn't normal.* Austin, TX: Keel Publications.

Bennett, G. G., Merritt, M. M., Sollers, J. J., Edwards, C. L., Whitfield, K. E., Brandon, D. T., & Tucker, R. D. (2004). Stress, coping and health outcomes among African-Americans: A review of the John Henryism hypothesis. *Psychology and Health, 19*, 369–383. Doi:10.1080/0887044042000193505

Berens, A. E., Jensen, S. K. G., & Nelson, C. A. (2017). Biological embedding of childhood adversity: From physiological mechanisms to clinical implications. *BMC Medicine, 15*, 135. Doi:10.1186/s12916-017-0895-4

Berry, C. (1981). The Nobel scientists and the origins of scientific achievement. *British Journal of Sociology, 32*, 381–391. Doi:10.2307/589284

Blackie, L. E. R., Jayawickreme, E., Tsukayama, E., Forgeard, M. J. C., Roepke, A-M., & Fleeson, W. (2017). Post-traumatic growth as positive personality change: Developing a measure to assess within-person variability. *Journal of Research in Personality, 69*, 22–32. Doi:10.1016/j.jrp.2016.04.001

Boerner, M., Joseph, S., & Murphy, D. (2020). A theory on reports of constructive (real) and illusory posttraumatic growth. *Journal of Humanistic Psychology, 60*, 384–399. Doi:10.1177/0022167817719597

Bonanno, G. A. (2004). Loss, trauma, and human resilience: Have we underestimated the human capacity to thrive after extremely adverse events? *American Psychologist, 59*, 20–28. Doi:10.1037/0003-066x.59.1.20

Bonanno, G. A., Romero, S. A., & Klein, S. I. (2015). The temporal elements of psychological resilience: An integrative framework for the study of individuals, families, and communities. *Psychological Inquiry, 26*, 139–169. Doi:10.1080/10 47840x.2015.992677

Bothers, R. B., & Ulman, D. (1993). *The shattered self: A psychoanalytic study of trauma.* Abingdon, UK: Routledge.

Bovin, M. R., & Marx, B. P. (2011). The importance of the peritraumatic experience in defining traumatic stress. *Psychological Bulletin, 137*, 47–67. Doi:10.1037/a0021353

Bower, D. J., Diehr, S., Morzinski, J. A., & Simpson, D. E. (1998). Support—challenge—vision: A model for faculty mentoring. *Medical Teacher, 20*, 595–597. Doi:10.1080/01421599880373

Brady, A., & Alleyne, R. (2018). Resilience and growth mindset in sport and physical activity. In A. Brady & B. Grenville-Cleave (Eds.), *Positive psychology in sport and physical activity: An introduction* (pp. 102–114). Abingdon, UK: Routledge.

Brody, G. H., Yu, T., Chen, E., Miller, G. E., Kogan, S. M., & Beach, S. R. H. (2013). Is resilience only skin deep? Rural African Americans' socioeconomic status-related risk and competence in preadolescence and psychological adjustment and allostatic load at age 19. *Psychological Science, 24*, 1285–1293. Doi:10.1177/0956797612471954

Brody, G. H., Yu, T., Miller, G. E., & Chen, E. (2016). Resilience in adolescence, health, and psychosocial outcomes. *Pediatrics, 138*, 1–8. Doi:10.1542/peds.2016-1042

Brown, D. J., Arnold, R., Fletcher, D., & Standage, M. (2017). Human thriving: A conceptual debate and literature review. *European Psychologist, 22*, 167–179. Doi:10.1027/1016-9040/a000294

Bruce, J., Thornton, A. J., Scott, N. W., Marfizo, S., Powell, R., Johnston, M., . . . Thompson, A. M. (2012). Chronic preoperative pain and psychological robustness predict acute postoperative pain outcomes after surgery for breast cancer. *British Journal of Cancer, 107*, 937–946. Doi:10.1038/bjc.2012.341

Bryan, C., O'Shea, D., & MacIntyre, T. E. (2018). The what, how, where and when of resilience as a dynamic, episodic, self-regulating system: A response to Hill et al. (2018). *Sport, Exercise, and Performance Psychology, 7*, 355–362. Doi:10.1037/spy0000133

Calhoun, L. G., Cann, A., & Tedeschi, R. G. (2010). The posttraumatic growth model: Sociocultural considerations. In T. Weiss & R. Berger (Eds.), *Posttraumatic growth and culturally competent practice: Lessons learned from around the globe* (pp. 1–14). Hoboken, NJ: Wiley.

Calhoun, L. G., & Tedeschi, R. G. (1998). Posttraumatic growth: Future directions. In R. G. Tedeschi, C. L. Park, & L. G. Calhoun (Eds.), *Posttraumatic growth: Theory and research on change in the aftermath of crisis* (pp. 215–238). Mahwah, NJ: Erlbaum.

Cameron-Jones, M., & O'Hara, P. (1997). Support and challenge in teacher education. *British Educational Research Journal, 23*, 15–23.

Cappelli, P., & Crocker-Hefter, A. (1997). Distinctive human resources are firms' core competencies. *Organizational Dynamics, 24*, 7–22. Doi:10.1016/s0090-2616(96)90002-9

Carver, S. (1998). Resilience and thriving: Issues, models, and linkages. *Journal of Social Issues, 54*, 245–266. Doi:10.1111/j.1540-4560.1998.tb01217.x

Caspi, A., Roberts, B. W., & Shiner, R. L. (2005). Personality development: Stability and change. *Annual Review of Psychology, 56*, 453–484.

Cervone, D., & Pervin, L. A. (2013). *Personality: Theory and research* (12th ed.). Hoboken, NJ: John Wiley & Sons.

Cicchetti, D. (2010). Resilience under conditions of extreme stress: A multi-level perspective. *World Psychiatry, 9*, 145–154. Doi:10.1002/j.2051-5545.2010.tb00297.x

Cicchetti, D., & Blender, J. A. (2006). A multiple-levels-of-analysis perspective on resilience: Implications for the developing brain, neural plasticity, and preventive interventions. *Annuals of the New York Academy of Sciences, 1094*, 248–258. Doi:10.1196/annals.1376.029

Collins, D., MacNamara, Á., & McCarthy, N. (2016). Super champions, champions, and almost: Important differences and commonalities on the rocky road. *Frontiers in Psychology, 6*, 1–11. Doi:10.3389/fpsyg.2015.02009

Connor, J. M., & Mazanov, J. (2009). Would you dope? A general population test of the Goldman Dilemma. *British Journal of Sports Medicine, 43*, 871–872. Doi:10.1136/bjsm.2009.057596

Crane, M. F., Searle, B. J., Kangas, M., & Nwiran, Y. (2019). How resilience is strengthened by exposure to stressors: The systematic self-reflection model of resilience strengthening. *Anxiety, Stress, and & Coping: An International Journal, 32*, 1–17. Doi:10.1080/10615806.2018.1506640

Crawford, J. J., Gayman, A. M., & Tracey, J. (2014). An examination of post-traumatic growth in Canadian and American ParaSport athletes with acquired spinal cord injury. *Psychology of Sport and Exercise, 15*, 399–406. Doi:10.1016/j.psychsport.2014.03.008

Cskikszentmihalyi, M. (1990). *Flow: The psychology of optimal experience.* New York: Harper and Row.

Csikszentmihalyi, M., Rathunde, K., & Whalen, S. (1993). *Talented teenagers: The roots of success and failure.* Cambridge, UK: Cambridge University Press.

Cutrona, C. E. (1990). Stress and social support: In search of optimal matching. *Journal of Social and Clinical Psychology, 9*, 3–14. Doi:10.1521/jscp.1990.9.1.3

Cutrona, C. E., & Russell, D. W. (1990). Type of social support and specific stress: Toward a theory of optimal matching. In B. R. Sarason, I. G. Sarason, & G. R. Pierce (Eds.), *Wiley series on personality processes. Social support: An interactional view* (pp. 319–366). Oxford, UK: John Wiley & Sons.

Daloz, L. (1986). *Effective teaching and mentoring: Realizing the transformational power of adult learning experiences.* San Francisco, CA: Jossey-Bass.

Damian, R. I., & Simonton, D. K. (2014). Diversifying experiences in the development of genius and their impact on creative cognition. In D. K. Simonton (Ed.), *The Wiley handbook of genius* (pp. 375–394). Oxford, UK: Wiley-Blackwell.

Damian, R. I., & Simonton, D. K. (2015). Psychopathology, adversity, and creativity: Diversifying experiences in the development of eminent African Americans. *Journal of Personality and Social Psychology, 108*, 623–636. Doi:10.1037/pspi0000011

Day, M. C. (2013). The role of initial physical activity experiences in promoting posttraumatic growth in Paralympic athletes with an acquired disability. *Disability & Rehabilitation, 35*, 2064–2072. Doi:10.3109/09638288.2013.805822

Day, M. C., & Wadey, R. (2017). Researching growth following adversity in sport and exercise: Methodological implications and future recommendations. *Qualitative Research in Sport, Exercise and Health, 9*, 499–513. Doi:10.1080/2159 676x.2017.1328460

Dweck, C. S. (2017). From needs to goals and representations: Foundations for a unified theory of motivation, personality, and development. *Psychological Review, 124*, 689–719. Doi:10.1037/rev0000082

Edmonds, G. W., Jackson, J. J., Fayard, J. V., & Roberts, B. W. (2008). Is character fate, or is there hope to change my personality yet? *Social and Personality Psychology Compass, 2*, 399–413. Doi:10.1111/j.1751-9004.2007.00037.x

Feder, A., Nestler, E. J., Westphal, M., & Charney, D. S. (2010). Psychobiological mechanisms of resilience to stress. In J. W. Reich, A. J. Zautra, & J. S. Hall (Eds.), *Handbook of adult resilience* (pp. 35–54). New York: Springer.

Fletcher, D. (2019). Psychological resilience and adversarial growth in sport and performance. In E. O. Acevedo (Ed.), *The Oxford encyclopedia of sport, exercise, and performance psychology* (pp. 731–756). New York: Oxford University Press.

Fletcher, D., Hanton, S., & Mellalieu, S. D. (2006). An organizational stress review: Conceptual and theoretical issues in competitive sport. In S. Hanton & S. D. Mellalieu (Eds.), *Literature reviews in sport psychology* (pp. 321–374). Hauppauge, NY: Nova Science Publishers.

Fletcher, D., & Sarkar, M. (2012). A grounded theory of psychological resilience in Olympic champions. *Psychology of Sport and Exercise, 5,* 669–678. Doi:10.1016/j.psychsport.2012.04.007

Fletcher, D., & Sarkar, M. (2013). Psychological resilience: A review and critique of definitions, concepts and theory. *European Psychologist, 18,* 12–23. Doi:10.1027/1016-9040/a000124

Fletcher, D., & Sarkar, M. (2016a). An introduction to the special issue: Developing resilience. *Journal of Sport Psychology in Action, 7,* 133–134.

Fletcher, D., & Sarkar, M. (2016b). Mental fortitude training: An evidence-based approach to developing psychological resilience for sustained success. *Journal of Sport Psychology in Action, 7,* 135–157. Doi:10.1080/21520704.2016.1255496

Fletcher, D., & Streeter, A. P. (2016). A case study analysis of the high performance environment model in elite swimming. *Journal of Change Management, 16,* 123–141. Doi:10.1080/14697017.2015.1128470

Fletcher, D., & Wagstaff, C. R. D. (2009). Organizational psychology in elite sport: Its emergence, application and future. *Psychology of Sport and Exercise, 10,* 427–434. Doi:10.1016/j.psychsport.2009.03.009

Fox, K. R., & Lindwall, M. (2014). Self-esteem and self-perceptions in sport and exercise. In A. G. Papaioannou & D. Hackfort (Eds.), *Routledge companion to sport and exercise psychology: Global perspectives and fundamental concepts* (pp. 34–48). Abingdon, UK: Routledge.

Friedman, H. L., & Robbins, B. D. (2012). The negative shadow case by positive psychology: Contrasting views and implications of humanistic and positive psychology on resiliency. *The Humanistic Psychologist, 40,* 87–102. Doi:10.1080/08 873267.2012.643720

Galatzer-Levy, I. R., & Bonanno, G. A. (2016). It's not so easy to make resilience go away: Commentary on Infurna and Luthar (2016). *Perspectives on Psychological Science, 11,* 195–198. Doi:10.1177/1745691615621277

Galatzer-Levy, I. R., Huang, S. H., & Bonanno, G. A. (2018). Trajectories of resilience and dysfunction following potential trauma: A review and statistical evaluation. *Clinical Psychology Review, 63,* 41–55. Doi:10.1016/j.cpr.2018.05.008

Galli, N., & Gonzalez, S. P. (2015). Psychological resilience in sport: A review of the literature and implications for research and practice. *International Journal of Sport and Exercise Psychology, 3,* 243–257. Doi:10.1080/1612197x.2014.946947

Galli, N., & Pagano, K. (2018). Furthering the discussion on the use of dynamical systems theory for investigating resilience in sport. *Sport, Exercise, and Performance Psychology, 7,* 351–354. Doi:10.1037/spy0000128

Galli, N., & Vealey, R. S. (2008). "Bouncing back" from adversity: Athletes' experiences of resilience. *The Sport Psychologist, 22,* 316–335. Doi:10.1123/tsp.22.3.316

Gardner, H. (1994). The fruits of asynchrony: A psychological examination of creativity. In D. H. Feldman, M. Csikszentmihalyi, & H. Gardner (Eds.), *Changing the world: A framework for the study of creativity* (pp. 47–68). Westport, CT: Praeger.

Goclowska, M. A., Damian, R. I., & Mor, S. (2018). The diversifying experience model: Taking a broader conceptual view of the multiculturalism-creativity link. *Journal of Cross-Cultural Psychology, 49*, 303–322. Doi:10.1177/0022022116650258

Goertzel, V., & Goertzel, M. G. (1962). *Cradles of eminence: A provocative and eye-opening study of the childhoods of over 400 famous twentieth-century men and women.* London, UK: Little Brown.

Gogarty, P., & Williamson, I. (2009). *Winning at all costs: Sporting gods and their demons.* London, UK: JR Books.

Goldman, B., Bush, P. J., & Klatz, R. (1984). *Death in the locker room.* London, UK: Century.

Gucciardi, D. F. (2017). The psychosocial development of world-class athletes: Additional considerations for understanding the whole person and salience of adversity. In V. Walsh, M. Wilson, & B. Parkin (Eds.), *Sport and the brain: The science of preparing, enduring and winning, Part A* (pp. 127–132). London, UK: Academic Press.

Gulliver, A., Griffiths, K. M., Mackinnon, A., Batterham, P. J., & Stanimirovic, R. (2015). The mental health of Australian elite athletes. *Journal of Science and Medicine in Sport, 18*, 255–261. Doi:10.1016/j.jsams.2014.04.006

Hamilton, T., & Coyle, D. (2013). *The secret race: Inside the hidden world of the Tour de France.* London, UK: Transworld.

Hammond, T., Gialloreto, C., Kubas, H., & Hap Davis, H. (2013). The prevalence of failure-based depression among elite athletes. *Clinical Journal of Sport Medicine, 23*, 273–277. Doi:10.1097/jsm.0b013e318287b870

Hamrick, F. A., Evans, N. J., & Schuh, J. H. (2002). *Foundations of student affairs practice: How philosophy, theory, and research strengthen educational outcomes.* San Francisco, CA: Jossey-Bass.

Hardt, J., & Rutter, M. (2004). Validity of adult retrospective report of adverse childhood experiences: Review of the evidence. *Journal of Child Psychology and Psychiatry, 45*, 260–273. Doi:10.1111/j.1469-7610.2004.00218.x

Hardy, L., Barlow, M., Evans, L., Rees, T., Woodman, T., & Warr, C. (2017a). Great British medalists: Psychosocial biographies of super-elite and elite athletes from Olympic sports. In V. Walsh, M. Wilson, & B. Parkin (Eds.), *Sport and the brain: The science of preparing, enduring and winning, Part A* (pp. 1–119). London, UK: Academic Press.

Hardy, L., Barlow, M., Evans, L., Rees, T., Woodman, T., & Warr, C. (2017b). Great British medalists: Response to the commentaries. In V. Walsh, M. Wilson, & B. Parkin (Eds.), *Sport and the brain: The science of preparing, enduring and winning, Part A* (pp. 207–216). London, UK: Academic Press.

Hayes, A. M., Laurenceau, J-P., Feldman, G., Strauss, J. L., & Cardaciotto, L. (2007). Change is not always linear: The study of nonlinear and discontinuous patterns of change in psychotherapy. *Clinical Psychology Review, 27*, 715–723. Doi:10.1016/j.cpr.2007.01.008

Haynal, A. (2003). Childhood lost and recovered. *International Forum of Psychoanalysis, 12*, 30–37. Doi:10.1080/083037060310005241

Helmreich, I., Kunzler, A., Chmitorz, A., König, J., Binder, H., Wessa, M., & Lieb, K. (2017). Psychological interventions for resilience enhancement in adults. *Cochrane Database of Systematic Reviews, 2*, 1–43. Doi:10.1002/14651858.cd012527

Henley, R., Schweizer, I., de Gara, F., & Vetter, S. (2007). How psychosocial sport and play programs help youth manage adversity: A review of what we know and what we should research. *International Journal of Psychosocial Rehabilitation, 12,* 51–58. Doi:10.5167/uzh-9849

Hill, Y., Den Hartigh, R. J. R., Meijer, R. R., De Jonge, P., & Van Yperen, N. W. (2018a). Resilience in sports from a dynamic perspective. *Sport, Exercise, and Performance Psychology, 4,* 333–341. Doi:10.1037/spy0000118

Hill, Y., Den Hartigh, R. J. R., Meijer, R. R., De Jonge, P., & Van Yperen, N. W. (2018b). The temporal process of resilience. *Sport, Exercise, and Performance Psychology, 4,* 333–341. Doi:10.1037/spy0000143

Höltge, J., Mc Gee, S. L., Maercker, A., & Thoma, M. V. (2018). A salutogenic perspective on adverse experiences: The curvilinear relationship of adversity and well-being. *European Journal of Health Psychology, 25,* 53–69. Doi:10.1027/2512-8442/a000011

Howell, E. F., & Itzkowitz, S. (2016). The everywhereness of trauma and the dissociative structuring of the mind. In E. F. Howell & S. Itzkowitz (Eds.), *The dissociative mind in psychoanalysis: Understanding and working with trauma* (pp. 33–43). Abingdon, UK: Routledge.

Howells, K., & Fletcher, D. (2015). Sink or swim: Adversity- and growth-related experiences in Olympic swimming champions. *Psychology of Sport and Exercise, 16,* 37–48. Doi:10.1016/j.psychsport.2014.08.004

Howells, K., & Fletcher, D. (2016). Adversarial growth in Olympic swimmers: Constructive reality or illusionary self-deception? *Journal of Sport and Exercise Psychology, 38,* 173–186. Doi:10.1123/jsep.2015-0159

Howells, K., Sarkar, M., & Fletcher, D. (2017). Can athletes benefit from adversity? A systematic review of growth following adversity in competitive sport. *Progress in Brain Research, 234,* 117–159. Doi:10.1016/bs.pbr.2017.06.002

Hughes, K., Bellis, M. A., Hardcastle, K. A., Sethi, D., Butchart, A., Mikton, C., . . . Dunne, M. P. (2017). The effect of multiple adverse childhood experiences on health: A systematic review and meta-analysis. *Lancet Public Health, 2,* 356–366. Doi:10.1016/s2468-2667(17)30118-4

Huntjens, R. J. C., Wessel, I., Ostafin, B. D., Boelen, P. A., Behrens, F., & van Minnen, A. (2016). Trauma-related self-defining memories and future goals in dissociative identity order. *Behavior Research and Therapy, 87,* 216–224. Doi:10.1016/j.brat.2016.10.002

Infurna, F. L., & Jayawickreme, E. (2019). Fixing the growth illusion: New directions for research in resilience and posttraumatic growth. *Current Directions in Psychological Science, 28,* 152–158. Doi:10.1177/0963721419827017

Infurna, F. J., & Luthar, S. S. (2016a). Resilience to major life stressors is not as common as thought. *Perspectives on Psychological Science, 11,* 175–194. Doi:10.1177/1745691615621271

Infurna, F. J., & Luthar, S. S. (2016b). Resilience has been and will be always be, but rates declare are inevitably suspect: Reply to Galatzer-Levy & Bonanno (2016). *Perspectives on Psychological Science, 11,* 199–201. Doi:10.1177/1745691615621281

Infurna, F. J., & Luthar, S. S. (2018). Re-evaluating the notion that resilience is commonplace: A review and distillation of directions for future research, practice, and policy. *Clinical Psychology Review, 65,* 43–56. Doi:10.1016/j.cpr.2018.07.003

Iremonger, L. (1970). *The fiery chariot: A study of British prime ministers and the search for love.* London, UK: Secker & Warburg.

James, S. A. (1994). John Henryism and the health of African-Americans. *Culture, Medicine and Psychiatry, 18*, 163–182. Doi:10.1007/bf01379448

James, S. A., Hartnett, S., & Kalsbeek, W. D. (1983). John Henryism and blood differences among black men. *Journal of Behavioral Medicine, 6*, 259–278. Doi:10.1007/bf01315113

Janoff-Bulman, R. (1989). Assumptive worlds and the stress of traumatic events: Applications of the schema construct. *Social Cognition, 7*, 113–136. Doi:10.1521/soco.1989.7.2.113

Janoff-Bulman, R. (1992). *Shattered assumptions: Towards a new psychology of trauma.* New York: Free Press.

Jayawickreme, E., & Blackie, L. E. R. (2014). Post-traumatic growth as positive personality change: Evidence, controversies and future directions. *European Journal of Personality, 28*, 312–331. Doi:10.1002/per.1963

Jimjoe bobjacktom. (2013, January 18). *Part 6 — HD Oprah Lance Armstrong interview—Win at all costs.mp4 [Video file].* Retrieved from www.youtube.com/watch?v=MhSyct1gqz8

Jones, G., Gittins, M., & Hardy, L. (2009). Creating an environment where high performance is inevitable and sustainable: The high performance environment model. *Annual Review of High Performance Coaching and Consulting, 1*, 139–149.

Joseph, S., & Linley, A. (2005). Positive adjustment to threatening events: An organismic valuing theory of growth through adversity. *Review of General Psychology, 9*, 262–280. Doi:10.1037/1089-2680.9.3.262

Joseph, S., Murphy, D., & Regel, S. (2012). An affective-cognitive processing model of posttraumatic growth. *Clinical Psychology & Psychotherapy, 19*, 316–324. Doi:10.1002/cpp.1798

Kalisch, R., Müller, M. B., & Tüscher, O. (2015). A conceptual framework for the neurobiological study of resilience. *Behavioral and Brain Sciences, 38*, 1–79. Doi:10.1017/s0140525x1400082x

Kent, M., Davis, M. C., & Reich, J. W. (Eds.). (2014). *The resilience handbook: Approaches to stress and trauma.* New York: Routledge.

Kumar, U. (Ed.). (2017). *The Routledge international handbook of psychosocial resilience.* Abingdon, UK: Routledge.

Linley, P. A., & Joseph, S. (2004). Positive change following trauma and adversity: A review. *Journal of Traumatic Stress, 17*, 11–21. Doi:10.1023/b:jots.0000014671.27856.7e

Liu, R. T. (2015). A developmentally informed perspective on the relation between stress and psychopathology: When the problem with stress is that there is not enough. *Journal of Abnormal Psychology, 124*, 80–92. Doi:10.1037/abn0000043

Lomas, T., & Ivtzan, I. (2016). Second wave positive psychology: Exploring the positive-negative dialectics of wellbeing. *Journal of Happiness Studies, 17*, 1753–1768. Doi:10.1007/s10902-015-9668-y

Low, W. R., Sandercock, G., Freeman, P., Winter, M. E., Butt, J., & Maynard, I. (in press). Pressure training for performance domains: A meta-analysis. *Sport, Exercise and Performance Psychology.* Doi:10.1037/spy0000202

Ludwig, A. M. (1995). *The price of greatness: Resolving the creativity and madness controversy.* New York: Guildford Press.

Luthar, S. S., & Cicchetti, D. (2000). The construct of resilience: Implications for interventions and social policies. *Development and Psychopathology, 12,* 857–885. Doi:10.1017/s0954579400004156

Luthar, S. S., Cicchetti, D., & Becker, B. (2000). The construct of resilience: A critical evaluation and guidelines for future work. *Child Development, 71,* 543–562. Doi:10.1111/1467-8624.00164

Machida, M., Irwin, B., & Feltz, D. (2013). Resilience in competitive athletes with spinal cord injury: The role of sport participation. *Qualitative Health Research, 23,* 1054–1065. Doi:10.1177/1049732313493673

Macur, J. (2014). *Cycle of lies: The fall of Lance Armstrong.* New York: Harper Collins.

Maercker, A., & Zoellner, T. (2004). The Janus face of self-perceived growth: Toward a two-component model of posttraumatic growth. *Psychological Inquiry, 15,* 41–48.

Mangelsdorf, J., & Eid, M. (2015). What makes a thriver? Unifying the concepts of posttrumatic and postestecstatic growth. *Frontiers in Psychology, 6,* 813. Doi:10.3389/fpsyg.2015.00813

Martin, S. (1996). Support and challenge: Conflicting or complementary aspects of mentoring novice teachers? *Teachers and Teaching: Theory and Practice, 2,* 41–56. Doi:10.1080/1354060960020104

Massey, W. V., & Williams, T. (2019). Sporting activities for individuals who experienced trauma during their youth: A meta-study. *Qualitative Health Research, 30,* 73–87. Doi:10.1177/1049732319849563

Masten, A. S. (2001). Ordinary magic: Resilience processes in development. *American Psychologist, 56,* 227–238. Doi:10.1037/0003-066x.56.3.227

McClelland, D. C. (1965). Toward a theory of motive acquisition. *American Psychologist, 20,* 321–333. Doi:10.1037/h0022225

McClelland, D. C., Atkinson, J. W., Clark, R. A., & Lowell, E. L. (1953). *The achievement motive.* New York: Appleton-Century-Crofts.

Miller, F., Osbahr, H., Boyd, E., Thomalla, F., Bharwani, S., Ziervogel, G., . . . Nelson, D. (2010). Resilience and vulnerability: Complementary or conflicting concepts? *Ecology and Society, 15,* 11. Doi:10.5751/es-03378-150311

Morgan, P. B. C., Fletcher, D., & Sarkar, M. (2015). Understanding team resilience in the world's best athletes: A case study of a rugby union world cup winning team. *Psychology of Sport and Exercise, 16,* 91–100. Doi:10.1016/j.psychsport.2014.08.007

Morgan, P. B. C., Fletcher, D., & Sarkar, M. (2017). Recent developments in team resilience in elite sport. *Current Opinion in Psychology, 16,* 159–164. Doi:10.1016/j.copsyc.2017.05.013

Norris, F. H., Tracy, M., & Galea, S. (2009). Looking for resilience: Understanding the longitudinal trajectories. *Social Science & Medicine, 68,* 2190–2198. Doi:10.1016/j.socscimed.2009.03.043

O'Boyle, E., & Aguinas, H. (2012). The best and the rest: Revisiting the norm of normality of individual performance. *Personnel Psychology, 65,* 79–119. Doi:10.1111/j.1744-6570.2011.01239.x

Ogawa, J. R., Sroufe, A., Weinfield, N. S., Carlson, E. A., & Egeland, B. (1997). Development and the fragmented self: Longitudinal study of dissociative symptomatology in a nonclinical sample. *Development and Psychopathology, 9,* 855–879. Doi:10.1017/s0954579497001478

Olszewski-Kubilius, P. (2000). The transition from childhood giftedness to adult creative productiveness: Psychological characteristics and social supports. *Roeper Review, 2,* 65–71. Doi:10.1080/02783190009554068

O'Reilly, E. (2014). *The race to truth: Blowing the whistle on Lance Armstrong and cycling's doping culture.* London, UK: Transworld.

Park, C. L., Cohen, L. H., & Murch, R. L. (1996). Assessment and prediction of stress-related growth. *Journal of Personality, 64,* 71–105. Doi:10.1111/j.1467-6494. 1996.tb00815.x

Pashler, H. (1998). *The psychology of attention.* Cambridge, MA: MIT Press.

Piirto, J. (1992). *Understanding those who create.* Dayton, OH: Ohio Psychology Press.

Rees, T., Hardy, L., Güllich, A., Abernethy, B., Côté, J., Woodman, T., . . . Warr, C. (2016). The Great British medalists project: A review of current knowledge on the development of the world's best sporting talent. *Sports Medicine, 48,* 1041–1058. Doi:10.1007/s40279-017-0804-1

Reiner, M., Niermann, C., Jekauc, D., & Woll, A. (2013). Long-term health benefits of physical activity—A systematic review of longitudinal studies. *BMC Public Health, 13,* 1–9. Doi:10.1186/1471-2458-13-813

Reuben, A., Moffitt, T. E., Caspi, A., Belsky, D. W., Harrington, H., Schroeder, F., . . . Danese, A. (2016). Lest we forget: Comparing retrospective and prospective assessments of adverse childhood experiences in the prediction of adult health. *Journal of Child Psychology and Psychiatry, 57,* 1103–1112. Doi:10.1111/jcpp.12621

Rice, S. M., Purcell, R., De Silva, S., Mawren, D., McGorry, P. D., & Parker, A. G. (2016). The mental health of elite athletes: A narrative systematic review. *Sports Medicine, 46,* 1333–1353. Doi:10.1007/s40279-016-0492-2

Ringrose, J. L. (2018). *Understanding and treating dissociative identity disorder (or multiple personality disorder).* Abingdon, UK: Routledge.

Rinn, A. N., & Bishop, J. (2015). Gifted adults: A systematic review and analysis of the literature. *Gifted Child Quarterly, 59,* 213–235. Doi:10.1177/0016986 215600795

Rodewald, F., Dell, P. F., Wilhelm-Gossling, C., & Gast, U. (2011). Are major dissociative disorders characterized by a qualitatively different kind of dissociation? *Journal of Trauma Dissociation, 12,* 9–24. Doi:10.1080/15299732.2010.51 4847

Roepke, A. M. (2013). Gains without pains? Growth after positive events. *The Journal of Positive Psychology, 8,* 280–291. Doi:10.1080/17439760.2013 .791715

Russell, J. S. (2015). Resilience. *Journal of the Philosophy of Sport, 42,* 159–183. Doi :10.1080/00948705.2015.1009838

Rutten, B. P. F., Hammels, C., Geschwind, N., Menne-Lothmann, C., Pishva, E., Schruers, K., . . . Wichers, M. (2013). Resilience in mental health: Linking psychological and neurobiological perspectives. *Acta Psychiatrica Scandinavica, 128,* 3–20. Doi:10.1111/acps.12095

Rutter, M. (1981). Stress, coping and development: Some issues and some questions. *Journal of Child Psychology and Psychiatry and Allied Disciplines, 22,* 323–356. Doi:10.1111/j.1469-7610.1981.tb00560.x

Rutter, M. (1985). Resilience in the face of adversity: Protective factors and resistance to psychiatric disorders. *British Journal of Psychiatry, 147*, 598–611. Doi:10.1192/bjp.147.6.598

Rutter, M. (1987). Psychosocial resilience and protective mechanisms. *American Journal of Orthopsychiatry, 57*, 316–331. Doi:10.1111/j.1939-0025.1987. tb03541.x

Sameroff, A., Gutman, L. M., & Peck, S. C. (2003). Adaptation among youth facing multiple risks: Prospective research findings. In S. S. Luthar (Ed.), *Resilience and vulnerability: Adaptation in the context of childhood adversities* (pp. 364–392). New York: Cambridge University Press.

Sanford, N. (1967). *Where colleges fail: A study of the student as a person.* San Francisco, CA: Jossey-Bass.

Sarkar, M., & Fletcher, D. (2013). How should we measure psychological resilience in sport performers? *Measurement in Physical Education and Exercise Science, 17*, 264–280. Doi:10.1080/1091367x.2013.805141

Sarkar, M., & Fletcher, D. (2014a). Ordinary magic, extraordinary performance: Psychological resilience and thriving in high achievers. *Sport, Exercise and Performance Psychology, 3*, 46–60. Doi:10.1037/spy0000003

Sarkar, M., & Fletcher, D. (2014b). Psychological resilience in sport performers: A narrative review of stressors and protective factors. *Journal of Sports Sciences, 32*, 1419–1434. Doi:10.1080/02640414.2014.901551

Sarkar, M., & Fletcher, D. (2017). Adversity-related experiences are essential for Olympic success: Additional evidence and considerations. In V. Walsh, M. Wilson, & B. Parkin (Eds.), *Sport and the brain: The science of preparing, enduring and winning, Part A* (pp. 159–165). London, UK: Academic Press.

Sarkar, M., Fletcher, D., & Brown, D. J. (2015). What doesn't kill me . . . : Adversity-related experiences are vital in the development of superior Olympic performance. *Journal of Science and Medicine in Sport, 18*, 475–479. Doi:10.1016/j. jsams.2014.06.010

Savage, J., Collins, D., & Cruickshank, A. (2017). Exploring traumas in the development of talent: What are they, what do they do, and what do they require? *Journal of Applied Sport Psychology, 29*, 101–117. Doi:10.1080/10413200.2016.1 194910

Seery, M. D. (2011). Resilience: A silver lining to experiencing adverse life events? *Current Directions in Psychological Science, 20*, 390–394.

Seery, M. D., & Quinton, W. J. (2016). Understanding resilience: From negative life events to everyday stressors. *Advances in Experimental Psychology, 54*, 181–245.

Shumaker, S. A., & Brownell, A. (1984). Toward a theory of social support: Closing conceptual gaps. *Journal of Social Issues, 40*, 11–36. Doi:10.1111/j.1540-4560.1984. tb01105.x

Simonton, D. K. (2000). Creativity: Cognitive, personal, developmental, and social aspects. *American Psychologist, 55*, 151–158. Doi:10.1037/0003-066x.55.1.151

Simonton, D. K. (2014). The mad-genius paradox: Can creative people be more mentally healthy but highly creative people more mentally ill? *Perspectives on Psychological Science, 9*, 470–480. Doi:10.1177/1745691614543973

Simonton, D. K. (2016). Reverse engineering genius: Historiometric studies of superlative talent. *Annals of the New York Academy of Sciences, 1377*, 3–9. Doi:10.1111/nyas.13054

Smith, B. W., Tooley, E. M., Christopher, P. J., & Kay, V. S. (2010). Resilience as the ability to bounce back from stress: A neglected personal resource. *Journal of Positive Psychology, 5*, 166–176. Doi:10.1080/17439760.2010.482186

Standing, L. G., & Ringo, P. (2016). Parental loss and eminence: Is there a critical period for the Phaeton Effect? *North American Journal of Psychology, 18*, 147–160.

Tamminen, K. A., Holt, N. L., & Neely, K. C. (2013). Exploring adversity and the potential for growth among elite female athletes. *Psychology of Sport and Exercise, 14*, 28–36. Doi:10.1016/j.psychsport.2012.07.002

Tamminen, K., & Neely, K. C. (2016). Positive growth in sport. In N. L. Holt (Ed.), *Positive youth development through sport* (2nd ed., pp. 193–204). New York: Routledge.

Tedeschi, R. G., & Blevins, C. L. (2017). Posttraumatic growth: A pathway to resilience. In U. Kumar (Ed.), *The Routledge international handbook of psychosocial resilience* (2nd ed., pp. 324–333). Abingdon, UK: Routledge.

Tedeschi, R. G., & Calhoun, L. G. (1995). *Trauma & transformation: Growing in the aftermath of suffering*. Thousand Oaks, CA: Sage.

Tedeschi, R. G., & Calhoun, L. G. (2004). Posttraumatic growth: Conceptual foundations and empirical evidence. *Psychological Inquiry, 15*, 1–18. Doi:10.1207/s15327965pli1501_02

Tedeschi, R. G., Shakespeare-Finch, J., Taku, K., & Calhoun, L. G. (2018). *Posttraumatic growth: Theory, research, and applications*. Abingdon, UK: Routledge.

Therival, W. A. (1999). Why are eccentrics not eminently creative? *Creativity Research Journal, 12*, 47–55. Doi:10.1207/s15326934crj1201_6

Trotta, A., Murray, R. M., & Fisher, H. L. (2015). The impact of childhood adversity on the persistence of psychotic symptoms: A systematic review and meta-analysis. *Psychological Medicine, 45*, 2481–2498. Doi:10.1017/s0033291715000574

Udry, E., Gould, D., Bridges, D., & Beck, L. (1997). Down but not out: Athlete responses to season-ending injuries. *Journal of Sport and Exercise Psychology, 19*, 229–248. Doi:10.1123/jsep.19.3.229

Updegraff, J. A., & Taylor, S. E. (2000). From vulnerability to growth: Positive and negative effects of stressful life events. In J. Harvey & E. Miller (Eds.), *Loss and trauma: General and close relationship perspectives* (pp. 3–28). Philadelphia, PA: Brunner-Routledge.

Uphill, M. A., & Hemmings, B. (2017). Vulnerability: Ripples from reflections on mental toughness. *The Sport Psychologist, 31*, 299–307. Doi:10.1123/tsp.2016-0034

Wagstaff, C. R. D., Sarkar, M., Davidson, C. L., & Fletcher, D. (2017). Resilience in sport: A critical review of psychological processes, sociocultural influences, and organizational dynamics. In C. R. D. Wagstaff (Ed.), *An organizational psychology of sport: Key issues and practical applications* (pp. 120–149). Abingdon, UK: Routledge.

Walberg, H. J., Strykowski, B. F., Rovai, E., & Hung, S. S. (1984). Exceptional performance. *Review of Educational Research, 54*, 87–112. Doi:10.3102/00346543054001087

Walsh, D. (2012). *Seven deadly sins: My pursuit of Lance Armstrong*. New York: Simon & Schuster.

Ward, K., Trautvetter, L., & Braskamp, L. (2005). Putting students first: Creating a climate of support and challenge. *Journal of College and Character, 6,* 1–6. Doi:10.2202/1940-1639.1492

Watson, N. J. (2007). 'Winning at all costs' in modern sport: Reflections on pride and humility in the writing of C. S. Lewis. In J. Parry, S. Robinson, N. J. Watson, & M. Nesti (Eds.), *Sport and spirituality: An introduction* (pp. 61–79). Abingdon, UK: Routledge.

Wood, A. W., Barker, J. B., & Turner, M. J. (2018). Rational emotive behaviour therapy to help young athletes build resilience and deal with adversity. In C. Knight, C. G. Harwood, & D. Gould (Eds.), *Sport psychology for young athletes* (pp. 265–2760). Abingdon, UK: Routledge.

Zoellner, T., & Maercker, A. (2006). Posttraumatic growth in clinical psychology— A critical review and introduction of a two component model. *Clinical Psychology Review, 26,* 626–653. Doi:10.1016/j.cpr.2006.01.008

10 Personality

Sylvain Laborde, Sinikka Heisler, and Emma Mosley

Introduction

Imagine a swimmer on the blocks, moments before their dive into the water, or a soccer player standing at the penalty spot waiting to take a crucial shot. Spectators are watching, cameras are rolling, and everyone is waiting for the athlete to show his/her best performance. Even though both of them have done this countless times in training and competition, they feel the pressure. Athletes can perceive pressure due to competitive and organizational demands (Hanton, Fletcher, & Coughlan, 2005; Hill, Hanton, Matthews, & Fleming, 2010; see also Chapter 1), and how athletes deal with upcoming stress and perceived pressure is diverse. For some athletes, this pressure helps to increase performance, while for others, it might lead to a performance drop (Baumeister, 1984). Research has labeled positive performance outcomes under pressure "clutch performance" or "excelling under pressure" (Hill et al., 2010; Otten, 2016). In contrast, "choking under pressure" defines negative performance outcomes when athletes are confronted with stress (Baumeister, 1984). The resulting performance can be best described as a continuum ranging from choking to excelling under pressure (Geukes, Mesagno, Hanrahan, & Kellmann, 2013). Several explanations have been proposed and empirically tested, to gain a better understanding of performance variability due to the perception of pressure. The most prominent approaches are the Self-focus Model and the Distraction Model (Baumeister & Showers, 1986). Both are addressing the intrapersonal psychological processes that are affected by situational characteristics (i.e., pressure). Within those intrapersonal psychological processes, personality and executive functions play a particular role. The aim of this chapter is to define personality, to provide an overview of personality research in sport as it relates to stress, and to clarify the influence of personality on the relationship between executive functions and performance when athletes perform under pressure.

Personality

Personality is defined as "psychological qualities that contribute to an individual's enduring and distinctive patterns of feeling, thinking, and behaving" (Pervin & Cervone, 2010). Personality refers to stable patterns; however, it is also subject to change and development across the lifespan (Caspi & Roberts, 2001; Caspi, Roberts, & Shiner, 2005; Roberts, Walton, & Viechtbauer, 2006) and can be specifically developed in line with targeted interventions (Roberts & Woodman, 2017). The relevance of personality traits for sporting performance and well-being has been considered for many years in the history of sport psychology (Eysenck, Nias, & Cox, 1982; Morgan, 1980). Several reviews have contributed to establish understanding of how personality functions within sport psychology and sport and exercise phenomena, with findings related to both performance and well-being (Allen, Greenlees, & Jones, 2013; Rhodes & Smith, 2006; Roberts & Woodman, 2015, 2016, 2017; Roberts, Woodman, & Sedikides, 2018). Themes regarding performance showed that elite athletes tend to display higher levels of conscientiousness and lower levels of neuroticism (Allen et al., 2013). Themes regarding well-being, triggered by involvement in physical activity (Blackburn et al., 2020), highlighted a positive relationship with extraversion and conscientiousness, and negative relationships with neuroticism (Rhodes & Smith, 2006). Research on personality in sport and exercise started in the first half of the 20th century, where the focus was first to identify particular traits among athletes (Fleming, 1934). In this study, athletic females' personality traits were not found to differ from personality traits of non-athletic females. Research then progressed to understand the bidirectional relationship between sport and exercise and personality, whether specific personality traits were related to the practice of specific sports (gravitation hypothesis), or whether the practice of specific sports influence personality traits (change hypothesis) (Allen et al., 2013). So far no conclusive evidence was put forward for either hypothesis, given the lack of longitudinal studies. However, some relationships would be interesting to further investigate, like the associations found in a meta-analysis regarding the participants engaging in risk-taking sports, displaying a higher degree of extraversion and sensation-seeking (McEwan, Boudreau, Curran, & Rhodes, 2019).

The main conceptualization for personality traits is represented by the Five-Factor Model, also known as the Big Five Model (McCrae & John, 1992). This framework considers that personality is best assessed through five broad trait dimensions (openness, conscientiousness, agreeableness, extraversion, and neuroticism). These five dimensions have already shown relationships with stress (Carver & Connor-Smith, 2010), well-being (DeNeve & Cooper, 1998), and performance (Allen et al., 2013;

Barrick, Mount, & Judge, 2001) in many different domains. Despite the evidence and the established relationships, the Big Five is not without criticisms. The key criticisms are centered around its absence of a theoretical background—the Big Five is based on a factorial analysis—and does not adequately capture the diversity of behaviors, thoughts, and feelings observed in sport and exercise phenomena (Laborde, Allen, Katschak, Mattonet, & Lachner, 2019). Consequently, it is necessary to consider other personality traits (Laborde & Allen, 2016; Laborde et al., 2019; Laborde, Breuer-Weissborn, & Dosseville, 2013; Mosley & Laborde, 2015; Roberts & Woodman, 2017). Finally, regarding assessment, if the most common way to assess personality traits is questionnaires (Laborde et al., 2019), sometimes broader personality perspectives are considered, for example, characteristic adaptations and life narrative through interviews to achieve a more complete picture of human complexity (Coulter, Mallett, Singer, & Gucciardi, 2016; McAdams & Pals, 2006).

A measure typically used in sport to assess the Big Five is the NEO-FFI (Costa & McCrae, 1992), employed in several studies with athletic samples (e.g., Allen, Frings, & Hunter, 2012; Allen, Greenlees, & Jones, 2014). For personality traits distinct from the Big Five, specific instruments are adopted, such as the Bar-On Inventory (Bar-On, 2002) and the Trait Emotional Intelligence Questionnaire (Petrides, 2009) to measure emotional intelligence. Given using instruments developed for the general population with athletic samples may present some conceptual validity issues (Allen et al., 2013), it is recommended that scholars assess the validity and factor structure of measures within athletic populations. Following with the example of emotional intelligence questionnaires used with athletic samples (Laborde, Dosseville, & Allen, 2016), the factor structure of well-established questionnaires has been investigated within athletic populations, like with the Bar-On Inventory (Stanimirovic & Hanrahan, 2012) and the Trait Emotional Intelligence Questionnaire (Laborde, Dosseville, Guillén, & Chávez, 2014; Laborde, Guillén, & Watson, 2017).

Given personality is reflected in patterns of feelings, thoughts, and behaviors (Pervin & Cervone, 2010), it is very likely to be linked to the processes underpinning our feelings, thoughts, and behaviors, driven by the so-called executive functions (Diamond, 2013). In the next section, we detail what executive functions are, before specifying their links with a range of personality traits, summarized in Figure 10.1.

Executive Functions

Executive functions serve as an umbrella term to encompass the goal-oriented control functions of the prefrontal cortex (Best, Miller, & Jones, 2009; see also Chapter 5). Several definitions and conceptualizations coexist (for an overview, see Jurado & Rosselli, 2007). Diamond

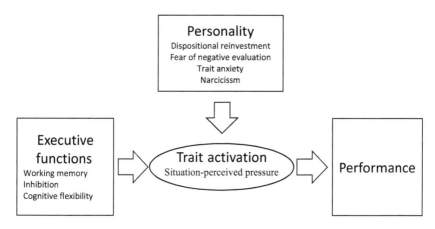

Figure 10.1 The Influence of Personality on the Relationship Between Executive Functions and Performance via Trait Activation

(2013) distinguishes between three core executive functions: working memory, inhibition, and cognitive flexibility. Those three core executive functions are involved in almost every aspect of sporting performance (e.g., thinking before moving, refreshing information within short term memory, resisting temptations, and staying focused). A more specific example would be the control of gaze, whereby the three executive functions influence an athlete's ability to master a steady gaze (Ducrocq, Wilson, Smith, & Derakshan, 2017). Specifically, to fixate the gaze "for long periods of time under high levels of pressure should not only necessitate good resistance to distraction (i.e., inhibition), but also efficient within-task attentional control (i.e., shifting) and the maintenance of accurate representations of non-fixated targets (i.e., updating)" (p. 5; see also Chapter 5). In the last two decades executive functions have received a lot of attention in the context of sports (Scharfen & Memmert, 2019; Voss, Kramer, Basak, Prakash, & Roberts, 2010). As executive functions are heavily involved in controlled cognitive functioning, the factors which influence this, both positively and negatively, are of major interest in performance research (Diamond, 2013), and in this chapter, we focus on the influence of certain personality traits under pressure.

Trait Activation

The personality of an athlete has a strong influence on performance and may predict behavior to a certain extent in particular situations (Allen, Vella, & Laborde, 2015; Laborde et al., 2019). As noted previously, personality is understood to be stable in nature and thereby cross-situational (Pervin & Cervone, 2010); however, there is also evidence that behavior may differ across situations. This is in line with previous personality theory, such as with Lewin's equation, stating that behavior is ultimately a function of the person interacting within his/her environment (Lewin, 1936). This idea was renewed at the beginning of the 21st century with the introduction of the concept of trait activation (Fleeson, 2001; Geukes, Mesagno, Hanrahan, & Kellmann, 2012; Tett & Guterman, 2000). Even though situational demands were already considered in personality research, their importance was not explicitly emphasized. Research on trait activation does not disagree on the stability assumption, but adds a new facet. Based on the trait activation concept, a person-situation interaction has to be considered, and the way personality shapes behavior will consequently depend on the context (Geukes et al., 2012). The concept of trait activation has been recently evidenced in the sports context (Geukes, Harvey, Trezise, & Mesagno, 2017; Geukes et al., 2012).

Returning to the example of the swimmer standing on the starting block. During practice, they do not perceive any pressure and can solely focus on the task, but when the situation changes and spectators are around, their focus may switch inwardly to themselves. The personality trait fear of negative evaluations (FNE) is suddenly activated and leads to a drop in performance, because the situation has changed. Geukes and colleagues (2013) tested this paradigm and showed that in a private high pressure condition self-focus traits got activated by situational demands, whereas in a low-pressure condition this was not the case. When assessing differing pressurized situations such as private, mixed, and public, a similar result was found in that with differing pressurized situational demands, self-focused traits were systematically activated (Geukes et al., 2013). Importantly, the traits have to be situation-relevant, meaning that in the aforementioned example, other traits such as openness to new experiences might not be activated because it is not relevant in this particular situation (Tett & Guterman, 2000).

Several studies have tested the concept of trait activation in the sports context, mostly related to stress and performance. The following list contains the psychological traits that have been investigated:

- **Athletic identity**—the degree (i.e., strength and exclusivity) to which individuals identify with the role of an athlete (Brewer, Van Raalte, & Linder, 1993; Geukes et al., 2017). Individuals scoring high on athletic identity are suggested to have a higher tendency to choke under pressure, although this still needs to be demonstrated experimentally (Geukes et al., 2017).
- **Dispositional reinvestment**—described in depth in the subsequent sections (Geukes et al., 2017; Kinrade, Jackson, & Ashford, 2010; Laborde, Furley, & Schempp, 2015).

- **Fear of negative evaluation**—described in depth in the subsequent sections (Geukes et al., 2017; Mesagno, Harvey, & Janelle, 2012).
- **Narcissism**—narcissist individuals are characterized by inflated self-appraisal, chronic self-glorification strivings, and their lack of concern for others except as sources of admiration (Wallace, Baumeister, & Vohs, 2005). Narcissists perform better when self-enhancement opportunities are high rather than low (Wallace & Baumeister, 2002), which may be the case when playing in front of a supportive audience under pressure (Wallace et al., 2005).
- **Private self-consciousness**—refers to the attention one gives to one's thought and feeling processes (Fenigstein, Scheier, & Buss, 1975; Geukes et al., 2013; Wang, Marchant, Morris, & Gibbs, 2004). Under private high-pressure situations (i.e., with a cover story outlining that the sporting task participants would undertake had been found to predict academic success and a monetary incentive but with no audience), private self-consciousness was associated with performance decrements (Geukes et al., 2013).

In the following sections, we focus on FNE and dispositional reinvestment, given their close interplay with executive functions (Kinrade et al., 2010; Laborde, Furley, et al., 2015).

Fear of Negative Evaluation

In the sports domain, performance evaluation is ubiquitous. Athletes are getting scouted for talent, contractually bounded to a club, and supported by fans. All of these situations involve subjective judgment of their talents, achievements, and development. Hence, athletes are confronted with many external expectations and evaluations (Left & Hoyle, 1995) and how individuals cope with this might differ. Watson and Friend (1970) defined FNE as the tendency to experience "apprehension about others' evaluations, distress over their negative evaluations, avoidance of evaluative situations, and the expectations that others would evaluate oneself negatively" (p. 449). Geukes and colleagues (2017) further described it as a cognitive sub-facet of competitive anxiety.

Personality traits that belong to or are closely bound to (competitive) anxiety are conceptually related to the Distraction Model of Choking (Mesagno, Harvey, & Janelle, 2012; Wang et al., 2004; Wine, 1971). Mesagno and colleagues (2012) studied the degree to which FNE as a personality trait can predict choking under pressure. Experienced basketball players performed basketball shots from different areas on the court under high- or low-pressure conditions. Results indicate that athletes high in FNE showed a significant increase in anxiety, and at the same time, a significant decrease in performance. However, athletes with low FNE only showed minimal changes between pressure situations, supporting the hypothesized influence of trait activation in a pressurized situation. In another study, Geukes and colleagues (2017) assessed experienced basketball players in a real-world high-pressure situation, namely during 12 basketball games. In comparison to a private low-pressure situation in the laboratory, athletes high on FNE showed a significant performance decrease in competition. These results again underpin the influence of self-presentation related concerns (such as FNE) in public pressure situations (Geukes et al., 2017). Further research should investigate the influence of FNE on executive functions during both low- and high-pressure situations, in order to clarify the mechanisms underlying its influence on performance.

Dispositional Reinvestment

The player is stood at the penalty spot during the penalty shoot-out of the Champions League final. If he/she scores, his/her team will win the Champions League, and if he/she misses, they will be out of the competition. The aim is to display a successful performance and thereby become the hero of the team. Due to this, the player starts to actively concentrate on his/her stance and thinks about their foot position and where to aim. As a result, he/she missed the goal by miles, which has never happened during practice.

What happened here could be due to a higher dispositional tendency to *reinvest*. Reinvestment is defined as the tendency to consciously control a well-learned skill under pressure (Masters, Polman, & Hammond, 1993). Most importantly, to reinvest means to disrupt the automatized processing by relating to explicit knowledge (Geukes et al., 2017). The result is that athletes revert back to a novice-like state in which all expertise is diminished. This can be explained by the fact that athletes are consciously controlling skills when facing stressful situations, which makes those skills more fragile and more susceptible to disruption. Another explanation is that the explicit processes used when reinvesting under pressure consume working memory, and the reduced function of working memory then debilitates automatic processing, causing skill breakdown under pressure (Masters & Maxwell, 2004). Reinvestment is considered as a stable disposition comparable to a personality trait and is assessed via trait instruments with the movement-specific (Masters, Eves, & Maxwell, 2005) and decision-specific (Kinrade et al., 2010) reinvestment scales. The trait nature of reinvestment has been further confirmed by test-retest reliability and convergent validity analyses with related personality traits (Laborde, Dosseville, & Kinrade, 2014; Laborde, Musculus, et al., 2015). Reinvestment has gained a large amount of attention in sports, accounting for performance variance in top-level athletes in different sports such as golf (Klämpfl, Lobinger, & Raab, 2013; Lobinger, Klämpfl, Altenmüller, & Altenmüller, 2014), basketball (Gray, 2004;

Kinrade, Jackson, & Ashford, 2015), and soccer (Chell, Graydon, Crowley, & Child, 2007).

The reinvestment definition of Masters and Maxwell (2004) emphasizes the importance of considering executive functions, particularly that of working memory. Reinvestment is defined as the "manipulation of conscious, explicit, rule-based knowledge, by working memory, to control the mechanics of one's movements during motor output" (p. 208). This relationship was further supported by the work of Laborde, Furley, et al. (2015) who investigated the link between reinvestment and working memory performance in different pressurized conditions (i.e., low vs. high). Additionally, the role of physiological measures, namely heart rate variability was addressed. Findings indicate that reinvestment was related to a drop in working memory performance under high pressure, which was also associated to a decrease in cardiac vagal activity, as measured with heart rate variability. Cardiac vagal activity indexes the activity of the vagus nerve regulating cardiac functioning and reflects self-regulation abilities of the individual linked with executive functions (Laborde, Mosley, & Mertgen, 2018; Laborde, Mosley, & Thayer, 2017). These results are in line with other studies, showing the negative influence of reinvestment in high pressure situations on physiological parameters (Mosley, Laborde, & Kavanagh, 2017, 2018a) as well as cognitive decision-making performance (Laborde, Raab, & Kinrade, 2014).

Choking Under Pressure: Links With Personality

Research on choking under pressure has considered different explanations, with the Distraction Model and the Self-focus Model being the most prominent standpoints (Beilock & Gray, 2007; Lewis & Linder, 1997). The Distraction Model suggest performance drop occurs because athletes become distracted due to task-irrelevant thoughts (see also Chapter 5). Through the increase of physical arousal, athletes shift their attention to irrelevant cues originating internally (e.g., negative thoughts and fear) or externally (e.g., the crowd). The aforementioned trait of FNE is directly linked to this hypothesis. It is proposed that the anxious thought about getting evaluated by others results in a distraction (Gröpel & Mesagno, 2017; Mesagno et al., 2012; Wine, 1971).

Within the Self-focus Model, researchers emphasize the role of the shift from automatized to controlled processing (e.g., Baumeister, 1984; Jackson, Ashford, & Norsworthy, 2016; Otten, 2016). When athletes perceive pressure they are directing attention to the task execution itself, aiming to put more effort into the task execution. However, well-skilled athletes have already performed task-relevant movements several times so that there is no need of conscious control. When those processes are then monitored or controlled, it leads to substandard performance (Geukes et al., 2012). The self-focus explanation was supported by several empirical studies (Beilock & Carr, 2001; Gucciardi & Dimmock, 2008; Mesagno, Marchant, & Morris, 2009). Dispositional reinvestment and its influence in explaining choking under pressure has been related to the Self-focus Model (Kinrade et al., 2010; Masters et al., 1993) and was supported by empirical evidence (Geukes et al., 2017; Laborde, Dosseville, & Kinrade, 2014; Mosley et al., 2018a). Both Distraction and Self-focus Models can account for decrements in executive functions (Furley & Memmert, 2010). For instance, the Distraction Model can explain why pressure-induced worries caused working memory deficits, by thinking about a dual task. According to Hill and colleagues (2010), resources are redistributed in order to cope with negative thoughts and thereby taken from task-relevant to task-irrelevant cognition. Interestingly, a self-focus appears not be detrimental per se, but can be beneficial in performing tasks that require working memory as part of their execution, or when someone learns a skill, like for novices. In contrast, for tasks that do not require any information updating and the skills required are well learnt (i.e., proceduralized skills), a self-focus remains negative (Geukes, Mesagno, Hanrahan, & Kellmann, 2016).

The self-focus and the Distraction Model were identified to be the most prominent explanatory models of choking under pressure and have showed a direct link to executive functions. The next section aims to offer a direct approach to cope with the activation of certain personality traits leading to choking under pressure with the introduction of practical training aiming to improve executive functions.

Practical Implications

Based on the aforementioned moderator role suggested for personality, certain traits may become particularly activated under pressure and provoke performance decrements. In this sense, we could then screen athletes for these traits to identify those who may be more susceptible to performance decrements under pressure and provide specific interventions to optimally support them. In this section, we suggest a novel intervention approach to counterbalance the negative effects of trait activation by training executive functions.

Athletes spend a vast amount of time and effort in the pursuit of improving athletic skills with the aim of reaching top-level performance even when confronted with pressure. Aside from physiological and tactical abilities, cognitive skills are necessary to perform more complex tasks, especially under perceived pressure (Nicholls, Holt, Polman, & James, 2005). Recent evidence shows that adding executive function training to normal training may result in positive benefits regarding performance under pressure (Ducrocq et al., 2017; Ducrocq, Wilson, Vine, & Derakshan, 2016). Recreational tennis players participated in the study of Ducrocq et al. (2017). The experimental group underwent a 10-day working memory training program, using the adaptive Dual N-back task (Owens, Koster, & Derakshan, 2013), while the control group accomplished the non-adaptive Dual 1-Back control task. With the Dual N-back task, participants were presented with a 3×3 grid where squares appear successively, together with a letter being spoken. Participants were then required to memorize the position of the square as well as the letter spoken and then asked to respond whenever either of the audio or visual stimuli previously matched the letter spoken or the position of the square "n" back trial. The difference between the adaptive and non-adaptive version of the task lies in the fact difficulty would increase in the adaptive task according to participants' success rate, while difficulty would remain at $n = 1$ for the non-adaptive task. Results showed that working memory capacity improved for the experimental group but not for the control group, being described as near effects of adaptive working memory training. The near effects represent the effects of N-back task practice on N-back task performance. Furthermore, tennis performance in a highly pressurized task also showed transfer effects after adaptive working memory training. Specifically, the negative influence of pressure on performance seemed to be buffered by working memory improvement, through the ability to have more facilitative attentional control on the tracked target via a delayed quiet eye offset. Consequently, not only was working memory capacity improved, but also more general athletic performance (i.e., tennis performance) was shown to increase. These findings add to another study of Ducrocq et al. (2016) who found enhanced inhibitory control on cognitive and motor tasks through a computer-based inhibition training. Both results highlight the potential of executive function training in the improvement of performance on the one hand and as a buffer against pressure-induced performance decrement on the other. Although this concept is not without limitations, research on executive function development showed that transfer effects from computerized training to real-life situations are overall very low (Diamond & Ling, 2016). In order to expect benefits, training should be realized in a situation as near to the ecological settings where the improvement is desired. In the following paragraph, we recommend some training ideas that can be applied to the sports context.

With respect to working memory, an activity adapted from the Dual N-back task (Gevins & Cutillo, 1993) could be, for example, to randomly distribute colored items on the field, and then announce a specific order of colors. Athletes are then asked to run in this order correctly after they have heard the whole list. The difficulty can be adjusted by adding or removing colors or items. In team sports, this can be adapted to players passing the ball to each other. When the signal comes, the player with the ball is asked to recall the N-back player with ball possession. Difficulty can be increased with incrementing the N-back number. For inhibition, the aim is to suppress any kind of behavioral response.

For example, two players engage in passing the ball, and when player A says "right", player B has to pass the ball with the left hand or foot. When player A says "Up", player B has to pass the ball toward the lower body part of player A. To improve cognitive flexibility, it is important to switch between rules. Based on the preceding example to train inhibition, one should not only inhibit movement but also switch to a second rule, for example, when player A says "Up", player B has to pass the ball toward the lower body part of player A only when player A used the left hand or foot. Consequently, when player A says "Up" and passes the ball with the right hand or foot, player B is required to pass the ball toward the upper body part of player A.

Future Research Directions

Future research on this topic may address a couple of challenges that were identified within this chapter. First, a systematic approach has to be undertaken to investigate the influence of personality traits both under low- and high-pressure conditions, in order to identify those which may have the tendency to trigger performance decrements, following previous research designs used to test trait activation in sport and exercise settings (Geukes et al., 2012, 2017). Additionally, extant trait activation research in sports should go beyond performance and investigate as well the impact of different contexts on well-being. Second, the role of executive performance in performance decrements linked to specific trait activation under pressure should be clarified. Third, the effectiveness of executive function training programs should be tested to see whether drops in performance under high pressure when people possess certain personality traits could be avoided. Finally, the relationship with physiological variables linked to personality and executive performance under pressure, like cardiac vagal activity (Laborde, Mosley, et al., 2017; Mosley et al., 2018a), should be investigated further.

Conclusion

In summary, this chapter defined personality, provided a brief overview of some personality research that has been conducted in sport, and then focused on explaining how the activation of certain personality traits in pressure situations can lead to a decrease in performance that is related to a deterioration in executive function (see Figure 10.1). As it is usually acknowledged, perceived pressure can lead to a decrease in performance either via inducing self-focus or distraction, and training executive functions is one method which is suggested to decrease these effects. Specifically, based on the findings of Ducrocq et al. (2017), the chapter illustrated how executive function training, and specifically targeting working memory, may help to counterbalance the negative effects of trait activation under pressure. Even if those findings should be considered with caution and be replicated, it seems that this field of research opens exciting training avenues for athletes and coaches, in order to become more resilient to the pressure faced during competitions.

References

Allen, M. S., Frings, D., & Hunter, S. (2012). Personality, coping, and challenge and threat states in athletes. *International Journal of Sport & Exercise Psychology, 10,* 37–41. Doi:10.1080/1612197X.2012.682375

Allen, M. S., Greenlees, I., & Jones, M. V. (2013). Personality in sport: A comprehensive review. *International Review of Sport and Exercise Psychology, 6,* 184–208.

Allen, M. S., Greenlees, I., & Jones, M. V. (2014). Personality, counterfactual thinking, and negative emotional reactivity. *Psychology of Sport and Exercise, 15,* 147–154. Doi:10.1016/j.psychsport.2013.10.011

Allen, M. S., Vella, S. A., & Laborde, S. (2015). Health-related behaviour and personality trait development in adulthood. *Journal of Research in Personality, 59,* 104–110. Doi:10.1016/j.jrp.2015.10.005

Bar-On, R. (2002). *Bar-On Emotional Quotient Inventory: Short. Technical manual.* Toronto, Canada: Multi-Health Systems.

Barrick, M. R., Mount, M. K., & Judge, T. A. (2001). Personality and performance at the beginning of the new millennium: What do we know and where do we go next? *International Journal of Selection and Assessment, 9,* 9–30. Doi:10.1111/1468-2389.00160

Baumeister, R. F. (1984). Choking under pressure: Self-consciousness and paradoxical effects of incentives on skillful performance. *Journal of Personality and Social Psychology, 46,* 610–620. Doi:10.1037/0022-3514.46.3.610

Baumeister, R. F., & Showers, C. J. (1986). A review of paradoxical performance effects: Choking under pressure in sports and mental tests. *European Journal of Social Psychology, 16,* 361–383. Doi:10.1002/ejsp.2420160405

Beilock, S. L., & Carr, T. (2001). On the fragility of skilled performance: What governs choking under pressure? *Journal of Experimental Psychology: General, 130,* 701–725. Doi:10.1037//096-3445.130.4.701

Beilock, S. L., & Gray, R. (2007). Why do athletes choke under pressure? In G. Tenenbaum & R. Eklund (Eds.), *Handbook of sport psychology* (pp. 425–444). Hoboken, NJ: John Wiley & Sons.

Best, J. R., Miller, P. H., & Jones, L. L. (2009). Executive functions after age 5: Changes and correlates. *Developmental Review, 29,* 180–200. Doi:10.1016/j.dr.2009.05.002

Blackburn, N. E., Wilson, J. J., McMullan, II, Caserotti, P., Gine-Garriga, M., Wirth, K., . . . Tully, M. A. (2020). The effectiveness and complexity of interventions targeting sedentary behaviour across the lifespan: A systematic review and meta-analysis. *International Journal of Behavioral Nutrition and Physical Activity, 17,* 53. Doi:10.1186/s12966-020-00957-0

Brewer, B. W., Van Raalte, J. L., & Linder, D. E. (1993). Athletic identity: Hercules' muscles or Achilles heel? *International Journal of Sport Psychology, 24,* 237–254.

Carver, C. S., & Connor-Smith, J. (2010). Personality and coping. *Annual Review of Psychology, 61*, 679–704. Doi:10.1146/annurev.psych.093008.100352

Caspi, A., & Roberts, B. W. (2001). Personality development across the life course: The argument for change and continuity. *Psychological Inquiry, 12*, 49–66. Doi:10.1207/s15327965pli1202_01

Caspi, A., Roberts, B. W., & Shiner, R. L. (2005). Personality development: Stability and change. *Annual Review of Psychology, 56*, 453–484. Doi:10.1146/annurev.psych.55.090902.141913

Chell, B., Graydon, J., Crowley, P., & Child, M. (2007). Manipulated stress and dispositional reinvestment in a wall-volley task: An investigation into controlled processing. *Perceptual and Motor Skills, 97*, 435–448. Doi:10.2466/pms.97.6.435-448

Costa, P. T., & McCrae, R. R. (1992). *Revised NEO personality inventory and NEO five-factor inventory: Professional manual.* Odessa, FL: Psychological Assessment Resources, Inc.

Coulter, T. J., Mallett, C. J., Singer, J. A., & Gucciardi, D. F. (2016). Personality in sport and exercise psychology: Integrating a whole person perspective. *International Journal of Sport and Exercise Psychology, 14*, 23–41.

DeNeve, K. M., & Cooper, H. (1998). The happy personality: A meta-analysis of 137 personality traits and subjective well-being. *Psychological Bulletin, 124*, 197–229. Doi:10.1037/0033-2909.124.2.197

Diamond, A. (2013). Executive functions. *Annual Review of Psychology, 64*, 135–168. Doi:10.1146/annurev-psych-113011-143750

Diamond, A., & Ling, D. S. (2016). Conclusions about interventions, programs, and approaches for improving executive functions that appear justified and those that, despite much hype, do not. *Developmental Cognitive Neuroscience, 18*, 34–48. Doi:10.1016/J.DCN.2015.11.005

Ducrocq, E., Wilson, M., Smith, T. J., & Derakshan, N. (2017). Adaptive working memory training reduces the negative impact of anxiety on competitive motor performance. *Journal of Sport and Exercise Psychology, 39*, 412–422. Doi:10.1123/jsep.2017-0217

Ducrocq, E., Wilson, M., Vine, S., & Derakshan, N. (2016). Training attentional control improves cognitive and motor task performance. *Journal of Sport & Exercise Psychology, 38*, 521–533. Doi:10.1123/jsep.2016-0052

Eysenck, H. J., Nias, D. K., & Cox, D. N. (1982). Sport and personality. *Advances in Behaviour Research & Therapy, 4*, 1–56. Doi:10.1016/0146-6402(82)90004-2

Fenigstein, A., Scheier, M. F., & Buss, A. H. (1975). Public and private self-consciousness: Assessment and theory. *Journal of Consulting and Clinical Psychology, 43*, 522–527.

Fleeson, W. (2001). Toward a structure- and process-integrated view of personality: Traits as density distributions of dates. *Journal of Personality and Social Psychology, 80*, 1011–1027. Doi:10.1037//0022-3514.80.6.1011

Fleming, E. G. (1934). Personality and the athletic girl. *School and Society, 39*, 166–169.

Furley, P. A., & Memmert, D. (2010). The role of working memory in sport. *International Review of Sport and Exercise Psychology, 3*, 171–194. Doi:10.1080/1750984X.2010.526238

Geukes, K., Harvey, J. T., Trezise, A., & Mesagno, C. (2017). Personality and performance in real-world competitions: Testing trait activation of fear of negative evaluation, dispositional reinvestment, and athletic identity in the field. *Psychology of Sport and Exercise, 30*, 101–109. Doi:10.1016/j.psychsport.2017.02.008

Geukes, K., Mesagno, C., Hanrahan, S. J., & Kellmann, M. (2012). Testing an interactionist perspective on the relationship between personality traits and performance under public pressure. *Psychology of Sport and Exercise, 13*, 243–250. Doi:10.1016/j.psychsport.2011.12.004

Geukes, K., Mesagno, C., Hanrahan, S. J., & Kellmann, M. (2013). Performing under pressure in private: Activation of self-focus traits. *International Journal of Sport and Exercise Psychology, 11*, 11–23. Doi:10.1080/16121 97X.2012.724195

Geukes, K., Mesagno, C., Hanrahan, S. J., & Kellmann, M. (2016). Activation of self-focus and self-presentation traits under private, mixed, and public pressure. *Journal of Sport and Exercise Psychology, 35*, 50–59. Doi:10.1123/jsep.35.1.50

Gevins, A., & Cutillo, B. (1993). Spatiotemporal dynamics of component processes in human working memory. *Electroencephalography and Clinical Neurophysiology, 87*, 128–143. Doi:10.1016/0013-4694(93)90119-G

Gray, R. (2004). Attending to the execution of a complex sensorimotor skill: Expertise differences, choking, and llumps. *Journal of Experimental Psychology, 10*, 42–54. Doi:10.1037/1076-898X.10.1.42

Gröpel, P., & Mesagno, C. (2017). Choking interventions in sports: A systematic review. *International Review of Sport and Exercise Psychology, 12*, 1–26. Doi:10.108 0/1750984x.2017.1408134

Gucciardi, D. F., & Dimmock, J. A. (2008). Choking under pressure in sensorimotor skills: Conscious processing or depleted attentional resources? *Psychology of Sport and Exercise, 9*, 45–59. Doi:10.1016/j.psychsport.2006.10.007

Hanton, S., Fletcher, D., & Coughlan, G. (2005). Stress in elite sport performers: A comparative study of competitive and organizational stressors. *Journal of Sports Sciences, 23*, 1129–1141. Doi:10.1080/02640410500131480

Hill, D. M., Hanton, S., Matthews, N., & Fleming, S. (2010). Choking in sport: A review. *International Review of Sport and Exercise Psychology, 3*, 24–39. Doi:10.1080/17509840903301199

Jackson, R. C., Ashford, K. J., & Norsworthy, G. (2016). Attentional focus, dispositional reinvestment, and skilled motor performance under pressure. *Journal of Sport and Exercise Psychology, 28*, 49–68. Doi:10.1123/jsep.28.1.49

Jurado, M. B., & Rosselli, M. (2007). The elusive nature of executive functions: A review of our current understanding. *Neuropsychology Review, 17*, 213–233. Doi:10.1007/s11065-007-9040-z

Kinrade, N. P., Jackson, R. C., & Ashford, K. J. (2010). Dispositional reinvestment and skill failure in cognitive and motor tasks. *Psychology of Sport and Exercise, 11*, 312–319. Doi:10.1016/j.psychsport.2010.02.005

Kinrade, N. P., Jackson, R. C., & Ashford, K. J. (2015). Reinvestment, task complexity and decision making under pressure in basketball. *Psychology of Sport and Exercise, 20*, 11–19. Doi:10.1016/j.psychsport.2015.03.007

Klämpfl, M. K., Lobinger, B. H., & Raab, M. (2013). Reinvestment—the cause of the yips? *PloS One, 8*, e82470. Doi:10.1371/journal.pone.0082470

Laborde, S., & Allen, M. S. (2016). Personality-trait-like individual differences: Much more than noise in the background for sport and exercise psychology. In M. Raab, P. Wylleman, R. Seiler, A.-M. Elbe, & A. Hatzigeorgiadis (Eds.),

Sport and exercise psychology research from theory to practice (pp. 201–210). Amsterdam, Holland: Elsevier.

Laborde, S., Allen, M. S., Katschak, K., Mattonet, K., & Lachner, N. (2019). Trait personality in sport and exercise psychology: A mapping review and research agenda, *International Journal of Sport and Exercise Psychology*. Advance online publication. Doi:10.1080/1612197x.2019.1570536

Laborde, S., Breuer-Weissborn, J., & Dosseville, F. (2013). Personality-trait-like individual differences in athletes. In C. Mohiyeddini (Ed.), *Advances in the psychology of sports and exercise* (pp. 25–60). New York: Nova Publishers.

Laborde, S., Dosseville, F., & Allen, M. S. (2016). Emotional intelligence in sport and exercise: A systematic review. *Scandinavian Journal of Medicine & Science in Sports, 26*, 862–874. Doi:10.1111/sms.12510

Laborde, S., Dosseville, F., Guillén, F., & Chávez, E. (2014). Validity of the trait emotional intelligence questionnaire in sports and its links with performance satisfaction. *Psychology of Sport and Exercise, 15*, 481–490. Doi:10.1016/j.psychsport.2014.05.001

Laborde, S., Dosseville, F., & Kinrade, N. P. (2014). Decision-specific Reinvestment Scale: An exploration of its construct validity, and association with stress and coping appraisals. *Psychology of Sport and Exercise, 15*, 238–246. Doi:10.1016/j.psychsport.2014.01.004

Laborde, S., Furley, P., & Schempp, C. (2015). The relationship between working memory, reinvestment, and heart rate variability. *Physiology and Behavior, 139*, 430–436. Doi:10.1016/j.physbeh.2014.11.036

Laborde, S., Guillén, F., & Watson, M. (2017). Trait emotional intelligence questionnaire full-form and short-form versions: Links with sport participation frequency and duration and type of sport practiced. *Personality and Individual Differences, 108*, 5–9. Doi:10.1016/j.paid.2016.11.061

Laborde, S., Mosley, E., & Mertgen, A. (2018). Vagal tank theory: The three Rs of cardiac vagal control functioning—resting, reactivity, and recovery. *Frontiers in Neuroscience, 12*, 458. Doi:10.3389/fnins.2018.00458

Laborde, S., Mosley, E., & Thayer, J. F. (2017). Heart rate variability and cardiac vagal tone in psychophysiological research—recommendations for experiment planning, data analysis, and data reporting. *Frontiers in Psychology, 8*, 213. Doi:10.3389/fpsyg.2017.00213

Laborde, S., Musculus, L., Kalicinski, M., Klaempfl, M. K., Kinrade, N. P., & Lobinger, B. H. (2015). Reinvestment: Examining convergent, discriminant, and criterion validity using psychometric and behavioral measures. *Personality and Individual Differences, 78*, 77–87. Doi:10.1016/j.paid.2015.01.020

Laborde, S., Raab, M., & Kinrade, N. P. (2014). Is the ability to keep your mind sharp under pressure reflected in your heart? Evidence for the neurophysiological bases of decision reinvestment. *Elsevier, 100*, 34–42. Doi:10.1016/j.biopsycho.2014.05.003

Left, S. S., & Hoyle, R. H. (1995). Young athletes' perceptions of parental support and pressure. *Journal of Youth and Adolescence, 24*, 187–203.

Lewin, K. (1936). *Principles of topological psychology*. New York: McGraw-Hill.

Lewis, B. P., & Linder, D. E. (1997). Thinking about choking? Attentional processes and paradoxical performance. *Personality and Social Psychology Bulletin, 23*, 937–944.

Lobinger, B. H., Klämpfl, M. K., Altenmüller, E., & Altenmüller, E. (2014). We are able, we intend, we act-but we do not succeed: A theoretical framework for a better understanding of paradoxical performance in sports. *Journal of Clinical Sport Psychology, 8*, 357–377. Doi:10.1123/jcsp.2014-0047

Masters, R. S. W., Eves, F. F., & Maxwell, J. P. (2005). Development of a movement specific Reinvestment Scale. In T. Morris, S. Gordon, S. Hanrahan, L. Ievleva, G. Kolt, & P. Tremayne (Eds.), *Proceedings of the ISSP 11th World Congress of Sport Psychology* (Vol. 11). Sydney, Australia: NSW, ISSP.

Masters, R. S. W., & Maxwell, J. P. (2004). Implicit motor learning, reinvestment and movement disruption: What you don't know won't hurt you? In A. M. Williams & N. J. Hodges (Eds.), *Skill acquisition in sport: Research, theory and practice* (pp. 207–228). London, UK: Routledge.

Masters, R. S. W., Polman, R. C. J., & Hammond, N. V. (1993). "Reinvestment": A dimension of personality implicated in skill breakdown under pressure. *Personality and Individual Differences, 14*, 655–666.

McAdams, D. P., & Pals, J. L. (2006). A new big five: Fundamental principles for an integrative science of personality. *American Psychologist, 61*, 204–217.

McCrae, R. R., & John, O. P. (1992). An introduction to the five-factor model and its applications. *Journal of Personality, 60*, 175–215.

McEwan, D., Boudreau, P., Curran, T., & Rhodes, R. E. (2019). Personality traits of high-risk sport participants: A meta-analysis. *Journal of Research in Personality, 79*, 83–93. Doi:10.1016/j.jrp.2019.02.006

Mesagno, C., Harvey, J. T., & Janelle, C. M. (2012). Choking under pressure: The role of fear of negative evaluation. *Psychology of Sport and Exercise, 13*, 60–68. Doi:10.1016/j.psychsport.2011.07.007

Mesagno, C., Marchant, D., & Morris, T. (2009). Alleviating choking: The sounds of distraction. *Journal of Applied Sport Psychology, 21*, 131–147. Doi:10.1080/10413200902795091

Morgan, W. P. (1980). The trait psychology controversy. *Research Quarterly for Exercise and Sport, 51*, 50–76.

Mosley, E., & Laborde, S. (2015). Performing with all my heart: Heart rate variability and its relationship with personality-trait-like-individual-differences (PTLIDs) in pressurized performance situations. In S. Walters (Ed.), *Heart rate variability (HRV): Prognostic significance, risk factors and clinical applications* (pp. 45–60). New York: Nova Publishers.

Mosley, E., Laborde, S., & Kavanagh, E. (2017). The contribution of coping related variables and cardiac vagal activity on the performance of a dart throwing task under pressure. *Physiology and Behavior, 179*, 116–125. Doi:10.1016/j.physbeh.2017.05.030

Mosley, E., Laborde, S., & Kavanagh, E. (2018a). Coping related variables, cardiac vagal activity and working memory performance under pressure. *Acta Psychologica, 191*, 179–189. Doi:10.1016/j.actpsy.2018.09.007

Nicholls, A. R., Holt, N. L., Polman, R. C. J., & James, D. W. D. (2005). Stress and coping among international adolescent golfers. *Journal of Applied Sport Psychology, 17*, 333–340. Doi:10.1080/10413200500313644

Otten, M. (2016). Choking vs. clutch performance: A study of sport performance under pressure. *Journal of Sport and Exercise Psychology, 31*, 583–601. Doi:10.1123/jsep.31.5.583

Owens, M., Koster, E. H. W., & Derakshan, N. (2013). Improving attention control in dysphoria through cognitive training: Transfer effects on working memory capacity and filtering efficiency. *Psychophysiology, 50,* 297–307. Doi:10.1111/psyp.12010

Pervin, L., & Cervone, D. (2010). *Personality: Theory and research* (11th ed.). New York: Wiley.

Petrides, K. V. (2009). *Technical manual for the trait emotional intelligence questionnaire (TEIQue)*. London, UK: London Psychometric Laboratory.

Rhodes, R. E., & Smith, N. E. I. (2006). Personality correlates of physical activity: A review and meta-analysis. *British Journal of Sports Medicine, 40,* 958–965. Doi:10.1136/bjsm.2006.028860

Roberts, B., Walton, K. E., & Viechtbauer, W. (2006). Patterns of mean-level change in personality traits across the life course: A meta-analysis of longitudinal studies. *Psychological Bulletin, 132,* 1–25. Doi:10.1037/0033-2909.132.1.1

Roberts, R., & Woodman, T. (2015). Contemporary personality perspectives in sport psychology. In S. Hanton & S. D. Mellalieu (Eds.), *Contemporary advances in sport psychology: A review* (pp. 1–27). Abingdon, UK: Routledge.

Roberts, R., & Woodman, T. (2016). Personality and performance: Beyond the Big 5. In R. J. Schinke, K. R. McGannon, & B. Smith (Eds.), *Routledge international handbook of sport psychology* (pp. 401–411). Abingdon, UK: Routledge.

Roberts, R., & Woodman, T. (2017). Personality and performance: Moving beyond the Big 5. *Current Opinion in Psychology, 16,* 104–108. Doi:10.1016/j.copsyc.2017.03.033

Roberts, R., Woodman, T., & Sedikides, C. (2018). Pass me the ball: Narcissism in performance settings. *International Review of Sport and Exercise Psychology, 11,* 190–213.

Scharfen, H.-E., & Memmert, D. (2019). Measurement of cognitive functions in experts and elite-athletes: A meta-analytic review. *Applied Cognitive Psychology, 33,* 843–860. Doi:10.1002/acp.3526

Stanimirovic, R., & Hanrahan, S. (2012). Examining the dimensional structure and factorial validity of the bar-on emotional quotient inventory in a sample of male athletes. *Psychology of Sport and Exercise, 13,* 44–50. Doi:10.1016/J.Psychsport.2011.07.009

Tett, R. P., & Guterman, H. A. (2000). Situation trait relevance, trait expression, and cross-situational consistency: Testing a principle of trait activation. *Journal of Research in Personality, 34,* 397–423. Doi:10.1006/jrpe.2000.2292

Voss, M. W., Kramer, A. F., Basak, C., Prakash, R. S., & Roberts, B. (2010). Are expert athletes "expert" in the cognitive laboratory? A meta-analytic review of cognition and sport expertise. *Applied Cognitive Psychology, 24,* 812–826. Doi:10.1002/acp.1588

Wallace, H. M., & Baumeister, R. F. (2002). The performance of narcissists rises and falls with perceived opportunity for glory. *Journal of Personality and Social Psychology, 82,* 819–834. Doi:10.1037//0022-3514.82.5.819

Wallace, H. M., Baumeister, R. F., & Vohs, K. D. (2005). Audience support and choking under pressure: A home disadvantage? *Journal of Sports Sciences, 23,* 429–438. Doi:10.1080/02640410400021666

Wang, J., Marchant, D., Morris, T., & Gibbs, P. (2004). Self-consciousness and trait anxiety as predictors of choking in sport. *Journal of Science and Medicine in Sport, 7,* 174–185. Doi:10.1016/S1440-2440(04)80007-0

Watson, D., & Friend, R. (1970). Measurement of social-evaluative anxiety. *Journal of Consulting and Clinical Psychology, 33,* 448–457. Doi:10.1037/h0020196

Wine, J. (1971). Test anxiety and direction of attention. *Psychological Bulletin, 76,* 92–104. Doi:10.1037/h00313322

11 Social Support

Paul Freeman

Introduction

Significant others are important for individuals' development, well-being, health, and performance both within and beyond sport contexts. Specifically, the presence of supportive relationships and the support that they convey is beneficial for mortality (Holt-Lunstad, Smith, & Layton, 2010), mental health (Rueger, Malecki, Pyun, Aycock, & Coyle, 2016), cognitive functioning (Kelly et al., 2017), and sleep outcomes (Kent de Grey, Uchino, Trettevik, Cronan, & Hogan, 2018). Importantly, the relationship between social support and health outcomes is comparable to common risk factors including smoking, obesity, and physical inactivity (Holt-Lunstad et al., 2010). Furthermore, social support is a key factor for success in numerous professions, including sport, business, and politics (Sarkar & Fletcher, 2014). In sport, support from family, friends, and coaches is crucial for the development of super-elite athletes (Rees et al., 2016). Contrastingly, social support may not be beneficial under certain circumstances and can even lead to negative outcomes including burnout and withdrawal from sport (Sheridan, Coffee, & Lavallee, 2014). This chapter identifies different types of social support and examines their impact in sport. A key focus is on how social support influences and interacts with stress, appraisals, and coping, along with theories that explain these processes. Contemporary literature is discussed, and factors that influence the effectiveness of social support are identified. The chapter closes with recommendations to help optimize supportive environments for athletes' development, well-being, and performance, along with directions for future research.

Definitions and Types of Social Support

Within the proliferation of research examining the impact of supportive relationships, social support has been conceptualized in various ways. Incorporating some of this diversity, social support can be defined as "the social resources that persons perceive to be available or that are actually provided to them by non-professionals in the context of both formal support groups and informal helping relationships" (Cohen, Gottlieb, & Underwood, 2000, p. 4). Social support is therefore a multifaceted construct, which includes structural aspects of social support, perceived support, and received support (Barrera, 1986; Gottlieb & Bergen, 2010), all of which can be assessed in terms of quantity and satisfaction. *Structural aspects of social support* focus on the number and type of relationships and groups which an individual engages with (e.g., social ties and integration). *Perceived support* typically refers to an individual's belief that resources and assistance would be available if required from members of their social network (Gottlieb & Bergen, 2010). *Received support* (sometimes referred to as *enacted support*) typically refers to the frequency with which an individual has received supportive resources from members of their social network during a specific time frame (Gottlieb & Bergen, 2010).

Different types of social support are only moderately correlated and can have unique relationships with outcomes (Barrera, 1986; Haber, Cohen, Lucas, & Baltes, 2007). To elaborate, being embedded in a social network (i.e., a structural aspect of support) does not determine how much support is perceived to be available or is actually received (Barrera, 1986). Furthermore, although perceived and received support are conceptually related under some conditions and can interact in important ways (Uchino, 2009), a meta-analysis found that the mean correlation between them is $r = 0.35$ (Haber et al., 2007). Moreover, compared to received support, perceived support is more strongly and consistently linked to physical and mental health (Lakey & Orehek, 2011; Prati & Pietrantoni, 2010; Rueger et al., 2016). In sport, perceived support can aid psychological resilience, thriving, flow, and self-confidence (Rees & Freeman, 2007; Rees & Hardy, 2004; Sarkar & Fletcher, 2014; see also Chapters 9 and 13). These links appear consistent across different samples, research designs, and when perceived support is examined alongside other types of support (DeFreese & Smith, 2013; Freeman & Rees, 2008; Rees & Freeman, 2010). For example, beyond the effect of satisfaction with received support from teammates, perceived support from teammates was positively related to self-determined motivation and inversely related to overall burnout, whereas the frequency of received support was not related to either (DeFreese & Smith, 2013; see also Chapter 7). Furthermore, received support can be viewed negatively by recipients and has been found to exacerbate burnout and maladaptive responses to injury if it is misguided or poorly communicated (Abgarov, Jeffrey-Tosoni, Baker, & Fraser-Thomas, 2012; Udry, Gould, Bridges, & Tuffey, 1997). Despite these findings, received support may improve affect, psychological well-being, self-talk, and self-confidence if it is appropriate (Freeman, Coffee, Moll, Rees, & Sammy, 2014; Katagami & Tsuchiya, 2017; Zourbanos et al., 2011; see also Chapters 4 and 6). To help explain the different effects of social support, research has adopted a range of theoretical perspectives.

Theoretical Perspectives

There are three key theoretical perspectives adopted in social support research: the social constructionist perspective, the relationship perspective, and the stress and coping perspective (see, for a review, Lakey & Cohen, 2000). Although the first two perspectives have provided important insights, particularly outside of sport, the stress and coping perspective has been particularly influential to social support research in sport. The stress and coping perspective draws heavily on the work of Lazarus (1999). Within this perspective, social support can influence various points from encountering a stressor, appraising and coping with that stressor, and subsequent outcomes. A number of specific models outline how social support may exert effects on various outcomes.

Main Effect Model

The main effect model (or the general or direct effect model) proposes that social support is related to outcomes irrespective of stress (Cohen et al., 2000). Main effects might occur through a number of mechanisms including social comparison, social control, self-esteem, behavioral guidance, or a sense of mastery (Thoits, 2011). Bianco and Eklund (2001) argued that perceived support is more closely related to the main effect model than received support, and perceived support can have main effects on burnout, self-confidence, motivation, and performance (DeFreese & Smith, 2013; Freeman & Rees, 2008; Rees & Freeman, 2007). Indeed, the main effect of social support on golf performance was primarily attributable to perceived support rather than received support (Freeman & Rees, 2008). Despite these findings, received support may have main effects on self-confidence, affect, psychological response to injuries, and performance (Freeman et al., 2014; Mitchell, Evans, Rees, & Hardy, 2014; Rees, Hardy, & Freeman, 2007). More evidence is required, however, which integrates measures of multiple types of support to better understand the relative strength of their main effects. Outside of sport, the beneficial effects of social support on health and well-being typically more strongly reflect main effects than stress-buffering effects, with evidence particularly highlighting the importance of perceived support (see, for reviews, Lakey & Orehek, 2011; Rueger et al., 2016).

Stress Prevention Model

The stress prevention model (Barrera, 1986) proposes that social support leads to favorable outcomes through reducing the stress that individuals experience. To elaborate, support may prevent the occurrence of demanding situations or alter how they are appraised (Barrera, 1986; see also Chapters 1 and 2). Raedeke and Smith (2004) found that satisfaction with received support was associated with lower athlete burnout and operated in a manner more consistent with the stress prevention model than the stress-buffering model. Specifically, perceived stress mediated the relationship between support satisfaction and overall burnout (see also Chapter 7). Furthermore, perceived support was positively associated with situational control appraisals, and in turn lower threat appraisals, higher challenge appraisals, and superior performance in high-level amateur golfers (Freeman & Rees, 2009; see also Chapter 2). Similarly, perceived support was one of five key factors found to promote challenge appraisals and psychological resilience in Olympic champions (Fletcher & Sarkar, 2012; see also Chapter 9). Outside of sport, Aspinwall and Taylor (1997) argued that social support may enhance proactive coping, defined as "efforts undertaken in advance of a potentially stressful event to prevent it or to modify its form before it occurs" (p. 417; see also Chapter 3). Although further research is needed into this role of support, perceived support may be particularly relevant for proactive coping and stress prevention pathways. Compared to received support, perceived support is a broader resource that influences a range of outcomes and daily experiences (Cohen et al., 2000; French, Dumani, Allen, & Shockley, 2018).

Stress-Buffering Model

The stress-buffering model proposes that social support moderates the relationship between stress and outcomes, and is typically evidenced by a stress × support interaction term predicting additional variance in outcomes beyond their respective main effects (Cohen et al., 2000). Specifically, the buffering model suggests that stress and outcomes (e.g., health and performance) are negatively related at low levels of social support, but unrelated at high levels of support. Social support may buffer stress by altering the emotional, physiological, or behavioral response to stress, offering a solution, reducing the importance of the situation, or facilitating coping efforts (Thoits, 2011). Theoretically, both perceived and received support can exert stress-buffering effects (Cohen et al., 2000), but Bianco and Eklund (2001) argued that received support is more strongly linked with the stress-buffering model than perceived support. In contrast to the broad nature of perceived support, received support is considered a situation-specific variable that is most beneficial when individuals are under high levels of stress (French et al., 2018; Uchino, 2009). When both types of support were examined simultaneously, the stress-buffering effect on self-confidence (Rees & Freeman, 2007) and performance (Freeman & Rees, 2008) was primarily attributable to received support rather than perceived support. However, evidence for stress-buffering effects in sport is mixed. Some studies have not found significant stress-buffering effects of received support (Mitchell et al., 2014; Rees et al., 2007), and others have found that perceived support can buffer the detrimental effects of stress (Mitchell et al., 2014; Rees & Hardy, 2004). Furthermore, perceived support buffered the effect of stress on psychological responses to injury in athletes at lower, but not higher, competitive levels (Rees, Mitchell, Evans, & Hardy, 2010). The authors speculated that higher level athletes might possess better coping skills and therefore be more equipped to cope with stress, whereas lower level athletes may require more external support. Recently, Arnold, Edwards, and Rees (2018) found that at high levels of organizational stressors, some dimensions of perceived support were actually negatively related to subjective ratings of performance—termed reverse buffering (cf. Rueger et al., 2016). Outside of sport, evidence for the stress-buffering model is also inconsistent (Lakey & Orehek, 2011; Rueger et al., 2016). It is important, therefore, that researchers explore factors that optimize the protective role of support during times of stress, including the context, recipient, provider, and the type of support.

Optimal Matching Model

The optimal matching model (Cutrona & Russell, 1990) complements the stress-buffering model and proposes that the dimension of support should be matched to the specific needs arising from a stressor. In this regard, it is important to highlight that both perceived and received support are often conceptualized as multidimensional constructs. Following interviews with high-level athletes, Rees and Hardy (2000) identified four dimensions of functional support: emotional, esteem, informational, and tangible (see Table 11.1). These dimensions are consistent with those identified in a review of multidimensional models of support (Cutrona & Russell, 1990).

Cutrona and Russell (1990) argued that the desirability, duration of consequences, life domain (assets, relationships, achievements, and social roles), and controllability of a stressor may all determine the most effective dimension of support. For example, consistent with the coping literature (see also Chapter 3), uncontrollable stressors were predicted to elicit a need for support that fosters emotion-focused forms of coping, and controllable events were predicted to elicit a need for support that fosters problem-focused coping (cf. Folkman & Lazarus, 1980; see also Chapter 1). In sport, Rees and Hardy (2004) found that perceived emotional and esteem support buffered the detrimental effect of competition pressure (an uncontrollable stressor) on processes underpinning performance, and perceived informational and tangible support buffered technical problems in training (a more controllable stressor).

Table 11.1 Definitions and Example Behaviors for Each Dimension of Social Support

Dimension	Definition	Examples
Emotional	Behaviors and messages that express comfort, security, and a sense of being loved	• Show concern • Listening
Esteem	Behaviors and messages that boost an individual's sense of competence and self-esteem	• Encouragement • Reinforce positives
Informational	Behaviors and messages that provide advice and guidance	• Advice about performing • Constructive criticism
Tangible	Behaviors and messages that focus on practical and instrumental assistance	• Transportation • Help with tasks

Furthermore, Mitchell et al. (2014) matched dimensions of social support to specific injury-related stressors and found stress-buffering effects for perceived support but not received support on psychological responses to injury. Other studies, however, have not provided support for the optimal matching model (Rees et al., 2007, 2010). Despite its intuitive appeal, there is inconsistent evidence for the optimal matching model outside of sport (Burleson & MacGeorge, 2002). Indeed, as recognized by Burleson and MacGeorge (2002), a supportive behavior can serve multiple functions, and different supportive behaviors can achieve similar outcomes. Researchers have offered extensions to the optimal matching model, including considering the outcome alongside the match between stressors and dimension of support (de Jonge & Dormann, 2006) and taking into consideration both the quantity and quality of support (Rini & Dunkel Schetter, 2010).

The Measurement of Social Support

The importance of accurate and appropriate measurement of social support has been consistently emphasized by researchers (Cohen et al., 2000; Holt & Hoar, 2006; Gottlieb & Bergen, 2010). Sheridan et al. (2014), however, found that nearly half of the studies of social support in youth sport had used different social support questionnaires. Across the social support literature in sport, there have been three broad types of questionnaires employed. First, researchers have utilized questionnaires originally developed in social and health psychology, such as the Inventory of Socially Supportive Behaviors (ISSB: Barrera, Sandler, & Ramsay, 1981), the Social Support Questionnaire (SSQ: Sarason, Levine, Basham, & Sarason, 1983), and the Social Support Survey (SSS: Richman, Rosenfeld, &

Hardy, 1993). These questionnaires have been used to collect valid and reliable data in the general population, can provide important insight into how general supportive resources benefit athletes, and allow direct comparison of the effects of social support observed with these measures within and outside of sport. They might not, however, capture the social support behaviors that are most relevant for athletes in sport contexts (Holt & Hoar, 2006; Rees, Ingledew, & Hardy, 1999). A second approach, therefore, has seen researchers design questionnaires for specific studies (e.g., Freeman & Rees, 2009; Lubans, Morgan, & McCormack, 2011; Rees & Hardy, 2004; Zourbanos et al., 2011). This addressed calls for social support questionnaires to be relevant to the experiences of athletes (Bianco & Eklund, 2001; Holt & Hoar, 2006), but the use of different measures limits the ability to synthesize the findings across studies (Holt & Hoar, 2006; Vangelisti, 2009). The third approach has been the development and use of two questionnaires to assess athletes' perceived support and received support respectively: the Perceived Available Support in Sport Questionnaire (PASS-Q; Freeman, Coffee, & Rees, 2011) and the Athletes' Received Support Questionnaire (ARSQ; Freeman et al., 2014). These measures were created from statements provided by high-level athletes about their social support experiences (Rees & Hardy, 2000), have good psychometric properties, and assess four dimensions of perceived/received support: emotional, esteem, informational, and tangible. To guide decisions on the measurement of social support, researchers should consider requirements such as the type of support (structural, perceived, or received; quantity or satisfaction), general life and/or sport-specific support, overall support or multiple dimensions, and specific providers or a summary judgment across a support network.

The Effects of Social Support

The models and empirical evidence in the previous section highlight how social support may influence a range of emotional, cognitive, and behavioral outcomes. The following section briefly reviews evidence for the relationship between social support and coping, well-being, and performance.

Social Support and Coping

The importance of social support in coping with demanding situations is implicit within the stress and coping theoretical perspective (Lakey & Cohen, 2000), and qualitative studies have demonstrated that the support received from coaches, family, and team members enables athletes to cope with competitive and organizational stressors (Hayward, Knight, & Mellalieu, 2017; Kristiansen & Roberts, 2010; see also Chapter 3). The specific relationship between social support and coping, however, is interpreted in different ways. First, social support may initiate coping efforts, and Lakey and Cohen (2000) recommended that researchers should examine whether coping mediates the relationship between received support and outcomes. Second, social support may be considered as one of many coping strategies available to individuals (Uchino, 2009), and various coping questionnaires have seeking support as subscales alongside other coping strategies (e.g., Crocker & Graham, 1995; see also Chapter 3). Third, Raedeke and Smith (2004) argued that social support is an external resource and coping behaviors are internal resources. Consistent with this position, researchers have examined whether social support and coping are associated with conjunctive (i.e., in combination) or disjunctive (i.e., independently) moderation effects on the relationship of stress with burnout (Raedeke & Smith, 2004) and injuries (Smith, Smoll, & Ptacek, 1990). In the latter study, it was found that only athletes low in both social support and coping skills experienced a significant detrimental relationship between stress and injury (a conjunctive effect). Future research should aim to provide a greater understanding of the relationship between social support and coping to advance theory and aid the development of interventions to enable athletes to effectively manage situational demands (see also Chapter 12).

Social Support and Well-Being

There is increasing evidence for beneficial effects of social support on health and well-being outcomes in sport (see also Chapters 6 and 8). Injured athletes generally recognize the importance of social support from a range of providers for their well-being and recovery (Bianco, 2001; Judge et al., 2012). Specifically, support can help athletes to maintain a positive outlook, improve their motivation, and enhance physical and emotional healing (Podlog et al., 2013). In a recent meta-analysis, Pacewicz, Mellano, and Smith (2019) found eight studies that typically reported significant, low-moderate inverse correlations between social support and burnout (see also Chapter 7). The eight studies assessed a range of types of support: satisfaction with overall support ($n = 5$), received support ($n = 2$), and perceived support ($n = 1$). Received support has also been linked to psychological well-being, self-confidence, and feelings of adaptation (Katagami & Tscuhiya, 2016, 2017). Furthermore, Katagami and Tscuhiya (2017) found that the effects of received support on feelings of adaptation varied as a function of both the provider and dimension. Specifically, esteem support from teammates and informational support from coaches were positively correlated with feelings of adaptation, whereas teammates' informational and tangible support and coaches' tangible support were associated with negative effects. Indeed, misguided support can exacerbate negative outcomes such as burnout and maladaptive responses to injury (Udry et al., 1997), so the provision of support should be carefully considered.

Social Support and Performance

Social support is positively linked with performance (Freeman & Rees, 2009; Sarkar & Fletcher, 2014) and is an important factor in the development of elite athletes (Rees et al., 2016). Specifically, in a review of current knowledge on the development of world leading talent, Rees and colleagues (2016) concluded that there is at least moderate evidence that super-elite athletes have benefitted from supportive networks (e.g., family and coaches). Furthermore, female Olympians and their main support provider reported that social support was vital for athletic success (Poucher, Tamminen, & Kerr, 2018), and over 90% of summer and winter Olympians reported that social support was beneficial for performance (Gould, Greenleaf, Chung, & Guinan, 2002). Despite this evidence, the nuances of support need to be better understood (Rees et al., 2016). Across the performance literature, perceived support has been consistently related to superior performance (e.g., Freeman & Rees, 2008; Rees & Freeman, 2010; Sarkar & Fletcher, 2014), whereas the impact of received support may depend on factors such as the presence of stress (Freeman & Rees, 2008), the support provider (Holt & Dunn, 2004), the visibility of support (Moll, Rees, & Freeman, 2017), and the recipient's level of perceived support (Rees & Freeman, 2010). For example, novice golfers with low perceived support benefited more from received support prior to a putting task compared to those with high perceived support (Rees & Freeman, 2010).

Factors That Influence the Effectiveness of Social Support

As highlighted previously, a number of factors may influence the effectiveness of social support including the type of support, presence of stress, and whether dimensions of support are matched to situational demands. Beyond these factors, characteristics of the recipient, the provider, and their relationship are also important.

Recipient-Related Factors

The effectiveness of social support may be contingent on a number of recipient-related factors, including age, gender, and how much support is wanted. Compared to older and more experienced athletes, younger individuals can possess less developed coping skills and be more reliant on social support from their parents and coaches (Hayward et al., 2017; Kristiansen & Roberts, 2010; see also Chapter 3). Furthermore, males and females can differ in terms of their perceptions of support. For example, Judge and colleagues (2012) found that females rated emotional support as more important for their well-being. Furthermore, females have been found to be more satisfied with emotional and practical support during injury rehabilitation (Johnston & Carroll, 2000). Understanding what support individuals actually want may also be crucial in ensuring the effectiveness of received support. The support adequacy model classifies support exchanges into three categories: (i) *underprovision* refers to receiving less support than wanted, (ii) *overprovision* refers to receiving more support than wanted, and (iii) *adequate support* refers to receiving the same amount of support as wanted (Dehle, Larsen, & Landers, 2001). Limited research has examined the support adequacy model in sport, but recently Fu, Hase, Goolamallee, Godwin, and Freeman (2020) examined its predictions in two golf-putting experiments. Compared to participants in the underprovision and overprovision of support conditions, those who received adequate support had better self-confidence and superior performance (Experiment 2 only). In the wider literature, adequate support has been associated with better health (e.g., Priem & Solomon, 2015), underprovision has consistently been associated with unfavorable outcomes (e.g., negative affect and perceived stress), whereas the effects of overprovision are less consistent (e.g., Brock & Lawrence, 2009; Siewert, Antoniw, Kubiak, & Weber, 2011).

Provider-Related Factors

The effectiveness of support may vary dependent on the provider, and their knowledge, experience, and how they communicate support. Parents and friends may be typically suited to providing emotional support, coaches to informational support, and teammates to tangible support (Poucher et al., 2018). Rather than the type of provider, however, the effectiveness of support may be more dependent on the specific knowledge and competencies of the individual. Generally, support providers should possess high levels of contextual intelligence and an awareness of the stressors faced by athletes (Knight, Harwood, & Sellars, 2018; see also Chapter 1). Having experience of similar situations faced by athletes may foster mutual understanding and underpin effective support provision (Brown, Webb, Robinson, & Cotgreave, 2018). The effectiveness of informational support in particular may be contingent on the specific knowledge and expertise of the provider (Bianco, 2001). Although informational support can be unhelpful from parents who lack knowledge of the sport (Hassell, Sabiston, & Bloom, 2010), sport-specific advice can be helpful if parents have knowledge and experience in sport (Holt & Dunn, 2004). Even informational support from medical professionals can be unhelpful if it is poorly communicated (Rees, Smith, & Sparkes, 2003).

Bolger and Amarel (2007) argued that the timing of received support and the way it is communicated are particularly important. When an individual has decided to seek help (termed the postrogotory period), any support received should be beneficial provided it matches the needs of the individual. When support is received before it has been requested (termed the anterogatory period), support could be interpreted as intrusive and controlling, and may lead to feelings of incompetence and inefficacy (Bolger & Amarel, 2007). Unrequested informational and tangible support in particular may lead to negative outcomes, as these dimensions are often more direct and less nurturing than emotional and esteem support (Trobst, 2000). Bolger and Amarel (2007), however, argued that social support received in the anterogatory phase can be effective if it is provided in a subtle, invisible manner, such that the recipient does not notice it or interpret it as support. Moll et al. (2017) examined the impact of the dimension (esteem and informational) and visibility (visible and invisible) of support on putting performance in novice golfers. Visible support messages were delivered directly to the participant, whereas invisible support messages were delivered indirectly as a comment to the experimenter so they would be helpful to the participant but not perceived as support. Esteem support was most effective when delivered in a visible manner, whereas informational support was most effective when delivered in an invisible manner.

Relationship-Related Factors

Beyond the separate impact of recipient- and provider-related factors, relationship-related factors can also influence the effectiveness of support. For example, support perceptions are linked to relationship quality, with close relationships conveying a sense of being loved and valued and thereby a feeling of being supported (Brown et al., 2018). Teammates of a similar cultural background were also rated as the most important support providers for elite Indigenous Australian Football League players (Nicholson, Hoye, & Gallant, 2011). Furthermore, social identity theory (Turner, 1982) has been used as a framework to understand the impact of support and how support perceptions are formed. Received support may be more effective when the provider and recipient share a common identity (Haslam, O'Brien, Jetten, Vormedal, & Penna, 2005). A shared social identity may also underpin the perceptions of coach support. Specifically, when athletes perceived themselves to share a common identity with particular coaches, they perceived those coaches to be particularly supportive compared to how the athletes rated other coaches and how those coaches were rated by other athletes (Coussens, Rees, & Freeman, 2015). Support providers might therefore seek to emphasize values or group memberships that they have in common with athletes to foster a sense of shared identity and thereby enhance perceptions of support.

Practical Implications

Support networks can help athletes in a myriad of ways, leading to numerous favorable outcomes. Different types of social support, however, can exert unique effects, and various factors can influence the effectiveness of support. Support interventions, therefore, should be evidence-based, and carefully designed and implemented (see also Chapter 12). Interventions providing support, however, may not always be effective (Hogan, Linden, & Najarian, 2002). For example, Freeman, Rees, and Hardy (2009) delivered a professionally led, single-subject design intervention with three high-level golfers. Even though all golfers reported higher levels of received support during the intervention, only one golfer experienced a significant improvement in performance.

Perceived support has been consistently associated with favorable outcomes and can help individuals experience less stress and appraise demanding situations more positively. Sport psychologists should therefore help athletes to recognize the support available from different individuals and facilitate the development of supportive environments. Interventions could seek to strengthen bonds between individuals by providing opportunities for social interactions or by using cognitive therapy techniques to modify maladaptive perceptions of support (Cutrona & Cole, 2000).

Although received support can be beneficial, positive intentions in providing support do not always lead to favorable outcomes. It is important to consider factors that influence the effectiveness of received support including characteristics of the recipient, provider, and their relationship. Sport psychologists could adopt an educational approach to enable individuals to provide the most appropriate dimension of support, at the right time, and in the optimal manner. For example, emotional support is best provided by individuals who are close to the athlete, whereas informational support should be provided by individuals with relevant knowledge and expertise. Individuals, however, may lack the skills to provide support in difficult situations (Brown et al., 2018). Communication training could help providers to deliver unrequested support, particularly informational and tangible dimensions in a subtle, invisible manner. More generally, optimal support should focus on the whole person, and efforts should be integrated across an athletes' support network (Knight et al., 2018). Athletes can experience frustrations when they receive conflicting advice and support from different individuals (Abgarov et al., 2012). Sport psychologists could, therefore, facilitate discussions between support providers and help to coordinate the provision of support. Furthermore, not all athletes and their support providers have explicit discussions around support preferences, yet open communication can be an important aspect of support provision (Poucher et al., 2018). Finally, sport psychologists should help athletes overcome any stigma or difficulty in seeking support (Brown et al., 2018; see also Chapter 8).

Future Research

Social support is a multifaceted construct, yet few studies have incorporated measures of multiple types of support. This is important to enhance understanding of their relative impact, whether they operate independently or conjunctively, and if they operate via different mechanisms. A greater insight is needed into social integration, how this relates to perceived and received support, and its impact upon outcomes including well-being and performance. For instance, Rodrigues and colleagues (2019) recently conducted a social network analysis within Brazilian Jiu-Jitsu. Individuals who were most central in a peer network reported greater ingroup ties and were more likely to continue involvement in the sport. Furthermore, technology such as Skype and WhatsApp allow regular communication regardless of geography (Poucher et al., 2018), which can be important in elite sport when athletes and their support networks are not in the same location. It is important to elucidate, however, whether support received via digital platforms is equivalent to that received in person. Moreover, a better understanding of the mechanisms through which support operates and factors that moderate the effectiveness of support is needed, so that interventions can target these specific processes (Thoits, 2011). Indeed, very few studies have examined social support interventions in sport and future research should develop and test evidence-based interventions.

Social support research has typically focused on the perspective of the athlete. Recently, Poucher et al. (2018) provided novel insight by examining the perspectives of both the athletes and their main support provider. Although support provision was found to be personally and professionally rewarding, it could be demanding. Future research should therefore consider the impact of support on both the provider and recipient. For example, providing support to others can facilitate adjustment to retirement from sport (Brown et al., 2018). Reciprocal support exchanges between athletes and providers can have mutual benefits (Hayward et al., 2017), and these should be explored using dyadic approaches. Research should also explore team-referent social support. Coffee, Freeman, and Allen (2017) demonstrated that team members' perceptions of the support available to their team predicted collective efficacy and team cohesion.

Conclusion

Social support is an important resource linked with stress, coping, well-being, and performance in sport and other contexts. Different types of support are only moderately correlated and may have unique effects and operate via different mechanisms. Perceived support is more strongly and consistently related to outcomes than received support, and sport psychologists should help athletes to recognize all of the supportive resources that they have available to them. Although evidence for the effects of received support is inconsistent, it can lead to positive outcomes and future research should examine factors that optimize the impact of support exchanges. A greater understanding of these issues will advance theory and contribute to the development of evidence-based social support interventions.

References

Abgarov, A., Jeffrey-Tosoni, S., Baker, J., & Fraser-Thomas, J. (2012). Understanding social support throughout the injury process among interuniversity swimmers. *Journal of Intercollegiate Sport, 5*, 213–229.

Arnold, R., Edwards, T., & Rees, T. (2018). Organizational stressors, social support, and implications for subjective performance in high-level sport. *Psychology of Sport & Exercise, 39*, 204–212. Doi:10.1016/j.psychsport.2018.08.010

Aspinwall, L. G., & Taylor, S. E. (1997). A stitch in time: Self-regulation and proactive coping. *Psychological Bulletin, 121*, 417–436. Doi:10.1037/0033-2909.121.3.417

Barrera, M., Jr. (1986). Distinctions between social support concepts, measures, and models. *American Journal of Community Psychology, 14*, 413–445. Doi:10.1007/BF00922627

Barrera, M., Jr., Sandler, I. N., & Ramsay, T. B. (1981). Preliminary development of a scale of social support: Studies on college students. *American Journal of Community Psychology, 9*, 435–447. Doi:10.1007/BF00918174

Bianco, T. (2001). Social support and recovery from sport injury: Elite skiers share their experiences. *Research Quarterly for Exercise and Sport, 72*, 376–388. Doi:10.1080/02701367.2001.10608974

Bianco, T., & Eklund, R. C. (2001). Conceptual considerations for social support research in sport and exercise settings: The case of sport injury. *Journal of Sport & Exercise Psychology, 23*, 85–107.

Bolger, N., & Amarel, D. (2007). Effects of social support visibility on adjustment to stress: Experimental evidence. *Journal of Personality and Social Psychology, 92*, 458–475. Doi:10.1037/0022-3514.92.3.458

Brock, R. L., & Lawrence, E. (2009). Too much of a good thing: Underprovision versus overprovision of partner support. *Journal of Family Psychology, 23*, 181–192. Doi:10.1037/a0015402

Brown, C. J., Webb, T. L., Robinson, M. A., & Cotgreave, R. (2018). Athletes' experiences of social support during their transition out of elite sport: An interpretive phenomenological analysis. *Psychology of Sport & Exercise, 36*, 71–80. Doi:10.1016/j.psychsport.2018.01.003

Burleson, B. R., & MacGeorge, E. L. (2002). Supportive communication. In M. L. Knapp & J. A. Daly (Eds.), *Handbook of interpersonal communication* (pp. 374–424). Thousand Oaks, CA: Sage Publications.

Coffee, P., Freeman, P., & Allen, M. S. (2017). The TASS: The team-referent availability of social support questionnaire. *Psychology of Sport and Exercise, 33*, 55–65. Doi:10.1016/j.psychsport.2017.08.003

Cohen, S., Gottlieb, B. H., & Underwood, L. G. (2000). Social support and health. In S. Cohen, L. G. Underwood, & B. H. Gottlieb (Eds.), *Social support measurement and intervention: A guide for health and social scientists* (pp. 3–25). New York: Oxford University Press.

Coussens, A. H., Rees, T., & Freeman, P. (2015). Applying generalizability theory to examine the antecedents of perceived coach support. *Journal of Sport & Exercise Psychology, 37,* 51–62. Doi:10.1123/jsep.2014-0087

Crocker, P. R. E., & Graham, T. R. (1995). Coping with competitive athletes with performance stress: Gender differences and relationships with affect. *The Sport Psychologist, 9,* 325–338. Doi:10.1123/tsp.9.3.325

Cutrona, C. E., & Cole, V. (2000). Optimizing support in the natural network. In S. Cohen, L. G. Underwood, & B. H. Gottlieb (Eds.), *Social support measurement and intervention: A guide for health and social scientists* (pp. 278–308). New York: Oxford University Press.

Cutrona, C. E., & Russell, D. W. (1990). Type of social support and specific stress: Toward a theory of optimal matching. In B. R. Sarason, I. G. Sarason, & G. R. Pierce (Eds.), *Social support: An interactional view* (pp. 319–366). New York: Wiley.

De Jonge, J., & Dormann, C. (2006). Stressors, resources, and strain at work: A longitudinal test of the triple-match principle. *Journal of Applied Psychology, 91,* 1359–1374. Doi:10.1037/0021-9010.91.5.1359

DeFreese, J. D., & Smith, A. L. (2013). Teammate social support, burnout, and self-determined motivation in collegiate athletes. *Psychology of Sport and Exercise, 14,* 258–265. Doi:10.1016/j.psychsport.2012.10.009

Dehle, C., Larsen, D., & Landers, J. E. (2001). Social support in marriage. *The American Journal of Family Therapy, 29,* 307–324.

Fletcher, D., & Sarkar, M. (2012). A grounded theory of psychological resilience in Olympic champions. *Psychology of Sport and Exercise, 13,* 669–678. Doi:10.1016/j.psychsport.2012.04.007

Folkman, S., & Lazarus, R. S. (1980). An analysis of coping in a middle-aged community sample. *Journal of Health and Social Behavior, 21,* 219–239. Doi:10.2307/2136617

Freeman, P., Coffee, P., Moll, T., Rees, T., & Sammy, N. (2014). The ARSQ: The athletes' received support questionnaire. *Journal of Sport & Exercise Psychology, 36,* 189–202. Doi:10.1123/jsep.2013-0080

Freeman, P., Coffee, P., & Rees, T. (2011). The PASS-Q: The perceived available support in sport questionnaire. *Journal of Sport & Exercise Psychology, 33,* 54–74.

Freeman, P., & Rees, T. (2008). The effects of perceived and received support upon objective performance outcome. *European Journal of Sport Science, 8,* 359–368. Doi:10.1080/17461390802261439

Freeman, P., & Rees, T. (2009). How does perceived support lead to better performance? An examination of potential mechanisms. *Journal of Applied Sport Psychology, 21,* 429–441. Doi:10.1080/10413200903222913

Freeman, P., Rees, T., & Hardy, L. (2009). An intervention to increase social support and improve performance. *Journal of Applied Sport Psychology, 21,* 186–200. Doi:10.1080/10413200902785829

French, K. A., Dumani, S., Allen, T. D., & Shockley, K. M. (2018). A meta-analysis of work-family conflict and social support. *Psychological Bulletin, 144,* 284–314. Doi:10.1037/bul0000120

Fu, D., Hase, A., Goolamallee, M., Godwin, G., & Freeman, P. (2020). The effects of support (in)adequacy on self-confidence and performance: Two experimental studies. *Sport, Exercise, and Performance Psychology*. Advance online publication. Doi:10.1037/spy0000206

Gottlieb, B. H., & Bergen, A. E. (2010). Social support concepts and measures. *Journal of Psychosomatic Research, 69*, 511–520. Doi:10.1016/j. jpsychores.2009.10.001

Gould, D., Greenleaf, C., Chung, Y., & Guinan, D. (2002). A survey of U.S. Atlanta and Nagano Olympians: Variables perceived to influence performance. *Research Quarterly for Exercise and Sport, 73*, 175–186. Doi:10.1080/02 701367.2002.10609006

Haber, M., Cohen, J., Lucas, T., & Baltes, B. (2007). The relationship between self-reported received and perceived social support. *American Journal of Community Psychology, 39*, 133–144. Doi:10.1007/s10464-007-9100-9

Haslam, S. A., O'Brien, A., Jetten, J., Vormedal, K., & Penna, S. (2005). Taking the strain: Social identity, social support and the experience of stress. *British Journal of Social Psychology, 44*, 355–370. Doi:10.1348/014466605X37468

Hassell, K., Sabiston, C. M, & Bloom, G. A. (2010). Exploring the multiple dimensions of social support among elite female adolescent swimmers. *International Journal of Sport Psychology, 41*, 340–359.

Hayward, F. P. I., Knight, C. J., & Mellalieu, S. D. (2017). A longitudinal examination of stressors, appraisals, and coping in youth swimming. *Psychology of Sport and Exercise, 29*, 56–68. Doi:10.1016/j.psychsport.2016.12.002

Hogan, B. E., Linden, W., & Najarian, B. (2002). Social support interventions: Do they work? *Clinical Psychology Review, 22*, 381–440.

Holt, N. L., & Dunn, J. G. H. (2004). Toward a grounded theory of the psychosocial competencies and environmental conditions associated with soccer success. *Journal of Applied Sport Psychology, 16*, 199–219. Doi:10.1080/10413200490437949

Holt, N. L., & Hoar, S. D. (2006). The multidimensional construct of social support. In S. Hanton & S. D. Mellalieu (Eds.), *Literature reviews in sport psychology* (pp. 199–225). Hauppauge, NY: Nova Science Publishers.

Holt-Lunstad, J., Smith, T. B., & Layton, B. (2010). Social relationships and mortality: A meta-analysis. *PloS Medicine, 7*, e1000316. Doi:10.1371/journal. pmed.1000316

Johnston, L. H., & Carroll, D. (2000). Coping, social support, and injury: Changes over time and the effects of level of sports involvement. *Journal of Sport Rehabilitation, 9*, 290–303.

Judge, L. W., Bellar, D., Blom, L. C., Lee, D., Harris, B., Turk, M., . . . Johnson, J. (2012). Perceived social support from strength and conditioning coaches among injured student athletes. *The Journal of Strength and Conditioning Research, 26*, 1154–1161. Doi:10.1519/JSC.0b013e31822e008b

Katagami, E., & Tsuchiya, H. (2016). Effects of social support on athletes' psychological well-being: The correlations among received support, perceived support, and personality. *Psychology, 7*, 1741–1752. Doi:10.4236/psych.2016.713163

Katagami, E., & Tsuchiya, H. (2017). Effects of received social support on athletes' psychological well-being. *International Journal of Sport and Health Sciences, 15*, 72–80. Doi:10.5432/ijshs.201612

Kelly, M. E., Duff, H., Kelly, S., McHugh Power, J. E., Brennan, S., Lawlor, B. A., . . . Loughrey, D. G. (2017). The impact of social activities, social networks, social support and social relationships on the cognitive functioning of healthy older adults: A systematic review. *Systematic Reviews, 6,* 259. Doi:10.1186/s13643-017-0632-2

Kent de Grey, R. G., Uchino, B. N., Trettevik, R., Cronan, S., & Hogan, J. N. (2018). Social support and sleep: A meta-analysis. *Health Psychology, 37,* 787–798. Doi:10.1037/hea0000628

Knight, C. J., Harwood, C. G., & Sellars, P. A. (2018). Supporting adolescent athletes' dual careers: The role of an athlete's social support network. *Psychology of Sport & Exercise, 38,* 137–147. Doi:10.1016/j.psychsport.2018.06.007

Kristiansen, E., & Roberts, G. C. (2010). Young elite athletes and social support: Coping with competitive and organizational stress in "Olympic" competition. *Scandinavian Journal of Medicine & Science in Sports, 20,* 686–695. Doi:10.1111/j.1600-0838.2009.00950.x

Lakey, B., & Cohen, S. (2000). Social support theory and measurement. In S. Cohen, L. G. Underwood & B. H. Gottlieb (Eds.), *Social support measurement and intervention: A guide for health and social scientists* (pp. 29–52). New York: Oxford University Press.

Lakey, B., & Orehek, E. (2011). Relational regulation theory: A new approach to explain the link between perceived social support and mental health. *Psychological Review, 118,* 482–495. Doi:10.1037/a0023477

Lazarus, R. S. (1999). *Stress and emotion: A new synthesis.* New York: Springer.

Lubans, D. R., Morgan, P. J., & McCormack, A. (2011). Adolescents and school sport: The relationship between beliefs, social support and physical self-perception. *Physical Education & Sport Pedagogy, 16,* 237–250. Doi:10.1080/17408989.2010.532784

Mitchell, I., Evans, L., Rees, T., & Hardy, L. (2014). Stressors, social support and the buffering hypothesis: Effects on psychological responses of injured athletes. *British Journal of Health Psychology, 19,* 486–508.

Moll, T., Rees, T., & Freeman, P. (2017). Enacted support and golf-putting performance: The role of support type and support visibility. *Psychology of Sport and Exercise, 30,* 30–37. Doi:10.1016/j.psychsport.2017.01.007

Nicholson, M., Hoye, R., & Gallant, D. (2011). The provision of social support for elite indigenous athletes in Australian football. *Journal of Sport Management, 25,* 131–142.

Pacewicz, C. E., Mellano, K. T., & Smith, A. L. (2019). A meta-analytic review of the relationship between social constructs and athlete burnout. *Psychology of Sport & Exercise, 43,* 155–164. Doi:10.1016/j.psychsport.2019.02.002

Podlog, L., Wadey, R., Stark, A., Lochbaum, M., Hannon, J., & Newton, M. (2013). An adolescent perspective on injury recovery and the return to sport. *Psychology of Sport and Exercise, 14,* 437–446. Doi:10.1016/j.psychsport.2012.12.005

Poucher, Z. A., Tamminen, K. A., & Kerr, G. (2018). Providing social support to female Olympic athletes. *Journal of Sport and Exercise Psychology, 40,* 217–228. Doi:10.1123/jsep.2018-0008

Prati, G., & Pietrantoni, L. (2010). The relationship of perceived and received social support to mental health among first responders: A meta-analytical review. *Journal of Community Psychology, 38,* 403–417. Doi:10.1002/jcop.20371

Priem, J. S., & Solomon, D. H. (2015). Emotional support and physiological stress recovery: The role of support matching, adequacy, and invisibility. *Communication Monographs, 82,* 88–112. Doi:10.1080/03637751.2014.971416

Raedeke, T. D., & Smith, A. L. (2004). Development and preliminary validation of an athlete burnout measure. *Journal of Sport & Exercise Psychology, 23*,
281–306.

Rees, T., & Freeman, P. (2007). The effects of perceived and received
support on self-confidence. *Journal of Sports Sciences, 25*, 1057–1065.
Doi:10.1080/02640410600702974

Rees, T., & Freeman, P. (2010). The effect of experimentally provided social support on golf-putting performance. *The Sport Psychologist, 18*, 333–348.

Rees, T., & Hardy, L. (2000). An investigation of the social support experiences of
high-level sports performers. *The Sport Psychologist, 14*, 327–347. Doi:10.1123/
tsp.14.4.327

Rees, T., & Hardy, L. (2004). Matching social support with stressors: Effects on
factors underlying performance in tennis. *Psychology of Sport and Exercise, 5*,
319–337. Doi:10.1016/S1469-0292(03)00018-9

Rees, T., Hardy, L., & Freeman, P. (2007). Stressors, social support and
effects upon performance in golf. *Journal of Sports Sciences, 25*, 33–42.
Doi:10.1080/02640410600982279

Rees, T., Hardy, L., Güllich, A., Abernethy, B., Côté, J., Woodman, T., . . . Warr,
C. (2016). The Great British medalists project: A review of current knowledge
into the development of the world's best sporting talent. *Sports Medicine, 46*,
1041–1058. Doi:10.1007/s40279-016-0476-2

Rees, T., Ingledew, D. K., & Hardy, L. (1999). Social support dimensions and
components of performance in tennis. *Journal of Sports Sciences, 17*, 421–429.
Doi:10.1080/026404199365948

Rees, T., Mitchell, I., Evans, L., & Hardy, L. (2010). Stressors, social support and
psychological responses to sport injury in high and low-performance standard participants. *Psychology of Sport and Exercise, 11*, 505–512. Doi:10.1016/j.
psychsport.2010.07.002

Rees, T., Smith, B., & Sparkes, A. (2003). The influence of social support on the
lived experiences of spinal cord injured sportsmen. *The Sport Psychologist, 17*,
135–156. Doi:10.1123/tsp.17.2.135

Richman, J. M., Rosenfeld, L. B., & Hardy, C. J. (1993). The social support survey: A validation of a clinical measure of the social support process. *Research on
Social Work Practice, 3*, 288–311. Doi:10.1177/104973159300300304

Rini, C., & Dunkel Schetter, C. (2010). The effectiveness of social support
attempts in intimate relationships. In K. T. Sullivan & J. Davila (Eds.), *Support processes in intimate relationships* (pp. 26–67). New York: Oxford University
Press.

Rodrigues, A. I. C., Evans, M. B., & Galatti, L. R. (2019). Social identity and
personal connections on the mat: Social network analysis within Brazilian Jiu-Jitsu. *Psychology of Sport & Exercise, 40*, 127–134. Doi:10.1016/j.
psychsport.2018.10.006.

Rueger, S. Y., Malecki, C. K., Pyun, Y., Aycock, C., & Coyle, S. (2016). A meta-
analytical review of the association between perceived social support and
depression in childhood and adolescence. *Psychological Bulletin, 142*, 1017–1067.
Doi:10.1037/bul0000058.

Sarason, I. G., Levine, H. M., Basham, R. B., & Sarason, B. R. (1983). Assessing social support: The social support questionnaire. *Journal of Personality and
Social Psychology, 44*, 127–139. Doi:10.1037/0022-3514.44.1.127

Sarkar, M., & Fletcher, D. (2014). Ordinary magic, extraordinary performance: Psychological resilience and thriving in high achievers. *Sport, Exercise, and Performance Psychology, 3*, 46–60. Doi:10.1037/spy0000003

Sheridan, D., Coffee, P., & Lavallee, D. (2014). A systematic review of social support in youth sport. *International Review of Sport and Exercise Psychology, 7*, 198–228. Doi:10.1080/1750984X.2014.931999

Siewert, K., Antoniw, K., Kubiak, T., & Weber, H. (2011). The more the better? The relationship between mismatches in social support and subjective well-being in daily life. *Journal of Health Psychology, 16*, 621–631. Doi:10.1177/1359105310385366

Smith, R. E., Smoll, F. E., & Ptacek, J. T. (1990). Conjunctive moderator variables in vulnerability and resiliency research: Life stress, social support, coping skills, and adolescent sport injuries. *Journal of Personality and Social Psychology, 58*, 360–370. Doi:10.1037/0022-3514.58.2.360

Thoits, P. A. (2011). Mechanisms linking social ties and support to physical and mental health. *Journal of Health and Social Behavior, 52*, 145–161. Doi:10.1177/0022146510395592

Trobst, K. K. (2000). An interpersonal conceptualization and quantification of social support transactions. *Personality and Social Psychology Bulletin, 26*, 971–986. Doi:10.1177/01461672002610007

Turner, J. C. (1982). Towards a cognitive redefinition of the social group. In H. Tajfel (Ed.), *Social identity and intergroup relations* (pp. 15–40). Cambridge, UK: Cambridge University Press.

Uchino, B. N. (2009). Understanding the links between social support and physical health: A lifespan perspective with emphasis on the separability of perceived and received support. *Perspectives in Psychological Science, 4*, 236–255. Doi:10.1111/j.1745-6924.2009.01122.x

Udry, E., Gould, D., Bridges, D., & Tuffey, S. (1997). People helping people? Examining the social ties of athletes coping with burnout and injury stress. *Journal of Sport & Exercise Psychology, 19*, 368–395.

Vangelisti, A. L. (2009). Challenges in conceptualizing social support. *Journal of Social and Personal Relationships, 26*, 39–51. Doi:10.1177/0265407509105521

Zourbanos, N., Hatzigeorgiadis, A., Goudas, M., Papaioannou, A., Chroni, S., & Theodorakis, Y. (2011). The social side of self-talk: Relationships between perceptions of support received from the coach and athletes' self-talk. *Psychology of Sport and Exercise, 12*, 407–414. Doi:10.1016/j.psychsport.2011.03.001

Section IV

Stress Management to Promote Thriving in Sport

12 Stress and Pressure Training

David Fletcher and Rachel Arnold

Stress is a ubiquitous feature of sport. By definition, athletes perform in physically, technically, and psychosocially demanding competitive situations (Jones, 1995). At the higher levels of sport, stressors are not restricted to the field of play; rather, they extend into other aspects of athletes' lives (Fletcher, Hanton, & Mellalieu, 2006). Although some stress in sport is avoidable, detrimental, and/or unethical (Fletcher & Arnold, 2017; Fletcher, Hanton, & Mellalieu, 2006; Fletcher & Scott, 2010; Hanton & Fletcher, 2005; see also Chapters 1 and 14), it is not always possible or appropriate to prevent, reduce, or eliminate stressors. Some stress is inherent, inevitable, and/or desirable (Arnold, Fletcher, & Daniels, 2017; Fletcher & Arnold, 2017; Fletcher et al., 2006, 2012; Rumbold, Fletcher, & Daniels, 2012; see also Chapters 3 and 9) and as such it needs to be prepared for and managed effectively. In a similar way that athletes train for the physical and technical demands of athletic competition, they also need to train for the psychosocial stress and pressure of performance sport.

As long ago as 1980, Smith remarked that "stress coping skills are no different than any other kind of skill. In order to be most effective, they must be rehearsed and practiced under conditions that approximate the "real-life" situations in which they will eventually be employed" (p. 65). Smith (1980) proposed that stress management training for athletes should incorporate a phase of psychological skill rehearsal involving exposure to a variety of stressors that induce affect (cf. Sipprelle, 1967) and high levels of emotional arousal. Simultaneously, Long (1980) explained why practicing under conditions of stress should form part of athletes' training:

> Prior experience with stress . . . [is] an important factor in the determination of an individual's stress reaction. . . . "paced mastery" with manageable units of stress provides "inoculations" against future stressors. . . . [and] exposure to a stimulus that is mildly stressful will enable one to tolerate a similar stimulus of somewhat greater

intensity. This is a technique coaches have used for some time to simulate "competition" situations for their athletes.

(p. 75)

This chapter discusses the psychosocial preparation of athletes for performance in pressurized competition. To begin, the historical origins of stress training are outlined to highlight the main underpinning concepts and theories. The empirical research that supports the notion that individuals can develop following stress-related experiences is then discussed. This evidence subsequently forms the basis for practical guidelines and recommendations to implement stress training in competitive sport.

Underpinning Concepts and Theories

The notion that humans can develop following stress-related experiences can be traced back to various religious and philosophical writings, and more recently to the emergence and evolution of psychology as a scientific discipline. Nearly a century ago, Sándor Ferenczi (1923) used a metaphor of a "wise baby" to describe how some traumatized children grow up to be more mature adults than their peers (Mészáros, 2014). According to Ferenczi (1933), there is:

> . . . a surprising rise of new faculties after a trauma, like a miracle that occurs with the wave of a magic wand, or like that of the fakirs who are said to raise from a tiny seed, before our very eyes, a plant, leaves and flowers. Great need, and more especially mortal anxiety, seem to possess the power to waken suddenly and to put into operation latent dispositions which, un-cathected, waited in deepest quietude for their development. . . . One is justified—as opposed to the familiar regression—to speak of a *traumatic progression*, or a *precocious maturity*. . . . Not only emotionally but also *intellectually*, can the trauma bring to maturity a part of the person.
>
> (pp. 164–165)

Since the publication of Ferenczi's seminal work, various lines of inquiry have shown that not only can some traumatized children experience psychological growth, but also that adverse childhood experiences, most notably the loss of a parent through death or absence, may for some individuals be associated with later life success (see, for reviews, Csikszentmihalyi, 1990; Fletcher, 2019; Gardner, 1994; Haynal, 2003; Olszewski-Kubilius, 2000; Piirto, 1992; Rinn & Bishop, 2015; Simonton, 1994). Within the psychology literature, childhood adversity that precedes adult achievement has been referred to as a diversifying experience (Fletcher, 2019; Goclowska, Damian, & Mor, 2018; Simonton, 2000, 2016), with the loss of a parent specifically known as the "Phaeton effect" (Iremonger, 1970; see also Fletcher, 2019; Standing, Aikins, Madigan, & Nohl, 2015; Standing & Ringo, 2016). Interestingly, from a sport perspective, a significant finding of the research in recent years is that early life, non-sport adversity appears to be a consistent feature of the world's best athletes' lives (Fletcher, 2019; Hardy et al., 2017; Howells & Fletcher, 2015; Sarkar & Fletcher, 2017; Sarkar, Fletcher, & Brown, 2015) but experienced less by lower elite-level athletes who, while performing in international competition, do not attain or sustain the highest possible success at this level (Collins, MacNamara, & McCarthy, 2016; Hardy et al., 2017; Savage, Collins, & Cruickshank, 2016).

Collectively, this body of work contributes to the understanding of the origin of and factors that support human health and well-being, known as salutogenesis (Antonovsky, 1979, 1987). More specifically, how and why some individuals remain healthy or even thrive despite exposure to stressful events (Antonovsky, 1979; Mittelmark et al., 2017). Pertinent are the concepts of adversarial growth (Linley & Joseph, 2004), emergent resilience (Bonanno & Diminich, 2013), and resilient reintegration (Richardson, 2002), which point to human development following stress-related experiences (see also Chapter 9, Fletcher, 2019; Howells, Sarkar, & Fletcher, 2017; Sarkar & Fletcher, 2014). The remainder of this subsection focuses on the main concepts and theories that underpin stress training in competitive sport.

Eustress

It would be remiss of a review of the historical roots of any stress-related phenomenon not to mention the pioneering work of Hans Selye. Although not the first person to use the word "stress", Selye's (1936) influential paper, "A syndrome produced by diverse nocuous agents", lay the foundations for the scientific study of stress. In his first comprehensive monograph on the topic, Selye (1950) used the word "stress" for the first time and followed this publication with a series of "annual reports of stress". He settled on a definition of stress as "the non-specific response of the body" (Selye, 1956) and recognized that not all stress responses are the same. John Mason (1971, 1975) was, however, critical of Selye's work arguing that the "afferent limb of the stress response" had been largely ignored and that the psychological components of stress were a vital part of the stress response. Indeed, as early as 1911, Walter Cannon recognized the role of emotionality, particularly fear and fright, in the stress response (Cannon & de la Paz, 1911).

Following Lazarus (1966), who distinguished between psychological challenge and threat stress appraisals (see also Chapter 2), Selye (1974, 1977) proposed the terms "eustress" (the Greek prefix "eu" meaning good) and "distress" to distinguish between positive and negative aspects of stress. Perhaps due in part to Selye's sometimes imprecise use of terminology, the term eustress has not been widely used in the psychology literature (Kupriyanov & Zhdanov, 2014; Nelson & Simmons, 2004). It nonetheless represents a recognition that something positive can come from stress experiences and, noteworthy in the context of this chapter, the term has been used to underpin the promotion of positive and challenging work (Hargrove, Becker, & Hargrove, 2015; Hargrove, Nelson, & Cooper, 2013). From a stress management and training perspective, Kupriyanov and Zhdanov's (2014) reflections are pertinent:

> When using the term "eustress", we want to emphasize the positive, constructive value of the stress response. The initial purpose of the body's reaction to stress and stressors is to overcome the adverse impact of the external environment. Nature created a mechanism that allows the body to activate all of its resources to survive in adverse conditions. Therefore, more anti-stress programs aimed at decreasing stress levels are misguided; they intend to reduce stress levels rather than to control the stress response by converting the response to a eustress reaction.
>
> (p. 181)

Systematic Desensitization

During the 1950s and 1960s, Joseph Wolpe (1958) developed a form of behavioral therapy to help people overcome phobias and other anxiety-related disorders. Known as systematic desensitization, the approach involves gradually and systematically exposing an individual to a stimulus while teaching him or her coping strategies to desensitize him or her to the stimulus. The process of systematic desensitization occurs in three phases. The first phase involves identifying the stimuli that induce the anxiety for an individual. In the second phase, the individual is taught and learns strategies, such as relaxation techniques, to cope with the stimuli. The third phase entails the individual using these coping strategies to overcome situations, based on a hierarchy of stimuli identified in the first phase. The aim of this process is for the individual to become less sensitive to the stimuli that triggered his or her phobias or anxiety-related disorder in a variety of anxiety-provoking situations. In the early 1970s, systematic desensitization procedures began to be modified to, for example, include the use of visualization (Suinn & Richardson, 1971) and enhance perceptions of self-control (Goldfried, 1971). Although limited, there are a couple of single case studies in basketball (Katahn, 1967) and American football (Gray, Haring, & Banks, 1984) that suggest that systematic desensitization might have some utility in helping athletes to cope with the pressure of sport competition (cf. Feltz & Landers, 1980).

Stress Inoculation

As long ago as the 10th century, inoculation has been used to combat disease by exposing potentially vulnerable individuals to weaker forms of a disease to prepare and protect them against future stronger forms (Gross & Sepkowitz, 1998; Gwei-djen & Sivin, 2000). The word "inoculation" is derived from the Latin "inoculare", meaning "to graft". In 1796, Edward Jenner successfully used the cowpox virus to inoculate a child against (the more deadly) smallpox virus and, after repeating the procedure with others, he privately published his observations two years later (Willis, 1997). During the 19th century, the medical practice of inoculation became widespread and established, involving exposing individuals to a small amount of an infectious disease, referred to as a vaccine (Pasteur, Chamberland, & Roux, 1881), to produce antibodies and develop immunity to the disease.

It was not until the latter half of 20th century that inoculation was applied to psychological-related phenomena. McGuire (1961, 1964) observed that exposure to weak arguments against an individual's views can "inoculate" him or her against subsequent stronger efforts. Such prior exposure to persuasion mobilizes counter arguments in support of one's own beliefs that can be used in future threats to the individual's views (see, for a review, Banas & Rains, 2010). Most notably in the context of this chapter, however, it was Donald Meichenbaum (1975, 1976, 1977) who extended the application to psychological stress and the therapeutic treatment of related symptoms and disorders, under the rubric of cognitive-behavioral modification. He proposed that exposing an individual to mild forms of a stressor(s) can inoculate via the development of psychosocial protective and coping mechanisms, to the extent that the individual is better prepared to function and perform in analogous future situations. In developing his work, Meichenbaum drew on contemporary psychological theories, including the transactional conceptualization of stress and coping (Lazarus & Folkman, 1984) and the constructive narrative perspective (Meichenbaum & Fitzpatrick, 1993), to theoretically underpin, refine, and generalize the concept of stress inoculation. Despite attracting initial attention from sport psychology researchers (see, for reviews, Feltz & Landers, 1980; Long, 1980; Mace, 1990; Smith, 1980), interest in stress inoculation has waned over the past few decades.

Steeling

In his writings on psychosocial resilience, Rutter (1987, 2012) argued that stress can have either a sensitizing (negative) effect or a strengthening (positive) effect in relation to an individual's response to subsequent adversity, the latter process he termed steeling. Drawing on related research, Rutter (2012) acknowledged that inoculation may play a role in steeling effects, but he also argued that broader factors were important to consider, including taking on new responsibilities to acquire a sense of self-efficacy and mastery, a personal agency involving a concern to act to overcome adversity, a self-reflective style to access what does and does not work, a commitment to relationships, and planning for the future. He also suggested that some genetic alleles and life turning point events (e.g., marriage and military service) may be associated with steeling effects. Despite its potential relevance to and application in sport, steeling has received limited, if any, attention in sport (see, for an exception, Bhana, 2016).

Toughness

Not long after Rutter's early writing on steeling, Dienstbier (1989, 1992) proposed a model illustrating how exposure to stress can lead to the development of toughness. He conceptualized stress exposure as three types of "manipulations": early experience involving regular exposure to stimuli that can elicit strong arousal responses, passive toughness involving similar intermittent exposure (i.e., shock and cold), and active toughness involving regular activity (e.g., swimming in cold water and aerobic activity). Dienstbier (1989) argued that these manipulations enhance toughness via physiological mechanisms leading to positive characteristics of performance, temperament, and stress tolerance. Although adaptive physiological change is at the heart of the model, Dienstbier suggested that these mechanisms enabled a toughened individual to generate more positive appraisals and cope mentally. Particularly worthy of note in the context of this chapter is that Dienstbier (1989) was critical of some psychological interventions that he perceived as undermining toughness:

> . . . an important part of adequate long-term coping depends on physiological toughness. Relaxation-based therapies (biofeedback, autogenic training, meditation, chemical tranquilizers, etc.) provide short-term solutions that may foster avoidance of the very situations that lead to toughness.
>
> (p. 96)

Researchers in sport have recognized the psychological aspect of toughness for some time and how mental toughness can be developed following stress-related experiences (see, for a review, Anthony, Gucciardi, & Gordon, 2016). Furthermore, there are several athlete- and coach-focused interventions specifically designed to develop mental toughness in sport (see, for a review, Beattie, Hardy, Cooke, & Gucciardi, 2019).

Stress Exposure

During the 1990s, Johnson and colleagues drew on and adapted stress inoculation principles (cf. Saunders, Driskell, Johnson, & Salas, 1996) to develop the concept of stress exposure (Driskell & Johnston, 1998; Johnston & Cannon-Bowers, 1996). Although fundamentally analogous to stress inoculation, stress exposure is less focused on therapeutic treatment and more focused on preparing "personnel to perform tasks effectively under high-demand, high-stress conditions" (Driskell & Johnston, 1998, p. 192), including sport competition (Driskell, Sclafani, & Driskell, 2014). Johnston and Cannon-Bowers (1996) stated that stress exposure has three main objectives: to build skills that promote effective performance under stress, to build performance confidence, and to enhance familiarity with the stress environment.

Psychological Preparedness

Researching torture survivors, Başoğlu et al. (1997) found that psychological preparedness for traumatic stress resulted in less distress during torture and less posttraumatic stress disorder symptoms. Although there was no evidence of any psychosocial development, the findings suggested that prior immunization to stressors can protect against the effects of traumatic stress. Başoğlu et al. (1997) suggested that repeated exposures to stressors coupled with prior learning of effective coping resources may have played an important role in enhancing the survivors' sense of control.

Antifragility

Over the past decade, the notion that humans or systems can increase in capability to thrive as a result of stressors has been termed antifragility (Taleb, 2011, 2012; see also Danchin, Binder, & Noria, 2011). In defining antifragility, Taleb (2011) opposed the fragility of Damocles' Sword (where something bad could happen at any time) not to the robustness of the Phoenix (who rises from the ashes) but to the inventiveness of the Hydra (who gets two heads each time one is cut off). According to this perspective, humans develop following stress-related experiences by acquiring novel coping strategies to deal with future events. From a mathematical perspective, Taleb (2013) defined antifragility as a convex response to a stressor leading to a positive sensitivity to future increases in stressors (see Taleb & Douady, 2013). The notion of antifragility has recently been applied to the sport context (Kiefer, Silva, Harison, & Araújo, 2018) and has received some preliminary empirical support (Hill et al., 2020).

Discretionary Vulnerability

In her discussion of vulnerability and resilience, Lotz (2016) proposed the term discretionary vulnerability to refer to vulnerability that arises as a result of intention and deliberate decision. Interestingly, Lotz (2016) distinguished between discretionary vulnerability that is assumed on the part of the individual and that which is imposed by one individual on another. When vulnerability is assumed, an individual knowingly and willingly (but not necessarily happily) voluntarily chooses to put him or herself into a position of vulnerability, perhaps to ultimately facilitate some good that he or she seeks for themselves or others. When vulnerability is imposed, however, someone else decides to and intentionally places an individual into conditions of vulnerability. Discretionary vulnerability is a pertinent concept for understanding how humans can develop following stress-related experiences because it points to the potential salience of choice and decision making of both self and others in stress training.

Pressure Inurement

Pressure inurement refers to accustoming or habituating an individual to stressors and adversity. As part of their work on the development of psychological resilience, Fletcher and Sarkar (2016) argued that the environment should, at appropriate times, be manipulated to evoke a stress-related response with the aim of an individual maintaining functioning and performance under pressure. A fundamental feature of this approach is a challenging but supportive climate (Fletcher, 2019; Fletcher & Sarkar, 2016). Regarding the challenge, a culture of high expectations should be promoted that stretches individuals and groups out of their comfort zones. Turning to the support, a culture that provides individuals and groups with assistance should be promoted to enable them to operate effectively (see also Chapter 11). Hence, stress or pressure training should not be about solely imposing pressure; rather, the focus should be on appropriately balancing challenge and support to enable performers to inure themselves to stressors and adversity (cf. Fletcher, 2019). Initial evidence from the sport domain suggests that pressure inurement can be trained in athletes preparing for pressurized competition (van Rens, Burgin, & Morris-Binelli, in press).

Supporting Empirical Research

Given the diversity of underpinning concepts and theories in stress training, it is perhaps inevitable that the supporting empirical research is similarly disparate coming from a range of psychology subdisciplines and performance domains. The research varies considerably in the extent to which it draws on the aforementioned work and with regard to the types of methods used to investigate individuals' stress responses. Although this lack of coherence could be construed as a drawback making it challenging to locate, interpret, and compare relevant work, it can also be perceived as a strength because of multiple lines of inquiry pointing to the potential of development following stress-related experiences.

Non-Human Studies

One body of supporting evidence comes from studies on non-human subjects, such as rats, mice, and monkeys (see, for reviews, Ashokan, Sivasubramanian, & Mitra, 2016; Levine & Mody, 2003; Liu, 2015; Lyons & Parker, 2007; Lyons, Parker, & Schatzberg, 2010). Since the publication of early studies in this area (Denenberg, 1962, 1964, 1967; Levine, 1957, 1959, 1960, 1961), research has consistently found that rodents and non-human primates subjected to moderate stress compared to those subjected to high or low stress display more adaptive neurobiological (e.g., optimal development of the hippocampus, amygdala, and prefrontal cortex), neuroendocrinological (e.g., attenuated hypothalamic-pituitary-adrenal axis activation and corticosterone production), cognitive (e.g., better decision making, greater control, and curiosity), affective (e.g., less anxiety, fear, and/or depression), and behavioral (e.g., greater exploratory and novelty seeking actions) reactions to stressors later in childhood and/or adulthood (cf. McEwen, Nasca, & Gray, 2016; Russo, Murrough, Han, Charney, & Nestler, 2012). Research findings suggest that exposure to intermittent stressors with a degree of control, predictability, and/or feedback appears to be particularly conducive for stimulating these adaptations (Ashokan et al., 2016; Lyons et al., 2010; Maier, Amat, Baratta, Paul, & Watkins, 2006). Although non-human studies often have the methodological strengths of reproduceable stress protocols and an experimental control group, a weakness of the research is the extent to which the findings can be transferred to humans.

Human Studies

Over the past few decades, momentum has gathered in the study of human development following stress-related experiences. The findings of the research generally, but not exclusively, indicate a curvilinear (i.e., nonlinear) relationship between stress and positive outcomes, whereby moderate stress is associated with the most adaptive development, whereas lower and higher stress are associated with less adaptation or no development (see, for reviews, Höltge, McGee, Maercker, & Thoma, 2018; Liu, 2015; Seery, 2011; Seery & Quinton, 2016; Updegraff & Taylor, 2000; see also DiCorcia & Tronick, 2011; Silver & Wortman, 1980). As noted earlier, a significant finding of the sport psychology research in recent years is that early life, non-sport adversity appears to be a consistent feature of the world's best athletes' lives (Fletcher, 2019; Hardy et al., 2017; Howells & Fletcher, 2015; Sarkar & Fletcher, 2017; Sarkar et al., 2015).

In terms of early life stress, researchers have reported a curvilinear relationship such that moderate early life stress is associated with lower cortisol (Bush, Obradović, Adler, & Boyce, 2011; Gunnar, Frenn, Wewerka, & Van Ryzin, 2009; Hagan, Roubinov, Purdom Marreiro, & Luecken, 2014), lower implicit anxiety (Edge et al., 2009), lower suicidality (McLafferty et al., 2018), better executive functioning (Finch & Obradović, 2017), greater posttraumatic growth (McCaslin et al., 2009), and higher quality of life and mental health (Höltge, McGee, & Thoma, 2019) in later life compared to low or high early life stress. One study has shown U-shaped quadratic relationships between lifetime exposure to adverse experiences and chronic back pain and healthcare utilization, whereby participants with some lifetime adversity reported less functional impairment and health utilization than participants with no or high lifetime adversity (Seery, Leo, Holman, & Silver, 2010). Neff and Broady (2011) found that newlywed couples who experienced moderate stress during the early months of marriage, together with exhibiting effective problem-solving behaviors and good relationship resources, reported greater marital adjustment than spouses who had similar behaviors and resources but less prior experience coping with stress. Another study has found that adults with moderate (poly)adversity reported more resilient resources (e.g., optimism) than participants with high or low (poly) adversity (Lines et al., 2020). Similar findings for nonlinear relationships and moderate stress have been observed in studies of war veterans and cancer patients, which have reported that moderate stress was associated with less healthcare exposure (McLean et al., 2013), increased solidarity with others (Fontana & Rosenheck, 1998), more adaptative coping (Suvak, Vogt, Savarese, King, & King, 2002), improvements in psychological functioning (Schnurr, Friedman, & Rosenberg, 1993), and higher wisdom (Jennings, Aldwin, Levenson, Spiro, & Mroczek, 2006) in veterans, and with fewer intrusive thoughts and more positive affect (Dooley, Slavich, Moreno, & Bower, 2017), higher benefit finding (Lechner et al., 2003), and greater posttraumatic growth (Coroiu, Körner, Burke, Meterissian, & Sabiston, 2016) in cancer patients.

Most researchers in this area tend to use cross-sectional self-report designs, although some have employed longitudinal approaches or conducted studies within controlled laboratory settings. Several longitudinal studies have found curvilinear relationships such that individuals (Seery, Holman, & Silver, 2010), students (Wildman & Johnson, 1977), and women (Ruch, Chandler, & Harter, 1980) with a moderate amount of adversity report more positive mental health, less distress, and less negative psychological impact respectively. Laboratory-based studies have demonstrated similar curvilinear relationships where moderate lifetime adversity was associated with lower levels of negative psychological responses and higher levels of positive physiological responses to a cold pressor task and an intelligence test (Seery, Leo, Lupien, Kondrak, & Almonte, 2013) and with better cardiovascular and task performances in response to a competitive dart throwing test (Moore, Young, Freeman, & Sarkar, 2018). Noteworthy in the context of this chapter is that the study employing dart throwing represents the only quantitative research in this area with participants who all reported competing in sport.

Despite the evidence for a curvilinear relationship between stress and positive outcomes, not all studies have reported unequivocal support for such a nonlinear effect (Arpawong et al., 2016; Jennings et al., 2006; Lines et al., 2020; McCaslin et al., 2009; Powell, Rosner, Butollo, Tedeschi, & Calhoun, 2003). Furthermore, some studies have reported positive linear relationships such that increases in stress are associated with greater perceived benefits (Aldwin, Levenson, & Spiro, 1994) and more posttraumatic growth (Kleim & Ehlers, 2009; Kunst, 2010; see also Chapter 9), whereas other studies have reported increases in stress are associated with increased basal cortisol (Bush et al., 2011), increased cortisol during a stress test (Hagan et al., 2014), higher explicit anxiety (Edge et al., 2009), greater negative affect (Dooley et al., 2017), greater mental health problems (McLafferty et al., 2018; see also Chapter 8), increased posttraumatic stress and/or major depressive disorder (Fernandez et al., in press), and poorer physical health (Höltge et al., 2019). It is likely that these differences in findings and the effects of stress on individuals can be explained by the combined influence of a range of personal and situational factors during and after stress-related experiences (Liu, 2015; Seery & Quinton, 2016; Updegraff & Taylor, 2000).

Although the majority of studies indicate that humans can develop following stress-related experiences, this is different to showing that exposing individuals to stress or imposing stress on individuals can promote development. This is an important distinction to strengthen an evidence-based rationale for stress training. Fortunately, researchers have used experimental, quasi-experimental, or intervention designs to investigate how the environment can be manipulated to evoke a stress-related response to enhance performance under pressure (cf. Gröpel & Mesagno, 2017; Kent, Devonport, Lane, Nicholls, & Friesen, 2018; Low et al., in press; Mace, 1990). Using a variety of approaches, including laboratory manipulation and randomized controlled trials, researchers have studied the effects of pressure training on individuals from multiple performance domains, including competitive sport (Alder, Ford, Causer, & Williams, 2016; Beilock, & Carr, 2001; Bell, Hardy, & Beattie, 2013; Beseler, Mesagno, Young, & Harvey, 2016; Gustafsson, Lundqvist, & Tod, 2017; Kegelaers, Wylleman, Bunigh, & Oudejans, in press; Kegelaers, Wylleman, & Oudejans, 2020; Kent, Devonport, Lane, & Nicholls, 2020; Kinrade, Jackson, & Ashford, 2010, 2015; Kinrade, Jackson, Ashford, & Bishop, 2010; Lawrence et al., 2014; Lewis & Linder, 1997; Mace & Carroll, 1985, 1986; Mace, Carroll, & Eastman, 1986; Mace, Eastman, & Carroll, 1986a, 1986b; Moore, Vine, Wilson, & Freeman, 2012, 2015; Moore, Wilson, Vine, Coussens, & Freeman, 2013; Oudejans & Pijpers, 2009, 2010; Reeves, Tenenbaum, & Lidor, 2007; Sammy et al., 2017; Stoker, Lindsay, Butt, Bawden, & Maynard, 2016; Stoker, Maynard, Butt, Hays, & Hughes, 2019; Stoker et al., 2017; van Rens et al., in press; Ziegler, Klinzing, & Williamson, 1982), business, law enforcement, firefighting, medicine, aviation, and education (see Kent et al., 2018; Low et al., in press).

Within pressure training interventions, the environment is typically manipulated by increasing the demand imposed by stressors and/or increasing the appraised significance of stressors (Fletcher & Sarkar, 2016). Most evaluations of pressure training interventions show that they enhance performance under pressure for athletes of all abilities (Gröpel & Mesagno, 2017; Low et al., in press), although one study in sport has failed to find support for their effectiveness (Beseler et al., 2016). These performance enhancements have been reported following a single pressure training session (see, e.g., Lewis & Linder, 1997) or multiple, prolonged sessions (see, e.g., Bell et al., 2013), and for a variety of closed (e.g., golf putting; Lawrence et al., 2014) and open (e.g., reading the location of badminton opponent serves; Alder et al., 2016) athletic skills.

Practical Guidelines and Recommendations

As should be apparent to the reader, preventative or reductive stress management is an insufficient, and sometimes an inappropriate, approach to supporting athletes for performance in pressurized competition; rather, enabling athletes to learn and practice skills under conditions of pressure will likely be essential to attain and sustain the highest levels of performance. It is, therefore, important that coaches and psychologists have access to evidence-based guidelines to inform practice in this area (cf. Beattie et al., 2019; Driskell et al., 2014; Fletcher & Sarkar, 2016; Headrick, Renshaw, Davids, Pinder, & Araújo, 2015; Kiefer et al., 2018; Low et al., in press; Mace, 1990; see also Driskell & Johnston, 1998; Johnston & Cannon-Bowers, 1996; Keinan & Friedland, 1996; Meichenbaum, 2007). It is recommended that practitioners adopt a multi-phased (cf. Friedland & Keinan, 1986; Keinan, Friedland, & Sarig-Naor, 1990) approach to stress and pressure training consisting of three main phases: preparation and design, delivery and implementation, and debrief and review (see Figure 12.1).

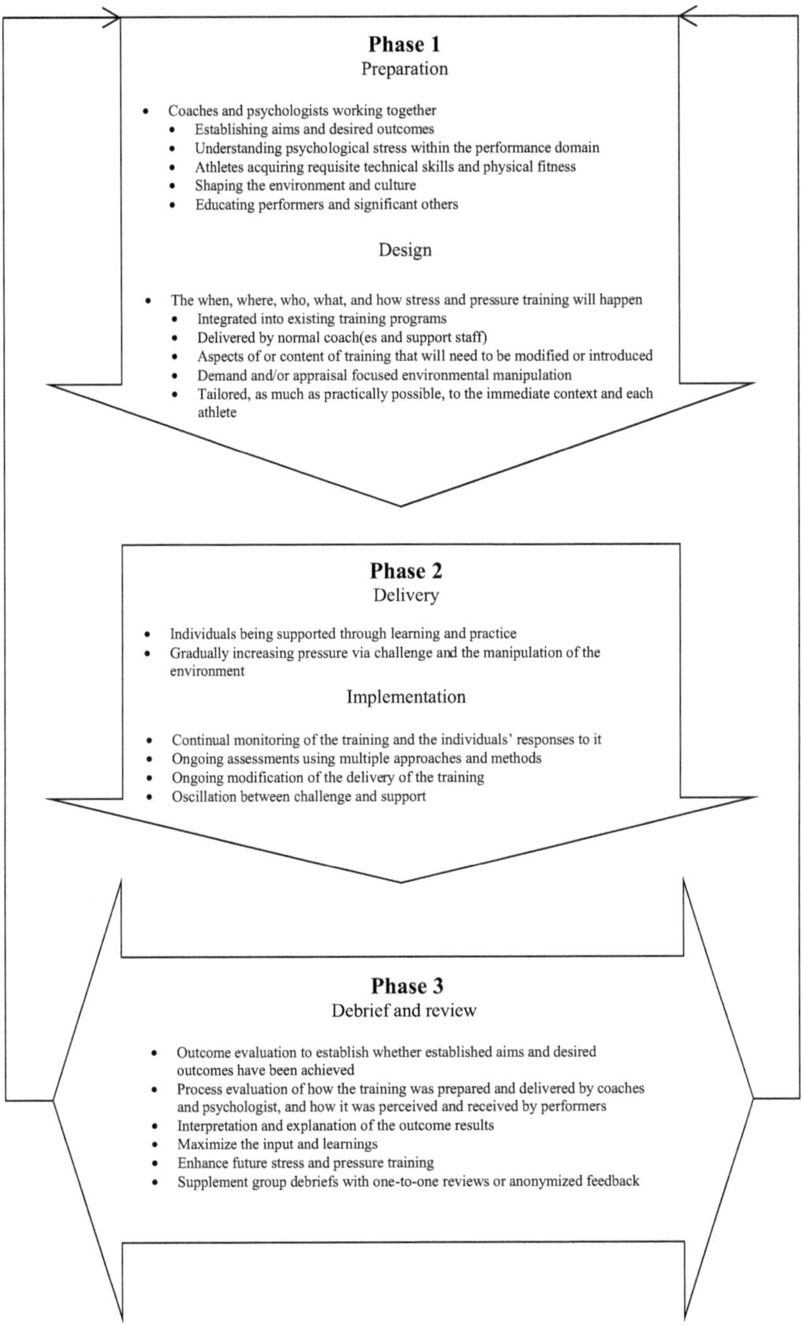

Phase 1
Preparation

- Coaches and psychologists working together
  - Establishing aims and desired outcomes
  - Understanding psychological stress within the performance domain
  - Athletes acquiring requisite technical skills and physical fitness
  - Shaping the environment and culture
  - Educating performers and significant others

Design

- The when, where, who, what, and how stress and pressure training will happen
  - Integrated into existing training programs
  - Delivered by normal coach(es and support staff)
  - Aspects of or content of training that will need to be modified or introduced
  - Demand and/or appraisal focused environmental manipulation
  - Tailored, as much as practically possible, to the immediate context and each athlete

Phase 2
Delivery

- Individuals being supported through learning and practice
- Gradually increasing pressure via challenge and the manipulation of the environment

Implementation

- Continual monitoring of the training and the individuals' responses to it
- Ongoing assessments using multiple approaches and methods
- Ongoing modification of the delivery of the training
- Oscillation between challenge and support

Phase 3
Debrief and review

- Outcome evaluation to establish whether established aims and desired outcomes have been achieved
- Process evaluation of how the training was prepared and delivered by coaches and psychologist, and how it was perceived and received by performers
- Interpretation and explanation of the outcome results
- Maximize the input and learnings
- Enhance future stress and pressure training
- Supplement group debriefs with one-to-one reviews or anonymized feedback

Figure 12.1 A Multi-Phased Approach to Stress and Pressure Training

Phase 1: Preparation and Design

Before commencing stress and pressure training, practitioners should undertake a period of planning to strategize this type of training. Preparation should involve coaches and psychologists working together toward the following: establishing aims and desired outcomes, understanding psychological stress within the performance domain, athletes acquiring requisite technical skills and physical fitness, shaping the environment and culture, and educating performers and significant others. Stress and pressure training should involve manipulating the environment to evoke a stress-related response with the aim of an individual maintaining functioning and performance under pressure (Fletcher, 2019; Fletcher & Sarkar, 2016). To achieve this, practitioners should begin by identifying what performances, components of performance, stressors and pressures, and psychological responses are most relevant and, therefore, to be the main foci of the training (see also Chapters 1–4). Baseline assessments of these areas should be recorded and used in combination with effective goal-setting strategies to establish the desired improvements, timescales, and outcomes following the training. As part of this process, coaches may need to educate themselves about psychological stress and its effect on individuals and their performance, and psychologists may need to better understand the nature and context of the performance domain they are operating in. Hence, it is important from the outset that coaches and psychologists collaborate with a view to developing an effective working alliance (Bell et al., 2013; Stoker et al., 2016; van Rens et al., in press).

In parallel to the aforementioned point, coaches should be training athletes to acquire the requisite technical skills and physical fitness to enhance performance, ideally with the support of skill acquisition and physiology specialists. Although research suggests that stress and pressure training can be effective for performers of all abilities ranging from novice to expert (see, for a review, Gröpel & Mesagno, 2017; Low et al., in press), athletes should possess the technique and fitness to perform the desired actions in conditions of minimal pressure before commencing stress training. To this end, it is important that coaches have a sound understanding of skill acquisition and expertise development (Baker & Farrow, 2015; Farrow, Baker, & MacMahon, 2013; Hodges & Williams, 2019) and, in particular in the context of the present discussion, the specific role of the environment and emotions in learning (see Headrick et al., 2015; Pinder, Davids, Renshaw, & Araújo, 2011; Pinder, Renshaw, Headrick, & Davids, 2014). For example, this body of work suggests that, in the early stages of skill development, the focus should be on creating environments that stimulate positive emotions, perceptions of competence, and intrinsic motivation, before beginning to manipulate the environment to better simulate the demands of and anxieties commonly associated with competitive performance (see also Chapters 1 and 4; Bell et al., 2013; Lawrence et al., 2014).

To prepare performers to operate in stressful conditions, coaches and psychologists should attempt to shape the team environment such that a challenge culture predominates where individuals view pressure as an opportunity to perform (Fletcher & Sarkar, 2016). As Fletcher and Sarkar (2016) observed, the leadership, management, coaching, support staff, and parents all play important roles in creating and role-modeling the desired culture, through appropriate motivational and developmental feedback (Bell et al., 2013; see also Chapter 11). Furthermore, the organization's vision should inspire those within it to establish a collective identity that embodies cultural and behavioral norms of reacting positively to pressure (Fletcher & Sarkar, 2016). The vision should also be authentic, drawing on the organization's heritage and desired legacy. To support the shaping of the environment and culture, performers and significant others (e.g., support staff and parents) will likely need some education about why stress and pressure training is important and how it can benefit athletes' performance (Bell et al., 2013; Keinan & Friedland, 1996; van Rens et al., in press). To facilitate this educational process, Driskell and colleagues (Driskell & Johnston, 1998; Driskell et al., 2014; Inzana, Driskell, Salas, & Johnson, 1996) emphasized the provision of three important types of preparatory information: sensory (regarding how the individual is likely to feel under stress), procedural (describing the events that are likely to occur in the stress environment), and instrumental (outlining what to do to counter the undesirable consequences of stress). This educational aspect of the preparation should include opportunities for performers and others to input into how the training could be designed in their context and, in doing so, hopefully engender trust, buy-in, ownership, and responsibility (Bell et al., 2013; Kegelaers et al., 2020; Kent et al., 2020; Pierce, Gould, Cowburn, & Driska, 2016).

Educating performers and significant others about stress and pressure training should involve a process of informed consent (cf. Faden & Beauchamp, 1986; Knapp, VandeCreek, & Fingerhut, 2017). Informed consent is a shared decision-making process in which the coach and psychologist communicate sufficient information, so that performers and others may make an informed decision about participation in the training. According to Gross (2001), three conditions must be met for informed consent to be considered valid: the individual involved must understand the information presented, the consent must be given voluntary, and the individual must be competent to give consent. In terms of stress and pressure training, dilemmas exist for coaches and psychologists knowing when to share information, how much information to share, and when this process may be counterproductive (cf. Barnett, 2007; Keinan & Friedland, 1996). From a performer perspective, diversity of physical and/psychosocial competence, understanding of preparatory information, and extent of voluntariness represent further challenges. Barnett (2007) also emphasized that consideration should also be given to the potential impact of diversity-related factors on the informed consent process, including language, age (and developmental level), cultural background, and physical and/or psychological impairment. In discussing these and other issues, Wise (2007) highlighted some of the limitations of the notion of informed consent, leading her to encourage greater use of the terms choice and decision because they arguably imply more active engagement and agency (cf. Keinan & Friedland, 1996; Lotz, 2016). It is, therefore, important that coaches and psychologists collaborate with performers and significant others to establish mutually agreeable boundaries of acceptableness (and unacceptableness) in the design, delivery, and implementation of pressure training.

Following this preparation, coaches and psychologists should begin to design the stress and pressure training focusing on when, where, who, what, and how it will happen. Why the training will take place should have already been addressed as part of the aforementioned preparatory establishment of aims, but consideration will need to be given to when and where the training will take place and who will deliver the content. Stress and pressure training should usually be integrated into existing training programs (Bell et al., 2013; van Rens et al., in press), typically at similar locations and times delivered by the normal coach(es and support staff) (cf. Brown & Fletcher, 2017), although there may be occasions when changing the location and/or time is an appropriate way of developing novel stressors (Kegelaers et al., 2020). If changes are made in these areas, for example, a psychologist assisting in the delivery and evaluation of the training because of his or her knowledge of psychology, then the participants should, if they have not previously, be introduced to the psychologist during the aforementioned preparatory education process. It is also important to note that it appears that the timing of this type of training can be optimized by delivering it at critical periods of performance growth (Kiefer et al., 2018), most likely involving introducing anxiety later in the learning process (Keinan & Friedland, 1996), particularly for complex skills (Lawrence et al., 2014).

In terms of designing the content of the stress and pressure training and how it will be delivered, an important consideration is what aspects or content of training will need to be modified or introduced and how this will be done. Known as active ingredients, these core training-specific components serve as key levers of change to realize the desired outcomes (Abry, Hulleman, & Rimm-Kaufman, 2015). As noted earlier, in stress and pressure training, the environment is typically manipulated in ways that can be broadly classified as demand and/or appraisal focused (Fletcher & Sarkar, 2016). The demand imposed by stressors can be increased through the manipulation of their type, property, or dimension (see also Chapter 1) and the appraised significance of stressors increased through the manipulation of their relevance, importance, and consequences (see also Chapter 2). Ideally, but not always necessarily (cf. Driskell & Johnston, 1998; Driskell, Johnston, & Salas, 2001; Keinan & Friedland, 1996; Kiefer et al., 2018; Stoker et al., 2016), these modifications should simulate, where possible, features of the environment where high or peak performance is desired (Alder et al., 2016; Bell et al., 2013; van Rens et al., in press; Ward, Williams, & Hancock, 2006).

Coaches and psychologists should be mindful of a range of contextual and individual differences when integrating environmental manipulations into existing training programs (Kent et al., 2020; Keinan & Friedland, 1996; Stoker et al., 2016, 2017). Contextual differences include the nature of the sport (e.g., individual vs. team sports), the technical skills and physical activities required to perform (e.g., discrete vs. continuous skills), the training location and layout (e.g., visible vs. hidden arena), and the accessible equipment and resources (e.g., unavailability vs. availability of virtual reality technology). Individual differences include personality traits (e.g., neuroticism vs. hardiness; see also Chapter 10), mental health (e.g., clinical disorders vs. minimal symptoms; see also Chapter 8), learning disability (e.g., attention-deficit/hyperactivity disorder vs. normal functioning), psychological skills (e.g., singular techniques vs. advanced combinations), interpersonal skills (e.g., communication difficulties vs. emotional intelligence; see also Chapter 4), coping strategies (e.g., consciously vs. automatically deployed; see also Chapter 3), and anticipated support (e.g., perceived unavailable vs. available assistance; see also Chapter 11). All of this means that stress and pressure training design should be tailored, as much as practically possible, to the immediate context and each athlete.

Phase 2: Delivery and Implementation

In terms of the delivery of stress and pressure training, the content of the training should involve individuals being supported through learning and practice to enhance their psychological and interpersonal skills, coping strategies, and perceived support (Fletcher & Sarkar, 2016; see also Chapters 3 and 11). The aim being to enable individuals to better manage and deal with the stressors and pressures encountered. Drawing on both the research evidence (see, e.g., Bell et al., 2013; Pierce et al., 2016; Hardy, Jones, & Gould, 1996; Mace, 1990) and coaches' and psychologists' combined expertise, psychological skills and coping strategy training (e.g., relaxation and imagery) should be initially rehearsed in non-pressurized and simulated pressurized situations prior to actual pressurized training and competition (Suinn, 1972a, 1972b; see also Quinton et al., 2019; Williams & Cumming, 2012) and in such a way that individuals are enabled to detect threatening cues earlier and develop an appropriate response (Bell et al., 2013). Furthermore, the learning, training, and support should, as far as practically possible, be tailored to meet the needs of each individual (Bell et al., 2013; van Rens et al., in press; see also Lotz, 2016). For example, stressors that are more uncontrollable in nature may require more emotional and/or esteem support, whereas stressors that are more controllable in nature may require more informational and/or tangible support (Cutrona & Russell, 1990; Rees & Hardy, 2004; see also Chapters 1 and 11).

As psychosocial development becomes evident, the pressure on an individual can be gradually increased via challenge and the manipulation of the environment (Fletcher & Sarkar, 2016), sometimes referred to as stressor exposure (cf. Gustafsson et al., 2017) or planned disruptions (Kegelaers et al., 2020). The demand and/or appraisal focused manipulations (Fletcher & Sarkar, 2016) can be facilitated by the use of imagery (Hale & Whitehouse, 1998; Williams, Cumming, & Balanos, 2010), equipment, and technology such as mixed reality devices that support virtual and augmented reality environments (Argelaguet Sanz, Multon, & Lécuyer, 2015; Kiefer et al., 2018; see also Keinan & Friedland, 1996). The demand imposed by stressors is increased through the manipulation of their type, property, or dimension (see also Chapter 1) and includes exposure to different types of stressors, introducing new stressors, and/or increasing how frequently they are encountered (Kegelaers et al., 2020, in press; Kent et al., 2020; Stoker et al., 2016, 2017, 2019). The appraised significance of stressors is increased through the manipulation of their relevance, importance, and consequences (see also Chapter 2) and includes changing individuals' beliefs, setting different types of goals, and/or using punishments (Bell et al., 2013; Kegelaers et al., 2020; Kent et al., 2020; Seifried, 2008, 2010; Stoker et al., 2016, 2017, 2019; van Rens et al., in press). Such manipulations should involve opportunities for individuals to acclimatize to heightened self-consciousness (cf. Baumeister, 1984) and/or increased anxiety (cf. Mace, 1990; Oudejans & Nieuwenhuys, 2009) typically experienced in pressurized situations. Similar to the support, the challenge should, as far as practically possible, be tailored to meet the aims of each individual (Bell et al., 2013; Stoker et al., 2016, 2017). For example, the environment could be manipulated to expose individuals to stressors that they know normally stretch them out of their comfort zone and/or they will likely encounter in pressurized performance situations.

As most practitioners know only too well, "no plan survives contact with the enemy" (von Moltke, 1892) and the implementation of stress and pressure training is no exception. No amount of planning can account for all of the potential contextual and individual differences mentioned in the previous subsection and the ongoing changes that occur over time in individuals' training and lives. These complex psychosocial dynamics emphasize the importance of continually monitoring the training and the individuals' responses to it (Bell et al., 2013;

Stoker et al., 2016, 2017; van Rens et al., in press; see also Lotz, 2016). This is soberingly underscored by the potential of individuals responding negatively to pressure for prolonged periods of time; in particular, the psychosocial implications for athletes (e.g., loss of confidence and burnout; see also Chapter 7) and ethical implications for coaches and psychologists (e.g., ineffective practice and abuse; see also Chapter 14).

Monitoring of the training should generally align with the baseline assessments of performances, components of performance, stressors and pressures, and psychological responses undertaken during the preparation and design phase. Ideally, ongoing assessments should use multiple approaches and methods that capture psychological, social, and physiological responses to the training, although pragmatically the range of assessments will likely be limited by the available resources, expertise, and time. Hence, coaches and psychologists will need to establish which assessments are particularly important and how often to record them. Clearly, the less intrusive an assessment, the better.

The information from the continual monitoring should inform the ongoing modification of the delivery of the training (Stoker et al., 2017; van Rens et al., in press). For example, the findings of the assessment may indicate that the training is not having the desired psychological and/or performance effects, and that changes are required. It may be, for example, that a shift from increasing the demands to increasing the appraised significance of stressors is required. Indeed, there is some evidence to suggest that focusing on consequences may be a more effective approach to stress exposure than focusing on demands (Stoker et al., 2017, 2019). In reality, it is likely that individuals will respond to stress and pressure training differently (Mace, 1990), and will therefore require different modifications to the training to optimize their experiences.

The information from the continual monitoring should also inform the oscillation between challenge and support (Fletcher, 2019; Fletcher & Sarkar, 2016). To elaborate, when assessment findings indicate that an individual is reacting with more debilitative responses and negative outcomes it is likely that the pressure is exceeding his or her available resources. When this occurs, support and motivational feedback should be increased, together with possibly temporarily decreasing the challenge. Conversely, when assessment findings indicate that an individual is reacting with more facilitative responses and positive outcomes it is likely that he or she has adapted to the pressure. When this occurs, challenge and developmental feedback should be increased. This is very much the "art" of coaching and consulting in stress and pressure training; the ability to know when and how much to stretch an individual out of their comfort zone, but also knowing when enough is enough and when to step back. As alluded earlier, having an effective coach-psychologist working alliance, based on robust ethical and evidence-based principles, is critical to getting the oscillation between challenge and support right.

Phase 3: Debrief and Review

Coaches and psychologists are, like most individuals operating in performance environments, busy people. As should be apparent, preparing and delivering stress and pressure training is a time-consuming activity (Beseler et al., 2016) that is important to get right otherwise the consequences could be severe. An understandable temptation given the multiple demands on coaches' and psychologists' time is to complete the training and draw conclusions about its effectiveness based solely on the findings of the aforementioned monitoring. It is true that the findings of the monitoring, if based on valid and reliable assessment methods, should give a good indication of whether the training has worked or not, otherwise known as outcome evaluation. However, a more comprehensive reflection on the entire training process is needed to maximize benefits and learning (e.g., develop resilience; Crane, Searle, Kangas, & Nwiran, 2019; Kegelaers et al., 2020, in press).

Although a debrief should clearly review whether the established aims and desired outcomes have been achieved and to what extent (Bell et al., 2013; van Rens et al., in press), it is also important and informative to reflect on how the training was prepared and delivered by coaches and psychologists, and how it was perceived and received by performers (cf. McArdle, Martin, Lennon, & Moore, 2010; Macquet, Ferrand, & Stanton, 2015). For example, what went well in terms of the design of the training and what could have gone better? Was the training implemented as planned? How did the performers react to the training? Known as process evaluation, this approach goes beyond the findings of the monitoring and the evaluation of outcomes, and explores the context, implementation, and appraisal of the training (Oakley, Strange, Bonell, Allen, & Stephenson, 2006). Rather than focusing on the results of the training (i.e., did it work or not?), the focus is on how the training was delivered and received, with particular attention paid to any changes or nuances that unfold across settings and/or over time (Nielsen, Randall, & Albertsen, 2007; Randall, Griffiths, & Cox, 2005; Saksvik, Nytrø, Dahl-Jørgensen, & Mikkelsen, 2002). Included in the debrief and review should be the extent to which an intervention and its core components were delivered as intended (known as intervention fidelity and integrity; Dane & Schneider, 1998; Gearing, El-Bassel, Ghesquiere, Baldwin, Gillies, & Ngeow, 2011), how the participants perceived the training (known as manipulation check; Kidd, 1976), and to what extent the performers are satisfied with the training (known as social validation; Page & Thelwell, 2013). Sound insight and intelligence in these areas can help with the interpretation and explanation of the outcome results (i.e., why did the training work or not?), maximize input and learnings (i.e., what can we take away from understanding everyone's perspective of what happened?), and enhance future stress and pressure training (i.e., what can we do differently and better next time?).

In addition to evaluating the processes and outcomes of stress and pressure training, a debrief and review should also present opportunities for ventilation in a context of group support, normalization of responses, and education about posttraining psychological reactions. Although focused on experiences of more extreme stress, there are several clinical approaches to stress-related debriefing that have potential to inform this process (cf. Raphael & Wilson, 2000), including critical incident stress debriefing (Mitchell, 1983; Elhart, Dotson, & Smart, 2019), psychological debriefing (Dyregov, 1989; Kaplan, Iancu, & Bodner, 2001), and multiple stressor debriefing (Armstrong, 2000; Armstrong, O'Callahan, & Mannar, 1991). Regardless of the specific approach adopted, it should be recognized that group debriefs may need to be supplemented with one-to-one reviews (Bell et al., 2013) or anonymized feedback because of inhibitors to the debriefing process in sport such as coach-athlete power differentials and athletes' potential reluctance to speak honestly in front of their teammates and coaches (McArdle et al., 2010).

Conclusion

Stress and pressure training should be used as part of the effective psychosocial preparation of athletes for performance in pressurized competition. Although further research is needed to investigate the effectiveness and efficacy of such interventions (cf. Beattie et al., 2019; Driskell et al., 2014; Fletcher & Sarkar, 2016; Headrick et al., 2015; Kiefer et al., 2018; Low et al., in press; Mace, 1990; see also Driskell & Johnston, 1998; Johnston & Cannon-Bowers, 1996; Keinan & Friedland, 1996; Meichenbaum, 2007), a multitude of concepts and theories, together with a convergence of research findings, collectively provide a robust evidence-based foundation to inform practice in this area. Coaches and psychologists should use the practical guidelines and recommendations outlined in this chapter to assist them in developing stress and pressure training. Given that the ability to perform under pressure and that extensive deliberate practice appear to be prerequisites for performing at the highest level in sports (Rees et al., 2016), their fusion in the form of effective stress and pressure training is likely to become an increasingly important aspect of athletes' preparation for competition.

References

Abry, T., Hulleman, C. S., & Rimm-Kaufman, S. E. (2015). Using indices of fidelity to intervention core components to identify program active ingredients. *American Journal of Evaluation, 36*, 320–338. Doi:10.1177/1098214014557009

Alder, D., Ford, P. R., Causer, J., & Williams, A. M. (2016). The effects of high- and low anxiety training on the anticipation judgments of elite performers. *Journal of Sport and Exercise Psychology, 38*, 93–104. Doi:10.1123/jsep.2015-0145

Anthony, D. R., Gucciardi, D. F., & Gordon, S. (2016). A meta-study of qualitative research on mental toughness development. *International Review of Sport and Exercise Psychology, 9*, 160–190. Doi:10.1080/1750984x.2016.1146787

Antonovsky, A. (1979). *Health, stress and coping.* San Francisco, CA: Jossey-Bass.

Antonovsky, A. (1987). *Unravelling the mystery of health: How people manage stress and stay well.* San Francisco, CA: Jossey-Bass.

Aldwin, C. M., Levenson, M. R., & Spiro, A. (1994). Vulnerability and resilience to combat exposure: Can stress have lifelong effects? *Psychology and Aging, 9*, 34–44. Doi:10.1037/0882-7974.9.1.34

Argelaguet Sanz, F., Multon, F., & Lécuyer, A. (2015). A methodology for introducing competitive anxiety and pressure in VR sports training. *Frontiers in Robotics and AI, 2*, 10. Doi:10.3389/frobt.2015.00010

Armstrong, K. (2000). Multiple stressor debriefing as a model for intervention. In B. Raphael & J. P. Wilson (Eds.), *Psychological debriefing: Theory, practice and evidence* (pp. 290–301). Cambridge, UK: Cambridge University Press.

Armstrong, K., O'Callahan, W., & Mannar, C. R. (1991). Debriefing red cross disaster personnel: The multiple stressor debriefing model. *Journal of Traumatic Stress, 4*, 581–593. Doi:10.1002/jts.2490040410

Arnold, R., Fletcher, D., & Daniels, K. (2017). Organizational stressors, coping, and outcomes in competitive sport. *Journal of Sports Sciences, 35*, 694–703. Doi: 10.1080/02640414.2016.1184299

Arpawong, T. E., Rohrback, L. A., Milam, J. E., Unger, J. B., Land, H., Sun, P., . . . Sussman, S. (2016). Stressful life events and predictors of post-traumatic growth among high-risk early adults. *The Journal of Positive Psychology, 11*, 1–14. Doi:10.1037/e574802013-302

Ashokan, A., Sivasubramanian, M., & Mitra, R. (2016). Seeding stress resilience through inoculation. *Neural Plasticity*, 4928081. Doi:10.1155/2016/4928081

Baker, J., & Farrow, D. (Eds.). (2015). *Routledge handbook of sport expertise.* Abingdon, UK: Routledge.

Banas, J. A., & Rains, S. A. (2010). A meta-analysis of research on inoculation theory. *Communication Monographs, 77*, 281–311. Doi:10.1080/0363775 1003758193

Barnett, J. E. (2007). Seeking an understanding of informed consent. *Professional Psychology: Research and Practice, 38*, 179–182. Doi:10.1037/0735-7028. 38.2.179

Başoğlu, M., Mineka, S., Paker, M., Aker, T., Livanou, M., & Gök, S. (1997). Psychological preparedness for trauma as a protective factor in survivors of torture. *Psychological Medicine, 27*, 1421–1433. Doi:10.1017/s0033291797005679

Baumeister, R. F. (1984). Choking under pressure: Self-consciousness and paradoxical effects of incentives on skillful performance. *Journal of Personality and Social Psychology, 46*, 610–620. Doi:10.1037/0022-3514.46.3.610

Beattie, S., Hardy, L., Cooke, A., & Gucciardi, D. (2019). Mental toughness training. In N. Hodges & A. M. Williams (Eds.), *Skill acquisition in sport: Research, theory and practice* (pp. 255–270). Abingdon, UK: Routledge.

Beilock, S. L., & Carr, T. H. (2001). On the fragility of skilled performance: What governs choking under pressure? *Journal of Experimental Psychology: General, 130*, 701–725. Doi:10.1037/e413792005-051

Bell, J. J., Hardy, L., & Beattie, S. (2013). Enhancing mental toughness and performance under pressure in elite young cricketers: A 2-year longitudinal intervention. *Sport, Exercise, and Performance Psychology, 2*, 281–297. Doi:10.1037/a0033129

Beseler, B., Mesagno, C., Young, W., & Harvey, J. (2016). Igniting the pressure acclimatization training debate: Contradictory pilot-study evidence from Australian football. *Journal of Sport Behavior, 39*, 22–38.

Bhana, D. (2016). Steeling the junior body: Learning sport and masculinities in the early years. In J. Coffey, S. Budgeon, & H. Cahill (Eds.), *Learning bodies* (pp. 53–68). Amsterdam, Holland: Springer.

Bonanno, G. A., & Diminich, E. D. (2013). Annual research review: Positive adjustment to adversity—trajectories of minimal—impact resilience and emergent resilience. *The Journal of Child Psychology and Psychiatry, 54*, 378–401. Doi:10.1111/jcpp.12021

Brown, D. J., & Fletcher, D. (2017). Effects of psychological and psychosocial interventions on sport performance: A meta-analysis. *Sports Medicine, 47*, 77–99. Doi:10.1007/s40279-016-0552-7

Bush, N. R., Obradović, J., Adler, N., & Boyce, W. T. (2011). Kindergarten stressors and cumulative adrenocortical activation: The "first straws" of allostatic load? *Development and Psychopathology, 23*, 1089–1106. Doi:10.1017/s0954579411000514

Cannon, W. B., & De La Paz, D. (1911). Emotional stimulation of adrenal secretion. *American Journal of Physiology, 27*, 65. Doi:10.1152/ajplegacy.1911.28.1.64

Collins, D., MacNamara, Á., & McCarthy, N. (2016). Super champions, champions, and almost: Important differences and commonalities on the rocky road. *Frontiers in Psychology, 6*, 1–11. Doi:10.3389/fpsyg.2015.02009

Coroiu, A., Körner, A., Burke, S., Meterissian, S., & Sabiston, C. M. (2016). Stress and posttraumatic growth among survivors of breast cancer: A test of curvilinear effects. *International Journal of Stress Management, 23*, 84–97. Doi:10.1037/a0039247

Crane, M. F., Searle, B. J., Kangas, M., & Nwiran, Y. (2019). How resilience is strengthened by exposure to stressors: The systematic self-reflection model of resilience strengthening. *Anxiety, Stress and Coping, 32*, 1–17. Doi:10.1080/10615806.2018.1506640

Csikszentmihalyi, M. (1990). *Flow: The psychology of optimal experience.* New York: Harper & Row.

Cutrona, C. E., & Russell, D. W. (1990). Type of social support and specific stress: Toward a theory of optimal matching. In B. R. Sarason, I. G. Sarason, & G. R. Pierce (Eds.), *Social support: An interactional view* (pp. 319–366). New York: Wiley.

Danchin, A., Binder, P. M., & Noria, S. (2011). Antifragility and tinkering in biology (and in business) flexibility provide an efficient epigenetic way to manage risk. *Genes, 2*, 998–1016. Doi:10.3390/genes2040998

Dane, A. V., & Schneider, B. H. (1998). Program integrity in primary and early secondary prevention: Are implementation effects out of control? *Clinical Psychology Review, 18,* 23–45. Doi:10.1016/s0272-7358(97)00043-3

Denenberg, V. H. (1962). The effects of early experience. In E. S. E. Hafez (Ed.), *The behaviour of domestic animals* (pp. 109–138). London, UK: Balliere, Tindall & Cox.

Denenberg, V. H. (1964). Critical periods, stimulus input, and emotional reactivity: A theory of infantile stimulation. *Psychological Review, 71,* 335–351. Doi:10.1037/h0042567

Denenberg, V. H. (1967). Stimulation in infancy, emotional reactivity, and exploratory behaviour. In D. C. Glass (Ed.), *Neurophysiology and emotion* (pp. 161–222). New York: Rockefeller University Press.

DiCorcia, J. A., & Tronick, E. (2011). Quotidian resilience: Exploring mechanisms that drive resilience from a perspective of everyday stress and coping. *Neuroscience and Biobehavioral Reviews, 35,* 1593–1602. Doi:10.1016/j. neubiorev.2011.04.008

Dienstbier, R. A. (1989). Arousal and physiological toughness: Implications for mental and physical health. *Psychological Bulletin, 96,* 84–100. Doi:10.1037/0033-295x.96.1.84

Dienstbier, R. A. (1992). Mutual impacts of toughening on crises and losses. In L. Montada, S.-H. Filipp, & M. J. Lerner (Eds.), *Life crises and experiences of loss in adulthood* (pp. 367–384). Hillsdale, NJ: Erlbaum.

Dooley, L. N., Slavich, G. M., Moreno, P. I., & Bower, J. E. (2017). Strength through adversity: Moderate lifetime stress exposure is associated with psychological resilience in breast cancer survivors. *Stress and Health, 33,* 549–557. Doi:10.1002/smi.2739

Driskell, T., & Johnston, J. H. (1998). Stress exposure training. In J. A. Cannon-Bowers & E. Salas (Eds.), *Making decision under stress: Implications for individual and team training* (pp. 191–217). Washington, DC: American Psychological Association.

Driskell, T., Johnston, J. H., & Salas, E. (2001). Does stress training generalize to novel settings? *Human Factors, 43,* 99–110. Doi:10.1518 %2F001872001775992471

Driskell, T., Sclafani, S., & Driskell, J. E. (2014). Reducing the effects of game day pressures through stress exposure training. *Journal of Sport Psychology in Action, 5,* 28–43. Doi:10.1080/21520704.2013.866603

Dyregov, A. (1989). Caring for helpers in disaster situations: Psychological debriefing. *Disaster Management, 2,* 25–30.

Edge, M. D., Ramel, W., Drabant, E. M., Kuo, J. R., Parker, K. J., & Gross, J. J. (2009). For better or worse? Stress inoculation effects for implicit but not explicit anxiety. *Depression and Anxiety, 26,* 831–837. Doi:10.1002/da.20592

Elhart, M. A., Dotson, J., & Smart, D. (2019). Psychological debriefing of hospital emergency personnel: Review of critical incident stress debriefing. *International Journal of Nursing Student Scholarship, 6,* 37.

Faden, R. R., & Beauchamp, T. L. (1986). *A history and theory of informed consent.* New York: Oxford University Press.

Farrow, D., Baker, J., & MacMahon, C. (2013). *Developing sport expertise.* Abingdon, UK: Routledge.

Feltz, D. L., & Landers, D. M. (1980). Stress management techniques for sport and physical education. *Journal of Physical Education and Recreation, 51*, 41–43. Doi:10.1080/00971170.1980.10624087

Ferenczi, S. (1923). The dream of the wise baby. In *Further contributions to the theory and technique of psych-analysis* (p. 349). London, UK: Maresfield Library.

Ferenczi, S. (1933). Confusion of tongues between adults and the child. In *Final contributions to the problems and methods of psych-analysis* (pp. 156–167). London, UK: Maresfield Library.

Fernandez, C. A., Choi, K. W., Marshall, B. D. L., Vicentre, B., Saldivia, S., Kohn, R., . . . Buka, S. L. (in press). Assessing the relationship between psychosocial stressors and psychiatric resilience among Chilean disaster survivors. *The British Journal of Psychiatry.* Advance online publication. Doi:10.1192/bjp.2020.88

Finch, J. E., & Obradović, J. (2017). Unique effects of socioeconomic and emotional parental challenges on children's executive functions. *Journal of Applied Developmental Psychology, 52*, 126–137. Doi:10.1016/j.appdev.2017.07.004

Fletcher, D. (2019). Psychological resilience and adversarial growth in sport and performance. In E. O. Acevedo (Ed.), *The Oxford encyclopedia of sport, exercise, and performance psychology* (pp. 731–756). New York: Oxford University Press.

Fletcher, D., & Arnold, R. (2017). Stress in sport: The role of the organizational environment. In C. R. D. Wagstaff (Ed.), *The organizational psychology of sport: Key issues and practical applications* (pp. 83–100). New York: Routledge.

Fletcher, D., Hanton, S., & Mellalieu, S. D. (2006). An organizational stress review: Conceptual and theoretical issues in competitive sport. In S. Hanton & S. D. Mellalieu (Eds.), *Literature reviews in sport psychology* (pp. 321–374). Hauppauge, NY: Nova Science Publishers.

Fletcher, D., Hanton, S., & Wagstaff, C. R. D. (2012). Performers' responses to stressors encountered in sport organizations. *Journal of Sports Sciences, 30*, 349–358. Doi:10.1080/02640414.2011.633545

Fletcher, D., & Sarkar, M. (2016). Mental fortitude training: An evidence-based approach to developing psychological resilience for sustained success. *Journal of Sport Psychology in Action, 7*, 135–157. Doi:10.1080/21520704.2016.1255496

Fletcher, D., & Scott, M. (2010). Psychological stress in sports coaches: A review of concepts, research, and practice. *Journal of Sports Sciences, 28*, 127–137. Doi:10.1080/02640410903406208

Fontana, A., & Rosenheck, R. (1998). Psychological benefits and liabilities of traumatic exposure in the war zone. *Journal of Traumatic Stress, 11*, 485–503. Doi:10.1023/a:1024452612412

Friedland, N., & Keinan, G. (1986). Stressors and tasks: How and when should stressors be introduced during training for task performance in stressful situations. *Journal of Human Stress, 12*, 71–76. Doi:10.1080/0097840X.1986.9936770

Gardner, H. (1994). The fruits of asynchrony: A psychological examination of creativity. In D. H. Feldman, M. Csikszentmihalyi, & H. Gardner (Eds.), *Changing the world: A framework for the study of creativity* (pp. 47–68). Westport, CT: Praeger.

Gearing, R. E., El-Bassel, N., Ghesquiere, A., Baldwin, S., Gillies, J., & Ngeow, E. (2011). Major ingredients of fidelity: A review and scientific guide to improving quality of intervention research implementation. *Clinical Psychology Review, 31*, 79–88. Doi:10.1016/j.cpr.2010.09.007

Goclowska, M. A., Damian, R. I., & Mor, S. (2018). The diversifying experience model: Taking a broader conceptual view of the multiculturalism-creativity link. *Journal of Cross-Cultural Psychology, 49*, 303–322. Doi:10.1177/0022022116650258

Goldfried, M. R. (1971). Systematic desensitization as training in self-control. *Journal of Consulting and Clinical Psychology, 37*, 228–234. Doi:10.1037/h0031974

Gray, J. J., Haring, M. J., & Banks, N. M. (1984). Mental rehearsal for sport performance: Exploring the relaxation-imagery paradigm. *Journal of Sport Behavior, 7*, 68–78.

Gröpel, P., & Mesagno, C. (2017). Choking interventions in sports: A systematic review. *International Review of Sport and Exercise Psychology, 10*, 1–26. Doi:10.108 0/1750984x.2017.1408134

Gross, B. H. (2001). Informed consent. *Annals of the American Psychotherapy Association, 4*, 24.

Gross, C. P., & Sepkowitz, K. A. (1998). The myth of the medical breakthrough: Smallpox, vaccination, and Jenner reconsidered. *International Journal of Infectious Diseases, 3*, 54–60. Doi:10.1016/s1201-9712(98)90096-0

Gunnar, M. R., Frenn, K., Wewerka, S. S., & Van Ryzin, M. J. (2009). Moderate versus severe early life stress: Associations with stress reactivity and regulation in 10–12-year-old children. *Psychoneuroendocrinology, 34*, 62–75. Doi:10.1016/j.psyneuen.2008.08.013

Gustafsson, H., Lundqvist, C., & Tod, D. (2017). Cognitive behavioural intervention in sport psychology: A case illustration of the exposure method with an elite athlete. *Journal of Sport Psychology in Action, 8*, 152–162. Doi:10.1080/215 20704.2016.1235649

Gwei-djen, L., & Sivin, N. (2000). Biology and biological technology: Medicine. In J. Needham (Ed.), *Science and civilisation in China Vol. VI:6*. Cambridge, UK: Cambridge University Press.

Hagan, M. J., Roubinov, D. S., Purdom Marreiro, C. L., & Luecken, L. J. (2014). Childhood interpersonal conflict and HPA axis activity in young adulthood: Examining nonlinear relations. *Developmental Psychobiology, 56*, 871–880. Doi:10.1002/dev.21157

Hale, B. D., & Whitehouse, A. (1998). The effects of imagery manipulated appraisal on intensity and direction of competitive anxiety. *The Sport Psychologist, 12*, 40–51.

Hanton, S., & Fletcher, D. (2005). Organizational stress in competitive sport: More than we bargained for? *International Journal of Sport Psychology, 36*, 273–283.

Hardy, L., Barlow, M., Evans, L., Rees, T., Woodman, T., & Warr, C. (2017). Great British medalists: Psychosocial biographies of super-elite and elite athletes from Olympic sports. In V. Walsh, M. Wilson, & B. Parkin (Eds.), *Sport and the brain: The science of preparing, enduring and winning, Part A* (pp. 1–119). London, UK: Academic Press.

Hardy, L., Jones, J. G., & Gould, D. (1996). *Understanding psychological preparation for sport: Theory and practice of elite performers*. Chichester, UK: John Wiley & Sons.

Hargrove, M. B., Becker, W. S., & Hargrove, D. F. (2015). The HRD eustress model: Generating positive stress with challenging work. *Human Resource Development Review, 14*, 279–298. Doi:10.1177/1534484315598086

Hargrove, M. B., Nelson, D. L., & Cooper, C. L. (2013). Generating eustress by challenging employees: Helping people savour their work. *Organizational Dynamics, 42*, 61–69. Doi:10.1016/j.orgdyn.2012.12.008

Haynal, A. (2003). Childhood lost and recovered. *International Forum of Psychoanalysis, 12*, 30–37. Doi:10.1080/08037060304585

Headrick, J., Renshaw, I., Davids, K., Pinder, R. A., & Araújo, D. (2015). The dynamics of expertise acquisition in sport: The role of affective learning design. *Psychology of Sport and Exercise, 16*, 83–90. Doi:10.1016/j.psychsport.2014.08.006

Hill, Y., Kiefer, A. W., Silva, P. L., Van Yperen, N. W., Meijer, R. R., Fischer, N., & Den Hartigh, R. J. R. (2020). Antifragility in climbing: Determining optimal stress loads for athletic performance training. *Frontiers in Psychology: Movement Science and Sport Psychology, 11*, 272. Doi:10.3389/fpsyg.2020.00272

Hodges, N. J., & Williams, A. M. (Eds.). (2019). *Skill acquisition in sport: Research, theory and practice.* Abingdon, UK: Routledge.

Höltge, J., McGee, S. L., Maercker, A., & Thoma, M. V. (2018). A salutogenic perspective on adverse experiences: The curvilinear relationship of adversity and well-being. *European Journal of Health Psychology, 25*, 53–69. Doi:10.1027/2512-8442/a000011

Höltge, J., McGee, S. L., & Thoma, M. V. (2019). The curvilinear relationship of early-life adversity and successful aging: The mediating role of mental health. *Aging and Mental Health, 23*, 608–617. Doi:10.1080/13607863.2018.1433635

Howells, K., & Fletcher, D. (2015). Sink or swim: Adversity- and growth-related experiences in Olympic swimming champions. *Psychology of Sport and Exercise, 16*, 37–48. Doi:10.1016/j.psychsport.2014.08.004

Howells, K., Sarkar, M., & Fletcher, D. (2017). Can athletes benefit from difficulty? A systematic review of growth following adversity in competitive sport. In M. R. Wilson, V. Walsh, & B. Parkin (Eds.), *Sport and the brain: The science of preparing, enduring and winning, part B* (pp. 117–159). London, UK: Academic Press.

Inzana, C. M., Driskell, J. E., Salas, E., & Johnson, J. (1996). Effects of preparatory information on enhancing performance under stress. *Journal of Applied Psychology, 81*, 429–435. Doi:10.1037/0021-9010.81.4.429

Iremonger, L. (1970). *The fiery chariot: A study of British prime ministers and the search for love.* London, UK: Secker & Warburg.

Jennings, P. A., Aldwin, C. M., Levenson, M. R., Spiro, A. III., & Mroczek, D. K. (2006). Combat exposure, perceived benefits of military service, and wisdom in later life: Findings from the normative aging study. *Research on Aging, 28*, 115–134. Doi:10.1177/0164027505281549

Johnston, J. H., & Cannon-Bowers, J. A. (1996). Training for stress exposure. In J. E. Driskell & E. Salas (Eds.), *Stress and human performance* (pp. 223–256). Mahwah, NJ: Erlbaum.

Jones, G. (1995). More than just a game: Research developments and issues in competitive anxiety in sport. *British Journal of Psychology, 86*, 449–478. Doi:10.1111/j.2044-8295.1995.tb02565.x

Kaplan, Z., Iancu, I., & Bodner, E. (2001). A review of psychological debriefing after extreme stress. *Psychiatric Services, 52*, 824–827. Doi:10.1176/appi.ps.52.6.824

Katahn, M. (1967). Systematic desensitization and counseling for anxiety in a college basketball player. *The Journal of Special Education, 1,* 309–314. Doi:10.1177/002246696700100308

Kegelaers, J., Wylleman, P., Bunigh, A., & Oudejans, R. R. D. (in press). A mixed methods evaluation of a pressure training intervention to develop resilience in female basketball players. *Journal of Applied Sport Psychology.* Advance online publication. Doi:10.1080/10413200.2019.1630864

Kegelaers, J., Wylleman, P., & Oudejans, R. R. D. (2020). A coach perspective on the use of planned disruptions in high-performance sports. *Sport, Exercise, and Performance Psychology, 9,* 29–44. Doi:10.1037/spy0000167

Keinan, G., & Friedland, N. (1996). Training effective performance under stress: Queries, dilemmas, and possible solutions. In J. E. Driskell & E. Salas (Eds.), *Stress and human performance* (pp. 257–277). Mahwah, NJ: Erlbaum.

Keinan, G., Friedland, N., & Sarig-Naor, V. (1990). Training for task performance under stress: The effectiveness of phased training methods. *Journal of Applied Social Psychology, 20,* 1514–1529. Doi:10.1111/j.1559-1816.1990.tb01490.x

Kent, S., Devonport, T., Lane, A., & Nicholls, W. (2020). The importance of contextualization when developing pressure intervention: An illustration among age-group professional soccer players. *Psychreg Journal of Psychology, 4,* 22–45. Doi:10.5281/zenodo.3871272

Kent, S., Devonport, T. J., Lane, A. M., Nicholls, W., & Friesen, A. P. (2018). The effects of coping interventions on ability to perform under pressure. *Journal of Sports Science and Medicine, 17,* 40–55.

Kidd, R. F. (1976). Manipulation checks: Advantage or disadvantage? *Representative Research in Social Psychology, 7,* 160–165.

Kiefer, A. W., Silva, P. L., Harison, H. S., & Araújo, D. (2018). Antifragility in sport: Leveraging adversity to enhance performance. *Sport, Exercise and Performance Psychology, 7,* 342–350. Doi:10.1037/spy0000130

Kinrade, N. P., Jackson, R. C., & Ashford, K. J. (2010). Dispositional reinvestment and skill failure cognitive and motor tasks. *Psychology of Sport & Exercise, 11,* 312–319. Doi:10.1016/j.psychsport.2010.02.005

Kinrade, N. P., Jackson, R. C., & Ashford, K. J. (2015). Reinvestment, task complexity and decision making under pressure in basketball. *Psychology of Sport and Exercise, 20,* 11–19. Doi:10.1016/j.psychsport.2015.03.007

Kinrade, N. P., Jackson, R. C., Ashford, K. J., & Bishop, D. T. (2010). Development and validation of the decision-specific reinvestment scale. *Journal of Sports Sciences, 28,* 1127–1135. Doi:10.1080/02640414.2010.499439

Kleim, B., & Ehlers, A. (2009). Evidence for a curvilinear relationship between posttraumatic growth and posttraumatic depression and PTSD in assault survivors. *Journal of Traumatic Stress, 22,* 45–52. Doi:10.1002/jts.20378

Knapp, S. J., VandeCreek, L. D., & Fingerhut, R. (2017). *Practical ethics for psychologists: A positive approach.* Washington, DC: American Psychological Association.

Kunst, M. J. J. (2010). Peritraumatic distress, posttraumatic stress disorder symptoms, and posttraumatic growth in victims of violence. *Journal of Traumatic Stress, 23,* 514–518. Doi:10.1002/jts.20556

Kupriyanov, R., & Zhdanov, R. (2014). The eustress concept: Problems and outlooks. *World Journal of Medical Sciences, 11,* 179–185.

Lawrence, G. P., Cassell, V. E., Beattie, S., Woodman, T., Khan, M. A., Hardy, L., . . . Gottwald, V. M. (2014). Practice with anxiety improves performance, but only when anxious: Evidence for the specificity of practice hypothesis. *Psychological Research, 78*, 634–650. Doi:10.1007/s00426-013-0521-9

Lazarus, R. S. (1966). *Psychological stress and the coping process.* New York: McGraw-Hill.

Lazarus, R. S., & Folkman, S. (1984). *Stress, appraisal and coping.* New York: Springer.

Lechner, S. C., Zakowski, S. G., Antoni, M. H., Greenhawt, M., Block, K., & Block, P. (2003). Do sociodemongraphic and disease-related variables influence benefit-finding in cancer patients? *Psychooncology, 12*, 491–499. Doi:10.1002/pon.671

Levine, S. (1957). Infantile experience and resistance to physiological stress. *Science, 126*, 405–406. Doi:10.1126/science.126.3270.405

Levine, S. (1959). The effects of differential infantile stimulation on emotionality at weaning. *Canadian Journal of Psychology, 13*, 253–247. Doi:10.1037/h0083784

Levine, S. (1960). Stimulation in infancy. *Scientific American, 202*, 80–86. Doi:10.1038/scientificamerican0560-80

Levine, S. (1961). Psychophysiological effects of early stimulation. In E. Bliss (Ed.), *Roots of behaviour.* New York: Hoeber.

Levine, S., & Mody, T. (2003). The long-term psychobiological consequences of intermittent postnatal separation in the squirrel monkey. *Neuroscience and Biobehavioral Reviews, 27*, 83–89. Doi:10.1016/s0149-7634(03)00011-3

Lewis, B. P., & Linder, D. E. (1997). Thinking about choking? Attentional processes and paradoxical performance. *Personality and Social Psychology Bulletin, 23*, 937–944. Doi:10.1177/0146167297239003

Lines, R. L. J., Crane, M., Ducker, K., Ntoumanis, N., Thøgersen-Ntoumani, C., Fletcher, D., & Gucciardi, D. F. (2020). Profiles of adversity and individual-level resilience resources: A latent class analysis across two samples. *British Journal of Psychology, 111*, 174–199. Doi:10.1111/bjop.12397

Linley, A. P., & Joseph, S. (2004). Positive change following trauma and adversity: A review. *Journal of Traumatic Stress, 17*, 11–21. Doi:10.1023/b:jots.0000014671.27856.7e

Liu, R. T. (2015). A developmentally informed perspective on the relation between stress and psychopathology: When the problem with stress is that there is not enough. *Journal of Abnormal Psychology, 124*, 80–92. Doi:10.1037/abn0000043

Long, B. C. (1980). Stress management for the athlete: A cognitive-behavioral model. In C. H. Nadeau, W. R. Halliwell, K. M. Newell, & G. C. Roberts (Eds.), *Psychology of motor behaviour and sport—1979* (pp. 73–83). Champaign, IL: Human Kinetics.

Lotz, M. (2016). Vulnerability and resilience: A critical nexus. *Theoretical Medicine and Bioethics, 37*, 45–59. Doi:10.1007/s11017-016-9355-y

Low, W. R., Sandercock, G., Freeman, P., Winter, M. E., Butt, J., & Maynard, I. (in press). Pressure training for performance domains: A meta-analysis. *Sport, Exercise and Performance Psychology.* Advance online publication. Doi:10.1037/spy0000202

Lyons, D. M., & Parker, K. J. (2007). Stress inoculation-induced indications of resilience in monkeys. *Journal of Traumatic Stress, 20*, 423–433. Doi:10.1002/jts.20265

Lyons, D. M., Parker, K. J., & Schatzberg, A. F. (2010). Animal models of early life stress: Implications for understanding resilience. *Developmental Psychobiology, 52*, 402–410. Doi:10.1002/dev.20429

Mace, R. D. (1990). Cognitive behavioural interventions in sport. In J. G. Jones & L. Hardy (Eds.), *Stress and performance in sport* (pp. 203–230). Chichester, UK: John Wiley & Sons.

Mace, R. D., & Carroll, D. (1985). The control of anxiety in sport: Stress inoculation training prior to abseiling. *International Journal of Sport Psychology, 16*, 165–175.

Mace, R. D., & Carroll, D. (1986). Stress inoculation training to control anxiety in sport: Two case studies in squash. *British Journal of Sports Medicine, 20*, 115–117. Doi:10.1136/bjsm.20.3.115

Mace, R. D., Carroll, D., & Eastman, C. (1986). Effects of stress inoculation training on self-report, behavioural and psychophysiological reactions to abseiling. *Journal of Sports Sciences, 4*, 229–236. Doi:10.1080/02640418608732121

Mace, R. D., Eastman, C., & Carroll, D. (1986a). Stress inoculation training to control anxiety in sport: A case study in gymnastics. *British Journal of Sports Medicine, 10*, 139–141. Doi:10.1136/bjsm.20.3.139

Mace, R. D., Eastman, C., & Carroll, D. (1986b). The effects of stress inoculation training on gymnastics performance on the pommelled horse: A case study. *Behavioural Psychotherapy, 15*, 272–279. Doi:10.1017/s0141347300012349

Macquet, A.-C., Ferrand, C., & Stanton, N. A. (2015). Divide and rule: A qualitative analysis of the debriefing process in elite team sports. *Applied Ergonomics, 51*, 30–38. Doi:10.1016/j.apergo.2015.04.005

Maier, S. F., Amat, J., Baratta, M. V., Paul, E., & Watkins, L. R. (2006). Behavioral control, the medial prefrontal cortex, and resilience. *Dialogues Clinical Neuroscience, 8*, 397–406.

Mason, J. W. (1971). A re-evaluation of the concept of nonspecificity in stress theory. *Journal of Psychiatric Research, 8*, 323–333. Doi:10.1016/0022-3956(71)90028-8

Mason, J. W. (1975). A historical view of the stress field. *Journal of Human Stress, 1*, 6–12. Doi:10.1080/0097840x.1975.9940399

McArdle, S., Martin, D., Lennon, A., & Moore, P. (2010). Exploring debriefing in sports: A qualitative perspective. *Journal of Applied Sport Psychology, 22*, 320–332. Doi:10.1080/10413200.2010.481566

McCaslin, S. E., de Zoysa, P., Butler, L. D., Hart, S., Marmar, C. R., Metzler, C. R., & Koopman, C. (2009). The relationship of posttraumatic growth to peritraumatic reactions and posttraumatic stress symptoms among Sri Lankan university students. *Journal of Traumatic Stress, 22*, 334–339. Doi:10.1002/jts.20426

McEwen, B. S., Nasca, C., & Gray, J. D. (2016). Stress effects on neuronal structure: Hippocampus, amygdala, and prefrontal cortex. *Neuropsychopharmacology, 41*, 3–23. Doi:10.1038/npp.2015.171

McGuire, W. J. (1961). Resistance to persuasion conferred by active and passive prior refutation of the same and alternative counterarguments. *The Journal of Abnormal and Social Psychology, 63*, 326–332. Doi:10.1037/h0048344

McGuire, W. J. (1964). Inducing resistance to persuasion: Some contemporary approaches. In L. Berkowitz (Ed.), *Advances in social psychology* (Vol. 1). New York: Academic Press.

McLafferty, M., O'Neil, S., Murphy, S., Armour, C., Ferry, F., & Bunting, B. (2018). The moderating impact of childhood adversity profiles and conflict on psychological health and suicidal behaviour in the Northern Ireland population. *Psychiatry Research, 262,* 213–220. Doi:10.1016/j.psychres.2018.02.024

McLean, C. P., Handa, S., Dickstein, B. D., Benson, T. A., Baker, M. T., Isler, W. C . . . Litz, B. T. (2013). Posttraumatic growth and posttraumatic stress among military medical personnel. *Psychological Trauma: Theory, Research, and Policy, 5,* 62–68. Doi:10.1037/a0022949

Meichenbaum, D. (1975). Self-instructional methods. In F. H. Kanfer & A. P. Goldstein (Eds.), *Helping people change* (pp. 357–391). New York: Pergamon Press.

Meichenbaum, D. (1976). A self-instructional approach to stress management: A proposal for stress inoculation training. In C. Spielberger & I. Sarason (Eds.), *Stress and anxiety in modern life.* New York: Winston.

Meichenbaum, D. (1977). *Cognitive behavior modification: An integrative approach.* New York: Plenum Press.

Meichenbaum, D. (2007). Stress inoculation training: A preventative and treatment approach. In P. M. Lehrer, R. L. Woolfolk, & W. E. Sime (Eds.), *Principles and practice of stress management* (pp. 497–516). New York: Guilford Press.

Meichenbaum, D., & Fitzpatrick, D. (1993). A constructivist narrative perspective on stress and coping: Stress inoculation applications. In L. Goldberger & S. Breznitz (Eds.), *Handbook of stress: Theoretical and clinical aspects* (pp. 706–723). New York: Free Press.

Mészáros, J. (2014). Ferenczi's "wise baby" phenomenon and resilience. *International Forum of Psychanalysis, 23,* 3–10. Doi:10.1080/0803706x.2013.773074

Mitchell, J. (1983). When disaster strikes: The critical incident stress debriefing process. *Journal of Emergency and Medical Services, 8,* 36–39.

Mittelmark, M. B., Sagy, S., Eriksson, M., Bauer, G., Pelikan, J. M., Lindström, B., & Espnes, G. A. (Eds.). (2017). *The handbook of salutogenesis.* New York: Springer.

Moore, L. J., Vine, S. J., Wilson, M. R., & Freeman, P. (2012). The effect of challenge and threat states on performance: An examination of potential mechanisms. *Psychophysiology, 49,* 1417–1425. Doi:10.1111/j.1469-8986.2012.01449.x

Moore, L. J., Vine, S. J., Wilson, M. R., & Freeman, P. (2015). Reappraising threat: How to optimize preference under pressure. *Journal of Sport and Exercise Psychology, 37,* 339–343. Doi:10.1123/jsep.2014-0186

Moore, L. J., Wilson, M., Vine, S. J., Coussens, A. H., & Freeman, P. (2013). Champ or chump? Challenge and threat states during pressurized competition. *Journal of Sport and Exercise Psychology, 35,* 551–562. Doi:10.1123/jsep.35.6.551

Moore, L. J., Young, T., Freeman, P., & Sarkar, M. (2018). Adverse life event, cardiovascular responses, and sports performance under pressure. *Scandinavian Journal of Medicine and Science in Sports, 28,* 340–347. Doi:10.1111/sms.12928

Neff, L. A., & Broady, E. F. (2011). Stress resilience in early marriage: Can practice make perfect? *Journal of Personality and Social Psychology, 101,* 1050–1067. Doi:10.1037/a0023809

Nelson, D. L., & Simmons, B. L. (2004). Eustress: An elusive construct, an engaging pursuit. In P. L. Perrewe & D. C. Ganster (Eds.), *Research in occupational stress and well-being (Vol 3): Emotional and physiological processes and positive intervention strategies* (pp. 265–322). Oxford, UK: Elsevier.

Nielsen, K., Randall, R., & Albertsen, K. (2007). Participants' appraisals of process issues and the effects of stress management interventions. *Journal of Organizational Behavior, 28,* 793–810. Doi:10.1002/job.450

Oakley, A., Strange, V., Bonell, C., Allen, E., & Stephenson, J. (2006). Process evaluation in randomised controlled trials of complex interventions. *British Medical Journal, 332,* 413–416. Doi:10.1136/bmj.332.7538.413

Olszewski-Kubilius, P. (2000). The transition from childhood giftedness to adult creative productiveness: Psychological characteristics and social supports. *Roeper Review, 2,* 65–71. Doi:10.1080/02783190009554068

Oudejans, R. R. D., & Nieuwenhuys, A. (2009). Perceiving and moving in sports and other high-pressure contexts. *Progress in Brain Research, 174,* 35–48. Doi:10.1016/S0079-6123(09)01304-1

Oudejans, R. R. D., & Pijpers, J. R. (2009). Training with anxiety has a positive effect on expert perceptual-motor performance under pressure. *Quarterly Journal of Experimental Psychology, 62,* 1631–1647. Doi:10.1080/17470210802557702

Oudejans, R. R. D., & Pijpers, J. R. (2010). Training with mild anxiety may prevent choking under higher levels of anxiety. *Psychology of Sport and Exercise, 11,* 44–50. Doi:10.1016/j.psychsport.2009.05.002

Page, J., & Thelwell, R. (2013). The value of social validation in single-case methods in sport and exercise psychology. *Journal of Applied Sport Psychology, 25,* 61–71. Doi:10.1080/10413200.2012.663859

Pasteur, L., Chamberland, C., & Roux, E. (1881). Del'attenuation des viruset-deleurretourala virulence. *Comptes rendus de l'Académie des Sciences, 92,* 430–435.

Pierce, S., Gould, D., Cowburn, I., & Driska, A. (2016). Understanding the process of psychological development in youth athletes attending an intensive wrestling camp. *Qualitative Research in Sport, Exercise and Health, 8,* 332–351. Doi:10.1080/2159676X.2016.1176067

Piirto, J. (1992). *Understanding those who create.* Dayton, OH: Ohio Psychology Press.

Pinder, R. A., Davids, K., Renshaw, L., & Araújo, D. (2011). Representative learning design and functionality of research and practice in sport. *Journal of Sport and Exercise Psychology, 33,* 146–155. Doi:10.1123/jsep.33.1.146

Pinder, R. A., Renshaw, L., Headrick, J., & Davids, K. (2014). Skill acquisition and representative task design. In K. Davids, R. Hristovski, D. Araújo, N. Balague, C. Button, & P. Passos (Eds.), *Complex systems in sport* (pp. 319–333). London, UK: Routledge.

Powell, S., Rosner, R., Butollo, W., Tedeschi, R. G., & Calhoun, L. G. (2003). Post-traumatic growth after war: A study with former refugees and displaced people in Sarajevo. *Journal of Clinical Psychology, 59,* 71–83. Doi:10.1002/jclp.10117

Quinton, M. L., Veldhuijzen van Zanten, J., Trotman, G. P., Cumming, J., & Williams, S. E. (2019). Investigating the protective role of mastery imagery ability in buffering debilitative stress responses. *Frontiers in Psychology, 10,* 1657. Doi:10.3389/fpsyg.2019.01657

Randall, R., Griffiths, A., & Cox, T. (2005). Evaluating organisational stress-management interventions using adapted study designs. *European Journal of Work and Organizational Psychology, 14,* 23–41. Doi:10.1080/13594320444000209

Raphael, B., & Wilson, J. P. (Eds.). (2000). *Psychological debriefing: Theory, practice and evidence.* Cambridge, UK: Cambridge University Press.

Rees, T., & Hardy, L. (2004). Matching social support with stressors: Effect on factors underlying performance in tennis. *Psychology of Sport and Exercise, 5,* 319–337. Doi:10.1016/s1469-0292(03)00018-9

Rees, T., Hardy, L., Güllich, A., Abernethy, B., Côté, J., Woodman, T., . . . Warr, C. (2016). The Great British medalists project: A review of current knowledge on the development of the world's best sporting talent. *Sports Medicine, 48,* 1041–1058. Doi:10.1007/s40279-016-0476-2

Reeves, J. L., Tenenbaum, G., & Lidor, R. (2007). Choking in front of the goal: The effects of self-consciousness training. *International Journal of Sport and Exercise Psychology, 5,* 240–254. Doi:10.1080/1612197X.2007.9671834

Richardson, G. E. (2002). The metatheory of resilience and resiliency. *Journal of Clinical Psychology, 58,* 307–321. Doi:10.1002/jclp.10020

Rinn, A. N., & Bishop, J. (2015). Gifted adults: A systematic review and analysis of the literature. *Gifted Child Quarterly, 59,* 213–235. Doi:10.1177/0016986215600795

Ruch, L. O., Chandler, S. M., & Harter, R. A. (1980). Life change and rape impact. *Journal of Health and Social Behavior, 21,* 248–260. Doi:10.2307/2136619

Rumbold, J. L., Fletcher, D., & Daniels, K. (2012). A systematic review of stress management interventions with sport performers. *Sport, Exercise and Performance Psychology, 1,* 173–193. Doi:10.1037/a0026628

Russo, S. J., Murrough, J. W., Han, M.-H., Charney, D. S., & Nestler, E. J. (2012). Neurobiology of resilience. *Nature Neuroscience, 15,* 1475–1484.

Rutter, M. (1987). Psychosocial resilience and protective mechanisms. *American Journal of Orthopsychiatry, 57,* 316–331. Doi:10.1111/j.1939-0025.1987. tb03541.x

Rutter, M. (2012). Resilience as a dynamic concept. *Development and Psychopathology, 24,* 335–344. Doi:10.1017/s0954579412000028

Saksvik, P. Ø., Nytrø, K., Dahl-Jørgensen, C., & Mikkelsen, A. (2002). A process evaluation of individual and organizational occupational health and stress interventions. *Work & Stress: An International Journal of Work, Health & Organisations, 16,* 37–57. Doi:10.1080/02678370110118744

Sammy, N., Anstiss, P. A., Moore, L. J., Freeman, P., Wilson, M. R., & Vine, S. J. (2017). The effects of arousal reappraisal on stress responses, performance and attention. *Anxiety, Stress, and Coping: An International Journal, 30,* 619–629. Doi:10.1080/10615806.2017.1330952

Sarkar, M., & Fletcher, D. (2014). Psychological resilience in sport performers: A narrative review of stressors and protective factors. *Journal of Sports Sciences, 32,* 1419–1434. Doi:10.1080/02640414.2014.901551

Sarkar, M., & Fletcher, D. (2017). Adversity-related experiences are essential for Olympic success: Additional evidence and considerations. In V. Walsh, M. Wilson, & B. Parkin (Eds.), *Sport and the brain: The science of preparing, enduring and winning, Part A* (pp. 159–165). London, UK: Academic Press.

Sarkar, M., Fletcher, D., & Brown, D. J. (2015). What doesn't kill me . . . : Adversity-related experiences are vital in the development of superior Olympic performance. *Journal of Science and Medicine in Sport, 18,* 475–479. Doi:10.1016/j. jsams.2014.06.010

Saunders, T., Driskell, J. E., Johnson, J. H., & Salas, E. (1996). The effect of stress inoculation training on anxiety and performance. *Journal of Occupational Health Psychology, 1,* 170–186. Doi:10.1037/1076-8998.1.2.170

Savage, J., Collins, D., & Cruickshank, A. (2016). Exploring traumas in the development of talent: What are they, what do they do, and what do they require? *Journal of Applied Sport Psychology, 29,* 101–117. Doi:10.1080/10413200.2016.1194910

Schnurr, P. P., Friedman, M. J., & Rosenberg, S. D. (1993). Preliminary MMPI scores as predictors of combat-related PTSD symptoms. *The American Journal of Psychiatry, 150,* 479–483. Doi:10.1176/ajp.150.3.479

Seery, M. D. (2011). Resilience: A silver lining to experiencing adverse life events? *Current Directions in Psychological Science, 20,* 390–394.

Seery, M. D., Holman, E. A., & Silver, R. C. (2010). Whatever does not kill us: Cumulative lifetime adversity, vulnerability, and resilience. *Journal of Personality and Social Psychology, 99,* 1025–1041. Doi:10.1037/a0021344

Seery, M. D., Leo, R. J., Holman, E. A., & Silver, R. C. (2010). Lifetime exposure to adversity predicts functional impairment and healthcare utilization among individuals with chronic back pain. *Pain, 150,* 507–515. Doi:10.1016/j.pain.2010.06.007

Seery, M. D., Leo, R. J., Lupien, S. P., Kondrak, C. L., & Almonte, J. L. (2013). An upside to adversity? Moderate cumulative lifetime adversity is associated with resilient responses in the face of controlled stressors. *Psychological Science, 24,* 1181–1189. Doi:10.1177/0956797612469210

Seery, M. D., & Quinton, W. J. (2016). Understanding resilience: From negative life events to everyday stressors. *Advances in Experimental Psychology, 54,* 181–245.

Seifried, C. (2008). Examining punishment and discipline: Defending the use of punishment by coaches. *Quest, 60,* 370–386. Doi:10.1080/00336297.2008.10483587

Seifried, C. (2010). The misconception of corporal punishment: A rejoin to Albrecht's "Drop and give us 20, Seifried: A practical response to defending the use of punishment by coaches". *Quest, 62,* 218–223. Doi:10.1080/00336297.2010.10483643

Selye, H. (1936). A syndrome produced by diverse nocuous agents. *Nature, 138,* 32. Doi:10.1038/138032a0

Selye, H. (1950). *The physiology and pathology of exposure to stress, a treatise based on the concepts of the general-adaptation-syndrome and the diseases of adaptation.* Montreal, Canada: ACTA, Inc., Medical Publishers.

Selye, H. (1956). *The stress of life.* New York: McGraw-Hill.

Selye, H. (1974). *Stress without distress.* Philadelphia, PA: J. B. Lippincott Co.

Selye, H. (1977). *The stress of my life: A scientist's memoirs.* Toronto, Canada: McClelland and Stewart.

Silver, R. L., & Wortman, C. B. (1980). Coping with undesirable life events. In J. Garber & M. E. P. Seligman (Eds.), *Human helplessness: Theory and applications* (pp. 279–340). New York: Academic Press.

Simonton, D. K. (1994). *Greatness: Who makes history and why.* New York: Guilford Press.

Simonton, D. K. (2000). Creativity: Cognitive, personal, developmental, and social aspects. *American Psychologist, 55,* 151–158. Doi:10.1037/0003-066x.55.1.151

Simonton, D. K. (2016). Reverse engineering genius: Historiometric studies of superlative talent. *Annals of the New York Academy of Sciences, 1377,* 3–9. Doi:10.1111/nyas.13054

Sipprelle, C. N. (1967). Induced anxiety. *Psychotherapy: Theory, Research and Practice, 4*, 36–40.

Smith, R. E. (1980). A cognitive-affective approach to stress management training for athletes. In C. H. Nadeau, W. R. Halliwell, K. M. Newell, & G. C. Roberts (Eds.), *Psychology of motor behaviour and sport—1979* (pp. 54–72). Champaign, IL: Human Kinetics.

Standing, L. G., Aikins, S., Madigan, B., & Nohl, W. (2015). Exceptional achievement and early parental loss: The Phaeton Effect in American writers, presidents, and eminent individuals. *Journal of Psychohistory, 42*, 188–199.

Standing, L. G., & Ringo, P. (2016). Parental loss and eminence: Is there a critical period for the Phaeton Effect? *North American Journal of Psychology, 18*, 147–160.

Stoker, M., Lindsay, P., Butt, J., Bawden, M., & Maynard, I. (2016). Elite coaches' experiences of creating pressure training environments. *International Journal of Sport Psychology, 47*, 262–281.

Stoker, M., Maynard, I., Butt, J., Hays, K., & Hughes, P. (2019). The effect of manipulating individual consequences and training demands on experiences of pressure with elite disability shooters. *The Sport Psychologist, 33*, 221–227. Doi:10.1123/tsp.2017-0045

Stoker, M., Maynard, I., Butt, J., Hays, K., Lindsay, P., & Norenberg, D. A. (2017). The effect of manipulating training demands and consequences on experiences of pressure in elite netball. *Journal of Applied Sport Psychology, 29*, 434–448. Doi:10.1080/10413200.2017.1298166

Suinn, R. M. (1972a). Behavior rehearsal training for ski racers. *Behavior Therapy, 3*, 519–520. Doi:10.1016/S0005-7894(72)80191-6

Suinn, R. M. (1972b). Removing emotional obstacles to learning and performance by visuomotor behavior rehearsal. *Behavior Therapy, 3*, 308–310. Doi:10.1016/S0005-7894(72)80096-0

Suinn, R. M., & Richardson, F. (1971). Anxiety management training: A nonspecific behavior therapy program for anxiety control. *Behavior Therapy, 2*, 498–510. Doi:10.1016/S0005-7894(71)80096-5

Suvak, M. K., Vogt, D. S., Savarese, V. W., King, L. A., & King, D. W. (2002). Relationship of war-zone coping strategies to long-term general life adjustment among Vietnam veterans: Combat exposure as a moderator variable. *Personality and Social Psychology Bulletin, 28*, 974–985. Doi:10.1177/014616720202800710

Taleb, N. N. (2011). Antifragility—or—the property of disorder-loving systems. *Edge*. Retrieved from http://edge.org/response-detail/819/what-scientific-concept-would-improve-everybodys-cognitivetoolkit

Taleb, N. N. (2012). *Antifragile: Things that gain from disorder*. London, UK: Penguin.

Taleb, N. N. (2013). 'Antifragility' as a mathematical idea. *Nature, 494*, 430. Doi:10.1038/494430e

Taleb, N. N., & Douady, R. (2013). Mathematical definition, mapping, and detection of (anti)fragility. *Quantitative Finance, 13*, 1677–1689. Doi:10.1080/1469 7688.2013.800219

Updegraff, J. A., & Taylor, S. E. (2000). From vulnerability to growth: Positive and negative effects of stressful life events. In J. Harvey, & E. Miller (Eds.), *Loss and trauma: General and close relationship perspectives* (pp. 3–28). Philadelphia, PA: Brunner-Routledge.

Van Rens, F. E. C. A., Burgin, M., & Morris-Binelli, K. (in press). Implementing a pressure inurement training program to optimize cognitive appraisal, emotion regulation, and sport self-confidence in a women's state cricket team. *Journal of Applied Sport Psychology*. Advance online publication. Doi:10.1080/1 0413200.2019.1706664

von Moltke, H. K. B. G. (1892). *MilitÄrische werke (Band 2, Teil 2)*. Berlin, Germany: E. S. Mittler & Sohn.

Ward, P., Williams, A. M., & Hancock, P. A. (2006). Simulation for performance and training. In K. A. Ericsson, N. Charness, P. J. Feltovich, & R. R. Hoffman (Eds.), *The Cambridge handbook of expertise and expert performance* (pp. 243–262). Cambridge, UK: Cambridge University Press. Doi:10.1017/ CBO9780511816796.014

Wildman, R. C., & Johnson, D. R. (1977). Life change and Langner's 22-item mental health index: A study and partial replication. *Journal of Health and Social Behavior, 18*, 179–188. Doi:10.2307/2955381

Williams, S. E., & Cumming, J. (2012). Challenge vs. threat: Investigating the effect of using imagery to manipulate stress appraisal of a dart throwing task. *Sport and Exercise Psychology Review, 8*, 4–21.

Williams, S. E., Cumming, J., & Balanos, G. M. (2010). The use of imagery to manipulate challenge and threat appraisal states in athletes. *Journal of Sport and Exercise Psychology, 32*, 339–358.

Willis, N. J. (1997). Edward Jenner and the eradication of smallpox. *Scottish Medical Journal, 42*, 118–121. Doi:10.1177/003693309704200407

Wise, E. H. (2007). Informed consent: Complexities and meanings. *Professional Psychology: Research and Practice, 38*, 182–183. Doi:10.1037/0735-7028.38.2.179

Wolpe, J. (1958). *Psychotherapy by reciprocal inhibition*. Stanford, CA: Stanford University Press.

Ziegler, S. G., Klinzing, J., & Williamson, K. (1982). The effects of two stress management training programs on cardiorespiratory efficiency. *Journal of Sport Psychology, 4*, 280–289. Doi:10.1123/jsp.4.3.280

13 Thriving

Daniel J. Brown, Michael Passaportis, and Kate Hays

The implications of achieving success in sport (e.g., continued access to funding and enhancing job security) make it a fundamental concern for elite sport organizations (Fletcher & Wagstaff, 2009). This need to succeed can foster a win-at-all-costs mentality and create sporting environments that prioritize results and performance at the expense of athlete welfare. Indeed, recent accusations of maltreatment have exposed the detrimental impact that this mindset can have on athlete well-being and highlighted the need to reconsider what is deemed as acceptable practice in these settings (see also Chapters 6 and 14). An emerging line of research that may be helpful in redressing this imbalance is that on the topic of thriving. Broadly defined as "the joint experience of development and success" (Brown, Arnold, Fletcher, & Standage, 2017, p. 168), thriving encapsulates an experience of full or holistic functioning and, within sport, this has been characterized by perceiving a high level of performance and experiencing a high level of well-being (Brown, Arnold, Standage, & Fletcher, 2017; Brown, Arnold, Reid, & Roberts, 2018). Understanding how to facilitate thriving may, therefore, offer researchers and practitioners mechanisms to promote sporting success without sacrificing athlete well-being. This chapter will introduce and discuss the nascent literature on human thriving, and explore how high levels of athletic performance can be achieved while simultaneously promoting athlete well-being. This discussion is composed of three parts: Conceptual Overview, Prediction and Promotion of Thriving, and Recommendations for Future Research on Thriving in Sport.

Conceptual Overview

What Is Thriving?

The topic of thriving in humans has received growing attention over the past 25 years with scholars considering the construct across a variety of contexts such as following adversity (e.g., O'Leary & Ickovics, 1995), at work (e.g., Sumsion, 2004), and in youth development (e.g., Lerner, 2004). In each of these settings, scholars have forwarded differing interpretations of what it means to thrive, and these have resulted in a lack of consensus on the characteristics of thriving and the processes that underpin it (Brown, Arnold, Fletcher et al., 2017). For example, in developmental domains (e.g., positive youth development), thriving is considered to be a process characterized by development and growth (e.g., Benson & Scales, 2009; Bundick, Yeager, King, & Damon, 2010), and realized through high levels of competence, character, connection, confidence, and compassion (Lerner, Dowling, & Anderson, 2003). In contrast, in performance domains (e.g., work), thriving tends to refer to outcome-oriented aspects, such as a sense of accomplishment, success, and wealth (see, e.g., Bakker, van Veldhoven, & Xanthopoulou, 2010; Sarkar & Fletcher, 2014). These contextual variations have meant that, until recently, it has been difficult to establish a definition that is applicable across multiple settings and to ascertain whether thriving is a context-specific or a more global experience.

Recognizing the need for conceptual consensus, Brown, Arnold, Fletcher et al. (2017) reviewed and consolidated the extant literature on thriving in an attempt to establish a robust, global definition of the construct. Through this review, two overarching themes were identified: development and success (Brown, Arnold, Fletcher et al., 2017). These themes were suggested to be experienced in tandem (cf. Su, Tay, & Diener, 2014), thus inferring thriving to be a multifaceted construct (see, e.g., Spreitzer, Sutcliffe, Dutton, Sonenshein, & Grant, 2005). Incorporating these observations, Brown, Arnold, Fletcher et al. (2017) broadly defined thriving as "the joint experience of development and success" (p. 168). The development component encapsulates the innate human drive for self-fulfillment and growth (Ryan & Deci, 2017), whereby humans are making progressive enhancements to their lives. These can be either physical (e.g., an infant learning to walk), psychological (e.g., learning adaptive coping styles), or social (e.g., establishing a friendship group) in nature. The success component is characterized by the attainment of outcomes that are meaningful and tangible to an individual's current context (e.g., key performance indicators, wealth, and cardiovascular capacity). Brown, Arnold, Fletcher et al.'s (2017) conceptualization of thriving advanced understanding in this area in three main ways. First, it overcame the temporal constraints applied by previous definitions that restrict the construct to certain age groups (e.g., Benson & Scales, 2009). Second, it provided a broader focus than those taken by previous context-specific definitions (e.g., Spreitzer et al., 2005), enabling thriving to be explored across different domains. Last, it provided flexibility in the construct, allowing thriving to be both a global and scenario-specific experience. To expand on the last point, this conceptualization of thriving recognized that an individual can be thriving in all areas of their lives, or alternatively, that he or she may be experiencing development and success in one area (e.g., in their work), but not necessarily in others (e.g., their home life; Brown, Arnold, Fletcher et al., 2017).

In order to thrive (i.e., experience development and success), an individual must experience full or holistic functioning (Brown, Arnold, Fletcher et al., 2017; Ryan & Deci, 2017; Su et al., 2014). To elaborate, Su et al. (2014) suggest, "*Thriving* denotes that state of positive functioning at its fullest range—mentally, physically, and socially" (p. 256), and Brown, Arnold, Fletcher et al. (2017) state that, "thriving can be realized through effective holistic functioning" (p. 169). Furthermore, Ryan and Deci (2017) infer that thriving is akin to being fully functioning. To determine the level of human functioning, scholars have typically examined indices of well-being (e.g., positive affect and vitality) and performance (e.g., high-achievement and informant-rated performance; Ryan & Frederick, 1997; McNeill, Durand-Bush, & Lemyre, 2018; Sarkar & Fletcher, 2014; Verner-Filion & Vallerand, 2018; see also Chapter 6). High levels of well-being suggest a state of being or doing well in life, and are essential for thriving as they indicate that an individual has the necessary social and personal functioning for development to occur (Ryan & Deci, 2001). Performance is the extent of quality displayed when executing an action, operation, or process, and the level of performance shown on the task is considered to represent an individual's level of functioning (cf. Sarkar & Fletcher, 2014). Achieving elevated levels of performance on temporally and contextual appropriate tasks are thus important for thriving as they underpin success (cf. Lerner et al., 2003; Scales, Benson, Leffert, & Blyth, 2000). Importantly, as is illustrated in the previous descriptions, it is when individuals demonstrate high levels on both well-being and performance indices that they can be considered to be functioning fully and, therefore, thriving.

Characterizing Thriving in Sport

Thriving has driven interest from researchers investigating humans across a variety of domains (e.g., work and youth development) and, at the turn of the century, it began to receive attention from scholars in sport psychology. To illustrate, thriving in sport initially emerged from research exploring mental toughness in elite athletes (see Bull, Shambrook, & Brooks, 2005; Jones, Hanton, & Connaughton, 2002). Subsequently, it featured in research investigating youth (e.g., Gucciardi, Jackson, Hodge, Anthony, & Brooke, 2015; Gucciardi & Jones, 2012; Gucciardi, Stamatis, & Ntoumanis, 2017; Jones, Dunn, Holt, Sullivan, & Bloom, 2011) and adult sport populations (e.g., Galli & Reel, 2012; Harris, Myhill, & Walker, 2012; McNeill et al., 2018). Within these studies, sports researchers have applied various interpretations of thriving including those developed in work settings (e.g., Gucciardi et al., 2015) and within a positive youth development framework (e.g., Jones et al.,

2011), while others consider thriving as a response to significant challenge akin to stress-related growth (e.g., Galli & Reel, 2012). The divergent approaches therefore mirrored those observed in the wider thriving literature, and this variance restricted the development of a coherent or systematic line of research into thriving in sport. In summary, although interest in the notion of thriving in sport performers continued to grow, the absence of a comprehensive exploration of thriving in this context meant that it was impossible to elicit whether the previous definitions of thriving accurately captured thriving in sport performers.

To construct a sport-based understanding of thriving for comparison with the interpretations previously applied to athletes, Brown et al. (2018) conducted an inductive exploration of thriving in elite sport. Couched in the perspectives of athletes, coaches, and sport psychologists, thriving in sport performers was suggested to be characterized by a sustained high level of performance and dimension of eudaimonic well-being (i.e., the extent to which a person is fully functioning; Brown et al., 2018; see also Chapter 6). When these findings are considered against the previous work on thriving in sport (e.g., Gucciardi et al., 2017), it is important to recognize the similar expression of well-being in individuals who thrive, but also to highlight the additional role of performance as a critical component of thriving in sport performers. In 2017, Brown, Arnold, Standage, and Fletcher[1] examined whether it was possible to identify performers who thrived in competitive sporting encounters using indices of subjective performance and well-being (i.e., positive affect and subjective vitality). Sampling 535 performers, the analysis identified common response patterns to the encounters and revealed a group of "thriving" performers who displayed the highest levels on all measures. In a similar study examining the experiences of sport coaches, McNeill et al. (2018) identified a thriving profile of coaches who scored highest for personal accomplishment and emotional, social, and psychological well-being. The ability to distinguish between those who thrive and those who do not is an important advancement, as this allows researchers to begin testing and examining potential factors that may result in individuals residing in these differing categories. Furthermore, finding that sport performers (athletes or coaches) are able to function fully while facing the demands of competitive sport is particularly encouraging, as it highlights that high-level performance can be achieved without sacrificing well-being (see also Chapter 14).

Prediction and Promotion of Thriving

Understanding the Role of Enabler and Process Variables

The previous discussion has established the characteristics of both human thriving and thriving in sport and provided a conceptualization that can offer a robust foundation upon which to build a systematic inquiry into thriving. The next step in this process is to explore the factors that can predict and promote thriving in individuals, both in general and in sport. Beginning with thriving in general, when reviewing previous literature on thriving, Brown, Arnold, Fletcher et al. (2017) identified a number of psychosocial variables that may facilitate thriving. These variables can be broadly separated into enabler and process variables.

Enabler variables consist of both personal and contextual types, where personal enablers are the attitudes, cognitions, and behaviors of an individual that help him or her to thrive (cf. Park, 1998), and contextual enablers are the characteristics of an environment that can foster continued task engagement and subsequent thriving (Carver, 1998). Brown, Arnold, Fletcher et al. (2017) found the most prevalent personal enablers associated with thriving were: positive perspective (see, e.g., Sarkar & Fletcher, 2014), religiosity and spirituality (see, e.g., Park, 1998), proactive personality (see, e.g., Sumsion, 2004), being motivated (see, e.g., Benson & Scales, 2009), commitment to knowledge and learning (see, e.g., Niessen, Sonnentag, & Sach, 2012), psychological resilience (see, e.g., Gan, Xie, Wang, Rodriguez, & Tang, 2013), and social competence (see, e.g., Tedeschi & Calhoun, 1996). Examples of contextual enablers identified in the thriving literature include: a challenge environment (see, e.g., O'Leary & Ickovics, 1995), attachment and trust (see, e.g., Carmeli & Spreitzer, 2009), family support (see, e.g., Weine et al., 2013), and colleague/employer support (see, e.g., Paterson, Luthans, & Jeung, 2014). Some of these enablers were suggested to apply across the majority of contexts (e.g., the opportunity for challenge), whereas others were considered to be more context specific (e.g., employer support; Brown, Arnold, Fletcher et al., 2017).

Process variables can be described as the mechanisms through which enabler variables may influence thriving. Throughout the extant literature, two process variables have been espoused as potentially facilitating thriving: the satisfaction of basic psychological needs and the manifestation of a challenge appraisal (Brown, Arnold, Fletcher et al., 2017; see also Chapter 2). Basic psychological needs theory (Ryan & Deci, 2017) proposes that human beings have three basic psychological needs for autonomy (i.e., feelings of volition), competence (i.e., feeling capable), and relatedness (i.e., feeling a connection to others), and that the satisfaction of these needs is fundamental for ongoing growth, wellness, and thriving. Based on this premise, personal and contextual enablers are believed to play a direct role in supporting an individual's level of need satisfaction and his or her subsequent experience of thriving (Ryan & Deci, 2017; see also Spreitzer & Porath, 2014). Turning to the second process variable, Lazarus and Folkman (1984) claim that individuals who view potentially stressful situations as opportunities for gain or growth are making a challenge appraisal (see also Chapter 2). Challenge appraisals thus encourage task engagement and create opportunities for positive change, and it is for these reasons that it has previously been associated with thriving (see Carver, 1998, O'Leary & Ickovics, 1995). In this regard, Bakker et al. (2010) suggest that perceiving one can meet the challenges in his or her environment results in high levels of task enjoyment and organizational commitment, which they consider as describing thriving at work.

Enabler and Process Variables for Thriving in Sport

Scholars have also begun to qualitatively explore (Brown & Arnold, 2019; Brown et al., 2018; Harris et al., 2012) and quantitatively examine (Brown, Arnold, Standage et al., 2017; Gucciardi et al., 2017) the factors that may predict thriving in sport performers. Within these studies, a range of personal and contextual enablers, and process variables have been identified as potentially relevant to thriving. These factors may contribute to the creation of greater task engagement, maintaining high work ethic, and enabling the athletes to cope with the stressors inherent in elite sport (Brown et al., 2018). To expand on the first of these categories, Brown et al. (2018) identified a number of personal enablers that were believed to facilitate sport performers' thriving in elite sport. Examples include, but are not limited to, desire and motivation, goal setting and creating challenge, positive mental state, and self-belief (Brown et al., 2018). Interestingly, similarities can be drawn between some of these personal enablers (e.g., positive mental state) and the personal resilient qualities (e.g., positive and proactive personality) previously associated with thriving in demanding situations (see Sarkar & Fletcher, 2014; see also Chapter 9). Brown, Arnold, Standage et al. (2017) provided further evidence for this relationship when they found that levels of personal resilient qualities positively predicted sport performers' membership to a thriving profile compared to lower levels of functioning. Similarly, Gucciardi et al. (2017) found a significant relationship between mental toughness, which they suggested "can be considered a resilience (personal) resource" (p. 719) and thriving. Beyond the promotion of thriving in athletes, it appears that similar personal enablers may be important for thriving in other sport populations, as some of the personal enablers forwarded by Brown et al. (2018; e.g., ability to control and manage potentially stressful situations and goal setting) align with the self-regulatory processes (e.g., self-control and goal setting) found to predict thriving in sport coaches (see McNeill et al., 2018).

Contextual enablers of thriving are believed to comprise the social agents and features of an environment that support performance and well-being (Brown, Arnold, Standage et al., 2017). Brown et al. (2018) explored these enablers in elite sport performers and identified some comparable factors (e.g., parental support and colleague/teammate support) to those previously recognized to be important for thriving in non-sport populations (see, e.g., workers, Spreitzer & Porath, 2014; adolescents, Theokas et al., 2005). In addition to these factors, Brown et al. (2018) also identified support staff as an important source of support in elite sport, highlighting the breadth of social agents that may enable thriving (see also Harris et al., 2012; see also Chapter 11). Although the perception of social support and of key individuals in the environment who can provide assistance appears important for thriving, Brown and Arnold (2019) recognized the additional importance of the depth and sincerity of these relationships. To elaborate, professional rugby players espoused a desire to operate within an integrated, inclusive, and trusting environment, and that their thriving was contingent on establishing strong bonds with teammates and fostering a meaningful connection to coaching staff and the club (Brown & Arnold, 2019). Despite sport performers' repeated emphasis on the role of social agents in their experience of thriving, statistical support for these relationships is equivocal. For example, Gucciardi et al. (2017) found significant negative associations between coach interpersonal control and thriving (indexed using learning and vitality); however, contrastingly, Brown, Arnold, Standage et al. (2017) found no significant predictive effects between perceived social support, coach need support, or coach need thwart variables and membership to a thriving profile. Further understanding the relationships between these contextual enablers (e.g., coaching behaviors) and thriving therefore appears to be important in progressing our understanding of thriving promotion.

As previously alluded to, humans are thought to achieve thriving (or full functioning) through the satisfaction of three basic and universal needs for autonomy, competence, and relatedness (Ryan & Deci, 2017). Ryan and Deci (2017) propose that environmental factors that are needs supportive will enhance the satisfaction of these needs, whereas environmental factors that are controlling will thwart or hinder them. Within sporting contexts, an array of studies have been conducted that substantiate the suggested sequential relationships between need supportive/thwarting environments, need satisfaction/frustration, and well-being and performance as separate outcomes (see, e.g., Adie, Duda, & Ntoumanis, 2012; Carpentier & Mageau, 2013; Fransen, Boen, Vansteenkiste, Mertens, & Vande Broek, 2018; Kipp & Weiss, 2015). Furthermore, Brown, Arnold, Standage et al. (2017) found that greater levels of need satisfaction significantly predicted sport performers' membership to a thriving profile, whereas higher levels of need frustration significantly predicted membership to a below-average functioning profile. In addition to examining the effects of basic psychological need satisfaction on thriving in sport performers, studies have also begun to test the predictive effects of challenge appraisal on thriving. For example, within their study, Brown, Arnold, Standage et al. (2017)

found a statistically significant prediction, with performers who were more likely to thrive perceiving their demanding competitive sporting encounters as a challenge compared with those who experienced low functioning. This finding offers some evidence to support the previous theoretical suggestions linking challenge appraisal to thriving (see Carver, 1998).

Promotion of Thriving in Sport

The previous sections have identified a number of personal and contextual variables that are believed to facilitate thriving in athletes. With regard to personal characteristics, research suggests that possessing personal resilient qualities and exhibiting self-regulatory capacities can promote thriving. In their grounded theory of resilience, Fletcher and Sarkar (2012) identified five psychological factors (viz., positive personality, motivation, confidence, focus, and perceived social support) or resilient qualities that they believed influenced challenge appraisals and meta-cognitions. Within their subsequent work (see, e.g., Fletcher & Sarkar, 2016), the authors forward a model of pressure inurement training for the development of these qualities based on the premise of creating an optimal balance of challenge and support in the environment (see also Chapters 9 and 12). This method, along with alternative approaches for developing resilience (see, e.g., Gonzalez, Detling, & Galli, 2016; Schinke, Peterson, & Couture, 2004; Turner, 2016), could therefore offer a strategy for developing resilient qualities with the view of, ultimately, enhancing thriving. Turning to performers' capacities to self-regulate, McNeill et al. (2018) espouse the importance of setting high but realistic well-being-related goals, identifying obstacles to self-regulation (e.g., lack of energy), employing self-monitoring, and increasing one's self-awareness for enabling thriving. Practitioners are thus encouraged to help clients develop these self-regulatory skills to support them in overcoming the demands of sport and to, ultimately, thrive.

Of the enabler variables purported to facilitate thriving, Spreitzer et al. (2005) previously argued that greater contributions to theory and knowledge can be generated from "understanding the contexts that enable thriving" (p. 539), with Ryan and Deci (2017) also suggesting that thriving is predicated on the features of the environments in which individuals act. Therefore, identifying the thriving-enabling features of an environment and the key social agents operating within it are likely to be of benefit to practitioners wanting to promote thriving. Brown and Arnold (2019) highlighted two such environmental features being the creation of strong bonds between teammates and fostering a meaningful connection between players and the coaching staff and sporting organization. To develop these relationships, the findings emphasize the need to provide opportunities for high-quality interactions between performers, establish a collective and shared "voice" among them, develop a club/organization collective identity, create a climate of transparency and fairness, and invest in the performers and their family (Brown & Arnold, 2019). To elaborate, high-quality interactions between performers were those which were open and honest, and where communication styles were empathic and constructive. In addition, creating a climate of transparency and fairness centered on fostering a psychological-safe environment whereby players could express themselves without fear of negative consequences. A number of these themes and ideas are increasingly being implemented by psychologists working to create environments for the promotion of thriving in elite sport. Figure 13.1 presents just one example of how some thriving principles developed in research are being applied in elite sport. Specifically, it details a case study of the English Institute of Sport's framework for promoting thriving when delivering sport psychology in Olympic and Paralympic Sport.

#ProjectTHRIVE: A framework for delivering psychology in Olympic and Paralympic Sport

Background: Consultation following the 2016 Olympic and Paralympic Games led the English Institute of Sport (EIS) performance psychology team to advance a consistent approach to delivering impactful psychology systematically, enabling athletes (and the staff that support them) to thrive in the Olympic and Paralympic environment. The purpose of this project was to (i) help sports facilitate the best version of their "performers" when it counts, (ii) optimize positive mental health alongside performance, (iii) ensure that the EIS psychology team is as consistent and effective as its potential, and (iv) increase knowledge share and access across the high-performance system.

Project Framework: By drawing on the acquired knowledge and expertise of the EIS psychology team and extant literature, and in collaboration with athletes, coaches, and military personnel, we developed 10 guiding principles to underpin the eventual project aim and present purpose of the EIS Psychology team:

Facilitate the creation of psychologically informed environments that develop the person as well as the performer to thrive.

Figure 13.1 An Example of An Approach To Enable Thriving in Elite Sport

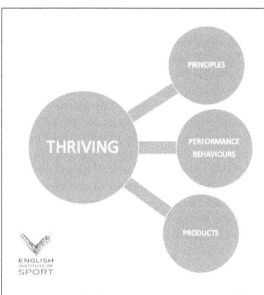

There are 10 *Guiding Principles* that drive the EIS Psychology approach. Aligned to each guiding principle are critical and observable *Behaviors* that indicate the principles are being lived (i.e., performance behaviors that encourage thriving). Finally, the *Products* are essentially interventions that can be delivered by the performance psychology team to enhance thriving. Thus, the products are underpinned by the guiding principles and targeted toward enhancing performance behaviors.

Practical Example: Guiding Principle: Performance environments require appropriate balance of challenge and support Example Behaviors: (i) Individualized responses to challenge and support are understood and acted on, and (ii) Interventions are designed to balance challenge and support appropriately over time.

Example Products: (i) Case Formulation (to best understand and determine challenge and support needs) and (ii) Multi-phased pressure exposure (to evoke stress-related responses with feedback and upskilling of individualized strategies). *Dr. Kate Hays, Head of Psychology, English Institute of Sport*

Figure 13.1 (Continued)

Recommendations for Future Research on Thriving in Sport

Existing research on thriving in sport has advanced our understanding about what it means to thrive and has begun to identify the factors that may be important to facilitating it; however, many questions remain unaddressed and worthy of consideration in the future. First, little is known about the lasting effect of thriving. For example, do cumulative or enduring effects exist after experiencing thriving? Within the youth development research, the consequences of thriving on future contribution and risk behaviors have been tracked longitudinally (see, e.g., Corbett & Drewett, 2004; Jelicic, Bobek, Phelps, Lerner, & Lerner, 2007), yet, no research exists on the lasting effect of thriving in adults. In part, these questions remain unaddressed because studies have typically adopted a cross-sectional design; scholars are therefore encouraged to use longitudinal techniques to track thriving over time. Specifically, researchers are encouraged to examine how thriving in one context (e.g., specific match/race) may related to thriving in subsequent similar (e.g., the next match/race) and broader contexts (e.g., entire competition). The adoption of such techniques will also enable the more rigorous examination of the predictive factors for thriving by separating the measurement of the enablers, process variables, and thriving. As a further extension of this work, researchers may want to consider the impact of thriving in one scenario (e.g., a sporting fixture) on other areas of an individual's life (e.g., academic attainment).

Second, scholars are encouraged to continue to strive toward the refinement and validation of the measurement of thriving in sport. Initial evidence suggests that the scales of subjective performance, subjective vitality, and positive affect are effective measures of full and holistic functioning (e.g., Brown, Arnold, Standage et al., 2017), but further studies employing this approach are warranted to examine the reliability of this method. In addition, conducting multiple studies using the same approach may enable standardized thresholds for thriving to be established to allow consistent classification of sport performers' responses. Establishing a valid and reliable measure will also be important for determining the effectiveness and efficacy of strategies designed to promote thriving. To elaborate, a robust thriving assessment method would allow interventions to be tested and compared, and to identify any complementary or counterproductive techniques.

Third, future research could be designed to extend existing work through the examination of additional personal and contextual enablers of thriving (e.g., personality), thriving in different populations (e.g., support staff), the co-facilitation of thriving in athlete and coach populations (see, e.g., Kerr, Stirling, & Gurgis, 2017), and the contagious effect of thriving. To elaborate on this latter point, research is yet to examine questions pertaining to dyadic or collective thriving in sport (e.g., If one person is thriving in a team, does that influence another player? How many team members need to be thriving for an organization to thrive?) If, as highlighted in the previous discussion, the promotion of thriving increasingly focuses on the contextual enablers and process variables of thriving, it may be important to explore how environments can be developed to facilitate thriving across athletes collectively, rather than for individual athletes in isolation. In this future inquiry, it will likely be necessary to consider organizational-level approaches as athletes cannot be viewed as separate from the environments that they train and compete in; rather, they function within complex organizational environments that exert significant influences on their well-being and performance (see Chapter 1; see also Fletcher & Streeter, 2016; Fletcher & Wagstaff, 2009; Wagstaff, Fletcher, & Hanton, 2012).

Fourth, given the early position of scholarly work on thriving in sport, it would be prudent to ensure that existing frameworks and interventions (see, e.g., Figure 13.1) designed to promote thriving in sport performers are rigorously tested for efficacy and real-world effectiveness. In part, this will depend on measure development as aforementioned, but it will also depend on establishing key indicators of thriving that can be documented through process evaluation (e.g., qualitative accounts of the athletes or coaches who have received, or are receiving, the intervention). Such developments will allow thriving frameworks and interventions to be refined and modified to best fit the context or population for which they are intended, and to ensure that the desired outcomes are being met.

Conclusion

This chapter has provided an introduction to thriving and traced its emergence as a construct of interest in sport. Specifically, thriving is considered a multifaceted construct that encompasses both development and success and represents a state of full or holistic functioning. Within a sporting context, full functioning has been characterized by the simultaneous display of perceiving a high level of performance and experiencing a high level of well-being. To promote this experience, coaches and practitioners can develop personal (e.g., resilient qualities) and contextual (e.g., bonds between teammates) enablers, and create environments that satisfy athletes' basic psychological needs and facilitate challenge appraisals. Future research into the lasting effect of thriving, its measurement, collective and organizational influences, and intervention evaluation may represent some of the most fruitful avenues to advancing knowledge in this area. In closing, thriving offers researchers and practitioners a mechanism through which to explore how to promote sporting success while simultaneously ensuring athlete well-being. This inquiry may, therefore, be critical in determining what is deemed as acceptable practice in the promotion of elite sporting success.

Note

1 Please note that differing time frames for publication in print form for Brown et al. (2018) and Brown et al. (2017) mean that publication dates for these articles appear reversed.

References

Adie, J. W., Duda, J. L., & Ntoumanis, N. (2012). Perceived coach-autonomy support, basic need satisfaction and the well- and ill-being of elite youth soccer players: A longitudinal investigation. *Psychology of Sport and Exercise, 13*, 51–59. Doi:10.1016/j.psychsport.2011.07.008

Bakker, A. B., van Veldhoven, M., & Xanthopoulou, D. (2010). Beyond the demand-control model: Thriving on high job demands and resources. *Journal of Personnel Psychology, 9*, 3–16. Doi:10.1027/1866-5888/a000006

Benson, P. L., & Scales, P. C. (2009). The definition and preliminary measurement of thriving in adolescence. *Journal of Positive Psychology, 4*, 85–104. Doi:10.1080/17439760802399240

Brown, D. J., & Arnold, R. (2019). Sports performers' perspectives on facilitating thriving in professional rugby contexts. *Psychology of Sport and Exercise, 40*, 71–81. Doi:10.1016/j.psychsport.2018.09.008

Brown, D. J., Arnold, R., Fletcher, D., & Standage, M. (2017). Human thriving: A conceptual debate and literature review. *European Psychologist, 22*, 167–179. Doi:10.1027/1016-9040/a000294

Brown, D. J., Arnold, R., Reid, T., & Roberts, G. (2018). A qualitative exploration of thriving in elite sport. *Journal of Applied Sport Psychology, 30*, 129–149. Doi:10.1080/10413200.2017.1354339

Brown, D. J., Arnold, R., Standage, M., & Fletcher, D. (2017). Thriving on pressure: A factor mixture analysis of sport performers' responses to competitive encounters. *Journal of Sport and Exercise Psychology, 39*, 423–437. Doi:10.1123/jsep.2016–0293

Bull, S. J., Shambrook, C. J., & Brooks, J. E. (2005). Towards an understanding of mental toughness in elite English cricketers. *Journal of Applied Sport Psychology, 17*, 209–227. Doi:10.1080/10413200591010085

Bundick, M. J., Yeager, D. S., King, P. E., & Damon, W. (2010). Thriving across the life span. In R. M. Lerner, M. E. Lamb, & A. M. Freund (Eds.), *The handbook of life-span development* (pp. 882–923). Hoboken, NJ: John Wiley & Sons.

Carmeli, A., & Spreitzer, G. M. (2009). Trust, connectivity, and thriving: Implications for innovative behaviors at work. *Journal of Creative Behavior, 43*, 169–191. Doi:10.1002/j.2162-6057.2009.tb01313.x

Carpentier, J., & Mageau, G. A. (2013). When change-oriented feedback enhances motivation, well-being and performance: A look at autonomy-supportive feedback in sport. *Psychology of Sport and Exercise, 14*, 423–435. Doi:10.1016/j. psychsport.2013.01.003

Carver, C. S. (1998). Resilience and thriving: Issues, models, and linkages. *Journal of Social Issues, 54*, 245–266. Doi:10.1111/0022-4537.641998064

Corbett, S. S., & Drewett, R. F. (2004). To what extent is failure to thrive in infancy associated with poorer cognitive development? A review and meta-analysis. *Journal of Child Psychology and Psychiatry, 45*, 641–654. Doi:10.1111/j.1469-7610.2004.00253.x

Fletcher, D., & Sarkar, M. (2012). A grounded theory of psychological resilience in Olympic champions. *Psychology of Sport and Exercise, 13*, 669–678. Doi:10.1016/j.psychsport.2012.04.007

Fletcher, D., & Sarkar, M. (2016). Mental fortitude training: An evidence-based approach to developing psychological resilience for sustained success. *Journal of Sport Psychology in Action, 7*, 135–157. Doi:10.1080/21520704.2016.1255496

Fletcher, D., & Streeter, A. (2016). A case study analysis of a high performance environment in elite swimming. *Journal of Change Management, 16,* 123–141. Doi:10.1080/14697017.2015.1128470

Fletcher, D., & Wagstaff, C. R. D. (2009). Organizational psychology in elite sport: Its emergence, application and future. *Psychology of Sport and Exercise, 10,* 427–434. Doi:10.1016/j.psychsport.2009.03.009

Fransen, K., Boen, F., Vansteenkiste, M., Mertens, N., & Vande Broek, G. (2018). The power of competence support: The impact of coaches and athlete leaders on intrinsic motivation and performance. *Scandinavian Journal of Medicine & Science in Sports, 28,* 725–745. Doi:10.1111/sms.12950

Galli, N., & Reel, J. J. (2012). "It was hard, but it was good": A qualitative exploration of stress-related growth in Division I intercollegiate athletes. *Qualitative Research in Sport, Exercise and Health, 4,* 297–319. Doi:10.1080/21596 76X.2012.693524

Gan, Y. Q., Xie, X. F., Wang, T., Rodriguez, M. A., & Tang, C. S. (2013). Thriving in the shadow of the 2008 Sichuan Earthquake: Two studies on resilience in adolescents. *Journal of Health Psychology, 18,* 1232–1241. Doi:10.1177/1359105312459897

Gonzalez, S. P., Detling, N., & Galli, N. A. (2016). Case studies of developing resilience in elite sport: Applying theory to guide interventions. *Journal of Sport Psychology in Action, 7,* 158–169. Doi:10.1080/21520704.2016.1236050

Gucciardi, D. F., Jackson, B., Hodge, K., Anthony, D. R., & Brooke, L. E. (2015). Implicit theories of mental toughness: Relations with cognitive, motivational, and behavioral correlates. *Sport, Exercise, and Performance Psychology, 4,* 100–112. Doi:10.1037/spy0000024

Gucciardi, D. F., & Jones, M. I. (2012). Beyond optimal performance: Mental toughness profiles and developmental success in adolescent cricketers. *Journal of Sport and Exercise Psychology, 34,* 16–36. Doi:10.1123/jsep.34.1.16

Gucciardi, D. F., Stamatis, A., & Ntoumanis, N. (2017). Controlling coaching and athlete thriving in elite adolescent netballers: The buffering effect of athletes' mental toughness. *Journal of Science and Medicine in Sport, 20,* 718–722. Doi:10.1016/j.jsams.2017.02.007

Harris, M., Myhill, M., & Walker, J. (2012). Thriving in the challenge of geographical dislocation: A case study of elite Australian footballers. *International Journal of Sports Science, 2,* 51–60. Doi:10.5923/j.sports.20120205.02

Jelicic, H., Bobek, D. L., Phelps, E., Lerner, R. M., & Lerner, J. V. (2007). Using positive youth development to predict contribution and risk behaviors in early adolescence: Findings from the first two waves of the 4-H study of positive youth development. *International Journal of Behavioral Development, 31,* 263–273. Doi:10.1177/0165025407076439

Jones, G., Hanton, S., & Connaughton, D. (2002). What is this thing called mental toughness? An investigation of elite sport performers. *Journal of Applied Sport Psychology, 14,* 205–218. Doi:10.1016/j.sbspro.2010.07.156

Jones, M. I., Dunn, J. G. H., Holt, N. L., Sullivan, P. J., & Bloom, G. A. (2011). Exploring the '5Cs' of positive youth development in sport. *Journal of Sport Behavior, 34,* 250–267. Doi:1016/j.psychsport.2008.06.005

Kerr, G., Stirling, A., & Gurgis, J. (2017). An athlete-centred approach to enhance thriving within athletes and coaches. In S. Pill (Ed.), *Perspectives on athlete-centred coaching* (pp. 24–36). London, UK: Routledge.

Kipp, L. E., & Weiss, M. R. (2015). Social predictors of psychological need satisfaction and well-being among female adolescent gymnasts: A longitudinal analysis. *Sport, Exercise, and Performance Psychology, 4,* 153–169. Doi:10.1037/spy0000033

Lazarus, R. S., & Folkman, S. (1984). *Stress, appraisal, and coping.* New York: Springer.

Lerner, R. M. (2004). *Liberty: Thriving and civic engagement among America's youth.* Thousand Oaks, CA: Sage.

Lerner, R. M., Dowling, E. M., & Anderson, P. M. (2003). Positive youth development: Thriving as a basis of personhood and civil society. *Applied Developmental Science, 7,* 172–180. Doi:10.1207/S1532480XADS0703_8

McNeill, K., Durand-Bush, N., & Lemyre, P.-N. (2018). Thriving, depleted, and at-risk Canadian coaches: Profiles of psychological functioning linked to self-regulation and stress. *International Sport Coaching Journal, 5,* 145–155. Doi:10.1123/iscj.2017-0042

Niessen, C., Sonnentag, S., & Sach, F. (2012). Thriving at work: A diary study. *Journal of Organizational Behavior, 33,* 468–487. Doi:10.1002/Job.763

O'Leary, V. E., & Ickovics, J. R. (1995). Resilience and thriving in response to challenge: An opportunity for a paradigm shift in women's health. *Women's Health, 1,* 121–142.

Park, C. L. (1998). Stress-related growth and thriving through coping: The roles of personality and cognitive processes. *Journal of Social Issues, 54,* 267–277. Doi:10.1111/ j.1540-4560.1998.tb01218.x

Paterson, T. A., Luthans, F., & Jeung, W. (2014). Thriving at work: Impact of psychological capital and supervisor support. *Journal of Organizational Behavior, 35,* 434–446. Doi:10.1002/job.1907

Ryan, R. M., & Deci, E. L. (2001). On happiness and human potentials: A review of research on hedonic and eudaimonic well-being. *Annual Review of Psychology, 52,* 141–166. Doi:10.1146/annurev.psych.52.1.141

Ryan, R. M., & Deci, E. L. (2017). *Self-determination theory: Basic psychological needs in motivation, development, and wellness.* New York: Guilford Press.

Ryan, R. M., & Frederick, C. (1997). On energy, personality, and health: Subjective vitality as a dynamic reflection of well-being. *Journal of Personality, 65,* 529–565. Doi:10.1111/j.1467-6494.1997.tb00326.x

Sarkar, M., & Fletcher, D. (2014). Ordinary magic, extraordinary performance: Psychological resilience and thriving in high achievers. *Sport, Exercise, and Performance Psychology, 3,* 46–60. Doi:10.1037/spy0000003

Scales, P. C., Benson, P. L., Leffert, N., & Blyth, D. A. (2000). Contribution of developmental assets to the prediction of thriving among adolescents. *Applied Developmental Science, 4,* 27–46. Doi:10.1207/S1532480XADS0401_3

Schinke, R. J., Peterson, C., & Couture, R. (2004). A protocol for teaching resilience to high performance athletes. *Journal of Excellence, 9,* 9–18.

Spreitzer, G. M., & Porath, C. L. (2014). Self-determination as nutriment for thriving: Building an integrative model of human growth at work. In M. Gagne (Ed.), *Oxford handbook of work engagement, motivation, and self-determination theory* (pp. 245–258). New York: Oxford University Press.

Spreitzer, G. M., Sutcliffe, K., Dutton, J., Sonenshein, S., & Grant, A. M. (2005). A socially embedded model of thriving at work. *Organization Science, 16,* 537–549. Doi:10.1287/orsc.1050.0153

Su, R., Tay, L., & Diener, E. (2014). The development and validation of the Comprehensive Inventory of Thriving (CIT) and the Brief Inventory of Thriving (BIT). *Applied Psychology: Health and Well-Being, 6*, 251–279. Doi:10.1111/aphw.12027

Sumsion, J. (2004). Early childhood teachers' constructions of their resilience and thriving: A continuing investigation. *International Journal of Early Years Education, 12*, 275–290. Doi:10.1080/0966976042000268735

Tedeschi, R. G., & Calhoun, L. G. (1996). The posttraumatic growth inventory: Measuring the positive legacy of trauma. *Journal of Traumatic Stress, 9*, 455–471. Doi:10.1007/BF02103658

Theokas, C., Almerigi, J. B., Lerner, R. M., Dowling, E. M., Benson, P. L., Scales, P. C., & Von Eye, A. (2005). Conceptualizing and modeling individual and ecological asset components of thriving in early adolescence. *Journal of Early Adolescence, 25*, 113–143. Doi:10.1177/0272431604272460

Turner, M. J. (2016). Proposing a rational resilience credo for use with athletes. *Journal of Sport Psychology in Action, 7*, 170–181. Doi:10.1080/21520704.2016.1236051

Verner-Filion, J., & Vallerand, R. J. (2018). A longitudinal examination of elite youth soccer players: The role of passion and basic need satisfaction in athletes' optimal functioning. *Psychology of Sport and Exercise, 39*, 20–28. Doi:10.1016/j.psychsport.2018.07.005

Wagstaff, C. R. D., Fletcher, D., & Hanton, S. (2012). Positive organizational psychology in sport. *International Review of Sport and Exercise Psychology, 5*, 87–103. Doi:10.1080/1750984X.2011.634920

Weine, S. M., Ware, N., Tugenberg, T., Hakizimana, L., Dahnweih, G., Currie, M., . . . Levin, E. (2013). Thriving, managing, and struggling: A mixed methods study of adolescent African refugees' psychosocial adjustment. *Adolescent Psychiatry, 3*, 72–81. Doi:10.2174/2210676611303010013

14 Duties of Care and Welfare Practices

Emma Kavanagh, Daniel Rhind, and Genevieve Gordon-Thomson

In 2017, the British Government published the Duty of Care in Sport Review (Grey-Thompson, 2017) sharing the findings of a critical inquiry into the culture and climate of elite sport in the United Kingdom. High-performance sport came under significant scrutiny linked to a number of high-profile accounts in the media that raised serious questions concerning the safety of elite sporting spaces and the threats they can pose to athlete welfare. Allegations of bullying, racial, sexual, and gender abuse alongside other forms of discrimination have been made across Olympic and Paralympic sports. Such findings were echoed within a number of independent reviews of sports around the world: as an example, "a culture of fear, intimidation and bullying" was presented in a report on British Cycling (Phelps, Kelly, Lancaster, Mehrzad, & Panter, 2017). Cultures similar to this are suggested to have proliferated elite sport under the banner of a no compromise approach to performance. Within the United Kingdom, UK Sport responded to allegations with positive action through the implementation of various initiatives including the launch of a new Code for Sports Governance, a "Culture Health Check" which was conducted across funded programs, the launch of a mental health strategy (UK Sport, 2018), and a clear focus on sporting integrity (UK Sport, 2017a). The impact of these initiatives is yet to be observed, as is the evidence of a pledged commitment to long-term cultural change in high-performance environments.

The notion of a duty of care has nominally been put forward as a solution to the challenges faced in high-performance sport (UK Sport, 2017a, 2017b); however, to date it has failed to gain significant attention within the sporting literature and its meaning has not been clearly articulated. Currently, the duty of care remains a Western centric proposition with the United Kingdom at the world's epicenter for the rapid emergence and prominence of this concept in sport. Therefore, the aims of this chapter are three-fold: (i) to examine the term duty of care and consider its scope within sport, (ii) to explore potential factors which can threaten athlete welfare in performance environments (linked to the recommendations of the Duty of Care Report; see also Chapter 6); and

(iii) to outline safeguarding mechanisms and make suggestions toward promoting a duty of care for all in sport.

Introducing the Duty of Care

Sport organizations are increasingly being held accountable for their role in developing and maintaining cultures that promote a duty of care and further support the well-being of all individuals within their realm of influence (Wagstaff, 2018); as a result, the term duty of care is increasingly being adopted within the sporting world. It is imperative that a distinction be drawn between moral and legal obligations. From a legal perspective, duty of care is encapsulated within the tort of negligence (Gordon, 2016). This considers when damage caused by another's carelessness becomes actionable (Plunkett, 2015). The basis of the tort of negligence and the duty of care is that a necessary standard of care is owed to a claimant. As in sport and society at large, the legal duty of care owed is higher for children, young people, and vulnerable adults. Traditionally, a legal duty of care amounts to risk and whether reasonable steps to prevent foreseeable risk have been identified and action taken to reduce the risks. It was announced in 2016 that UK sports bodies wishing to receive centralized funding through Sport England, UK Sport, and National Lottery awards would have to adhere to a new code of governance to help ensure that the highest levels of transparency, ethical standards, and leadership are present across sport in the United Kingdom (Gordon, 2016). This goes some way to bridging the gap between the legal and moral stand points, relying on quasi-legal standards in sport such as governance and regulation.

A duty of care further relies on the moral obligation placed upon an individual (such as a coach or sport scientist) to understand their role in the prevention of foreseeable harm to others in order to ensure their safety or well-being. While the term "duty of care" has been adopted more recently in sport, it has a long-standing tradition in other professions, such as nursing, teaching, or social work, and is associated closely with caring professions that may require difficult, social and emotional work. In such professions, there is an obligation to maintain both legal standards of care and further to act in accordance with professional standards set out by a regulatory body. The duty of care assumes a responsibility for the care of another whereby care refers to the relational element of this duty and is linked to the interaction between people and or an organization. Such a climate aligns with the feminist tradition of an ethics of care (Brackenridge, 2001). As Noddings (2010) notes "Caring, in every approach, involves attention, empathic response, and a commitment to respond to legitimate needs" (p. 28). Whereby care consists of performed acts that have the potential to enhance relationships and promote well-being and flourishing of others (Hamington, 2019); as such, the duty of care relies upon ethical and moral behavior in the treatment of the self and others.

It is now accepted that there is a moral duty owed by sport to protect its participants, and that measures need to be in place to ensure individuals are safe to participate in the absence of reasonable or foreseeable harm (within the boundaries of the activity). In essence, a moral duty of care means that a sporting body and individuals working across its levels need to take such reasonable measures to ensure individuals will be safe while participating in sport or physical activity. A duty of care further relies upon the moral obligation of those engaging in sport to understand their role in the prevention of foreseeable harm. The language here is important and should be more widely adopted in order to consider the boundaries of practice and to ask stakeholders to consider more closely the duty owed in order to protect those in their charge from harm (physical and/or psychological).

In the United Kingdom, this duty gained greater focus through the publication of the Duty of Care in Sport Review (Grey-Thompson, 2017). The review challenged current practice in sport and asked for greater consideration of *how* we promote care in the elite environment. As a result, sports organizations are now tasked with taking greater account of their role in fostering a duty of care in practice, considering the importance of welfare at all stages of an athlete's career. The Duty of Care Review adopted a broad definition of care, spanning personal safety and injury, to mental health and consideration of the support provided to athletes at the elite level. The findings highlighted the importance of keeping people safe in sport as a central pillar around which talent, performance, and participation can be achieved. The current imbalance between winning and welfare was at the heart of the findings, as was the challenge to be more critical of current high-performance climates. "Putting people—their safety, wellbeing and welfare—at the center of what sport does" (Grey-Thompson, 2017, p. 5), was championed as a starting point for positive change toward addressing some of the current risks highlighted within the review.

Welfare in the Elite Performance Environment

Seven key themes were presented within the Duty of Care Review based on evidence of current risks posed to athlete well-being in sport. Furthermore, each theme incorporates core recommendations for implementation and monitoring across National Governing Bodies of sport (NGBs). The seven themes are given as follows: (i) education; (ii) transition; (iii) representation of the participants voice; (iv) equality, diversity, and inclusion; (v) safeguarding; (vi) mental welfare; and (vii) safety, injury, and medical issues (Grey-Thompson, 2017). These recommendations were made in order to raise the profile of a duty of care and call for industry wide adoption of improved standards of care from grass roots to performance sport. While it is outside the scope of this chapter to provide an overview of all of the recommendations arising from the Duty of Care Review (see Table 14.1 for an overview of the priority recommendations); instead, the chapter will consider two areas that have

Table 14.1 Priority Recommendations of the Duty of Care Review

1. A sports ombudsman	The government should create a Sports Ombudsman (or Sports Duty of Care Quality Commission). This organization should have powers to hold national governing bodies (NGBs) to account for the Duty of Care they provide to all athletes, coaching staff, and support staff, providing independent assurance and accountability to address many of the issues covered by the review
2. Measurement	The government should measure Duty of Care via an independent benchmark survey giving equal voice to all stakeholders in the system. The results of the survey, which could act as the basis for the Duty of Care key performance indicator mentioned in the "Sporting Future" strategy, would allow government and others in the sport sector to monitor whether sport duty of care policies intended to improve standards are successful and inform future policies and investment decisions. The survey should give an indication of levels of trust in the provision and receipt of support in sport
3. Named board member responsible for Duty of Care	All NGB boards should have a named Duty of Care guardian. The guardian should have an explicit responsibility and leadership role to engage with participants across the talent pathways and in community sport, and to provide assurance at board level. This assurance should be evidenced in a public statement from the Duty of Care guardian in the NGB's annual report. Duty of Care should be a mandatory condition of future funding and all funded sports bodies should demonstrably apply it
4. Induction process	An induction process should be carried out for all participants entering elite levels of sport (and, where relevant, their families should also be included). The content will change depending on the level the individual is at within the system but it should include the steps involved with entering the elite system, what can be expected while training and competing, and what to be aware of and prepare for regarding exiting the elite level
5. Exit survey for elite athletes	As participants leave formal programs, an independent exit interview should be conducted, the results of which would be taken account of in future funding discussions

6. Duty of Care Charter	A Duty of Care Charter should be established by the government, explicitly setting out how participants, coaches, and support staff can expect to be treated and where they can go if they need advice, support, and guidance. As part of this, participants who receive funding (in any part of the system) should be offered honorary contracts, which set out the roles and responsibilities of both the sport and the participant
7. The British Athletes Commission (BAC)	Government should independently fund the BAC to enable it to provide the best support to participants on talent pathways in Olympic and Paralympic sports. This will increase confidence in grievance and dispute resolution, reducing the need for escalation, saving time, money and emotion

Source: Grey-Thompson (2017, p. 6).

gained recent attention both within the media and academic research: (i) risks to mental welfare and (ii) abuse and non-accidental violence. Both present significant challenges and opportunities for the promotion of safety in sport.

Risks to Mental Welfare in Elite Sport

The pressures faced by elite athletes and the need to consider the mental health and well-being of those involved in sport are recognized to be a critical shift in the promotion of care in high-performance settings (Grey-Thompson, 2017). Reardon and Factor (2010) suggest that the tendency to idealize elite athletes has led the general public to assume a low prevalence of mental health issues in sport; research and anecdotal accounts in the media, however, demonstrate that elite athletes are not immune to poor mental health (Coyle, Gorczynski, & Gibson, 2017; Ingle, 2019; see also Chapter 8).

While taking part in sport can positively reinforce a number of protective factors (e.g., increased confidence, enhanced self-esteem, and increased satisfaction with body image) and be viewed as a mental health asset (Doherty, Hannigan, & Campbell, 2016; Hill, MacNamara, & Collins, 2015; Uphill, Sly, & Swain, 2016), it is also acknowledged that performance environments can present a range of factors that have the potential to magnify mental health issues. For example, athletes face numerous stressors that are unique to the sporting environment (such as injury, career transitions, selection and de-selection, living away from home, and concussion-related problems; see also Chapter 1) many of which have the potential to increase risks to mental health (Newman, Howells, & Fletcher, 2016) and were presented as areas of risk within the Duty of Care Review. Continuous exposure to some, if not all of these challenges, has the potential to cause a deterioration in athlete well-being (Roberts, Faull, & Tod, 2016; see also Chapters 6 and 8).

It remains contested whether poor mental health is more prevalent in athletic populations, or if the patterns are simply consistent with those present in the "general population" (Rice et al., 2016; see also Chapter 8). That said, the stigma surrounding reporting or acknowledging problems is considered to be higher in athletic settings (Uphill et al., 2016). This can be compounded by the culture of sport which has a tendency to dictate that "mental toughness and mental health are seen as contradictory terms in the world of elite performance" (Bauman, 2016, p. 135). An emphasis on toughness and the minimization of perceived weakness (Reardon & Factor, 2010) may contribute, in part, to under-recognition of mental illness in the athletic population. In addition, the sporting environment may exacerbate pre-existing mental ill-health, as Bauman (2016) suggests mental ill-health that presented prior to involvement in sport may "become more evident when athletes are faced with stressors associated with elite sport" (p. 135; see also Chapters 1 and 8).

Gorczynski et al. (2019) believe that one of the most problematic elements of mental health is that it is almost always viewed negatively, with the focus primarily being placed on mental ill-health, rather than a broader and more holistic understanding of mental health and well-being. Such misunderstanding has increased the stigma surrounding mental health in sport, and this, in turn, can increase barriers to reporting mental ill-health in athletic populations. Increasing mental health literacy has been championed as a strategy to better inform athletes of the broader scope of mental health and well-being (MacIntyre et al., 2018). Such a strategy aims to enhance education surrounding mental health problems, improve attitudes toward mental health, and increase understanding of how to seek help (Gorczynski et al., 2019). Increasing mental health literacy may better enable individuals to understand the potential for optimizing their own mental well-being while further recognizing the signs of mental illness and where to seek support. Coaches and support staff are currently not required to undergo any formal mental health training, yet these frontline staff are argued to be well placed to promote mental health within sport systems (Sebbens, Hassmen, Crisp, & Wensley, 2016).

In theme 6 of the Duty of Care Review, mental welfare was indicated as a core priority and further a major concern in British performance sport (Grey-Thompson, 2017). In the United Kingdom, a Mental Health Strategy, developed by the Mental Health Steering Group, was launched by UK Sport and the English Institute of Sport in 2018 in response to the recommendations provided by the Duty of Care Review. NGBs have been tasked by UK Sport with placing greater emphasis on mental health support across the Tokyo Olympic Cycle. The strategy consists of four key pillars: education, provision, communication, and assurance—with a clear overall vision to "create a positive mental health environment for everyone in the UK high performance system" (UK Sport, 2018, p. 1). Such a focus has not just been present in British sport, the Australian Institute of Sport (2020) held a summit focused on the promotion of athlete well-being designed to develop sustainable high-performance programs where athletic well-being was prioritized. The impact of such strategies is yet to be seen; however, the priority placed on athlete mental health and further discussions concerning the well-being of athletes are positive steps forward in challenging the concerns surrounding the negative culture of high-performance environments and making a critical shift toward the promotion of health and well-being. An increased focus on mental well-being in sport (albeit mostly in Western nations) could lead the way for other countries looking to emphasize the importance of the mental and physical health of (elite) performers and support staff (see also Chapter 8).

Abuse and Non-Accidental Violence

In Great Britain, safeguarding was given a priority within the Duty of Care Review (theme 6). All athletes have a right to engage in "safe sport", defined as "an athletic environment that is respectful, equitable, and free from all forms of non-accidental violence to athletes" (Mountjoy et al., 2016, p. 1). However, recent global media accounts have been replete with reports of incidents suggesting that sport has not always provided a safe space for those who compete within it (Kavanagh, Lock, Adams, Stewart, & Clelland, 2020). For example, the case of Larry Nassar and the systemic abuse of over 150 gymnasts, spanning decades, perpetrated while in his privileged position as team doctor for U.S. Gymnastics (Fisher & Anders, 2020); in South Korea, female athletes have spoken out about the culture of abuse in skating (BBC, 2019a); in the United Kingdom, numerous sports including cycling, rowing, canoeing, and gymnastics have each been indicted as having practices that have allowed athletes to have been bullied by coaches, managers, and teammates (Adams & Kavanagh, 2020; Phelps et al., 2017); and English football has been investigated concerning a history of child sexual abuse committed over more than 30 years (BBC, 2019b). Fisher and Anders (2020) highlight how sport provides an optimal space for violence, oppression, sexism, and exploitation to occur, often without question.

Collectively, various types of abuse have been referred to as maltreatment (Stirling, 2009), non-accidental violence (Mountjoy et al., 2016), and/or interpersonal violence (Vertommen et al., 2016), in order to encompass a variety of behaviors (including, but not limited to sexual, emotional and physical abuse, neglect, bullying, and harassment, see Table 14.2 for definitions). Studies have reported prevalence rates of sexual abuse in sport as between 2% and 42% (Kerr & Stirling, 2019). Emotional abuse is recognized as potentially the most prevalent safeguarding concern, yet this remains one of the most accepted forms of abuse and therefore the least reported (Hartill & Lang, 2018). Less

Table 14.2 Definitions of Abuse Types in Sport

Sexual abuse	Any sexual interaction or conduct of a sexual nature with person(s) of any age that is perpetrated against the victims will, where consent is coerced/manipulated or is not or cannot be provided
Psychological abuse	Sustained and repeated pattern of deliberate non-contact behaviors by a person in a critical relationship role that has the potential to be harmful to an individual's affective, behavioral, cognitive, or physical wellbeing. While often referred to as emotional abuse, the adoption of psychological abuse recognizes the broader impact of this abuse type beyond emotional affect. It also consists of cognitions, values and beliefs about oneself, and the world. "The behaviors that constitute psychological abuse target a person's inner life in all its profound scope" (Mountjoy et al., 2016, p. 1021)
Physical abuse	Non-accidental trauma or physical injury caused by punching, beating, kicking, biting, burning, or otherwise harming an athlete. Can be experienced as contact or non-contact abuse. Contact abuse can relate to non-accidental trauma or physical injury inflicted by a person or caregiver (examples include punching, striking with an object or shoving). Non-contact physical abuse can stem from punishments or actions that can cause physical discomfort but do not necessarily have to involve physical contact from the perpetrator (e.g., physically aggressive displays, the use of physical punishments, and doping practices)
Bullying	Bullying is likely to occur in peer-to-peer relationships and can include physical, verbal, or psychological attacks or intimidations that are intended to cause fear, distress, or harm. Can include overt and covert hostility, such as repeated criticism or belittling, making threats, spreading rumors, and verbal and/or physical attacks
Harassment	Any unwanted and unwelcome conduct of a sexual nature, whether verbal, non-verbal, or physical
Neglect	A failure to meet the physical and/or emotional needs of an individual or the failure to protect a person from exposure to danger
Negligence	Acts of omission regarding the provision of safety for an athlete. For example, depriving an athlete of food and/or drink, insufficient rest and recovery, failure to provide a safe physical training environment, or developmental age-inappropriate or physique-inappropriate training methods

Source: Adapted from Mountjoy et al. (2016), Kavanagh (2014), and Stirling (2009, 2013).

is known about the prevalence of physical abuse and other forms of interpersonal violence.

In 2011, a total of 652 cases of a range of abuses were recorded as occurring in NGBs in the United Kingdom, including physical, sexual, and emotional abuse; bullying; inappropriate behavior via technology; racial abuse; sexual harassment; and poor practice (Rhind, McDermott, Lambert, & Koleva, 2014). Alexander, Stafford, and Lewis (2011) surveyed over 6,000 young people on their experience of taking part in sport in the United Kingdom; 75% reported to have experienced some form of emotional harm while taking part in sport. More recently, Hartill and Lang (2018) outlined findings concerning reports of child abuse in sport received by local authorities (LAs) in England (between 2010 and 2015). Of the LAs that responded (70 returning usable data), 1013 distinct safeguarding reports were recorded during this time. Reports concerning sexual abuse were by far the most common accounting for nearly 50% of those recorded.

The impact of abuse in sport can be long-term and extremely damaging (Mountjoy et al., 2016) and is correlated with a plethora of long-term sequelae, including depression, anxiety, maladaptive eating behavior, social withdrawal, self-harm, detriments to academic or work performance, and long-term posttraumatic stress symptomatology (Mountjoy et al., 2016; Parent & Fortier, 2018). Furthermore, the experience can have an impact both on the athlete and those closest to them (friends, family, partners, and teammates). Such an impact can both present in the moment and persist long after the abuse ends (McMahon & McGannon, 2020). As Kerr and Stirling (2019) suggest, we cannot deny the existence of abuse in sport and the recent media cases firmly place this issue in the spotlight.

The International Olympic Committee (IOC) has developed a number of guiding documents that place an emphasis on its mission toward protecting the safety and well-being of athletes and which acknowledge that this topic is of global importance. For example, the Olympic Movement Medical Code (2009) underscores that all stakeholders "should take care that sport is practiced without danger to the health of the athletes and with respect for fair play and sports ethics . . . [and should take] measures necessary to protect the health of participants and to minimize the risks of physical injury and psychological harm". The IOC consensus statement on harassment and abuse (non-accidental violence) in sport states that eliminating abuse against athletes should be part of a broad international conversation which reflects wider societal discourse regarding the need to eradicate abusive and unethical practices in institutional settings (Mountjoy et al., 2016). Evidently there is a legal and moral duty of care incumbent on those who organize, administer, and take part in sport to ensure that risks are identified and mitigated (Mountjoy, Rhind, Tiivas, & Leglise, 2015). An emphasis on safeguarding is of great importance in articulating the duty of care and enhancing the safety of all participants.

Safeguarding in Sport

The initial response to managing welfare issues in sport focused on protecting specific children who were deemed to be at increased risk. These strategies drew upon the broader concept of child protection as developed in the context of social work. Child protection has been defined as: "A set of activities that are required for specific children who are at risk of/or are suffering from significant harm" (Rhind, Brackenridge, Kay, & Owusu-Sekyere, 2015, p. 73). Mountjoy, Rhind, Tiivas, and Leglise (2015) argued that the scope of the issues to be addressed by those working to protect children in sport are much broader than the traditional approach of preventing abuse through child protection. As a result, there has been a move toward a more holistic approach, called safeguarding, which serves to promote the welfare and well-being of *everyone* in sport. Safeguarding has been defined as "the reasonable actions taken to ensure that everyone involved in sport are safe from harm" (Rhind et al., 2014, p. 73) and is therefore seen as a central tenant to keeping people safe in sport when considering a duty of care for all.

International Safeguards for Children in Sport

A significant development in this field was the launch of the International Safeguards for Children in Sport (Rhind & Owusu-Sekyere, 2018). The International Safeguards outline the guidance and processes that should be put in place by any organization providing sports activities to children and young people (Rhind & Owusu-Sekyere, 2018). The safeguards should be viewed as guides, which facilitate an organization's journey toward safeguarding individuals rather than as an end in themselves. The safeguards reflect the United Nations Convention on the Rights of the Child (United Nations, 1989), relevant legislation (Chroni et al., 2012), and existing child protection/safeguarding good practice (Boocock, 2002). These safeguards represent collective good practice at a point in time and will be subject to periodic review to ensure they reflect developments within safeguarding practice.

The International Safeguards aim to help create a safe sporting environment (for children) wherever they participate and at whatever level, provide a benchmark to assist sports providers and funders to make informed decisions, promote good practice and challenge practice that is harmful, and provide clarity on safeguarding to all involved in sport. Specifically, eight safeguards have been identified: (i) developing your policy, (ii) procedures for responding to safeguarding concerns, (iii) advice and support, (iv) minimizing risk (to children), (v) guidelines for behavior, (vi) recruiting, training, and communicating, (vii) working with partners, and (viii) monitoring and evaluating. Each of these safeguards are explained in Table 14.3. Mountjoy et al. (2016) outlined how the issues encapsulated under the umbrella of safeguarding in sport have broadened in three key areas. First, the range of potential threats that an individual can be exposed to in sport is now recognized at three levels: the individual level (e.g., depression, self-harm, substance abuse, and disordered eating), the relational level (e.g., sexual, physical, and emotional abuse), and the organizational level (e.g., systems which promote over training or competing with an injury, institutional doping, or an unhealthy organizational culture). Second, it is now

Table 14.3 International Safeguards for Children in Sport

Safeguard 1: Developing your policy	Any organization providing or with responsibility for sports activities should have a safeguarding policy. This is a statement of intent that demonstrates a commitment to safeguard everyone involved in sport from harm and provides the framework within which procedures are developed. A safeguarding policy makes clear to all what is required. It also helps to create a safe and positive environment and to show that the organization is taking its duty of care seriously
Safeguard 2: Procedures for responding to safeguarding concerns	Procedures describe the operational processes required to implement organizational policy and provide clear step-by-step guidance on what to do in different circumstances. They clarify roles and responsibilities, and lines of communication. Procedures help to ensure a prompt response to concerns about a person's safety or wellbeing
Safeguard 3: Advice and support	Arrangements made to provide essential information and support to those responsible for safeguarding. People should be advised on where to access help and support. An organization has a duty to ensure advice and support is in place to help people to play their part in safeguarding such that they know who they can turn to for help
Safeguard 4: Minimizing risks (to children)	The measures that are taken to assess and minimize the risks to people in the organization. Some people, who work or seek to work in sport in a paid or voluntary capacity, pose a risk. People can also be at risk when placed in unsuitable places or asked to participate in unsuitable activities. It is possible to minimize these risks by putting safeguards in place
Safeguard 5: Guidelines for behavior	An organization should have codes of conduct to describe what an acceptable standard of behavior is and promote current best practice. Standards of behavior set a benchmark of what is acceptable for all and codes of conduct can help to remove ambiguity and clarify the grey areas around what is viewed as acceptable behavior

(Continued)

Table 14.3 (Continued)

Safeguard 6: Recruiting, training and communicating	Recruiting appropriate members of staff, creating opportunities to develop and maintain the necessary skills and communicating regarding safeguarding. Everyone within an organization has a role to play in safeguarding. Organizations providing sporting activities have a responsibility to provide training and development opportunities for staff and volunteers
Safeguard 7: Working with partners	The actions taken by the organization to influence and promote the adoption and implementation of measures to safeguard people by partner organizations. Sports organizations have both a strategic and a delivery role. Where organizational partnership, membership, funding, or commissioning relationships exist or develop with other organizations, the organization should use its influence to promote the implementation of safeguarding measures
Safeguard 8: Monitoring and evaluating	It is essential that there is ongoing monitoring of compliance and effectiveness, involving all key stakeholders. This is necessary because organizations need to know whether safeguarding is effective and where improvements and adaptations are needed, or recognize patterns of risk

Source: Adapted with permission from Rhind and Owusu-Sekyere (2018).

acknowledged that anyone can be involved in such issues as a perpetrator, victim, or bystander. This includes all stakeholders from athletes, peers, and coaches through to parents, members of the support team, and managers. Third, the context in which these issues can take place has expanded beyond the environment of training or competition; for example, recent research has highlighted that athletes can be subject to online abuse via social media (Kavanagh, Jones, & Sheppard-Marks, 2016; Sanderson & Weathers, 2020); abuse that occurs far beyond the sports field. In addition, research has also highlighted that sport can be a context in which people disclose abuse which has occurred outside of sport (Rhind et al., 2014).

Although the International Safeguards for Children in Sport refer to child athletes, the underlying principles and strategies are applicable to adults. Safeguarding adults in sport has remained a significant blind spot for many organizations and requires far greater attention both in research and practice.

Safeguarding the Adult Athlete

When a person turns 18, the need for him/her to be safeguarded in sport does not stop overnight. Rather, safeguarding measures need to be implemented to help manage such transitions and mitigate any increased areas of risk (e.g., associated with participating at an elite level). An important contribution is the work of the Ann Craft Trust which is based at Nottingham University. The Ann Craft Trust offer resources, training, and advice regarding how to safeguard adults within sport (with a focus on those with additional vulnerabilities). Such developments are necessary because although the principles of safeguarding children can be applied to adults, there is also a need to acknowledge the specific safeguarding issues that are more salient in adult sport. For example, consent is often implied when adults continue to train in environments that may incorporate harmful practices or toxic relationships. Indeed, there should be an understanding of how tolerance of such practices can result in compliance, and thus increase vulnerability of those participating in such environments.

Safeguarding for adult athletes is currently characterized by the implementation of welfare policies that are inconsistently applied across sports; these policies often rely upon whistleblowing and/or grievance policies in the reporting of incidents. Clearly, there are implications for the relationship between sporting bodies and the criminal justice system when dealing with adult safeguarding. Some allegations may require legal intervention; others, which are unlikely to lead to criminal conviction, may need to be dealt with through disciplinary channels managed by the NGBs. Consistency in the approach to dealing with cases across sports is a necessity, as is a transparent approach to safeguarding across sports at all age levels. It is also important that a holistic approach is adopted in which everyone is safeguarded within the context, including coaches and support staff (Rhind, Fletcher, & Scott, 2013).

Practical Implications of the Duty of Care

It seems we are at a critical tipping point in increasing focus on the promotion of care in practice in order to promote thriving and foster a greater balance between well-being and performance (see also Chapter 13). As Kavanagh et al. (2020) suggest, without greater focus on *how* to achieve the duty of care, there is a danger that such duties are treated as symbolic requirements that will remain overshadowed by performance expectations (e.g., medal targets). Newton, Fry, Gano-Overway, and Magyar (2007) define a caring climate as "the extent to which individuals perceive their particular setting to be interpersonally inviting, safe, supportive, and capable of providing the experience of being valued and respected" (p. 70). There is a collective responsibility to practice with compassion, treating the self and others with respect and dignity. Like safeguarding, the duty of care should be considered on a number of levels, including the self, relational, and organizational.

The call for a more joined-up approach concerning "safeguarding and welfare of all" is championed here as a significant step in the care in sport agenda. In order to achieve this ambition, there needs to be an alignment between the four key elements: (i) vision and structure, (ii) strategy and policy, (iii) program content, and (iv) practice. At the broad level, the vision and structure of performance sport, as well as individual governing bodies, need to emphasize and support a philosophy grounded in a duty of care. At the national level, this can be facilitated through having clear measures and indicators of duty of care which are tied to key drivers (e.g., government funding or the ability to participate in a given competition). Within sports organizations, a duty of care should be fundamental to the vision and structure of the organization. The most senior members of an organization and the management board play a key role in shaping this vision. There needs to be a translation of this vision clearly articulated in an organization's strategy and policy documents which are effectively communicated to key stakeholders. Those colleagues with specific responsibility for the duty of care can significantly influence this element (e.g., Director of Safeguarding or Integrity). The strategy should explain how the duty of care fits into the overall vision. This is supported by policies that clearly outline what is expected in relation to the promotion of a duty of care within the organization. The specific program should be coherent with a duty of care philosophy. This should feed through to the practice environment in which everyone behaves in a way which reflects their understanding and support for the duty of care; this includes all key stakeholders including athletes, coaches, and other support staff (e.g., sport scientists, sport psychologists, and strength and conditioning practitioners).

An organization's performance with respect to duty of care can be monitored through a periodic audit process, as is embedded within the International Safeguards for Children in Sport (Rhind & Owusu-Sekyere, 2018). This audit can assess the extent to which the vision/structure, strategy/policy, program, and practice reflect a duty of care. Areas of good practice can be identified and championed with action plans being developed for areas of potential improvement. At the individual level, coaches and/or other practitioners can conduct their own self-audit through asking: Do I know my responsibilities related to our reciprocal duty of care? Am I aware of the policies, procedures, resources, and support available to help meet these responsibilities? Am I confident that I am fulfilling my duty of care for others? Are other people fulfilling their duty of care for me? This reflection at both the organizational and individual levels can help to promote continual improvement through emphasizing that duty of care is a journey and not a destination.

Conclusion and a Call to Action

There remains a responsibility for all to question the integrity of current practices and consider the duty of care to athletes and other key stakeholders in performance environments (Adams & Kavanagh, 2020). Safeguarding *all* from foreseeable harm and enhancing knowledge concerning safety, integrity, and duty of care in sport is an essential next step in the commitment to optimizing safety and performance in sporting spaces. As Fletcher and Wagstaff (2009) rightly suggested, organizations collectively hold (i) duty of care to protect and support the mental well-being of its employees and members and (ii) an ethical obligation to create performance environments that facilitate individual and group flourishing. We would further this statement and call upon other practitioners such as coaches, sport scientists, and other performance support staff to consider their role in the promotion of caring climates and fulfilling their responsibility for the duty of care. We believe that there is still a distance to cover in making this a reality through the actions we see reflected in practice, policy, and substantial change to elite performance cultures.

Empowering individuals and organizations to prioritize environments, climates, and cultures that promote care and increase psychological safety for all stakeholders is intuitively appealing but requires far greater attention within academic literature. While we promote the benefits of such spaces, there needs to be far greater guidance concerning the strategies for implementing and committing to them. There are a range of associated avenues for future research which merit exploration. First, research is required to establish the nature and scope of duty in care from a range of perspectives. Second, the antecedents of duty of care can be studied such as the influence of sport type, culture, or competitive level. Finally, the consequences of duty of care should be investigated to include the performance, satisfaction, and well-being of athletes. Such evidence could help to strengthen the rationale for a duty of care beyond the legal and moral arguments.

A responsibility for addressing safeguarding issues lies with all stakeholders and, in turn, such a focus will serve to protect all those who work and perform in sporting spaces. Adhering to statutory requirements (in those countries where such requirements exist) is certainly a start (e.g., in the UK statutory guidance concerning safeguarding children in sport). However, these more formal protections must be built upon and exist within a culture, which values the importance of safeguarding and works toward promoting the welfare of all participants as a priority.

Elite sport in particular often strives for the Olympic motto in which athletes become faster, higher, and stronger. We need to facilitate the same motivation for sport to be safer for all participants. Through raising standards around duty of care and striving for the highest performance when it comes to safeguarding people in sport, we can go beyond the minimal professional requirements to create cultures in which people are able to thrive and flourish (see also Chapter 13). As such, it is not a choice between performance or duty of care. These factors are not mutually exclusive. Instead, it can be argued that they go hand in hand and it is only through providing a genuine duty of care that the optimal performance can be achieved.

References

Adams, A., & Kavanagh, E. J. (2020). The capabilities and human rights of high performance athletes. *International Review for the Sociology of Sport, 55*, 147–168. Doi:10.1177/1012690218791139

Alexander, K., Stafford, A., & Lewis, T. L. (2011). *The experiences of children participating in organised sport in the UK.* Edinburgh, UK: NSPCC Child Protection Research Centre.

Australian Institute of Sport. (2020). *Athlete wellbeing summit, Tokyo and beyond: The future of athlete wellbeing.* Retrieved from https://ais.gov.au/events/athlete-wellbeing-summit

Bauman, N. J. (2016). The stigma of mental health in athletes: Are mental toughness and mental health seen as contradictory in elite sport? *British Journal of Sports Medicine, 50*, 135–136. Doi:10.1136/bjsports-2015-095570

BBC. (2019a, January 22). *Sex abuse scandal hits South Korea's elite skating scene.* Retrieved from www.bbc.co.uk/news/world-asia-46942374

BBC. (2019b, August 6). *Football's child sex abuse scandal: A timeline.* Retrieved from www.bbc.co.uk/news/uk-49253181

Brackenridge, C. H. (2001). *Spoilsports: Understanding and preventing sexual exploitation in sport.* London, UK: Routledge.

Boocock, S. (2002). The child protection in sport unit. *Journal of Sexual Aggression, 8*, 99–106.

Coyle, M., Gorczynski, P., & Gibson, K. (2017). "You have to be mental to jump off a board any way": Elite divers' conceptualizations and perceptions of mental health. *Psychology of Sport and Exercise, 29*, 10–18. Doi:10.1016/j.psychsport.2016.11.005

Chroni, S., Fasting, K., Hartill, M., Knorre, N., Martin, M., Papaefstathiou, M., . . . Zurc, J. (2012). *Prevention of sexual and gender harassment and abuse in sport: Initiatives from Europe and beyond.* Berlin, Germany: German Sports Youth.

Doherty, S., Hannigan, B., & Campbell, M. J. (2016). The experience of depression during the careers of elite male athletes. *Frontiers in Psychology, 7*, 1–11. Doi:10.3389/fpsyg.2016.01069

Fisher, L. A., & Anders, A. D. (2020). Engaging with cultural sport psychology to explore systemic sexual exploitation in USA Gymnastics: A call to commitments. *Journal of Applied Sport Psychology, 32*, 129–145. Doi:10.1080/10413200.2018.1564944

Fletcher, D., & Wagstaff, C. R. D. (2009). Organizational psychology in elite sport: Its emergence, application and future. *Psychology of Sport and Exercise, 10*, 427–434. Doi:10.1016/j.psychsport.2009.03.009.

Grey-Thompson, T. (2017). *Duty of Care in Sport: Independent Report to Government.* London, UK: HMSO.

Gorczynski, P., Gibson, K., Thelwell, R., Papathomas, A., Harwood, C., & Kinnafick, F. (2019). The BASES expert statement on mental health literacy in elite sport. *The Sport and Exercise Scientist, 59*, 6–7.

Gordon, G. (2016). Extending the duty of care beyond the immediate: The pressure is on. *Global Sports Law and Taxation Reports, 7*, 25–28.

Hamington, M. (2019). Integrating care ethics and design thinking. *Journal of Business Ethics, 155*, 91–103. Doi:10.1007/s10551-017-3522-6

Hartill, M., & Lang, M. (2018). Reports of child protection and safeguarding concerns in sport and leisure settings: An analysis of English local authority data between 2010 and 2015. *Leisure Studies, 5*, 479–499. Doi:10.1080/026143 67.2018.1497076

Hill, A., MacNamara, Á., & Collins, D. (2015). Psycho-behaviourally based features of effective talent development in rugby union: A coach's perspective. *The Sport Psychologist, 29*, 201–212. Doi:10.1123/tsp.2014-0103

Ingle, S. (2019). *Elite sport is gradually waking up to widespread mental health issues.* Retrieved from www.theguardian.com/sport/blog/2019/mar/04/elite-sport-mental-health

International Olympic Committee. (2009). *Olympic movement medical code.* Retrieved from https://stillmed.olympic.org/AssetsDocs/importednews/documents/en_report_1022.p

Kavanagh, E. J. (2014). *The dark side of sport: Athlete narratives of maltreatment in high performance environments* (Unpublished PhD thesis). Bournemouth University, UK.

Kavanagh, E. J., Jones, I., & Sheppard-Marks, L. (2016). Towards typologies of virtual maltreatment: Sport, digital cultures and dark leisure. *Leisure Studies, 35*, 783–796. Doi:10.1080/02614367.2016.1216581

Kavanagh, E. J., Lock, D., Adams, A., Stewart, C., & Clelland, J. (2020). Managing abuse in sport: An introduction to the special issue. *Sport Management Review, 21*, 1–7. Doi:10.1016/j.smr.2019.12.002

Kerr, G., & Stirling, A. (2019). Where is safeguarding in sport psychology research and practice? *Journal of Applied Sport Psychology, 31*, 367–384. Doi:10.1080/1041 3200.2018.1559255

MacIntyre, T., Van Raalte, J., Brewer, B. W., Jones, M., O'Shea, D., & McCarthy, P. J. (2018). Mental health challenges in elite sport: Balancing risk with reward. *Frontiers in Psychology, 8*, 1–4. Doi:10.3389/978-2-88945-383-2

McMahon, J., & McGannon, K. R. (2020). Acting out what is inside of us: Self-management strategies of an abused ex-athlete. *Sport Management Review, 23*, 28–38. Doi:10.1016/j.smr.2019.03.0 08

Mountjoy, M., Brackenridge, C., Arrington, M., Blauwet, C., Carska-Sheppard, A., Fasting, K., . . . Budgett, R. (2016). The IOC consensus statement: Harassment and abuse (non-accidental violence) in sport. *British Journal of Sports Medicine, 50*, 1019–1029. Doi:10.1136/bjsports-2016-096121

Mountjoy, M., Rhind, D. J. A., Tiivas, A., & Leglise, M. (2015). Safeguarding the child athlete in sport: A review, a framework and recommendations for the IOC youth athlete development model. *British Journal of Sports Medicine, 49*, 883–886. Doi:10.1136/bjsports-2015-094619

Newman, H. J. H., Howells, K. L., & Fletcher, D. (2016). The dark side of top level sport: An autobiographic study of depressive experiences in elite sport performers. *Frontiers in Psychology, 868*, 10–21. Doi:10.3389/fpsyg.2016.00868

Newton, M., Fry, M., Gano-Overway, L. A., & Magyar, T. M. (2007). Psychometric properties of the caring climate scale in a physical activity setting. *Revista de Psicologia del Deporte, 16*, 67–84.

Noddings, N. (2010). *The maternal factor: Two paths to morality*. Berkeley, CA: University of California Press.

Parent, S., & Fortier, K. (2018). Comprehensive overview of the problem of violence against athletes in sport. *Journal of Sport and Social Issues, 42*, 227–246. Doi:10.1177/0193723518759448

Phelps, A., Kelly, J., Lancaster, S., Mehrzad, J., & Panter, A. (2017). *Report of the independent review panel into the climate and culture of the world class programme in British cycling*. London, UK: UK Sport.

Plunkett, J. C. (2015). The historical foundations of the duty of care. *Monash University Law Review, 41*, 716–744.

Reardon, C. L., & Factor, R. M. (2010). Sport psychiatry: A systematic review of diagnosis and medical treatment of mental illness in athletes. *Sports Medicine, 40*, 961–980. Doi:10.2165/11536580-000000000-00000

Rhind, D., Brackenridge, C. H., Kay, T., & Owusu-Sekyere, F. (2015). Child protection and SDP: The post-MDG agenda for policy, practice and research. In L. Hayhurst, T. Kay, & M. Chawansky (Eds.), *Beyond sport for development and peace: Transitional perspectives on theory policy and practice* (pp. 72–86). Oxfordshire, UK: Routledge.

Rhind, D. J. A., Fletcher, D., & Scott, M. (2013). Organizational stress in professional soccer coaches. *International Journal of Sport Psychology, 44*, 1–16. Doi:10.7352/IJSP.2013.44.001

Rhind, D. J. A., McDermott, J., Lambert, E., & Koleva, I. (2014). A review of safeguarding cases in sport. *Child Abuse Review, 24*, 418–426. Doi:10.1002/car.2306

Rhind, D. J. A., & Owusu-Sekyere, F. (2018). *International safeguards for children in sport: Developing and embedding a safeguarding culture*. London, UK: Routledge.

Rice, S. M., Purcell, R., De Silva, S., Mawren, D., McGorry, P. D., & Parker, A. G. (2016). The mental health of elite athletes: A narrative systematic review. *Sports Medicine, 46*, 1333–1353. Doi:10.1007/s40279-016-0492-2

Roberts, C., Faull, A. L., & Tod, D. (2016). Blurred lines: Performance enhancement, common mental disorders and referral in the U.K. athletic population. *Frontiers in Psychology, 1067*, 61–73. Doi:10.3389/fpsyg.2016.01067

Sanderson, J., & Weathers, M. R. (2020). Snapchat and child sexual abuse in sport: Protecting child athletes in the social media age. *Sport Management Review, 23*, 81–94. Doi:10.1016/j.smr.2019.04.006

Sebbens, J., Hassmen, P., Crisp, D., & Wensley, K. (2016). Mental health in sport (MHS): Improving the early intervention knowledge and confidence of elite sport staff. *Frontiers in Psychology, 7*, 1–9. Doi:10.3389/fpsyg.2016.00911

Stirling, A. (2009). Definitions and constituents of maltreatment in sport: Establishing a conceptual framework for research practitioners. *British Journal of Sports Medicine, 43*, 1091–1099. Doi:10.1136/bjsm.2008.051433

Stirling, A. E. (2013). Understanding the use of emotionally abusive coaching practices. *International Journal of Sports Science and Coaching, 8*, 625–639. Doi:10.1260/1747-9541.8.4.625

UK Sport. (2017a, June 14). *UK Sport set to drive a more sustainable winning culture across high performance system in response to independent review.* Retrieved from www.uksport.gov.uk/news/2017/06/14/british-cycling

UK Sport. (2017b, June 14). *Independent review into the climate and culture of the world class programme in British Cycling: UK sport action plan.* Retrieved from www.uksport.gov.uk/news/2017/06/14/british-cycling

UK Sport. (2018). *Summary of the mental health strategy for the high performance system.* London, UK: UK Sport.

United Nations General Assembly. (1989). *United nations rights of the child.* Retrieved from www.unicef.org.uk/what-we-do/un-convention-child-rights/

Uphill, M., Sly, D., & Swain, J. (2016). From mental health to mental wealth in athletes: Looking back and moving forward. *Frontiers in Psychology, 7*, 93–98. Doi:10.3389/fpsyg.2016.00935

Vertommen, T., Veldhoven, N. S., Wouters, K., Kampen, J. K., Brackenridge, C. H., Rhind, D., . . . Van Den Eedea, F. (2016). Interpersonal violence against children in sport in the Netherlands and Belgium. *Child Abuse and Neglect, 51*, 223–236. Doi:10.1016/j.chiabu.2015.10.006

Wagstaff, C. R. D. (2018): A commentary and reflections on the field of organizational sport psychology. *Journal of Applied Sport Psychology, 31*, 134–146. Doi: 10.1080/10413200.2018.1539885

Conclusion

Rachel Arnold and David Fletcher

Stress, Well-being, and Performance in Sport aimed to provide a comprehensive overview of stress in sport and the performance and well-being implications for those operating in this domain. Indeed, while Jones and Hardy's (1990) *Stress and Performance in Sport* text was a seminal classic, the current book provides more up-to-date coverage on the topic by bringing together and exploring recent theoretical advances, original and cutting-edge research, a series of best practice recommendations, and novel suggestions for stimulating future research. Certainly, as evident when comparing the two titles alone, one important advance of this book has been extending the focus from examining the impact of stress on performance to also include the timely and topical consideration of its effects on well-being and broader implications for welfare in sport. Furthermore, while previous books have typically focused on isolated or narrow components of the stress process, we hope that you will agree that this book has provided a more complete perspective by including sections that logically progress through the transactional stress process. Indeed, following on from the Introduction chapter, which charted the chronological developments in the field via the identification of four main periods (viz. The Early Years, Establishment of the Field, The Millennial Period, and Contemporary Focus), the remainder of the book showcases the work of scholars from across the globe to illustrate academic progress on both established themes and emerging areas of interest.

The first section of this book, *Appraisal and Coping With Stress in Sport*, comprised coverage of some of the more established themes in the field (e.g., stressors, appraisals, and coping). Indeed, it was very clear from reviewing the three chapters in this section that there was certainly emphasis toward, and an abundance of research conducted on, particular elements of each topic. For example, this related to identifying types of stressors, hassles, and adversity in Chapter 1; examining the pivotal role of primary and secondary appraising in Chapter 2; and conceptualizing the variety of coping strategies and how these relate to outcomes in Chapter 3. That said, all three chapters recognized the need for scholars working on these topics to broaden the focus moving forward, offering innovative suggestions for such endeavors. To elaborate, Chapter 1 made recommendations for considering multiple dimensions, properties, and other worthy characteristics of demands in future investigations (e.g., severity and conscious/unconscious stressors); Chapter 2 directed attention to examining influential person and situation factors that could influence appraising in sport; and Chapter 3 forwarded recommendations for extending knowledge on performers' proactive and communal coping. While the reader is directed to each individual chapter for specific future research directions, it is worth noting some universal proposals that have arisen across the first section of this book. First, the chapters urged scholars to advance measurement by developing new, and improving existing, tools (e.g., to measure competitive stressors holistically, effectively assess internal load, and standardize the normative measurement of appraisal). Second, the chapters collectively emphasized the necessity of considering multiple components of the transactional stress process simultaneously (e.g., the complete appraising process considering emotions and performance, links back to stressors for enhancing proactive and communal coping).

Turning to the second section of this book, *Responses to and Outcomes of Stress in Sport*, there are four main conclusions that can be drawn from across the five contributing chapters (viz. emotions, attention and visuomotor performance under pressure, well-being and quality of life, burnout, and mental health). First, various chapters in this section report struggles with the ambiguity of construct definitions, with scholars often failing to reach consensus (e.g., emotions, well-being, and quality of life). Second, for many topics in this section, it is clear that early work has focused on problematic or aversive states, before a noticeable shift in emphasis toward the importance of examining and promoting more positive and constructive alternatives (e.g., urges to examine positive emotions over an anxiety focus in Chapter 4, challenge states being consistently identified as more beneficial than threat states in Chapter 5, and a movement in line with positive psychology toward examination of well-being over psychological ill-health in Chapter 6). Third, several chapters in this section observe the importance of widening the lens beyond a within-person focus to also consider the interpersonal interactions between performers (e.g., group-based emotions in Chapter 4) and the role of the broader context and environment (e.g., burnout as a product of the individual and environment in Chapter 7, the importance of developing an environment to optimize individuals' mental health in Chapter 8). Fourth, the chapters in this section have underscored the importance of developing and drawing from integrative models to best understand responses to and outcomes of stress in sport, rather than models which consider isolated components of respective stress-related topics or frameworks ignoring underpinning mechanisms. Examples include the following: The Integrative Framework of Stress, Attention, and Visuomotor Performance (Vine, Moore, & Wilson, 2016) in Chapter 5, Lundqvist's (2011) Integrated Model of Global and Sport-specific Well-being in Chapter 6, the eclectically Integrated Model of Burnout (Gustafsson, Kenttä, & Hassmén, 2011) in Chapter 7, and the Biopsychosocial Model (Engel, 1980) being increasingly applied to athletic settings (e.g., DeFreese, 2017) in Chapter 8. Interestingly, Self-Determination Theory has also been referenced across various chapters in this section as being a useful framework to explain certain topics (e.g., well-being and burnout) or develop models (e.g., mental health).

With regard to common future research directions proposed across this second section, these relate to conducting longitudinal studies (Chapters 4 and 7) which have a multilevel focus across micro (e.g., individual), meso (e.g., team), and macro (e.g., organizational) dimensions and are underpinned by, and continue to contribute to, extant theoretical frameworks (Chapters 4–7). Furthermore, there was a shared plea to create and test applied techniques—be that evaluating new techniques to optimize attentional control and performance during stressful competition in Chapter 5, creating tailored interventions for promoting well-being and quality of life in Chapter 6, developing sports-based cognitive-behavioral therapy for treating burnout in Chapter 7, or conducting randomized controlled trials for evaluating elite athlete mental health interventions in Chapter 8.

The third section, *Moderators of the Stress Process in Sport*, presented coverage of two personal characteristics (resilience and personality) and one situational characteristic (social support) which can moderate the transactional stress process. What became clear from reviewing the chapters in this section is that while these characteristics might be clearly distinguished conceptually, operationally it is not as black and white given that personal moderators depend on the situation and situational moderators on the person. To elaborate, Chapter 10 detailed that the way personality shapes behavior will depend on the context (i.e., certain stressors activating particular traits), and Chapter 11 illustrated that the effectiveness of social support depends on the characteristics of the person (both provider and recipient of the support). To best examine the complexity of such moderators, novel and advanced future research designs and methodologies will be required. Indeed, the chapters in this section made innovative suggestions for considering relatively new methodologies for their topic (e.g., social network analysis in Chapter 11) and measures (e.g., cardiac vagal activity to capture physiological variables linked to personality and executive function in Chapter 10). Original suggestions were also extended to practice, with Chapter 10 highlighting the need to test the effectiveness of executive function training programs in sport, and Chapter 11 illustrating the importance of testing how novel forms of support (e.g., Skype and WhatsApp) are received by sport performers.

The final section, *Stress Management to Promote Thriving in Sport*, forwarded a collection of three chapters which can be classified as emerging areas of interest in the field of stress in sport (viz. pressure training, thriving, and duties of care). In view of this, across all three chapters in this section, the authors effectively draw from literature outside of sport psychology and discuss the application of this to the sports setting to optimally support performers. A fundamental distinction relevant to all chapters in this section centers around first ascertaining which stressors in sport should be avoided given their detrimental and unethical premise (e.g., abuse in sport) and which might be more inherent and even desirable (e.g., crowd pressures at competition). Once disentangled, scholars and practitioners will then be best positioned to determine the most appropriate stress management strategies to support the performers with whom they work (i.e., Chapter 14's safeguarding and duty of care-related interventions for the former example, Chapter 12's pressure training applications for the latter example). Furthermore, it is likely that a combination of both approaches will be necessary in sport moving forward to ensure an environment is created which promotes an optimal balance between welfare and winning in the future and, in doing so, enables performers to thrive. Furthermore, while these topics are highly prevalent in the current elite sport climate and there exists a pressing need to ensure they are addressed within sports organizations, all three chapters make the case for ensuring that interventions relating to pressure training (Chapter 12), thriving (Chapter 13), and safeguarding/duties of care (Chapter 14) are theoretically informed, evidence-based, carefully planned, and their efficacy and effectiveness rigorously tested. Finally, all chapters emphasized the applicability of the topics for all performers in sport (i.e., not just athletes) and forwarded that future research and practice should consider and support multiple stakeholders' experiences in sport.

In addition to drawing conclusions from across the chapters in this book and synthesizing universal future research directions recommended, it is also important to reflect on work outside the covers of this book. Indeed, by boundary crossing both within and outside sport psychology, we can encourage scholars to ask new questions and think differently and, in doing so, collectively grow the field in vibrant and creative ways (McGannon, Smith, & Schinke, 2016). Within sport, there are some noteworthy example topics which have relevance to stress, well-being, and performance in sport but have not been extensively covered in this book. While it is beyond the scope of this book to provide exhaustive coverage, examples of such areas include the following: social identity as the basis for support and stress appraisals (cf. Rees, Haslam, Coffee, & Lavallee, 2015), risk taking and sensation seeking in competitive sport (see, e.g., Woodman, MacGregor, & Hardy, 2020), the role of stress in sport and physical activity involvement (see, e.g., Gucciardi et al., 2020), mood profiling (see, e.g., Terry & Parsons-Smith, 2019), stress and doping (see, e.g., Didymus & Backhouse, 2020), self-compassion as a predictor of appraisal and coping (see, e.g., Mosewich, Sabiston, Kowalkski, Gaudreau, & Crocker, 2019), psychosocial stress and injury risk (see, e.g., Pensgaard, Ivarsson, Nilstad, Solstaf, & Steffen, 2018), and novel techniques for stress and mental health management (e.g., Rational Emotive Behavioral Therapy; see, e.g., Turner, 2016).

Outside of sport, two recent handbooks illustrate some of the lines of enquiry that sport scholars may look to consider pursuing in the future (Cooper & Campbell-Quick, 2017; Harkness & Hayden, 2020). Examples include the following: early life adversity and psychopathology (McLaughlin, 2020; see also Slavich, 2019), the relationships between stress and particular disorders (e.g., depression; Vrshek-Schallhorn, Ditcheve, & Corneau, 2020) and conditions (e.g., chronic fatigue syndrome; Grinde, 2017), stress and the co-morbidity of physical and mental health (Vig, El-Gabalawy, & Asmundson, 2020), stress mindsets and the judgments of others' strain (Ben-Avi, Toker, & Heller, 2018), and the impact of stress on organizational well-being (Bennett, Weaver, Senft, & Neeper, 2017). As well as new topics, scholars can also draw from domains outside of sport to discover and upskill knowledge on novel study designs, methodologies, and analytical processes. Examples relevant to the study of stress may include the following: advanced quantitative modeling for stress and coping (Neufeld & Grant, 2020), utilizing different time lags in longitudinal studies (Ford, Matthews, Wooldridge, Mishra, Kakar, & Strahan, 2014), structural and functional neuroimaging for examining stress and the brain (Pagliaccio & Barch, 2020), psychoneuroimmunological methods for investigating stress and mental health (Slavich, 2020), novel in situ assessment methods for tracking momentary stress experiences that may influence health and other outcomes (cf. Segerstrom & O' Connor, 2012), machine-learning techniques for stress detection (Smets et al., 2015), and artificial intelligence-enabled wearable tools which can act as emotion and stress sensors (cf. Carneiro, Novais, Augusto, & Payne, 2019).

Turning from the future of scholarly work on stress, well-being, and performance in sport to the future of applied work, four themes are proposed which we anticipate will come to the fore and be emphasized as pressing priorities for sport psychology practitioners. First, it is suggested that the role of technology will become more prominent when supporting performers in sport in the future to manage the stress experienced and in doing so, enhance their performance, well-being, and ability to ultimately thrive. This could include the increased prevalence of athletes wearing portable digital devices so that the stress experience can be tracked and supported in situ (see, e.g., Bellido, Ruisoto, Beltran-Velasco, & Clemente-Suárez, 2018), or the use of virtual reality to expose athletes to particular stressors and enhance their responses (see, e.g., Sanz, Multon, & Lécuyer, 2015; Sárkány et al., 2016). Second, writing this conclusion at a time when the 2020 Tokyo Olympics have been postponed by a year due to coronavirus (BBC, 2020), it is proposed that practitioners will need to continue to develop and test the effectiveness of remote support methods and demonstrate adaptability and flexibility in their provisions to respond to this and equivalent global and societal trends (see also Bliese, Edwards, & Sonnentag, 2017). Third, while the importance of achieving high levels of performance while simultaneously promoting well-being has been repeatedly emphasized in this book (see, e.g., Chapters 13 and 14), how this and the oscillation between winning and welfare is actually implemented and monitored effectively in elite sport moving forward will likely be a pressing priority for those involved in supporting athletes. Linked to this, the fourth observation is that sport psychology practitioners will likely need to increasingly work as part of, and provide support to, a multidisciplinary team (cf. Arnold & Sarkar, 2015; McCalla & Fitzpatrick, 2016) to respond to high-performance and well-being issues simultaneously. This will likely involve moving away from a predominant focus on reactive 1:1 work with athletes to adopt, via an organizational psychology lens (cf. Sly, Mellalieu, & Wagstaff, 2020), a more systemic approach to creating an environment which enables multiple stakeholders to thrive.

In closing, we would like to sincerely thank all authors for their contributions to this book, and Professor Daniel Gould and Professor Sir Cary L. Cooper for their foreword and epilogue contributions respectively. We are grateful to all for your initial willingness and collegiality to engage with the project, and for giving your time to create a contribution which helped us to achieve our vision for the book—thank you.

References

Arnold, R., & Sarkar, M. (2015). Preparing athletes and teams for the Olympic games: Experiences and lessons learned from the world's best sport psychologists. *International Journal of Sport and Exercise Psychology, 13,* 4–20. Doi:10.1080/1612197X.2014.932827

BBC. (2020). *Tokyo 2020: Olympic and paralympic games postponed because of coronavirus.* Retrieved May 21, 2020, from www.bbc.co.uk/sport/olympics/52020134

Bellido, A., Ruisoto, P., Beltran-Velasco, A., & Clemente-Suárez, V. J. (2018). State of the art on the use of portable digital devices to assess stress in humans. *Journal of Medical Systems, 42,* 100. Doi:10.1007/s10916-018-0955-0

Ben-Avi, N., Toker, S., & Heller, D. (2018). "If stress is good for me, it's probably good for you too": Stress mindset and judgement of others' strain. *Journal of Experimental Social Psychology, 74,* 98–110. Doi:10.1016/j.jesp.2017.09.002

Bennett, J. B., Weaver, J., Senft, M., & Neeper, M. (2017). Creating workplace well-being: Time for practical wisdom. In C. Cooper & J. Campbell-Quick (Eds.), *The handbook of stress and health: A guide to research and practice* (pp. 570–604). Chichester, UK: John Wiley & Sons.

Bliese, P. D., Edwards, J. R., & Sonnentag, S. (2017). Stress and wellbeing at work: A century of empirical trends reflecting theoretical and societal influences. *Journal of Applied Psychology, 102*, 389–402. Doi:10.1037/apl0000109

Carneiro, D., Novais, P., Augusto, J. C., & Payne, N. (2019). New methods for stress assessment and monitoring at the workplace. *IEEE Transactions on Affective Computing, 10*, 237–254. Doi:10.1109/taffc.2017.2699633

Cooper, C., & Campbell-Quick, J. (2017). *The handbook of stress and health: A guide to research and practice.* Chichester, UK: John Wiley & Sons.

DeFreese, J. D. (2017). Athlete mental health care within the biopsychosocial model. *Athletic Training and Sports Health Care, 9*, 243–245. Doi:10.3928/19425864-20170703-03

Didymus, F. F., & Backhouse, S. H. (2020). Coping by doping? A qualitative inquiry into permitted and prohibited substance use in competitive rugby. *Psychology of Sport and Exercise, 49*. Advance online publication. Doi:10.1016/j.psychsport.2020.101680

Engel, G. (1980). The clinical application of the biopsychosocial model. *American Journal of Psychiatry, 137*, 535–544. Doi:10.1176/ajp.137.5.535

Ford, M. T., Matthews, R. A., Wooldridge, J. D., Mishra, V., Kakar, U. M., & Strahan, S. R. (2014). How do occupational stressor-strain effects vary with time? A review and meta-analysis of the relevance of time lags in longitudinal studies. *Work and Stress, 28*, 9–30. Doi:10.1080/02678373.2013.877096

Grinde, B. (2017). Stress and chronic fatigue syndrome. In C. Cooper & J. Campbell-Quick (Eds.), *The handbook of stress and health: A guide to research and practice* (pp. 135–146). Chichester, UK: John Wiley & Sons.

Gucciardi, D. F., Law, K. H., Guerrero, M. D., Quested, E., Thøgersen-Ntoumani, C., Ntoumanis, N., & Jackson, B. (2020). Longitudinal relations between psychological distress and moderate-to-vigorous physical activity: A latent change score approach. *Psychology of Sport and Exercise.* Advance online publication. Doi:10.1016/j.psychsport.2019.02.005

Gustafsson, H., Kenttä, G., & Hassmén, P. (2011). Athlete burnout: An integrated model and future research directions. *International Review of Sport and Exercise Psychology, 4*, 3–24. Doi:10.1080/1750984X.2010.541927

Harkness, K. L., & Hayden, E. P. (2020). *The Oxford handbook of stress and mental health.* Oxford, UK: Oxford University Press.

Jones, J. G., & Hardy, L. (1990). *Stress and performance in sport.* New York: John Wiley & Sons.

Lundqvist, C. (2011). Well-being in competitive sports—the feel-good factor? A review of conceptual considerations of well-being. *International Review of Sport and Exercise Psychology, 4*, 109–127. Doi:10.1080/1750984X.2011.584067

McCalla, T., & Fitzpatrick, S. (2016). Integrating sport psychology within a high performance team: Potential stakeholders, micropolitics, and culture. *Journal of Sport Psychology in Action, 7*, 33–42. Doi:10.1080/21520704.2015.1123208

McGannon, K. R., Smith, B., & Schinke, R. J. (2016). Conclusion: Closing the loop. In R. J. Schinke, K. R. McGannon, & B. Smith (Eds.), *Routledge international handbook of sport psychology* (pp. 830–836). New York: Routledge.

McLaughlin, K. A. (2020). Early life stress and psychopathology. In K. L. Harkness & E. P. Hayden (Eds.), *The Oxford handbook of stress and mental health* (pp. 45–74). Oxford, UK: Oxford University Press.

Mosewich, A. D., Sabiston, C. M., Kowalkski, K. C., Gaudreau, P., & Crocker, P. R. E. (2019). Self-compassion in the stress process in women athletes. *The Sport Psychologist, 33*, 23–34. Doi:10.1123/tsp.2017-0094

Neufeld, R. W. J., & Grant, B. (2020). Quantitative modeling of stress and coping. In K. L. Harkness & E. P. Hayden (Eds.), *The Oxford handbook of stress and mental health* (pp. 75–96). Oxford, UK: Oxford University Press.

Pagliaccio, D., & Barch, D. M. (2020). Stress and the brain: Structural and functional neuroimagining. In K. L. Harkness & E. P. Hayden (Eds.), *The Oxford handbook of stress and mental health* (pp. 435–462). Oxford, UK: Oxford University Press.

Pensgaard, A-M., Ivarsson, A., Nilstad, A., Solstaf, B. E., & Steffen, K. (2018). Psychosocial stress factors, including the relationship with the coach, and their influence on acute and overuse injury risk in elite female football players. *BMJ Open Sport and Exercise Medicine, 4*, e000317. Doi:10.1136/bmjsem-2017-000317

Rees, T., Haslam, S. A., Coffee, P., & Lavallee, D. (2015). A social identity approach to sport psychology: Principles, practice, and prospects. *Sports Medicine, 45*, 1083–1096. Doi:10.1007/s40279-015-0345-4

Sanz, F. A., Multon, F., & Lécuyer, A. (2015). A methodology for introducing competitive anxiety and pressure in VR sports training. *Frontiers in Robotics and AI, 2*, 1–11. Doi:10.3389/frobt.2015.00010

Sárkány, A., Töser, Z., Verö, A. L., Lörincz, A., Toyama, T., Toosi, E. N., & Sonntag, D. (2016). Maintain and improve mental health by smart virtual reality serious games. In S. Serino, A. Matic, D. Giakoumis, G. Lopez, & P. Cipresso (Eds.), *Pervasive computing paradigms for mental health* (pp. 220–229). Milan, Italy: MindCare.

Segerstrom, S. C., & O' Connor, D. B. (2012). Stress, health and illness: Four challenges for the future. *Psychology and Health, 27*, 128–140. Doi:10.1080/08 870446.2012.659516

Slavich, G. M. (2019). Stressnology: The primitive (and problematic) study of life stress exposure and pressing need for better measurement. *Brain, Behavior, and Immunity, 75*, 3–5. Doi:10.1016/j.bbi.2018.08.011

Slavich, G. M. (2020). Psychoneuroimmunology of stress and mental health. In K. L. Harkness & E. P. Hayden (Eds.), *The Oxford handbook of stress and mental health* (pp. 519–546). Oxford, UK: Oxford University Press.

Sly, D., Mellalieu, S. D., & Wagstaff, C. R. D. (2020). "It's psychology Jim, but not as we know it!": The changing face of applied sport psychology. *Sport, Exercise, and Performance Psychology, 9*, 87–101. Doi:10.1037/spy0000163

Smets, E., Casale, P., Großekathöfer, U., Lamichhane, B., De Raedt, W., Bogaerts, K . . . Van Hoof, C. (2015). Comparison of machine learning techniques for psychophysiological stress detection. In S. Serino, A. Matic, D. Giakoumis, G. Lopez, & P. Cipresso (Eds.), *Pervasive computing paradigms for mental health* (pp. 13–22). Milan, Italy: MindCare.

Terry, P., & Parsons-Smith, R. (2019). Identification and incidence of mood profile clusters among sport participants. *Journal of Science and Medicine in Sport, 22* (Supp. 2), S100. Doi:10.1016/j.jsams.2019.08.129

Turner, M. J. (2016). Rational emotive behavior therapy (REBT), irrational and rational beliefs, and the mental health of athletes. *Frontiers in Psychology, 7,* 1423. Doi:10.3389/fpsyg.2016.01423

Vig, K. D., El-Gabalawy, R., & Asmundson, G. J. G. (2020). Stress and comorbidity of physical and mental health. In K. L. Harkness & E. P. Hayden (Eds.), *The Oxford handbook of stress and mental health* (pp. 313–330). Oxford, UK: Oxford University Press.

Vine, S. J., Moore, L. J., & Wilson, M. R. (2016). An integrative framework of stress, attention, and visuomotor performance. *Frontiers in Psychology, 7*(1671), 1–10. Doi:10.3389/fpsyg.2016.01671.ss

Vrshek-Schallhorn, S., Ditcheve, M., & Corneau, G. (2020). Stress in depression. In K. L. Harkness & E. P. Hayden (Eds.), *The Oxford handbook of stress and mental health* (pp. 97–126). Oxford, UK: Oxford University Press.

Woodman, T., MacGregor, A., & Hardy, L. (2020). Risk can be good for self-esteem: Beyond self-determination theory. *Journal of Risk Research, 23,* 411–423. Doi:10.1080/13669877.2019.1588913

Epilogue

Cary L. Cooper

Stress in the workplace is now the leading cause of sickness absence in the most developed countries. In the United Kingdom, for example, the UK government's Health and Safety Executive reported that 57% of all long-term sickness absence was for stress, anxiety, and depression. The OECD reported that mental ill-health and stress costs the UK £70b per annum, equivalent to 4.5% of GDP. So, stress at work is very costly to employers but also to the individual in terms of their health, their family, and career.

Professional sport is not immune to work pressures, indeed, it thrives on them. There is a substantial difference between pressure and stress. While most competitive sports involve a great amount of pressure, which helps athletes get to their peak performance, when pressure exceeds their ability to cope, then we are in the arena of "stress". Stress in this context is dysfunctional, it leads to ill-health and poor performance, and unless dealt with, could lead to burnout and serious long-term health consequences.

If we can harness the pressures in our life, whether in sport or work more generally, we can perform to our maximum, with minimal negative consequences to our health and well-being. If however the pressures in our job escalate into stress, we need to recognize the symptoms and deal with the underlying causes before it leads to mental ill-health, burnout, or other negative manifestations. We all know of sportsmen/women who have suffered because of excessive pressure in the competitive world of sport, from football to cricket to rugby to tennis. As Winston Churchill once wrote about the stress he experienced: "Many remedies are suggested for the avoidance of worry and mental overstrain by persons who, over prolonged periods, have to bear exceptional responsibilities and discharge duties upon a very large scale. Some advise exercise, and others, repose. Some counsel travel, and others, retreat. Some praise solitude, and others, gaiety. No doubt all these may play their part according to the individual temperament. But the element which is constant and common in all of them is the need to change".

So being able to identify the sources of the stress, and dealing with them, is what we all need to do, whether a footballer or dentist or manager or tennis player. Competitive sport is intrinsically pressured, so we need to know what behavioral symptoms indicate a stress response, what can moderate the stressors in life (e.g., resilience, personality, coping strategies, and social support), and how we can cope with the stress to promote thriving in sport. This book has all these elements in it, from the sources of stress in sport, how to appraise it, how to cope with it, as well as coverage of the emotions and various outcomes of stress, and what might protect or make individuals more vulnerable to stress in sport. The book also contains a more positive section on stress management and promoting thriving in sport, plus topical inclusion of the duty of care that organizations have for those who participate and work within their sport. In doing so, the book provides content that will indeed be useful for various stakeholders (e.g., students, academics, and practitioners). I will never forget reading, at a time when I was a member of the track team in high school, and having a difficult time because another track student was undermining me, a quote from a Mark Twain book "keep away from people who try to belittle your ambitions. Small people always do that, but the really great make you feel that you, too, can somehow become great".

Stress, Well-being, and Performance in Sport will help many understand the pressures of competitive sport, alternative approaches to coping and how managing stress and enhancing well-being can benefit performance. At the beginning of the Industrial Revolution in Britain, John Ruskin, the social reformer, wrote in 1851 "in order that people may be happy in their work, these three things are needed. They must be fit for it, they must not do too much of it, and they must have a sense of success in it". These are the challenges in the frenetic, high pressure times we live in.

In closing, this collection of chapters captures the excellent contribution that scholars operating in the domain of sport can make, and are making, to wider knowledge on the topic of stress, well-being, and performance. While the Editors synthesize in the book's conclusion various cutting-edge future research directions that sport scholars might wish to draw from academic research being conducted outside of the sports domain, I urge this process to be reciprocal as there is much that can be learnt and applied from academic research conducted in the domain of sport to broader fields (e.g., general psychology), workplaces, and high-pressured domains. Indeed, as outlined by the Editors in their introduction chapter, sport can offer a natural laboratory for examining stress, and the implications it has for health and well-being, across the globe.

Professor Sir Cary L. Cooper.
Alliance Manchester Business School
University of Manchester, UK

Index

Note: **Boldface** page references indicate tables. *Italic* references indicate figures and boxed text.

Milton Keynes UK
Ingram Content Group UK Ltd.
UKHW021908310823
427871UK00025B/351